THE EARLIEST LIVES OF JESUS

THE EARLIEST
LIVES OF JESUS

ROBERT M. GRANT

HARPER & BROTHERS   PUBLISHERS, NEW YORK

CONTENTS

v

ABBREVIATIONS

ATR   *Anglican Theological Review*
HTR   *Harvard Theological Review*
JBL   *Journal of Biblical Literature*
JTS   *Journal of Theological Studies*
PG   *Patrologia graeca*
RE   *Real-Encyclopädie der classischen Altertumswissenschaft*
TU   *Texte und Untersuchungen*
ZNW   *Zeitschrift für die neutestamentliche Wissenschaft*

WORKS OF ORIGEN

C   *Contra Celsum*
E   *Exhortatio ad martyrium*
J   *Commentary on John*
L   *Homilies on Luke*
M   *Commentary on Matthew*
O   *De oratione*
P   *De principiis*
R   *Commentary on Romans*

METHOD OF CITATION

Greek rhetoricians are cited by volume, page, and line of the edition by L. Spengel, *Rhetores Graeci*, I–III (Leipzig, 1853–6); where no volume number is given, as often in the case of Theon, the reference is to volume II.

The works of Origen are cited as abbreviated above, with book, chapter, and section references as necessary (Greek Matthew with book and chapter, Latin Matthew with section), and the page number, in the Berlin edition when available, but otherwise in the edition of Lommatzsch or Migne.

PREFACE

THE PROBLEM of the way in which patristic exegetes viewed the New Testament, and indeed the whole Bible, has concerned scholars a good deal in recent years, especially since it has been discovered that many of the Fathers' methods were analogous to our own. The problem of historical criticism, however, does not seem to have occupied so much attention, though I should not fail to mention the work of Laeuchli, Daniélou, and the recent *Allegory and Event* by Hanson, which I have used in revising my own manuscript.

By concentrating on one problem, that of the life of Jesus, I have sought to see how early Christians up to and including Origen faced it, and what there is in their work which deserves retention or rejection.

The first chapter of this book was delivered in substance as a lecture in the autumn of 1957 at Union Theological Seminary, Brown University, the Philadelphia Divinity School, and the University of Chicago; it has been considerably revised since then. The whole book owes a good deal to the assistance given me by Professor Henry Chadwick and by my former student Professor W. R. Schoedel.

R. M. G.

The Divinity School,
University of Chicago

1

THE GOSPELS IN THE FIRST TWO CENTURIES

CONTEMPORARY New Testament critics are often rather proud of the degree to which they have been able to transcend the limitations of their predecessors, who lost themselves in minute details of textual, literary, and historical criticism and tried to find out something about the life of Jesus. Though there is considerable evidence that what has been contemporary is so no longer, the "contemporary" or almost contemporary attitude is so widespread that it deserves a little criticism.

The attitude seems to be based on two presuppositions. First, the "faith" or the proclamation of the "kerygma" was not really related to historical evidence. This presupposition can be supported to some extent by isolated verses from the Pauline epistles in which Paul is exaggerating the extent of his independence from the Church of Jerusalem. It can hardly be justified by the synoptic gospels or, for that matter, by John 20.30–1.

> Now Jesus did many other signs in the presence of his disciples, which are not written in this book; but these are written so that you may believe that Jesus is the Christ, the Son of God, and that by believing you may have life in his name.

Faith is not based on faith, or simply on events as events, but on the historical record of events, as in Paul's list of resurrection appearances and witnesses in 1 Cor. 15.

Second, literary and historical criticism are the creations of modern "rationalism". In the golden age of primitive faith, no one paid any attention to the literary and historical problems which the true believer ignored; only with the infiltration of Greek or Graeco-Roman conceptions into the pure stream of Hebrew-Christian revelation did such problems arise. Such a presupposition is based on the severance of the primitive Church from what succeeded it, on the sharp differentiation of "Hebrew" from "Greek" ideas, and upon all the host of related notions invented in order to create the notion that early Church history is nothing but a story of decline and fall.

In my opinion, both presuppositions are false, and it is the purpose of this book to show how the problems, historical in nature, which arise out of the canonical gospels whenever they are thoughtfully considered were faced by Christian writers in the first two or three centuries. I should not claim perfection for the methods, often borrowed from the Greek schools, which they followed, or for the results they achieved by using them. All I intend to do is to look carefully and critically at the procedures and achievements of the early Church Fathers, in the belief that we can learn something from them in regard not only to questions they themselves emphasized but also to questions, like that of writing the life of Jesus, which they did not emphasize. In other words, I am going to ask them a modern question, in the hope that the materials they provide will supply something of an answer to it. There is no reason to suppose that in historical matters their minds worked entirely differently from our own.

It must be admitted, however, that by asking a modern question we are likely to get a modernized answer. Ancient Christians had in mind a picture of a person with a "historical" life, but they were not primarily interested in dealing with that life either by using any psychological techniques or by employing historical tools to analyse the setting in time and place. They did not ask themselves, as we might ask ourselves of any historical character, what it was his nature to be and to do. They did not try to make Jesus comprehensible against his environment in the manner of a modern biographer. And once they had decided not only that Jesus himself was the divine logos but also that the sources for his life were written under divine inspiration, all the presuppositions which might make a "biographical" interest possible had disappeared.[1]

In spite of these difficulties we shall try to move back and forth

[1] For this paragraph I am indebted to Professor Henry Chadwick.

2

from ancient to modern times in the hope that some of the results will perhaps illuminate ideas held in both periods.

THE FOUR GOSPELS

Any attempt to recover the historical life of Jesus depends upon an analysis of the four gospels, of their interrelations, and of their sources. Analysis of the gospels themselves as literary documents means that we endeavour to observe and to understand what the individual evangelists say and how they say it; if possible, we may even be able to discover why they say what they say. Study of their interrelations means that we examine the extent to which Matthew, Mark, and Luke agree and the extent to which they disagree, in relation to matters of arrangement, of style, and of vocabulary, and try to explain both agreements and disagreements. Turning from these three gospels, called "synoptic" because to such a considerable extent they can be viewed together, we pass to the fourth gospel, which because of its unique arrangement and viewpoint, not to mention its content as a whole, has to be treated separately. When we consider the sources of the gospels we try to determine the extent to which any one of the evangelists may have made use of earlier documents (possibly including others of the gospels which we possess) and, behind such documents, various oral traditions or cycles of tradition which were in existence long before he wrote.

Like most of the early Fathers, we do not consider apocryphal gospels (those not preserved in the canon of the New Testament) or "unwritten sayings" as reliable sources for information about the life of Jesus. Too little control was exercised over the composition or transmission of these materials for us to be able to use them with any degree of confidence.

It is obvious that modern historical analysis of the gospels is somewhat different from the analysis provided in the early Church. The difference is due to several factors of varying importance. In the first place, the questions about authorship which have been raised, chiefly in modern times, mean that many of the questions we ask rarely entered the minds of the Fathers. In the patristic view, two of our gospels were written by apostles; the

3

other two were written by disciples of the apostles. Matthew and John were thus eyewitnesses to the events they described, while Mark derived his information from Peter, Luke from Paul. This traditional hypothesis meant that no questions could be asked about the sources, or possible sources, employed by either Matthew or John. The differences between these two gospels had to be explained exclusively by attempts to interpret the purposes which their authors had in view. In the second place, at least at Alexandria great emphasis was laid on the mantic inspiration of the evangelists, who by creating disagreements among their gospels were trying to lead their readers toward allegorical exegesis. In origin this theory may well have been intended to explain why there were disagreements of various kinds; but it tended to drive exegetes not to explain disagreements but to explain them away. Finally, when the Fathers dealt with literary and historical problems in the gospels they employed the methods traditionally taught in Greek schools of rhetoric. These methods could satisfactorily lead to the classification of literary forms and even to the assessment of degrees of credibility. Their use, however, meant that literary interrelations and the employment of sources could not be adequately handled. What was lacking was genuine historical criticism.

We shall see that even in the work of Origen, greatest of the early Christian exegetes, there is a failure to come to grips with the historical problem of the life of Jesus. In part this failure is due to Origen's Christological doctrine, in which the Incarnation is verbally accepted but effectively neglected; in part it is due to the methods of rhetorical analysis which he used. The two complement each other.

Before coming to Origen, however, we must look at some of the problems present in the gospels and see how they were faced or ignored by Christian writers before his time; then we shall deal with his own work in relation to some of the more important questions involved in writing a life of Jesus.

All three synoptic gospels begin the story of Jesus' public ministry with accounts of the mission of John the Baptist, of Jesus' baptism by him and the descent of the Spirit and the words

4

of a voice from heaven; then comes the account of the temptation in the wilderness, the arrest of John by Herod, preaching in Galilee, and the call of the first disciples. All three include the feeding of the five thousand, Peter's confession, Jesus' prediction of his own death, and his transfiguration. All three provide the story of the last journey to Jerusalem, the triumphal entry, the cleansing of the temple, teaching in and near Jerusalem (largely apocalyptic), the last supper, the Gethsemane scene, and the rest of the passion narrative. Their accounts of resurrection appearances are somewhat different. Matthew explicitly locates them in Galilee; Mark does so by implication; but Luke places them near Jerusalem.

Now when we turn from the synoptic gospels to John, we find a picture quite different in character. There is no infancy narrative; instead, John provides a theological prologue concerning the divine Logos. Next he tells of John the Baptist; he insists that he was not the Christ and does not mention Jesus' baptism by him; then he describes the call of the first disciples in Galilee. This event is followed by Jesus' changing water into wine at a wedding in Cana, a visit to Capernaum, and a journey to Jerusalem for the cleansing of the temple. John explicitly states (3.24) that the Baptist had not yet been imprisoned. Toward the middle of Jesus' ministry we find the feeding of the five thousand and something like Peter's confession, but there is no explicit prediction of Jesus' death, and no transfiguration. Jesus visits Jerusalem several times, not once as in the synoptics. The triumphal entry is not followed by the cleansing of the temple, an event which John has placed early in Jesus' ministry, and the words of institution are omitted, since John has paraphrased them in his account of the meaning of the feeding of the five thousand. The last supper, treated as a Passover meal by the synoptists, is not so regarded by John, who has Jesus crucified on the day of preparation for the Passover (18.28; 19.14). There is no Gethsemane scene. The synoptists have Simon of Cyrene carry Jesus' cross; according to John, Jesus himself carried it. The resurrection appearances take place in Jerusalem; only the appendix to John (21.1–23) describes an appearance in Galilee.

Apart from these differences related to events, there is also a difference between the teaching of Jesus as reported in the synoptics and the long Johannine discourses, which deal chiefly with the revelation of the Father through the Son. Only one such saying is preserved by the synoptic evangelists (Matt. 11.25–7; Luke 10.21–2). Without great exaggeration one can say that while the synoptists describe Jesus' proclamation of the imminent coming, or the inauguration, of the kingdom of God, John tells of the meaning of the revelation of the Son of God. It is hard to believe that, historically considered, both accounts of Jesus can be correct. And if the early Christian tradition that John wrote last is reliable, his gospel contains a theological meditation on the meaning of the Jesus described, and perhaps misunderstood, in the earlier gospels.

It is at this point that the problem of whether John knew the synoptic gospels or not becomes important. In recent years there have been several advocates of the hypothesis that he did not know them but drew on traditions partly like those they used, partly unlike them.[1] On the other hand, Windisch presented strong arguments on behalf of the theory that he wrote in order to supplant the synoptic gospels, which he knew.[2] And Bultmann has argued that most of the passages which have synoptic parallels are the work of an ecclesiastical redactor, determined to make the gospel acceptable in churches which used the synoptic gospels.[3] One may also mention the claim that affinities between John and the Dead Sea Scrolls prove that his gospel was written early;[4] it is hard to see what validity such a claim can have, for we know that Dead Sea documents were employed by Christians writing no earlier than the second century.[5]

The most likely solution of the problem seems to be that John's gospel is actually independent of the synoptics; he did

---

[1] P. Gardner-Smith, *St John and the Synoptic Gospels* (Cambridge, 1938); E. R. Goodenough in *JBL* 64 (1945), pp. 145–82; cf. also pp. 535–44 (R. P. Casey and Goodenough).

[2] H. Windisch, *Johannes und die Synoptiker* (Leipzig, 1926).

[3] R. Bultmann, *Das Evangelium des Johannes* (Göttingen, 1941).

[4] R. E. Brown in K. Stendahl, *The Scrolls and the New Testament* (New York, 1957), p. 206; F. M. Cross, Jr, *The Ancient Library of Qumran* (New York, 1958), pp. 161–2.

[5] Cf. M. de Jonge, *The Testaments of the Twelve Patriarchs* (Assen, 1953).

not use them among his sources. To date his gospel, however, is practically impossible. It probably comes from a time considerably before the end of the first century.

John's independence does not, however, mean that his record of events is more reliable than that of the other evangelists. The fact that his theology, like that of Paul, influenced the later Church more strongly than that of the synoptists is no guarantee of his work as an historian. And the anonymous statement at the end of his gospel, "This is the disciple who bears witness of these things, and wrote these things; and we know that his witness is true" (21.24), provides us with little information, since we do not know that by "true" is meant "historically accurate" (contrast Luke 1.3–4).

How do the evangelists actually know the words and deeds they report? Here it is significant that Mark represents the disciples as failing to comprehend some of the essential points of Jesus' teaching. They do not understand the inner meaning of parables and have to have them explained privately (4.13,34). They do not understand the meaning of the miraculous feedings of the five and four thousand (6.52; 8.16–21). And they cannot understand what Jesus means by foretelling resurrection after suffering (8.32–3; 9.32; 10.32–45). Both Luke and Matthew modify the disciples' understanding of parables; Luke omits most of the relevant materials, while Matthew adds (13.51) a significant bit of dialogue. "Have you understood all these things? They say to him, Yes." Luke omits all the material dealings with failure to understand the feeding, while Matthew, once more, alters it at some points (especially 14.33). As for the passion-predictions, Luke retains them, generally speaking, while Matthew omits, contradicts (17.23), or modifies them (20.20–8).

It is plain enough that the tendency after Mark is to soften the picture of the disciples' ignorance found in the earliest gospel. But it must be remembered that Mark himself is well aware of what the true teaching is—the true teaching on the grounds of which he can criticize the disciples' ignorance. And if he knows it, it must have become clear at some time after the earthly ministry of Jesus. It would be natural to assume that he knew the true

7

teaching because of the resurrection and the gift of the Spirit.

What is implicit in Mark and the other synoptics becomes explicit in the fourth gospel, where we find at two significant points that emphasis is laid on the disciples' remembering and interpreting earlier events. The first passage is that concerned with the cleansing of the temple. After the cleansing, "his disciples remembered that it was written, 'Zeal for thy house will consume me'" (John 2.17). After a discussion of Jesus' words after the cleansing, John goes on to say that, "When therefore he was raised from the dead, his disciples remembered that he had said this; and they believed the scripture and the word which Jesus had spoken" (2.22). A similar description of creative remembering is found in relation to the triumphal entry. Jesus enters on a colt and fulfils a prophecy in Zechariah: "his disciples did not understand this at first, but when Jesus was glorified, then they remembered that this had been written of him and had been done to him" (12.16). Since John, unlike the synoptic evangelists, has separated the triumphal entry from the cleansing of the temple,[1] he may be suggesting that his own chronology is right. Or he may be insisting on the importance of reflective meditation in the transmission of tradition. In any event, the "remembering" of the disciples is no merely human activity. John explicitly teaches that it is the Holy Spirit who, after the resurrection, teaches the disciples all things and brings to their remembrance all that Jesus taught them (14.26). This Spirit of Truth leads Christians into all the truth (15.13).

If John knew the synoptic gospels, then, he would have regarded them as inferior to his own work, for they reflect a standpoint earlier than the resurrection and therefore inadequate. To be sure, Luke tried to write history. He constantly refers to witnesses to the life, death, and resurrection of Jesus.[2] But his

[1] Luke apparently places them on the same day, while Mark and Matthew have a night intervene.

[2] Luke 1.2; 24.48; Acts 1.8,22; 2.32; 3.15; 4.33; 5.32; 10.36–43. Since the ordinary text of Luke 22.19–20 is close to 1 Cor. 11.23–5, ancient readers might assume that Luke's information came from Paul, Paul's (as he says) "from the Lord".

gospel is not a product of creative reminiscence as John's is. The fourth gospel is the only gospel explicitly based on post-resurrection reinterpretation.

It is also the only gospel which represents itself as the work of an eyewitness to the life of Jesus. Neither Mark nor Matthew has anything to say about authorship; it may be the mention of the name Matthew in Matthew 9.9 ("Levi" in the parallels, Mark 2.13 and Luke 5.27) which led ancient critics to ascribe the gospel to him. Luke explicitly claims to follow eyewitnesses, not to be an eyewitness himself (1.2-3). But of the Word of God the evangelist says that he "dwelt among us" and "we beheld his glory" (1.14), a glory manifested in the signs worked before the disciples (2.11). Who is the evangelist? In this gospel as not in the synoptics there is a mysterious "disciple whom Jesus loved" (13.23-5), who takes Mary to his own house (19.26-7) and first reaches the empty tomb (20.4). It is probably this disciple who "was known to the high priest" (18.15) and witnessed the coming of blood and water from Jesus' side (19.34-5). And at least according to the epilogue to the gospel, this disciple wrote the book (21.24). Who was he? Various answers have been given. "Tradition" suggests that he was John the son of Zebedee, but this conjecture has nothing to commend it. A more likely guess, based on the gospel itself, would be that the author was Nicodemus. Nicodemus had a private conversation with Jesus which is reported in the gospel (3.1-15 or 3.1-21); as a Pharisee, he was known to the high priest (7.50); and he was in Jerusalem at the time of the crucifixion (19.39-42). We may not be able to tell who the author actually was, but it is important to note that he seems to regard himself as an eyewitness. For this reason, as well as because of his concern for theology, early Christians valued his work highly.

DOCETIC-GNOSTIC IDEAS

Historical analysis did not arise in the course of the earliest controversies. Instead, in the early second century we find theological exegetes of doubtful orthodoxy insisting that Jesus, or more properly the Christ, since he was a divine being, was not born, did not suffer, and did not die. When Ignatius, Bishop of Antioch, insisted, in opposition to such persons, that Jesus "truly" did various things he did not enter into the question of historical evidence, since they did not raise it. Genuine debate could take place only when specific pieces of evidence were brought into the dispute.

A relatively early example of such specific evidence is provided in Irenaeus' account of the teaching of the gnostic Basilides.[1] According to this account, Basilides held that Jesus was not actually crucified because Simon of Cyrene took his place. Such an opinion seems ridiculous at first glance. But if we look at the gospel of Mark we see that while the author clearly intended to describe the crucifixion of Jesus, his words can be understood as referring to the crucifixion of Simon (Mark 15.21–5). And it appears that the later evangelists found Mark's account inadequate. According to Mark, the title on the cross read "King of the Jews" (15.26); Matthew changes it to "This is Jesus, king of the Jews" (27.37). Luke adds that Simon carried the cross behind Jesus (23.26), and John does not mention Simon but says that Jesus carried his own cross (19.17). This gnostic interpretation shows how severely literal gnostic exegesis could be, and how embarrassing it became to its opponents. On the other hand, alterations made in order to avoid one kind of difficulty could produce further difficulties, once the original occasion of the alterations was forgotten; for the stories of the crucifixion are now different in the various gospels.

A real exegetical crisis was produced in the Roman Church about the year 137, when a certain Marcion came from Pontus by the Black Sea and proceeded to argue not only that the authentic gospel contradicted the Old Testament (such a view was familiar from the teaching of earlier gnostics) but also that there was only one authentic gospel, at first transmitted orally, then put into writing and severely interpolated by enthusiasts for Judaism. Upon examination, this gospel proves to have been that traditionally ascribed to Luke; but Marcion presented it in a form

[1] *Adv. haer.* I, 24, 4, p. 200, Harvey.

considerably reduced by the removal of what he regarded as interpolations.

We need not pay too much attention to the many minor changes which Marcion made in the gospel of Luke, for the major ones clearly indicate the purpose he had in mind.[1] His gospel began with the words, "In the fifteenth year of Tiberius [Luke 3.1a] the saving Spirit Jesus came down to Capernaum [Luke 4.31]."[2] Thus he omitted the stories of Jesus' conception, birth, infancy, baptism, genealogy, temptation, preaching, and rejection at Nazareth. His gospel was therefore more like John than like Matthew and Mark, since among these items John records only the baptism, and he severely modifies the story. Such deletions would be appropriate in telling the story of a "saving spirit" or divine being, as Origen later suggests in regard to the fourth gospel. The other extensive omission is that of Luke 19.29–46: preparation for the entry into Jerusalem, the triumphal entry itself, Jesus' lament over Jerusalem, and the cleansing of the temple. Because of his hostility toward Judaism, Marcion did not like the notion that Jesus entered Jerusalem as its king and cleansed the temple there. But he may also have been aware that in John the cleansing is placed early rather than late in Jesus' ministry. He may have been given theological assistance by this chronological difficulty. In other words, at least at these two key points Marcion's gospel was synoptic in content but Johannine in framework.[3]

In Marcion's opinion Jesus had proclaimed a completely novel (in other words, non-Jewish) gospel which was corrupted by his Jewish disciples because they were slaves of tradition. This gospel was given again by revelation to Paul, whose letters were once more corrupted and interpolated. When properly corrected, however, they could serve as the key to the recovery of the true gospel. Marcion knew from his reading of the Pauline epistles that there had been a conflict between Paul and the more

---

[1] For his theological presuppositions cf. *The Letter and the Spirit*, pp. 115–19.

[2] He retained other verses from Luke 4 but rearranged them; cf. A. v. Harnack, *Marcion: das Evangelium vom fremden Gott* (2nd ed., Leipzig, 1924), pp. 183*–7*.

[3] For an attempt to solve the difficulty cf. O. Cullmann, *The Early Church* (Philadelphia, 1956), pp. 59–75.

Judaistic apostles of Jerusalem, especially James and Peter. And he knew that the apostle had received his gospel not from any man but by means of a revelation of Jesus Christ (Gal. 1.12). In 2 Cor. 12 he could read that Paul received a great many revelations, and from 1 Cor. 11.23 he could conclude that among them was the story of the last supper, since the only gospel was the authentic one which Paul had received. Yet Luke is not Pauline. It therefore had to be made Pauline, or semi-Pauline, by the removal of Judaizing interpolations. The basic ground of Marcion's work, then, was the Pauline doctrine, or part of the Pauline doctrine, which he found in parts of the major Pauline epistles. Either he did not know Acts and the pastoral epistles or else he rejected them. We have already suggested that he may have known something like the gospel of John and was able to use it for the framework of the life of Jesus.

The method Marcion employed is found among Graeco-Roman grammarians who believed that they were able to separate mythological additions from ancient theological texts. These additions had been made by poets in order to charm their readers or by priests in the interest of their own superstitions.[1] Marcion's theory is similar to that of the grammarians. In his view, Jewish apostles and others made additions in order to Judaize the gospel. We do not know whether he offered any proof for this theory or not. But since no evidence against it was available, his "heresy" created a sensation in the Roman Church and elsewhere. He was expelled from the Roman community.

Marcion had regarded Church history as the story of interpolation, or in other words the story of decline and fall. At Rome about the same time, the Valentinians interpreted it in the light of the ultimate gospel, their own Gospel of Truth; and they proceeded to interpret the other gospels allegorically so that the same doctrine could be found in all. In the school of Valentinus we find an attempt to classify the words and deeds of Jesus, ostensibly in relation to their form but really in relation to their content. The Valentinian Theodotus tells us that Jesus taught his disciples "at first, typically and mystically; later, parabolically

[1] *The Letter and the Spirit*, pp. 19–25.

and enigmatically; and thirdly, clearly and plainly, in private".[1] This scheme is presumably based on the gospels. There we read that Jesus' first sign involved the transformation of water from Jewish water-pots into wine (John 2.1–11). Later he taught his disciples in dark sayings (John 16.25) or in parables (Mark 4.33–4). Finally he spoke openly to them, when they were alone (John 16.25,29; cf. Mark 4.34).

The difference between public and private teaching was further emphasized by another Valentinian teacher. He held that Jesus secretly taught only those disciples who were able to understand "arguments, enigmas, and parables". In this way he taught them about the true Father, but elsewhere he used the term "God" to refer to the Demiurge or God of the Old Testament.[2] This point too is based on the gospels, where the term "Father" is used by Jesus only when he is alone with his disciples.

The Valentinian conception, then, involves a contrast between public teaching not literally true and private teaching which is genuinely theological. It also involves belief in the disciples' progressive understanding of the meaning of Jesus' ministry, an understanding presumably culminating in the theology of Valentinus himself.

With this exegetical key, the Valentinians proved to be remarkably subtle exegetes of Jesus' teaching, especially of his parables, which had already been treated as allegories by the synoptic evangelists. Ptolemaeus was able to read the doctrine of the heavenly aeons into the prologue of the fourth gospel, and Heracleon provided exegetical notes on at least the first eight chapters of the gospel. Heracleon was well aware of some of the stylistic difficulties in John. For example, he argues that while John 1.15–17 was quoted from John the Baptist, the following verse ("No one has ever seen God . . .") is a comment by the evangelist. Origen disagreed with him sharply, ascribing the whole section to the Baptist.[3] Actually, both commentators were wrong, since the evangelist's statements begin with John 1.16. But the fact that Heracleon was able to see a difficulty shows that he possessed the critical eye indispensable for the allegorist.

---

[1] Clement, *Exc. ex Theod.* 66.   [2] Irenaeus, *Adv. haer.* 2, 27, 3, p. 348.   [3] *J* 6, 2, p. 109.

Both Marcionites and Valentinians presented grave difficulties to the majority of early Christians, unaccustomed to read the gospels with such subtle criticisms in view. Both philology and historical criticism were practically unknown in Christianity before the rise of gnostic teachers. But as a result of this gnostic exegesis, it became necessary for Christians to present some literary and historical defence of the gospels. Examples of this new way of looking at things are to be found in the writings of Papias and Justin.

LITERARY AND HISTORICAL CRITICISM

Marcionites and Valentinians made trouble for their fellow-Christians by insisting that they possessed the true text of the gospel or the true exegesis of the gospel, or both. When Christians who were less heterodox tried to refute such claims, they were inevitably driven to make use of the critical methods taught in the grammatical and rhetorical schools of their time. Their use of these methods is not surprising, since those Christians who wrote books had almost certainly been educated in the schools. Jesus may (or may not) have been self-taught, but it is certain that the New Testament writers had learned how to write in schools, and that at least Paul, Luke, and the authors of 1–2 Peter, Hebrews, and James were acquainted with Greek rhetoric. Furthermore, the preface to Luke-Acts shows that its author stood, and intended to stand, in the tradition of Greek historical writing.[1] He tells us that he has had "many" predecessors, that he himself had followed everything carefully (ἀκριβῶς) for some time past, and that he is writing an orderly (καθεξῆς) account by means of which certainty may be attained (Luke 1.1–4). Marcion omitted this statement from his version of Luke, presumably because no emphasis on divine inspiration is to be found in it; besides, it refers to other gospel writings.

The first task which had to be undertaken by Christians who

[1] Theon tells us that the historian should mention his subject's ancestors and parents and note the Olympiads in which an Olympic victor won (83.29—84.1); Luke, unlike Mark, tells about the genealogy of Jesus (3.23–38), names his parents (1.27), and dates the mission of John the Baptist (3.1–2).

wanted to discuss the gospels was that of classifying them and their materials. Naturally enough, they used the classifications already available in the manuals composed by Graeco-Roman rhetoricians. Here they could find, apart from forms likely to be found only in rhetorical addresses, about five classifications which could be used in connection with the gospels or what was in them. Theon, who wrote his *Progymnasmata* early in the second century of our era, gives definitions and descriptions of myth (a false account portraying truth), narrative (an account descriptive of events which took place or might have taken place), and χρεία (a brief declaration or action referred to some definite person or to something like a person). The χρεία, says Theon, resembles both a proverbial saying (γνώμη) and an ἀπομνημόνευμα, but in some respects it is different from both. It is different from a proverbial saying because (1) it always refers to a particular person; (2) it is not always general in nature; (3) it does not always give a moral lesson; and (4) it is not always simply a saying. It is different from an ἀπομνημόνευμα because (1) it is shorter and (2) it always refers to a particular person.[1] Theon provides an elaborate classification of χρεῖαι,[2] but other rhetoricians, such as Hermogenes, regarded it as unnecessarily complicated,[3] and we do not need to discuss it at this point.

A Christian scholar of the second century would inevitably deny that the gospels had anything to do with the category of myth. He might well suggest that they were historical narratives (διήγησεις) which contained historical materials (διηγήματα).[4] But actually what our earliest witnesses had in mind was that the gospels were ἀπομνημονεύματα, materials worked up from χρεῖαι and γνῶμαι. In this way they were indirectly pointing toward the oral origin of the gospel traditions. Papias, Bishop of Hierapolis in Asia Minor early in the second century, himself relied on oral tradition and stated that it was preferable to written documents.[5] He described Mark's work with the verb ἀπομνημονεύειν;[6]

---

[1] Pp. 72.28; 78.15; 96.19—97.6. [2] Pp. 97.11—101.2. [3] P. 6.15 (7.10 Rabe).
[4] This distinction is drawn by Hermogenes, p. 4.21 (4.9 Rabe).
[5] Papias preferred the "living voice" of tradition; cf. Quintilian, *Inst.* 2, 2, 7.
[6] Eusebius, *H.E.* 3, 39, 15.

similarly Justin, who wrote at Rome about 150, classified the gospels as the ἀπομνημονεύματα of the apostles.[1]

Papias did not confine his historical studies to an analysis of literary forms. He tells us, in a passage preserved by Eusebius,[2] that he engaged in historical investigations which took him back to the first generation of Christian disciples.

> If someone happened to come along who had been a follower of the elders, I investigated his words—in regard to what Andrew or Peter or Philip or Thomas, or James or John or Matthew, or any other of the Lord's disciples, had said, or what Aristion and the elder John, the Lord's disciples, were saying.

Here we can probably differentiate two stages of tradition. The first group of seven disciples belongs to the earliest times of Christianity, to the apostolic generation itself. The next two names, those of Aristion and John, presumably are those of older contemporaries of Papias. The difficulty with Papias' words lies in the fact that he seems both to differentiate elders from disciples and at the same time to identify them. Since elsewhere, however, he calls his own informants "elders", it would appear that in general he recognized a difference between the two groups.

But who were the disciples of Jesus whose sayings were being reported? It is fairly obvious that Papias' list is based primarily upon the apostles or disciples named in the gospel of John. It is there, and only there that we meet, in the same order, Andrew (1.40), Peter (1.40–2), Philip (1.43), and Thomas (11.16). In the synoptic lists of apostles their names are never found in this order. We must therefore conclude that Papias knew either the gospel of John or its author, and perhaps both.

The fact that he knows John is confirmed by what he says about his own writing.[3]

> I did not take pleasure in those who say much, as the many do, but in those who teach the truth; nor did I record alien commandments but, instead, those given by the Lord to the faith and derived from the Truth itself.

Here he is criticizing the rise of false gospels in the light of his own tradition derived from the Jesus who was himself the Truth

---

[1] See p. 20 below.   [2] *H.E.* 3, 39, 4.   [3] Eusebius, *H.E.* 3, 39, 3.

(John 14.6). He may think that the apocryphal gospels are unduly lengthy. He may be emphasizing this point because he remembers that brevity is the soul of the χρεία-form which Jesus and his disciples used.[1]

His remarks about Matthew are not altogether unambiguous. He tells us that Matthew compiled either the oracles of Jesus or (less probably) the oracles about Jesus in a Hebrew dialect; afterwards, various translations were made into Greek. This statement presumably means that in Papias' time there were several Greek gospels which claimed the authority of Matthew. One of them was probably our gospel of Matthew; another may have been the gospel according to the Hebrews, which often resembles it. Papias was unwilling to choose between, or among, them. The fact that "each reader translated as he was able" suggests that the authority of the gospel had been considerably diminished by the diversity in the translations.

In discussing Mark, Papias does no more than to reproduce what "the elder John" had told him. Mark's gospel goes back in substance to the disciple Peter, whose translator Mark was.

> Mark, who was an interpreter of Peter, wrote down accurately whatever he recorded of what had been either said or done by the Lord, but ⟨his account was⟩ by no means in order. For he neither heard nor followed the Lord, but later, as I said, ⟨he heard and followed⟩ Peter.

The disorder of Mark's gospel is thus due to the circumstances under which Mark wrote—and also to the way in which Peter taught.[2]

> Peter gave his teachings in χρεία-form; he was not making a compilation (σύνταξις) of the dominical oracles.

In this way Peter differed from Matthew, who did make such a σύνταξις.

> Therefore Mark was not wrong when he wrote down single items in the form of ἀπομνημονεύματα ὡς ἀπομνηόνευσεν. For he had one purpose in mind; not to leave out anything he heard or to tell anything falsely among these items.

[1] Cf. Theon, p. 96.19; Hermogenes, p. 5.26 (6.5 Rabe).
[2] For this translation of χρεία cf. R. O. P. Taylor, *The Groundwork of the Gospels* (Oxford, 1946), pp. 75–90.

Obviously the elder is admitting the force of criticisms which have been made of Mark's gospel. At the same time he is trying to explain them away in relation to the circumstances under which Mark wrote and the purpose he had in view.

Mark's gospel is not a σύνταξις, a finished product of rhetorical art. It is an ἀπομνημόνευμα or a collection of ἀπομνημονεύματα based on the traditions which had already been shaped into χρεῖαι by Peter. Now according to the rules laid down by the rhetoricians, a χρεία can be criticized on the grounds (among others) that it leaves things out or that what it tells is false.[1] It cannot be criticized for its lack of order, because it has no special order. The fact that the elder and Papias clearly indicate that Mark's gospel has the virtues of truth and of relative completeness, while it does not have the order which was in any case unnecessary, shows that they were examining the gospel from the standpoint of Greek literary criticism.[2]

Now if we trace the process of composition and analysis from the beginning onwards, we see that there were originally memories and oral traditions about what Jesus had said and done. These were given shape in χρεία-form by the apostle Peter, and doubtless by others as well. The χρεῖαι which came from Peter were recorded by his disciple Mark, who intended to preserve all that Peter taught and to preserve it accurately. Whether he was successful or not, we do not know. He did not produce a finished composition, for his gospel lacks arrangement, whether chronological or literary or both. If the elder John was the author of the fourth gospel, he must have believed that his own book did possess a correct order. And to judge from Papias' relation to the gospel of John, he must have held the same view. But Papias must also have valued his own work highly. It was as close to the authentic oral tradition as the gospels of Mark and Luke; unlike Matthew, it was written in Greek. Unfortunately it was

[1] Theon, p. 104.15–18.
[2] According to Weinel (RE XIV, 1858) not more than the first sentence about Mark comes from the elder John; "as I said" shows that Papias is giving his own adaptation of the elder's remarks. F. C. Grant (The Earliest Gospel, New York, 1943, pp. 34–7) also ascribes much of the information to Papias' revision, but does not separate the two sources so sharply. Neither do I.

not preserved by many of the Christian churches and is now lost.

As a historian, Papias regarded the work of the evangelists as not unlike his own. He cannot have believed that they possessed some special gift of inspiration for their writing, since he describes Mark's efforts in purely historical terms. He may well have believed that John's gospel was more closely related to the Truth who was Jesus, but if this inference is correct he valued John's closeness to historical events more than any inspiration he may have been given as an evangelist.

Almost exactly the same kind of analysis of the gospels and their sources is to be found in the writings of the apologist Justin shortly after the middle of the second century. Critics have often regarded Justin as a rather inept philosophical theologian, and he himself describes some of the gaps in his philosophical education. But when he lists the subjects with which his acquaintance was slight, he does not include grammar and rhetoric among them.[1] From his writings we should assume that he had some training in a school of rhetoric. Such training seems to be reflected in what he says about the Christian books.

In Justin's opinion, the sayings of Jesus were "brief and concise" because he was not a sophist, a speaker devoted to words for their own sake.[2] What Justin has in mind is the form of the sayings in the sermon on the mount, from which he gives some quotations. In other words, for him the sayings are γνῶμαι, short sententious sayings characteristic of "gnomic" poets or philosophers. "A gnome", says Hermogenes, "is a summary statement given in a general declaration, discouraging or recommending something or explaining the nature of each kind of action."[3] Since it was gnomic, Jesus' teaching was more luminous than the sun,[4] even though on some occasions his words were "veiled"— as when he spoke about the "sign of Jonah" (Matt. 16.4).[5] Presumably Justin regarded the parables as "veiled" too; and he makes practically no allusions to them.[6]

[1] *Dial.* 2, 4; cf. *JTS* N.S. 7 (1956), pp. 246–8.   [2] *Apol.* 1, 14, 5; cf. *Dial.* 18, 1.
[3] II, 7, 12 Spengel (8, 16 Rabe).   [4] *Dial.* 121, 2.
[5] *Dial.* 107, 1; for similar speech in the Old Testament cf. *Dial.* 52, 1; 76, 2 and 6.
[6] A. Jülicher, *Die Gleichnisreden Jesu* I (2nd ed., Tübingen, 1910), pp. 210–11.

What of the accounts of Jesus' life? Outsiders might suppose that the stories about him are like myths composed by poets and are nothing but wonder stories (τερατολογία).[1] They would be wrong if they made such an analysis, first because the life of Jesus is the fulfilment of Old Testament prophecy and second because the literary form of the gospels is not that of myth. Like Papias, Justin classifies the gospels as ἀπομνημονεύματα. He may well be comparing them with the *Apomnēmoneumata of Socrates* by Xenophon, since he uses this work (though without mentioning its title) in his *Second Apology*, and frequently compares Jesus with Socrates.[2] The gospels are ἀπομνημονεύματα which come from the apostles.[3] More precisely, they can be described as "composed by the apostles and by those who followed them".[4] Here Justin is probably relying on the preface to Luke, where we find the same word for "follow" and a similar word for "compose" (Luke 1.1,3). Scholars have sometimes thought that he is referring to two gospels by apostles (Matthew, John) and two by followers (Mark, Luke). But soon afterwards he refers to a statement found only in Mark 3.16–17 and ascribes it to the *Apomnēmoneumata of Peter*.[5] It looks as if he was not concerned with any careful distinction between apostolic and sub-apostolic gospels. Indeed, to refer Mark's gospel to Peter means to emphasize its ultimate apostolic origin and to treat its authority as equal to that of either Matthew or John.

We should add that while Justin almost certainly knew the fourth gospel he rarely made use of it, and he never cites passages from it as derived from ἀπομνημονεύματα. It may be that at Rome the synoptic gospels were regarded more highly than John was. We know that at a later date at least one Roman Christian explicitly rejected the fourth gospel.[6] And the words of Jesus found in it can hardly be classified as "brief and concise".

Were these gospels inspired by the Spirit or Logos of God? Justin does not say so. But he does say that though the twelve apostles were unlearned and unable to speak (with any rhetorical skill) they were imbued with power from God which enabled them

---

[1] *Apol* 1, 54, 2.   [2] *Apol.* 2, 11, 2–7.   [3] *Apol.* 1, 66, 3; *Dial.* 100–7.
[4] *Dial.* 103, 8.   [5] *Dial.* 106, 3.   [6] See p. 28 below.

to proclaim the gospel.[1] Presumably this divine power, present in their oral preaching and teaching, was reflected in the work of those who compiled their words.

Justin's main concern, however, was not with divine inspiration but with historical accuracy. He believed that non-Christian readers could find evidence for the gospel story of Jesus' birth in tax declarations submitted under the procurator Quirinius and (*ex hypothesi?*) available at Rome a century and a half later.[2] Similarly he instructed his readers to look in the Acts of Pilate for confirmation of the miracles of Jesus and details about his crucifixion.[3] Presumably such official documents did exist, but it is not certain whether Justin has them in mind or is thinking of the Christian forgeries we encounter later.[4]

What Justin does not mention is also worth noting. While he believes that Jesus was born in a cave, he does not say that the cave is available for inspection; Origen, writing a century later, is the first to say so.[5] Again, while he thinks that as a carpenter Jesus made ploughs and yokes—presumably because they are mentioned in Luke 9.62 and Matt. 11.30—he does not say that they have been preserved.[6] Justin was not concerned with the later trend toward confirming New Testament statements by archaeology.

The four canonical gospels were not the only sources of information for the life of Jesus which Christians possessed in the first half of the second century. The oral tradition, from which these gospels had been compiled, continued to flourish, as we can see from the statement of Papias. And Papias himself, according to both Irenaeus and Eusebius, recorded in his writings some oral traditions which are not found in the gospels. Moreover, there were various apocryphal gospels, some circulated under the names of apostles supposedly responsible for their contents, others named

[1] *Apol.* 1, 39, 3. This statement implies the inspiration of the "gospel", however, not that of the written gospels (cf. 1.33,5).

[2] *Apol.* 1, 34, 2; for the translation cf. Kübler in *RE* IV A, 1899.

[3] *Apol.* 1, 48, 3; 35, 9.

[4] Cf. J. Quasten, *Patrology* I (Westminster, Md., 1950), pp. 115–18.

[5] *Dial.* 78, 5; Origen, *C* 1, 51, p. 102.

[6] *Dial.* 88, 8; cf. Irenaeus, *Adv. haer.* 4, 34, 4, p. 272. Origen (*C* 6, 36, p. 106) says that Jesus was not a carpenter.

for the groups of Christians who made use of them. The first class is represented by gospels ascribed to Peter and to Thomas, among others; the second includes the gospels "according to the Hebrews" (Jewish Christians) and "according to the Egyptians".

With his enthusiasm for oral tradition, Papias was willing to make use of a story of a woman "accused of many sins before the Lord"; and according to Eusebius this story was also to be found in the gospel according to the Hebrews.[1] It is by no means certain that Papias derived it from this book, but his preservation of it shows clearly that he did not confine himself to materials found in the four gospels. Indeed, his remarks about some of the gospels suggest that he was not very fond of them. They left out traditions which he thought ought to be retained.

Not only did Papias accept such traditions, but also Justin, who relied chiefly on the four gospels, made use of traditions not derived from them. It is likely that most, if not all, of these additional materials are derived from lost gospels.[2] Nevertheless, in Justin's time a reaction was evidently setting in against the use of materials not found in the four gospels. The four were regarded as authoritative by most Christians; the other gospels were not.

The most significant attempt during the second century to recover the life of Jesus was that made by a certain Tatian, trained in grammar and rhetoric according to his own testimony, and at one time a disciple of Justin at Rome. Tatian clearly built upon the results achieved by his predecessors in analysing the nature of the gospels. Papias had pointed out that the gospel of Mark was not written in order, and Tatian rarely followed Mark's order where it was not paralleled by that of Matthew. Papias had followed John's order in providing a list of the apostles, and Tatian, as we shall see, came close to the same sequence. Moreover Tatian's conception of the gospels as historical documents is very much like that set forth by both Papias and Justin. He differs from his predecessors however, because he probably did not make use of any material not found in the four canonical books.

---

[1] Eusebius, *H.E.* 3, 39, 17.
[2] Cf. E. R. Buckley in *JTS* 36 (1935), pp. 173–6.

No one knows precisely where or when Tatian compiled his *Diatessaron*, a synthesis of the four canonical gospels. The earliest references to it are found in the Syriac *Doctrine of Addai* and in Eusebius, but Irenaeus, Clement, and Origen make no mention of the work.[1] On the other hand, at Dura Carl Kraeling discovered a Greek fragment of the *Diatessaron* which comes from the early third century.[2] It was in existence even though ecclesiastical writers maintained silence about it.

To-day the *Diatessaron* is lost, as far as its original text is concerned; but its framework can be recovered from a group of late witnesses whose evidence is available in a treatise published by J. H. Hill in 1894. Hill relied almost exclusively on an Arabic version of a Syriac *Diatessaron*. His conclusion that this version probably represents the original arrangement of Tatian's work is still generally, and rightly, maintained by scholars.[3]

At first glance the *Diatessaron* resembles a patch-work, or more precisely a "crazy-quilt". After taking blocks of verses from John, Matthew, and Luke, Tatian began his real work of weaving together at a point where Marcan materials became available; and from that point onward his arrangement necessarily began to deviate from that provided by any one of the four gospels. One might suppose, since he begins and ends with verses from the fourth gospel, that the Johannine order was that which he favoured. This is not the case, however. At some points he corrects the synoptics by John, but more often he corrects John by the synoptics. Thus he follows the Johannine order from the beginning to the end of the first sign of Cana (John 2.11). But he transfers the cleansing of the temple (2.13–22) to Jesus' last visits to Jerusalem because the synoptic evangelists place it there. He removes from this point a comment on "signs" worked by Jesus (2.23–5), since only one has been performed. And he places Jesus' conversation with Nicodemus (3.1–21) in

---

[1] Eusebius, *H.E.* 4, 29. Both Clement and Origen knew the *Oration* of Tatian.

[2] C. H. Kraeling, *A Greek Fragment of Tatian's Diatessaron from Dura* (London, 1934).

[3] J. H. Hill, *The Earliest Life of Christ* (Edinburgh, 1894); cf. E. Preuschen and A. Pott, *Tatian's Diatessaron aus dem arabischen übersetzt* (Heidelberg, 1926); A. J. B. Higgins in *JTS* 45 (1944), pp. 187–99; B. M. Metzger in *JBL* 69 (1950), pp. 261–80.

Jerusalem because it refers back to "signs" (3.2) and because elsewhere (8.50; 19.39) Nicodemus is found only in Jerusalem. Similarly the discourse with the Samaritan woman (4.4–45a) is moved to a later point in Jesus' ministry because the synoptic outline does not allow for a journey through Samaria at this stage. The healing of a paralytic at Jerusalem and the discourse based on it (5.1–47) are set later because the witness of John the Baptist is regarded as past in the account (5.33–5).

Tatian feels free to rearrange the twelfth chapter of John. His own sequence is as follows: a plot against Lazarus (12.9–11), the anointing of Jesus (12.3–8), a comment by the evangelist (12.16),[1] the triumphal entry (12.12–15, 17–18), the discourse related to the Greeks (12.19–36a), Jesus' final words about judgement (12.42–50), and the evangelist's summary (12.36^b–41). It is evident that he regards the twelfth chapter as something rather artificially constructed by John. Its order is not chronological. And doubtless he reaches this conclusion not only by comparing John with the synoptics but also by observing the extent to which the evangelist has provided editorial comments.[2].

On the other hand, though he places the cleansing of the temple late he separates it from the triumphal entry, presumably because John does so, although the synoptic evangelists do not. And from John 13.1 (the beginning of the farewell discourses) to the end of the gospel Tatian is able to preserve the Johannine order, with one insignificant exception (19.19–22 follows 19.23–4). Indeed, he uses the Johannine passion narrative as the foundation of his own and correlates the synoptic accounts with it.

John, then, provides Tatian not with history—except for the passion narrative—but with materials for a history. What of the synoptic gospels? In recording the narrative of the birth and infancy of Jesus, as we have said, Tatian alternates blocks of material, not easily reconcilable, derived from Matthew and Luke. When these gospels begin to agree, since their order comes to be the same as that of Mark, he follows the common sequence. He

---

[1] The comment, originally applied to the entry as a whole, is now referred to the fulfilment of the prophecy of Zechariah.

[2] Tatian feels free to make transfers of synoptic summaries as well.

refrains, however, from using Matt. 4.12–16 (Mark 1.14) or Luke 3.19–20 at the beginning of Jesus' ministry. His reason for placing them later is that they state or imply that the ministry began after John's imprisonment. Tatian follows the gospel of John, which places the beginning of the ministry before that event (cf. 4.24). In other words, when he is confronted with a choice between statements explicitly historical-chronological in nature, he follows John against the synoptics. Usually he does not have to make choices of this sort.

Most of the time, in describing the ministry of Jesus, Tatian follows the order of Matthew. He pays absolutely no attention to Luke's arrangement of Jesus' teaching within the framework of a journey to Jerusalem (Luke 9.51—18.14). Indeed, the passage with which Luke introduces this peripatetic teaching (9.51–56) is removed from its context and placed after the cleansing of the temple, just before the triumphal entry. As for Mark, Tatian follows him chiefly where he agrees with Matthew.

Sometimes he follows sequences already established by Mark or Luke and thus diverges from the Matthaean order. Sometimes he follows sequences found in none of the three. For instance, at the end of a Matthaean collection of teachings (Matt. 11.1) he places the story of Martha and Mary (Luke 10.38–42) which illustrates these teachings, and adds a Marcan summary (Mark 6.12–13) and a word about the imprisoned Baptist from Matt. 11.12–19. Presumably he found these passages as difficult to locate as we do.

Sometimes he arranges his materials by subjects. For example, on riches and wages (following a Johannine discourse, John 7.2–31) he provides the parable of the rich fool (Luke 12.13–21); the story of the "rich young ruler" synthesized from Matt. 19.16–30, Mark 10.17–31, and Luke 18.18–30; the parable of the rich man and Lazarus (Luke 16.14–27); the parable of the labourers in the vineyard (Matt. 20.1–16); and two parables about banquets from Luke 14.1–24 (the second combined with Matt. 22.1–14).

The conclusion we should draw from this analysis of his methods is that he believed that Matthew provided the most reliable historical account of the ministry of Jesus before the passion,[1] while John's passion narrative was the most trustworthy of the four. Mark's order is accurate in so far as it corresponds with that of Matthew. But Luke's arrangements of the teaching of Jesus possess almost no historical validity whatever.

Tatian's admiration for Matthew did not require him to follow him all the time. For instance, where Matthew has the sermon on the mount (5.1), Tatian follows Luke 6.17 in placing it on level ground. Presumably he feels that Luke has corrected Matthew for the sake of historical accuracy. And as we have already seen, he does not hesitate to separate the cleansing of the temple from the triumphal entry, or to correct Matthew's Marcan notion that Jesus' ministry began after the arrest of John the Baptist.[2]

This means that in Tatian's view the evangelists cannot have been inspired in such a way that they were provided with absolutely accurate historical–chronological information about Jesus. He omits Luke 1.1–5, where the evangelist speaks of his intention to write accurate history. Of this omission Hill says that "the preface of St. Luke, dealing with his private reasons for writing a Gospel, was scarcely suitable for Tatian's work".[3] More than that: Luke indicated that his purpose was exactly the same as Tatian's; and since Tatian so often rejects the constructions of his predecessor he could hardly retain the passage. Indeed, in Tatian's opinion all the evangelists were subject to error. Though he made an effort to preserve every scrap of information they provided, he cannot have held the theory that their memories were infallible.

It was Tatian's intention to provide a way by which the seeming discrepancies in the four gospels could be reconciled. In place of the four, he wished to create a single gospel, based on the approved methods of historical research and going beyond the prejudices of the individual evangelists to the one true portrait of Jesus which they inadequately represented. His method

[1] Hence Matthew's call (Matt. 9.9) is placed early. The order in which the apostles were called (Andrew, Simon, Philip, Nathanael, James, John, Matthew) thus resembles that intimated by Papias.

[2] He thus gives the sequence Matt. 4.17–22 (Mark 1.15–20); Luke 4.14–22ᵃ; 5.1–11; John 3.22–4, 3ᵃ; Matt. 4.12 (Mark 1.14).

[3] Op. cit., p. 25.

was ultimately historical in character. Where the evangelists were in general agreement, he followed all four; where they disagreed, he gave the account which seemed most probable to him. In assessing probabilities he undoubtedly relied on the tradition of the priority of the apostolic Matthew to the sub-apostolic Mark and Luke, and he treated John as an apostolic writer who arranged his gospel for symbolical purposes. He felt free to provide a different arrangement from John's but he evidently believed that John did not invent symbolical narratives. John must have been using facts symbolically.

In other words, Tatian was an historian and was not concerned with philosophy or even with philosophical rhetoric. Questions of credibility lie completely outside the range of his interest. He was concerned not with what the evangelists may have meant but with what they reported. And like Papias and Justin he has no doctrine of the evangelists' infallibility or about a hidden meaning they intended to convey. Or rather—since such a conception of hidden meaning does appear in his Oration to the Greeks—no doctrine of this sort is intimated in the *Diatessaron*.[1]

We should suggest that Tatian viewed the gospels as Justin had viewed them. They were ἀπομνημονεύματα, memoranda which represented a point halfway between their sources in oral tradition and a finished product which could be regarded as the work of a competent historian. In Tatian's opinion he himself was such a competent historian, one who took the materials unfinished by others and worked them into a synthetic whole.

We thus reach a view of Tatian which makes him not unlike more modern critics of the gospels who have abandoned the outlines of the ministry of Jesus provided by the evangelists and have tried to create outlines of their own. The chief difference between him and his successors lies in their refusal to take the fourth gospel seriously, though in very recent times we can find signs of a return to his position. And his rearrangement of the gospels verse by verse, or sometimes phrase by phrase, suggests a comparison with the work of some critics of the fourth gospel.

The question of the adequacy of this method, however, still

[1] On Tatian and rhetorical methods cf. *HTR* 51 (1958), pp. 123–8.

remains. Without a foundation in a strange doctrine of verbal inspiration—verbal but non-contextual—it is hard to see how the method can be justified. And it is difficult to believe that a doctrine of inspiration which pays attention to syllables, so to speak, and neglects the sequences intended by the evangelists is a doctrine of inspiration at all. The real upshot of Tatian's method seems to be that the evangelists wrote neither scripture nor history.

The *Diatessaron* represents a radical effort to solve the problem created by the disagreement of the evangelists. But it was not a book which appealed to most Christians, and the difficulties in it both theological and historical finally led to its condemnation by leaders of the Church.

Continuing use of literary and historical criticism of the gospels can be seen in the debate related to Montanism, a debate in which the fourth gospel was especially important. The latter half of the second century saw the rise of the Montanist movement in Phrygia and the claim of its leaders that the coming of the Paraclete, prophesied in the gospel of John, had been fulfilled in the advent of their prophet Montanus. Against this claim Christians in Asia Minor, later joined by an influential Roman presbyter named Gaius, argued that the fourth gospel should not be accepted because of its disagreements with the synoptic gospels.[1]

According to Epiphanius, they quoted Johannine verses from John 1.1—2.1 in order to contrast them with the outline provided by the other evangelists, who "say that Jesus spent forty days in the wilderness, tempted by the devil, and that then he returned and received his disciples".[2] Again, Mark "nowhere speaks of the birth from above[3] but says, 'In the Jordan the Spirit came down upon him, and there was a voice which said, This is the beloved Son, in whom I am well pleased.' "[4] And while John mentions two Passovers (2.13; 6.4), the other gospels mention only one.[5]

In other words, for these Christians the synoptic gospels provided the historical norm for an account of the life of Jesus.

---

[1] Cf. A. Jülicher in Pauly-Wissowa, *RE* VII, pp. 509–10.   [2] *Haer.* 51, 4, 10.
[3] John 3.3,7 combined with 1.14.   [4] *Haer.* 51, 6, 14.   [5] Ibid., 51, 22, 1.

The gospel of John had to be rejected since it contradicted the synoptic account, especially on matters of chronology.

We know that Roman writers like Gaius were deeply concerned with the factuality of the Christian tradition. It was he who, in response to Asian claims probably related to John, told the Montanists that Roman Christians could point to the "trophies" of Peter and Paul.[1] The *aedicula* found under St Peter's is almost certainly one of the monuments he had in mind.[2] In his view, the search for fact meant maintaining the concrete reality of Peter and Paul and rejecting the unhistorical gospel of John. Gaius' rejection evoked an elaborate reply—now lost—from Hippolytus of Rome, and exercised considerable influence on the thought of Origen.[3] Two things were wrong with Gaius' attack on the Johannine literature. First, he wrote too late. At the time he criticized the Johannine books they had become firmly established in the life and thought of the Churches and could not be rejected from the canon in process of formation. Second, he assumed that the synoptic tradition was absolutely reliable as contrasted with the fourth gospel. Such an assumption could not have been justified by the simple comparisons he provided.

We might imagine that more light on Johannine–synoptic contradictions would be shed by those who wrote on the controversy over the celebration of Easter. This controversy arose because some Christians celebrated the Passover with Jews and others criticized them for doing so.[4] The divergence could be important in relation to the gospels, since the synoptics apparently regard the last supper as a Passover meal, while John indicates that the supper took place before the Passover.

Melito of Sardis was a Quartadeciman; that is, he advocated celebrating the Passover on the fourteenth (*quartadecima*) day of the Jewish month Nisan. But a fragment allegedly derived from his writings suggests that he combined the gospel of John with the synoptics.[5] According to this fragment, the "two natures"

[1] Eusebius, *H.E.* 2, 25, 6–7.
[2] J. Toynbee and J. W. Perkins, *The Shrine of St Peter* (New York, 1957).
[3] Cf. A. d'Alès, *La théologie de saint Hippolyte* (Paris, 1906), pp. xlvii–l.
[4] B. Lohse, *Das Passahfest der Quartadecimaner* (Gütersloh, 1953), pp. 50–89.
[5] Migne, *PG* 89, col. 229; Otto, *Corp. Apol.* IX, pp. 415–16.

of Christ are reflected in the gospels—his deity by the signs worked in the three years after his baptism (John 2.13; 6.4; 11.55), his humanity in the thirty years before it (Luke 3.23). If this fragment were indubitably genuine, as it is not, we should find not only a synthesis of the gospels but something like the later analysis of their differences. John emphasizes divinity; the synoptics emphasize humanity. But this doctrine seems to originate with Origen.

Apollinaris of Hierapolis wrote against the Quartadecimans. He said that his opponents relied on Matthew to show that Jesus ate the paschal lamb with his disciples on the fourteenth Nisan and suffered on the next day. "According to them the gospels seem to disagree."[1] Apollinaris' own principal authority must have been the gospel of John, to which he plainly alludes in a fragment from one of his writings. But since in his view the gospels did not disagree, he must have believed that they could be synthesized. Perhaps he held that John was the historical authority on this question and that the other gospels were to be interpreted in its light. In this way no disagreement would result.[2] We shall presently see that this procedure was followed by Clement of Alexandria.

THE UNITY OF THE GOSPELS

We find, then, that in the last quarter of the second century several leaders of Christian Churches were insisting upon the unity of the four gospels and their inspired authors. Theophilus, Bishop of Antioch, speaks of the unanimous teaching of "the holy scriptures and all the Spirit-inspired men, one of whom, John," wrote John 1.1–3. He provides collections of biblical passages to demonstrate the unity between the teaching of the prophets and that of "the gospel voice" or "the gospel". And he describes the Holy Spirit as "teaching and reminding" the Old Testament prophets, thus using a phrase derived from John 14.26.[3]

From this period comes the famous Muratorian fragment, of

[1] PG 92, col. 80–1; Otto, Corp. Apol. IX, pp. 486–7.
[2] Lohse, op. cit., pp. 136–7. [3] Ad Autolycum 2, 22. 3, 13. 3, 14. 3, 11.

doubtful provenance.[1] Its beginning is lost, and what we have starts with the words, *Quibus tamen interfuit et ita posuit*, "with whom (which?) he was present and thus wrote them down". Presumably the words refer to Mark, and to Mark's having been a companion not only of Peter but also of Paul and Barnabas. The fragment may be defending Mark from the charge that his gospel is not the work of an eyewitness, and that its order is wrong. *Tertium evangelii librum secundum Lucam*, "the third book of the gospel is that according to Luke". Like Mark, Luke "did not see the Lord in the flesh", but after the ascension he was a companion of Paul and wrote his gospel in his own name. Evidently for the author of the fragment both Mark and Luke are inferior to the gospels written by apostles. And the gospel of John seems to be the most valuable of the four. Encouraged by his fellow-disciples and bishops, John urged them to fast with him for three days and to tell one another whatever would be revealed to each of them. Revelation immediately came to the apostle Andrew; all were to give their assent, but John was to write down everything in his own name. This legend is presumably based on John 21.24, a mysterious statement about the evangelist, whose testimony "we" know is true.

The author of the fragment is obviously concerned with the historical, or rather legendary, details he is reporting. But he is even more concerned with the unity of the gospels. Because of the unanimity of the testimony to the authenticity of John's gospel, he can say that "therefore", while different beginnings (*principia*, probably an allusion to the contradictions in the opening chapters of the gospels) are taught in the various books of the gospels, there is no difference for the faith of believers. All the gospels are inspired by the Spirit. All have Jesus' nativity, his passion, his resurrection, his life with the disciples, and his double advent— first in humility, second with royal power.

Here we find a leap of faith which is not clearly related to reason. The details about the evangelists in the first part of the fragment do not prepare us to see how the contradictions make

[1] Cf. H. Koch in *ZNW* 25 (1926), pp. 154–60; J. Quasten, *Patrology* II (Westminster, Md., 1953), pp. 207–10.

no difference. No evidence is provided for the inspiration of the gospels beyond the legend about the fourth evangelist. And the list of the contents of the four gospels hardly does justice to what we actually find in them.

There was room for a more adequate analysis, and an attempt to provide it is what we find in the treatise *Adversus Haereses* by Irenaeus, Bishop of Lyons. Irenaeus was strongly convinced of the necessity for the unity of the Church, which in his mind was related to the unity of God, the unity of revelation, and the unity of the scriptures. He found such unity delineated in the book of Acts, which he used extensively in his writings. But he was aware that not everyone accepted Acts (the Muratorian fragment defends the book as containing the acts of all the apostles in one volume). And therefore he had to provide historical evidence of its reliability. Luke was present at most of the events he describes, says Irenaeus, because (1) there are "we-passages" in the book; (2) in describing Paul's journey to Rome he records precise data about persons, places, and times; and (3) he was with Paul at Rome because he is mentioned in 2 Tim. 4.10–11 and in Col. 4.14.[1] Moreover, if one compares Gal. 2 ("after three years . . . after fourteen years") with the book of Acts, one finds that the chronology is the same, and therefore the same apostolic council is described in both; this proves that the apostles were all in agreement.[2] One might suppose that Paul's letter contradicts such a pleasant picture, but Irenaeus' text of Gal. 2.5 read "we yielded in subjection for a time", not "we did not yield".[3] Paul has thus become a symbol of unity rather than the historical protagonist of gentile freedom whom we meet in some of his letters.

Since we find Irenaeus concerned with historical questions in dealing with Acts, we are not surprised to find the same concern exhibited in his treatment of the gospels. He knew Papias' treatise on the Dominical Oracles, and it may well be that his information is derived from this work. In any case, he is convinced that the information he has is correct. Matthew was the

---

[1] *Adv. haer* 3, 14, 1, pp. 74–5, Harvey.
[2] Ibid., 3, 13, 13, pp. 74; 3, 12, 13, pp. 69–71.   [3] Ibid., 3, 13, 13, p. 74.

first to write, at a time when Peter and Paul were still preaching the gospel at Rome. He composed his gospel among the Hebrews in their language. After the "exodus" of Peter and Paul (probably their deaths, as in 2 Pet. 1.15), Mark, Peter's disciple and interpreter, wrote down what Peter preached. Around the same time, Luke, the follower of Paul, wrote the gospel preached by the apostle. At a later date (*epeita*), John, the Lord's disciple who reclined on his bosom, wrote his gospel in Ephesus in Asia Minor.[1] The chronological sequence of the gospels is thus established as Matthew—Mark—Luke—John, though the relative priority of Mark to Luke is a matter of indifference, as Irenaeus soon makes clear.

He goes on to indicate something of the theological significance of the work of the various evangelists, though he is obviously considering only the opening chapters of their works. The three synoptists show that the story of Jesus fulfilled Old Testament prophecy; this can be proved from Matthew's story of the Magi, Luke's infancy narrative as a whole, and Mark's beginning with quotations from the prophets. John's purpose was different: he wrote against the Jewish-Christian heretic Cerinthus and spoke of the generation of the Logos.[2]

Finally Irenaeus starts over again, this time following an order based on that of the apocalyptic figures in Rev. 4.7. John wrote of the generation of the Logos; Luke emphasized Jesus' sacerdotal rôle; Matthew spoke of him as a human being; and Mark stressed the importance of prophecy. This sequence also has meaning in relation to the history of salvation in the Old Testament. The Logos or Word appeared to the Old Testament patriarchs; priestly office was given in the Mosaic law; the Word came to the Old Testament prophets; and finally the Word became man for us. It is evident that here we have passed far beyond history to a mystical-typological theory. If Irenaeus is still thinking about the sequence in which the gospels were written, he must mean that it implied a reversal of the order of revelation in the Old Testament. But we do not know that he has this sequence any longer in mind. History has been swallowed up in speculation, as it has when

[1] Ibid., 3, 1, 1, pp. 3–6. [2] Ibid., 3, 9–11, pp. 32–44.

Irenaeus tells us that there are four and only four gospels because there are four winds, four corners of the earth, and so forth.[1]

When Irenaeus deals with gospel chronology his mind turns to fantasy. The Valentinians held that Jesus' ministry lasted one year. They were wrong, for according to John, the Lord's disciple (John 8.56–7), Jesus was "not yet fifty years old". Since Jesus must have passed through all the stages of human development from infancy to old age, he was forty-nine years old at the time, and later reached fifty. But Luke 3.23 says that Jesus was about thirty years old, and Luke 3.1 refers to the fifteenth year of Tiberius. Therefore, if Jesus' ministry lasted for twenty years, Pontius Pilate must have been procurator of Judaea not under Tiberius but under his successor Claudius (41–54)—and so Irenaeus states in his later *Demonstration of the Apostolic Preaching*.[2] He does not say how he thinks this notion can be reconciled with the chronology of Paul's life. He must not have considered the question.

In his discussion of the gospel of Luke, important because distorted critically by Marcionites and exegetically by Valentinians, Irenaeus begins with the analysis of Acts which we have already mentioned. He then points out that Luke is the only source of information for many important features of the life and teaching of Jesus. First, there are passages in the first three chapters of Luke which are rejected by Marcion but allegorized by the Valentinians; second, there are sayings of Jesus which are accepted by Marcion and the Valentinians alike. His basic point is obviously that the heretics do not agree and that therefore the whole gospel ought to be accepted.[3] It should be noted that among the passages accepted by Marcion are Luke 17.5–6 (which Harnack wrongly called "un-attested")[4] and Luke 13.6–9 (which Epiphanius said Marcion deleted).[5] Because of Irenaeus' testimony both passages should be regarded as parts of Marcion's gospel.

This is a significant example of detailed literary criticism. Irenaeus evidently compared Luke with the other gospels and

[1] Ibid., 3, 11, 8, pp. 48–9.
[2] Ibid., 2, 22, 5, pp. 331–2; *Dem.* 74.   [3] Ibid., 3, 14, 3–4, pp. 76–8.
[4] Harnack, op cit., 223*.   [5] Ibid., 217*.

Marcion's version with the orthodox one. We may infer that his description of Marcion's gospel as omitting everything about the Lord's generation, as well as many of his sayings,[1] is probably based on comparative study, not on hearsay. We should conclude that Irenaeus, like other early Christian writers, was more competent in literary criticism than in historical analysis. He does not seem to be able to tell the difference between his rather sensible analysis of the authorship of Acts and his discussion of the Lord's age and the date of the crucifixion, and for this reason he cannot be regarded as a witness to the existence of historical study in the Christianity of his time.

CLEMENT OF ALEXANDRIA

At the end of the second century there were thus several solutions available for the problem presented by the four gospels. The field of investigation had been narrowed by the rejection, among most Christians, of any gospels not among the four, and the general insistence that no fewer than the four were to be used. But how were the four to be used? And how was the problem presented by their disagreements to be solved? In other words, what use was to be made of each in getting back to the life of Jesus?

It is in the writings of Clement of Alexandria that we find the beginnings of an attempt to synthesize information previously available. From "tradition"—more probably older learned conjecture—he knows that the gospels with genealogies (Matthew, Luke) were the first to be written.[2] He adds the detail that Matthew's diet consisted of seeds, leaves, and vegetables, with no meat.[3] In regard to Luke he reports the conjecture that he translated the epistle to the Hebrews from Hebrew, since its Greek style is the same as his.[4] It is hard to tell which of the two gospels Clement thought was written first. We should expect him to favour Matthew, but in discussing the sermon on the mount he says that Matthew "added" "in spirit" to the beatitude

[1] Irenaeus, *Adv. haer.* 1, 27, 2, p. 217.   [2] Eusebius, *H.E.* 6, 14, 5.

[3] *Paed.* 2, 16, 1. Could this be based on the fact that Matt. 3.4 reports the diet of John the Baptist, while Luke does not?

[4] Eusebius, *H.E.* 6, 14, 2. Actually they are not the same.

about the poor, and "for God's righteousness" to that concerning those who hunger and thirst.[1] Probably he has in view as a source the words of Jesus common to both Matthew and Luke.

What he says the elders told him about Mark looks like a garbled version of the report of Papias.[2]

> In Rome Peter preached the word and, inspired by the Spirit, proclaimed the gospel. Since Mark had followed Peter for a long time and remembered what had been said, many persons asked him to write down what was said. He did so, and delivered the gospel to those who had asked him. Peter knew of this gospel, but by way of recommending it neither discouraged nor encouraged the work.

This comment restricts the inspiration of Mark to the materials he derived from the inspired Peter. The composition of the gospel was at best neutral in character. In other words, among the elders whom Clement knew there was no unbounded enthusiasm for the work.

On the other hand, both Clement and the elders admired the gospel of John and undertook to explain why it differed from the synoptics. Its differences were both chronological and literary, as well as theological.

> Last of all John, aware that the "corporeal facts" (τα σωματικα) had been made plain in the ⟨previous⟩ gospels, and encouraged by his companions, and inspired by the Spirit, created a spiritual gospel.

What Clement says about the time, the circumstances, and the inspiration of the fourth gospel closely resembles what we have already found in the Muratorian fragment. What is new, however, is his idea that the gospel deals not so much with factual information as with spiritual meaning. Clement himself was devoted to allegorical exegesis,[3] and by treating John's gospel as primarily allegorical he believed that he could explain the difference between it and the synoptics.

Indeed, he may have held that it gave the true, post-resurrection "gnosis" delivered by Jesus to his disciples. This gnosis, says Clement, was given to Peter, James, and John; from them it passed to the other disciples and thence to the seventy.[4] Now

---

[1] *Quis dives salvetur?* 17, 4.   [2] Eusebius, *H.E.* 6, 14, 6–7.
[3] Cf. W. den Boer, *De Allegorese in het werk van Clemens Alexandrinus* (Leiden, 1940).
[4] Eusebius, *H.E.* 2, 1, 4.

since Peter did not write a gospel and did not commend that of Mark, and since James did not write a gospel, the gnosis must be contained in only one of the four gospels—that of John.

Of course Clement does not deny that John has any factual information. When he deals with the vexing question of the Last Supper, he argues that what Matthew calls the preparation for the Passover (26.17) was on the thirteenth of the month Nisan, and that this was the time of the footwashing in John 13.[1] "Our Saviour suffered on the following day"—i.e., the fourteenth of Nisan. This, he says, agrees with John 18.28, according to which the Passover meal is still future. "All the scriptures agree and the gospels are in concord." By relying on John as a historical document he has been able to refute the Quartadeciman arguments.[2]

Clement thus treats the synoptic gospels as histories (of varying quality) and the fourth gospel as a mixture of historical fact and spiritual truth. But since in spite of his concern for the religious history of mankind, to which Mondésert has drawn attention,[3] he is not really concerned with historical fact, we do not find in his writings any genuine feeling for the historical difficulties which still remain even when John is viewed symbolically. Such a feeling we encounter only in the writings of Origen.

Moreover, Clement insisted that the synoptic gospels, like that of John, contain symbols as well as history. This point becomes clear in his homily, *Who is the Rich Man who is Saved?* (a title itself based on allegory). Here he quotes Mark 10.17–31 in full, adding that the same general sense is found in the other accepted gospels. His basic concern is with the principle that "the Saviour teaches his people nothing in a merely human way, but everything by a divine and mystical wisdom". Therefore "we must not understand his words literally but with due inquiry and intelligence we must search out and master their hidden meaning".[4] Matthew is a witness to this mastery, as is shown by the additions we have already mentioned.

---

[1] The same sequence is found in Tatian (Matt. 26.14–17; John 13.1–20).
[2] Fragment *de Pascha*; Stählin III, pp. 216–17.
[3] C. Mondésert, *Clément d'Alexandrie* (Paris, 1944,) pp. 187–219.
[4] *Quis div. salv.?* 4–5.

GREEK LITERARY AND HISTORICAL CRITICISM

BEFORE we turn to examine the contribution which Origen made to the study of the gospels, it is time to say something about the methods which both he and his predecessors employed. We sometimes think that textual, literary, and historical criticism were created in the eighteenth and nineteenth centuries, or that at any rate they were not previously applied to the gospels. By this convenient fiction we can present ourselves with a picture of early Christianity in which we can see faith constantly triumphing over intelligence—a picture attractive, for different reasons, both to the very orthodox and to the very unorthodox.

Such an image, either of the ancient world in general or of ancient Christianity in particular, is thoroughly distorted. We have already seen methods of literary criticism and historical analysis being employed by such Christian writers as Papias, Justin, and Irenaeus; we know that these authors did not invent the methods they used; and we possess enough information about the work of textual, literary, and historical critics in the Graeco-Roman schools so that we can say something about the procedures they followed. In addition, we possess introductory manuals for the study of rhetoric, coming from the late first century and the early second, which enable us to obtain a fairly clear picture of what the educated Greek or Roman was taught in school. He learned how to analyse literary compositions with a rigour certainly unparalleled in modern education. And the methods he learned did not slip from his memory if he became a Christian.

We need say very little about textual criticism, for on the one hand it was not discussed in the manuals of rhetoricians and, on the other, it was not especially significant in Origen's work on the gospels. First, the work of ancient textual critics was almost entirely subjective; this is the case, for example, in their work on the *Odyssey*;[1] it is also the case in the work of such Christian writers as Marcion, Julius Africanus, and Origen himself. Second, while Origen knew how textual errors originated—he ascribes them to simple mistakes in copying, to misplaced ingenuity in emendation, and to theological bias[2]—his own practice is extremely unsatisfactory. He can discuss textual variants at considerable length,[3] or suggest the presence of interpolations;[4] but I can recall only one passage where he removes such an interpolation (Matt. 4.17: "repent"), and there his judgement is certainly wrong.[5]

LITERARY AND HISTORICAL CRITICISM: THEON

We are often tempted, as I have said, to suppose that ancient writers were incapable of undertaking the task of historical criticism. This temptation should be avoided, since they actually did undertake it. The proof comes not only from Graeco-Roman historians and from treatises like that of Lucian *On the writing of History*, but also from manuals of rhetoric in which the approved method of analysis was set forth, sometimes for students, sometimes for teachers. These manuals show not only that the method existed but also that it was taught in the schools.

The study of rhetoric as a science had been revived in the second century B.C. and although rhetoricians had often contended with philosophers for the prize of students' attention, by the first century of our era there were many who recognized the usefulness of philosophical conceptions and made use of them in their systems, though without adhering to any one philosophy. And while some rhetoricians kept alive the conflict between those who considered rhetoric an art and those who regarded it as a

---

[1] M. van der Valk, *Textual Criticism of the Odyssey* (Leiden, 1949).

[2] *M* 15, 14, pp. 387–8.

[3] Ibid. also *M* fr. 194, p. 93; *C* 1, 62, p. 113; cf. J.-P. Audet, *La Didaché* (Paris, 1958), pp. 63–7; pp. 420–1. On Romans 16.25–7 Origen discusses the readings of Marcion's text and of other witnesses but makes no attempt to explain them (*Rom. comm.*, PG 14, 1290A–B).

[4] *J* 32, 20, p. 462; *J* 32, 32, p. 479; *M* 134, p. 274 (but cf. Cant. II, p. 140; L fr. 83, pp. 273–4; *C* 2, 33, p. 159).

[5] *M* fr. 74, p. 45. Cf. Hanson, *Allegory and Event*, pp. 176–7.

science, most of them were prepared to go ahead without the benefit of a definition.

The point at which definition was important was that at which the various literary forms were differentiated. Thus for Theodore of Gadara in the first century B.C. the careful definition of historical narrative was obviously significant. "Narrative is the setting forth of an action, complete in itself, with mere statement, about things which have already happened."[1] The sole virtue of this form (i.e., that for which the narrator should aim) is "probability" or "persuasiveness" (πιθανότης).[2] Later writers criticized Theodore for his excessive technicality, but he thought that every word in his definitions was necessary. We shall meet the word "mere" again in Origen.

When we mention "probability" we have to consider criteria of probability, and the rhetoricians were also concerned with this problem. The student of rhetoric was expected to be able to apply the methods of ἀνασκευή (refutation) and κατασκευή (confirmation) to myths, narratives in general, brief sententious sayings, and laws.[3] We find these methods discussed in the *Institutio oratoria* of Quintilian and in the *Progymnasmata* of the Alexandrian Aelius Theon, who as Lana has shown was probably one of Quintilian's principal sources.[4]

Theon's list of the points to be discussed in providing refutations is practically the same when he considers various literary forms, but the number of points (τόποι) varies. Thus in dealing with myths he gives eleven points (76.19–22), for narratives ten (93.14–32), for sayings nine (104.15–18), and for laws eight (129.8–10). In the second century Hermogenes was able to reduce the list to six items.[5]

---

[1] Anonymous Seg., I, 434, 25 Spengel; W. Stegemann in *RE* V A, 1853.

[2] Ibid., 440, 1.

[3] This order is that of the manuscripts, though cross-references show that it is not the original one (Stegemann in *RE* V A, 2042).

[4] I. Lana, *Quintiliano, il "Sublime" e gli "Eserciẓi Preparatori" di Elio Teone (Università di Torino, Pubbl. della Facoltà di lettere e filosofia III, 4, 1951)*, pp. 110–51. On Theon's Stoic education, ibid., pp. 110–13; Stegemann in *RE* V A, 2049–50. Text in L. Spengel, *Rhetores Graeci*, II, pp. 57–130.

[5] Hermogenes, *Progymnasmata*, p. 9, 4–7 Spengel (11, 8–10 Rabe, Leipzig, 1913). In Hermogenes' view ἀνασκευή could not be applied to myths since they are absolutely false (8, 31 Spengel, 11, 4 Rabe).

The most complete analysis is thus that provided for myths, and we shall examine it while adding something of what Theon says on historical narratives. Since by Theon's definition a myth is "a false account portraying truth" (λόγος ψευδὴς εἰκονίζων ἀλήθειαν, 70.21; 72.28), he does not need to show that it is impossible (76.6); on the other hand, in dealing with narratives regarded as historical, he has to show that the events could not have taken place at all or that they could not have taken place at the time mentioned by the historian (93.18). Some say, Theon points out, that Heracles killed Bousiris; but according to Hesiod Bousiris lived eleven generations before Heracles (93.20).

Both myth and history can be criticized because of their obscurity, which arises either out of the matters being described or the diction used in describing them (76.22; 80.8). For instance, the subject matter of Thucydides is unclear because he presents various events in relation to summers and winters, and therefore has to keep going back and forth when he describes a single sequence of related events (80.15). "A narrative becomes obscure because of the omission of what it was necessary to mention, and because of the 'allegory' of the matters concealed" (81.4).

He can also show that either a myth or an historical narrative is incredible. "The incredible (ἀπίθανον) is something which can take place or be said, but is not believed to have taken place or to have been said" (76.32). Such an analysis does not rest upon mere assertion. It rests upon a detailed analysis of a story in relation to the person to whom the action or saying is referred; the place in which it is said to have happened; the time; the mode; and the reason assigned to the action (77.1–9).[1]

Theon gives an example of a story regarded as historical, and proceeds to show why it is incredible; this is the account of how Medea killed her children (94.12–32). The person, a mother, would not have harmed her children. The action itself is incredible, since she would not have slain them. She would not have done so in the place (Corinth) where their father Jason was living.

[1] Cf. also 77.12 and 94.10.

She would not have done so at the time when she had been humiliated and Jason possessed greater power than she did because he had married the king's daughter. The mode of action is an unlikely one; she would have tried to conceal her action, and since she was a sorceress she would have used not a sword but a poison. Finally, the reason assigned to her action is most improbable. Anger against her husband would not have driven her to kill the children who were hers as well as his; she harmed herself as well as him, and indeed she harmed herself more, since women are subject to emotion more than men are.

In the same way, he can show that a story is inappropriate (77.9)—though it is hard to see what the difference between the incredible and the inappropriate is, especially in view of the example Theon has provided.

He can also show that a myth or a narrative suffers from the omission of necessary information or the addition of irrelevant information about persons, actions, times, modes, places, reasons, etc. (77.10).

Then he can proceed to show that there is some disagreement with history as generally accepted or with suppositions generally held. For example, the writer may be saying that men were formed not by Prometheus but by some other god, or that the ass is intelligent and the fox is stupid (77.14). Such unusual statements would have to be rejected.

Perhaps the writer contradicts himself; perhaps he does not use the right sequence in telling his story. He may omit necessary information at the beginning, or he may fail to end the story as he should (77.18–23). The order of the chapters may be wrong (93.29). Again, he may be led astray by the prejudicial tone of his writing (77.27).

Finally, the conclusions or "morals" drawn from a myth may be wrong. They may not really be related to the story which has just been told. They may be false. "Those who desire more are deprived of what they have" is false, since it is not universally true (77.29—78.3).

Not all these topics are always relevant in dealing with historical narratives, says Theon (93.12). But the student of rhetoric should discuss them in the order set forth in the manual. "If we should suppose that the action is possible, we must say that it is incredible; if it turns out to be credible, we shall see whether it is false; if it should appear to be true, we shall go on to ask if there is some deficiency or redundance; next, that the author himself contradicts the narrative; in addition, we shall criticize the order of the chapters . . ." (93.24–30).

The method which rhetoricians had developed for the analysis both of myths and of historical narratives possessed several merits. It was logical; it could be understood easily; and it could be employed rather simply and straightforwardly. Unfortunately, its shortcomings were even more striking. Concentrating its emphasis on logical matters, it left no room for the operation of non-rational factors in historical events. And—perhaps the most important drawback—it was used in an effort to classify narratives as either true or false. In the conclusions there was room for either black or white, but no room for the grey tones in which much historical writing is painted. All that one could find in history consisted, on the one hand, of true history, an accurate record of real events, and, on the other hand, of fiction (what could have taken place but did not) and myth (what could not have taken place). The schematized logical analysis of the record, in short, resulted in a schematized logical conclusion.

Moreover, precisely the example which Theon used—the story of Medea's killing her children—was subject to other kinds of analysis which the rhetoricians did not employ. Writers who were concerned with understanding the human psyche recognized that in Medea there was an irrational power stronger than reason; though she knew that what she was about to do was evil, she proceeded to do it. And since she did it, an analysis of the event in relation to nothing but rational-prudential categories is ultimately meaningless.

This is to say that while some aspects of the rhetorical method are right—a single event cannot have taken place at two different places or on two different occasions, given the actuality of space and time—much of it involves applying purely external considerations which may well not be relevant. Since so much of the method depends on the analysis of psychological factors, it is a pity that the rhetoricians' psychology was so inadequate.

DIO AND OTHERS

Early in the second century the method of ἀνασκευή was applied to the Iliad by the rhetorician Dio Chrysostom. In his eleventh oration, *Troica*, he uses it in an effort to prove that the Trojan war never took place. And as W. Kroll pointed out, the oration follows the lines laid down for the ἀνασκευή;[1] indeed it could be regarded as an exercise in the method.

Dio begins by criticizing human credulity, which he ascribes to a desire for notoriety. Men prefer hearing slander about their ancestors to not hearing about them at all. Truth deserves defence, however, and Dio will provide a refutation of Homer's false statements, relying only on his own poetry.[2] The first thing he mentions is not actually from Homer's poems but from Homeric tradition. Homer is said to have been a beggar. If this is so, he is not likely to have been especially trustworthy. Moreover, the character of his poetry confirms one's doubts. His hero Odysseus told lies, and Homeric statements about the gods, as nearly everyone agrees, are not to be taken literally. Indeed, the conversations which the gods are supposed to have held often took place without any witnesses present. Perhaps Homer was not concerned with such a problem; but in the *Odyssey* Odysseus tells how he learned about the gods' debates from Calypso, and how she had heard about them from someone else. The problem therefore is a real one. It is not made less acute when Homer pretends that the gods have a language all their own and that he understands it.[3]

The basic difficulty with the story of Troy, however, is posed by the way in which Homer wrote it. He begins haphazardly, not with the proper beginning; he does not bring the story to an end. The real origin of the war was the abduction of Helen, and he describes this in such a way as to make it psychologically and historically incredible. The real end was the capture of Troy,

---

[1] *Rheinisches Museum* 70 (1915), 607–10; on the method in general, *RE* Suppl. VII, 1119.
[2] *Or.* 11, 1–11.   [3] Ibid., 15–23.

which he does not describe at all.[1] Many details and episodes in what Homer does relate are false, and the story of Patroclus and his death is simply a distortion of what must actually have happened to Achilles.[2]

Dio does not keep his promise to disprove Homer solely from Homer. Following a Hellenistic literary fashion, he introduces an aged Egyptian priest who knows the true story of Troy because it was told in Egypt by Menelaus and preserved in temple archives.[3] But this is simply a literary device; the priest uses the kinds of arguments employed by Dio himself. The basic substance of the oration is provided by the ἀνασκευή.

Later on, as we have said, Hermogenes simplified the method by reducing the number of categories to six. In his *Progymnasmata* he gives examples of each. An example of obscurity is the time when Narcissus lived; of improbability, that Arion would want to sing while in difficulties;[4] of impossibility, that Arion would be saved on a dolphin; of the inconsequent and inconsistent, to save the state and to wish to destroy it; of the unsuitable, for Apollo a god to have intercourse with a mortal woman; of the prejudicial, "when we say that it is by no means expedient to hear these things" (11.10).

G. Reichel tells us that such manuals as that of Theon were forgotten because they were used more by teachers than by their pupils, and because the method advocated by Theon was too complicated.[5] But what actually seems to have happened is that the textbook materials provided by Theon were simply absorbed into other textbooks. Such a process does not lack modern analogies. And as we shall see the complexity of the method did not deter writers who liked complexity from using it.

For example, in the later rhetorical manual of Aphthonius we see a method like that of Hermogenes being applied to a myth, a story of something which could not have taken place.[6]

---

[1] Ibid., 26–30. [2] Ibid., 97–102. [3] Ibid., 37–8.

[4] Cf. Theon, p. 93, 23 (an allusion to the story).

[5] *Quaestiones progymnasmaticae* (Leipzig, 1909), p. 46. In Hermogenes' curriculum more advanced students learned to deal with details about place, time, mode, person, reason, and action (*De inventione*, II 212–18 Spengel; 140–8 Rabe).

[6] II, 28–30 Spengel.

Aphthonius first sets forth the story of Daphne, daughter of the earth and the river Ladon, who, pursued by Apollo, was received back by the earth; a laurel sprang up in her stead. Then he proceeds to criticize lack of clarity, impossibility, unsuitability, inconsequence, and inconsistency. (1) How could Daphne have known that she came from the earth and a river? How could the earth and a river be united in marriage or bring forth a human being? (2) By whom was the infant fed? (3) How did a god love, and by desire betray his nature? (4) Why could Apollo not succeed in catching Daphne? Why did her mother help her avoid marriage, since marriage is good? And finally the story is inconsistent. Earth encouraged Apollo by bringing forth Daphne, but then she grieved him by rescuing the girl from him. On these grounds (which seem to overlap a good deal) Aphthonius has shown that the story is a myth. He has already criticized those who told it by pointing out their contradictions. "It is irrational for the poets to deny that they are eager to contradict one another when they first make up these stories about the gods. How then is it not irrational that none of the gods made an account for them but that we have the poets' account?"

In other words, the method of ἀνασκευή can involve criticism of both the theological content and the literary forms encountered in dealing with myths. And in Aphthonius' manual, the only result of κατασκευή, defence of the story, is a thorough going allegorization. First one can speak of the reputation of those who told the story—the poets, inspired by the Muses. Then one can say that (as an allegory) the story is perfectly clear, for all things are born from water and earth. It is quite possible, provided one remembers that virtues are acquired only by effort. It is consequent, since all mortals return to the earth. It is suitable, since the earth does receive men and does bring forth trees. And it is expedient or fitting, since Daphne is really Sophrosyne, temperance.[1]

From the passages we can see how closely related were grammatical-rhetorical criticism of stories on historical grounds and the use of the allegorical method in their defence. Many of the

[1] Ibid., 30–2.

ingredients with which a theologian like Origen was to be concerned are already present in the rhetorical manuals, including even the question of the inspiration of authors who contradict one another. And we shall later see that in dealing with the gospel stories he uses the method taught by the manuals.

As an example of the concern for the authenticity of religious literature in this period we may take the problem which arose in relation to Orphic literature. Did the very ancient seer Orpheus write the literature ascribed to him? Long before, Herodotus had said that Onomacritus of Athens had edited and published the oracles of Orpheus' disciple Musaeus; and a fourth-century Athenian historian had stated that Orpheus himself could not have written anything, for he was a Thracian and therefore illiterate.[1] In the second century of our era there was a great deal of theorizing about the work of Onomacritus. He collected, revised, and interpolated the Delphic oracles; he wrote the Orphic poems, or most of them; he wrote the oracles ascribed to Musaeus. Greek witnesses to this kind of analysis include Plutarch, Pausanias, and Sextus Empiricus; the Christian rhetoricians Tatian and Clement of Alexandria simply reproduce what had already been said.[2]

The analogy between the Orphic literature and the gospels is obvious. If Orpheus could not have written because he was illiterate, a similar claim could be made about the gospel writers, since according to the Christian tradition none of the apostles could write. The gap between oral tradition and written gospels was therefore bridged by means of a theory of inspiration such as Justin probably provided; Origen, as we shall see, certainly did so.

POSSIBLE ALTERNATIVES

We should not suppose that everyone accepted the rhetoricians' rules without question. Sextus Empiricus devotes a chapter to an attack on the grammarians who, like rhetoricians, claimed to be

---

[1] Androtion cited by Aelian (early third century after Christ), *Var. hist.* 8, 6.

[2] Plutarch, *De pyth. orac.* 25, 407b; Pausanias and Sextus Empiricus in I. M. Linforth, *The Arts of Orpheus* (Berkeley, Calif., 1941), pp. 350–3; Tatian, *Or.* 41, p. 42. 4 Schwartz; Clement, *Str.* 1, 131, 1, cf. 3.

able to analyse history by classifying it as factual, false, and like the truth.[1] Actually, says Sextus, there is no "scientific and general consideration" which would make it possible to deal with history in this way. "There is no technical knowledge either of things infinite or of things which vary from hour to hour. But particular histories are both infinite, because of their great number, and without fixity, because the same facts are not recorded by all respecting the same person."[2] It is all very well to classify history as real history, myth, and fiction, or to say that "though the subject-matter of history lacks method, yet the judging of it will be a matter of art". The trouble with this kind of analysis is that there is no criterion of true history, and there is no rule as to how history should rightly be written.[3] Therefore historical analysis is really impossible. As Sextus says when he discusses poetry, in distinguishing true and false statements "what is useful is not grammar but that which is capable of making the distinction, namely philosophy".[4] This kind of claim is, of course, characteristic of philosophers. Rhetoricians simply ignored it.

It is obvious that the discussions we have mentioned are concerned with what German writers call *Sachkritik*, analysis of the content of a narrative supposed to be historically true. In antiquity there was very little employment of *Quellenkritik*, analysis of the sources which narrators had used. There was considerable discussion of forgery and plagiarism,[5] but it was usually carried on in order to discredit one's opponents or predecessors. One of the rare statements to be found about sources occurs in Arrian's preface to his account of the expedition of Alexander the Great.

> Whenever Ptolemy son of Lagus and Aristobulus son of Aristobulus give an identical account, I follow this with complete confidence in its accuracy. Where they disagree, I choose the version which, in my judgment, is the more credible and at the same time the more interesting of the two.

These grounds of judgement are not as objective as one might

---

[1] *Adv. math.* I, 248–69. [2] Ibid., 259–60. [3] Ibid., 267–8.
[4] Ibid., 280. [5] Cf. K. Ziegler in *RE* XVIII 1, 1956–97.

wish. But Arrian goes on to explain why his sources deserve respect. Both writers were companions of Alexander, and Ptolemy was a king; both wrote after Alexander's death and therefore did not need to misrepresent the facts.

This kind of analysis was completely neglected by the Christian writers who, under the spell of *Sachkritik*, dealt with the gospels. Their emphasis on inspiration, valuable as it was, prevented them from asking how the evangelists knew what they wrote about.

3

ORIGEN AND THE GOSPELS

THE MOST important Christian critic in antiquity was Origen of Alexandria, born about 185 and brought up in a Christian home where Greek education was highly valued. At an early age he worked at both the Christian scriptures and the Greek "encyclical studies" such as grammar, rhetoric, geometry, and arithmetic.[1] His studies were directed not only in a Greek school but also at home, where his father Leonidas "advanced him in secular subjects".[2] It is probable that he also studied, perhaps a little later, with the Christian teachers Pantaenus and Clement; at any rate, Alexander of Jerusalem says that he became acquainted with Origen through these teachers,[3] even though Origen himself never mentions having been taught by either. After his father's martyrdom in 202, the family property was confiscated and Origen taught grammar and rhetoric, as well as the study of scripture, in the Christian catechetical school. Soon afterwards, when he was appointed dean, he sold his library of secular literature for an annuity of 4 obols a day. As A. S. Pease points out, Eusebius does not say to whom he sold it,[4] and it may well have remained available for his use. He continued to teach the encyclical subjects, and later did "graduate work" with the philosopher Ammonius Saccas.[5] By the year 217 he had decided to concentrate his attention on biblical and theological studies, and his pupil Heraclas took over the encyclical work.

This brief sketch of Origen's education and early life shows that until he was about thirty years old he was constantly engaged in the kind of rhetorical studies we discussed in the preceding chapter, and that rhetorical interpretation of literature had to be an important part of his exegetical method. The goal of his exegesis was the spiritual meaning. Its starting point was, and

---

[1] Eusebius, *H.E.* 6, 2, 7–8; 6, 18, 3.   [2] Ibid., 6, 2, 15.   [3] Ibid., 6, 14, 9.
[4] Ibid., 6, 3, 9; Pease in conversation 26 August 1958. The expression "four obols" was proverbial for any small amount (cf. Clement, *Quis div. salv.?* 21, 5; Aristaenetus *Ep.* 2, 16, p. 167 Hercher).   [5] Ibid., 6, 19, 12–14.

remained, historical-literal analysis. Both Cadiou and Klostermann have shown that school definitions are employed in his
writings both early and late.[1]

His critic Porphyry laments his exodus from secular studies
but insists that he was "always with" Plato, Numenius, Cronius,
Apollophanes, Longinus, Moderatus, Nicomachus, and other
Pythagorean writers, and that he used the books of the Stoic
Chaeremon and Cornutus. How did Porphyry know? Bidez is
undoubtedly right in suggesting that he had seen Origen's library
at Caesarea.[2]

What did these authors contribute? Origen undoubtedly used
Platonic theology in the development of his own. Most of the
other writers gave him insights into the relation between theology
and literature. For example, Cornutus could have shown him
how to separate ancient tradition from mythological interpolations (though this is not Origen's method);[3] Cronius insisted
that inconsistency in the *Odyssey* indicated the need for allegorical
exegesis.[4] Numenius himself interpreted the Old Testament
allegorically,[5] and Moderatus was an important first-century
teacher of number symbolism.[6] The only point at which Porphyry seems to have been quite wrong is in his mention of
Longinus; this rhetorician-philosopher was certainly Porphyry's
teacher, but hardly Origen's, since he was probably born when
Origen was about thirty.[7] We can perhaps save Porphyry's word
by taking it as a symbol of Origen's concern for rhetoric, not in
relation to style but as a method of analysis.

We learn something more of Origen's interests from the
panegyric addressed to him in 238 by Gregory Thaumaturgus
after five years of study with him at Caesarea. From this oration
it is quite clear that Origen taught a philological method. He was
not concerned with analysing vocabulary and style, but he did
provide a scientific background in "physiology" (the study of

[1] R. Cadiou, *La jeunesse d'Origène* (Paris, 1935), p. 28; E. Klostermann in *ZNW* 37 (1938), pp. 54–61.
[2] *Vie de Porphyre* (Ghent, 1913), 13; Eusebius, *H.E.* 6, 19, 8.
[3] *The Letter and the Spirit*, pp 21–2.
[4] Test. 9 Leemans, pp. 155–6; cf. *JTS* N.S. 10 (1959), p. 155.
[5] Test. 17 Leemans, p. 87= Origen, *C* 4, 51, p. 324.
[6] Cf. W. Capelle in *RE* XV, 2318–20.   [7] Aulitsky in *RE* XIII, 1401–15.

nature), geometry, and astronomy. This was useful for the study of scripture.[1] Since from Origen's commentaries we know that he was actually concerned with the biblical vocabulary we must assume that Gregory did not share this interest and therefore refrains from mentioning it.

Origen not only taught but wrote. Beginning about the year 215 he composed treatises such as that *On the Resurrection*, the *Stromateis*, and the great catechetical-theological work *De principiis*. These works show that exegetical problems were already important to him, and around the same time he began his commentaries on the first twenty-five psalms, on Lamentations, and on the beginning chapters of Genesis. Before he left Alexandria in 231 he had completed five books of his first New Testament commentary, that on the gospel of John, and perhaps some of his homilies on Luke.

After he was ordained priest at Caesarea he was removed from the catechetical school by Demetrius, Bishop of Alexandria, and expelled from the city. Thereafter he taught at Caesarea, with occasional visits elsewhere before his death about 253. There he composed the last twenty-seven books on John, apparently over a considerable period of time, as well as the rest of his homilies on Luke and his treatise *On Prayer*, much of which is devoted to exegesis of the Lord's Prayer. Between 244 and 249 he wrote the *Commentary on Matthew*. Since he ascribed no special significance to Mark he did not provide separate exegesis for this gospel. Finally, around 248 he composed his eight books *Contra Celsum*, an answer to an anti-Christian treatise written seventy years earlier.[2]

THE FOUR EVANGELISTS

What Origen tells us about the four evangelists comes to him partly from tradition and partly from his own detailed studies of their works. By "tradition" we mean the older information based sometimes on fact, sometimes on conjecture, and handed down

---

[1] *Pan.* 106–13; cf. 182. It is worth noting that the word "allegory" does not appear in this oration, though we find both *ainigma* (174, 180) and *kataskeuasma* (168) twice. For Origen's use of lexicographical works cf. R. Cadiou in *Revue des études grecques* 45 (1932), pp. 271–85; the citations from Origen are from works both early and late.

[2] For details about Origen's commentaries and homilies see Appendix.

without much, if any, investigation of its sources. Occasionally Origen modifies tradition or, at least, chooses between two alternative traditions. For example, before his time at Alexandria Clement had taught that the gospels were written in the order Matthew-Luke-Mark-John; Origen returns to the view, set forth by Irenaeus, that the sequence was Matthew-Mark-Luke-John.[1] In other words, while in Clement's view Luke preceded Mark, in that of Irenaeus and Origen Luke wrote after Mark. Does this conclusion have any historical or theological significance? No, it does not. Origen, like Irenaeus, is not interested in source-analysis. Indeed, he explicitly denies that Luke made use of any of the other canonical gospels when he wrote. One might conceivably suppose that the preface to Luke contains an implicit criticism of Matthew and Mark. But Origen rejects such a supposition. When Luke says (1.1) that previous writers "undertook" to compose an account of the life of Jesus, he must be referring to authors of apocryphal gospels. They are the ones who composed "rashly and without a gift of grace". None of the Church's four evangelists "undertook" to write anything; all were inspired by the Holy Spirit.[2] Origen's theory of inspiration excludes source-analysis.

His emphasis on the inspiration of the evangelists is the most striking feature of what he tells us about them. Probably observation rather than inspiration was responsible for their exact knowledge of Judaean geography.[3] But it is certain that Origen viewed the evangelists in much the same way as he viewed the apostles. "In them there was no power of speaking or of giving an orderly narrative by the standards of Greek dialectical or rhetorical arts." The apostles did not know even the rudiments of grammar.[4] But according to tradition two gospels were written by these men, two by their immediate followers. Given the reliability of the tradition, how could the gospels have been written at all? Origen's answer to this question is that their authors were inspired by the Holy Spirit. The Spirit taught them grammar and composition. In other words, their writings are the

[1] Eusebius, *H.E.* 6, 25, 4–6.
[2] *L* 1, p. 4.   [3] *J* 6, 41, p. 150.   [4] *C* 1, 62, pp. 113–14; cf. Acts 4.13.

result of the Spirit's work both in content and in form. No purely literary or historical explanation of their work is either necessary or possible.

Moreover, since their work was directed by the Spirit it cannot contain errors. At three different points in Origen's commentaries he explicitly states that inspiration implies freedom from error. (1) Some may suggest that the evangelists' narratives differ from one another because their memories were inaccurate; Origen denies that this is the case. (2) Critics of the gospels may suggest that they are "not true and not written by a more divine Spirit or recorded in orderly fashion, for the gospels are said to have been composed in various ways". Origen rejects this view. (3) His own opinion is this: "we believe that the gospels were accurately written by the aid of the Holy Spirit, and those who wrote them made no mistakes in recording".[1]

We have translated the Greek word ἀπομνημονεύειν in two of these passages by the English "record" even though it can also mean "remember" because it appears that Origen's primary emphasis is laid upon the written compositions involved rather than upon a pre-literary process. In this regard we may compare what he says about the epistle to the Hebrews, which in his view was not written by the apostle Paul. He states that the thoughts are the apostle's (hence, are divinely inspired) but the style and composition are the product of one who recorded (or remembered) the apostle's teachings and, as it were, made short notes on what his master said. Here it looks as if his emphasis lies not on the disciple's memory but on the recording of the master's words; the note-taking is simply a more precise description of the recording.[2] It is not clear whether the note-taking was the product of inspiration or not. In the case of the evangelists, however, their similar procedure was inspired.

Because of this emphasis on inspiration, Origen does not find the historical circumstances of the various evangelists especially meaningful. For example, in dealing with the evangelist Matthew he sometimes states that he had two names, Matthew and Levi, in accordance with Hebrew custom; but in the treatise *Contra*

[1] *J* 6, 34, p. 143; *J* 10, 3, p. 172; *M* 16, 12, p. 510.   [2] Eusebius, *H.E.* 6, 25, 11–14.

Celsum he says that Matthew and Levi were two different persons.[1] He knows something from tradition about Matthew's purpose in writing: he wrote for converts from Judaism, and in Hebrew.[2] Like the other synoptic evangelists, Matthew laid more emphasis on Jesus' humanity than on his divinity—though the importance of this emphasis can be exaggerated. Some suppose that the divinity is not stressed in his gospel, but according to Matt. 16.8 the Saviour can read men's thoughts; this is no merely human power.[3]

Origen raises but fails to solve one difficult problem in regard to Matthew's gospel. "Hosanna" in Matt. 21.9 makes sense neither in Hebrew nor in Greek, and Origen suggests that the word was added to the gospel by "Greek writers". Who could these Greek writers be? Harnack suggested that Origen meant the evangelist, but in Origen's view Matthew wrote in Hebrew. Klostermann claimed that he meant copyists of the gospel, and Origen certainly believed that copyists made mistakes.[4] We may tentatively suggest, however, that he meant those who translated the gospel from Hebrew into Greek, since it is a Hebrew word, not a Greek one, which is in question. If this suggestion is correct, a considerable difficulty arises in regard to the inspiration of the Greek text which we possess. Do we have an uninspired translation of an inspired document? Origen does not tell us. And while he does insist that the Greek translation of the Old Testament is inspired, he may not have been willing to say as much for that of the gospel of Matthew.

Of Mark Origen says very little; he only knows, following a tradition already criticized by Clement, that Mark was instructed to write by Peter and that Peter refers to his close relationship to Mark in 1 Pet. 5.13.[5]

Luke wrote an extremely accurate gospel. It is historically reliable, for Luke's opening words can be paraphrased as "I

[1] *L* fr. 7, p. 235; *R praef.* PG 14, 837*A*; *C* 1, 62, p. 113.
[2] Eusebius, *H.E.* 6, 25, 4; *J* 6, 32, p. 141.
[3] *J* 10, 8, p. 177; *M* 92, p. 210; *M* 126, p. 262; thoughts, *M* 12, 6, p. 77. The "some" may perhaps be Ebionites.
[4] Harnack in *Texte und Untersuchungen* 42, 4, 9; Klostermann, footnote ad loc., p. 542.
[5] Eusebius, *H.E.* 6, 25, 5.

write without accepting mere hearsay". On the other hand, it has a universal, non-historical quality. Some readers suppose that Luke wrote to a certain Theophilus, but actually all believers are θεοφίλοι, beloved of God, and therefore his gospel is not limited by historical particularity. Luke did not employ the expression "Father in the heavens" because he was not writing for Jews. Paul commends his gospel in 2 Cor. 8.18.[1]

Origen's favourite gospel is the fourth, that written by John, who reclined on the Lord's bosom. John emphasized the Lord's divinity; he preserved the "greater and more perfect words about Jesus"; he laid stress on the great works which Jesus did—works which were, however, more significant spiritually than literally. He was a theologian who used the Greek language with extreme care; this fact can be shown from his use of the definite article in reference to God the Father in John 17.3 and his omission of it in relation to the Son in John 1.1. He wrote for Greek readers and expected them to understand why he translated the name Thomas as "twin" in John 20.25.[2] Indeed, it is especially characteristic of John that he combines the seemingly historical with what has a deeper meaning (γυμναστικόν).[3]

One might suppose that this picture of John's work is contradicted by what Origen elsewhere says of it. In his view John, since he was "unskilled in speaking" (2 Cor. 11.6), expressed in a disjointed manner what he actually knew.[4] The seeming contradiction can probably be resolved, however, if one considers the fact that in Origen's view John possessed perfect knowledge, had been given the ability to write grammatically by the Holy Spirit, and wanted to use the common biblical method in recording revelation. This is to say that he wished to reveal some things plainly and to express other things obscurely so that men's minds would be directed toward deeper levels of reality. This purpose, given him by the Holy Spirit, coincided with his own lack of

---

[1] L 1, pp. 10–11; L fr. 42, p. 253; L 1, p. 6.

[2] John 13, 25; 21, 20; J 1, 4, p. 8; C 2, 73, p. 195; J 2, 2, p. 54; J fr. 106. pp. 516–2. The point about the definite article is ultimately derived from Philo, Somn. 1, 229.

[3] J fr. 74, p. 541; γυμναστικόν is dialectical rather than rhetorical. Thus John 4.6 is historical; John 4.10 is not.

[4] J 13, 54, p. 284.

ability to write clearly. Apparently Origen is trying to maintain both the complete inspiration of the sacred writings and the human characteristics of the sacred writers.

We have already seen that for Clement the fact that John wrote last of all had theological significance. A similar idea is expressed by Origen when he says that Christian preaching consists first of the "corporeal gospel", then of heavenly wisdom and the gospel of John.[1] From the synoptics he is aware that a certain process of development took place in the disciples' understanding of Jesus; at the beginning they did not understand the meaning of his mission (Matt. 16.20–1), and they first preached to Jews about Jesus, later about the Christ.[2] For the apostles came to be fully illuminated only after the resurrection, when they received the Holy Spirit.[3]

According to Origen a similar development took place in the life and thought of the apostle Paul, who gradually reached "a higher degree of perfection". By examining the Pauline epistles, Origen is able to place them in their chronological order. In Gal. 5.17 the flesh lusts against the spirit; in 1 Cor. 9.27 Paul still fears he may be rejected. But in 2 Cor. 4.8–10 he bears in his body the dying of Jesus; in Phil. 3.11–13 he is still imperfect but is reaching perfection; and in Rom. 8.35–9, nothing can separate him from the love of Christ.[4] Presumably Origen could have traced a similar process of development from Matthew to John, even though he does not explicitly do so. In any case, Origen certainly does not believe that the first gospel was the best.

We have observed what Origen did do and could have done with what information he had accumulated about the four evangelists. What he did is most conspicuous in his dealings with the differences between John and the synoptic gospels, which we

---

[1] *J* 1, 7, p. 13. [2] *M* 12, 16, p. 106; 12, 17, pp. 107–8.

[3] *C* 2, 2, pp. 128–9. This process has its limits, however; it is "absurd" to suppose that men later than the apostles were "more blessed" than the apostles themselves (*J* 10, 43, p. 221).

[4] *Rom. comm.* praef., Migne, *PG* 14, 833–5. Since Romans was written from Corinth (835B–C), Philippians must have come from Ephesus. The crude eschatology of the Thessalonian epistles was presumably due to Sylvanus and Timothy, with whom, as Origen points out (1297D–99A), Paul wrote the letters. (In *C* 3, 20, p. 217, the order Ephesians-Colossians-Thessalonians-Philippians-Romans is not necessarily, though it may be, chronological.)

shall presently discuss in more detail. But it is equally important to notice what he did not do. The notion that Matthew wrote his gospel in Hebrew is presumably intended to explain why the atmosphere of the book is more Jewish than that of the other gospels. Origen, as we have seen, is acquainted with this notion; and we should expect him to make some use of it in explaining the differences between Matthew and the other gospels. He does not do so. For him, the notion is apparently no more than a miscellaneous datum of history, essentially meaningless and unusable. It is evident that although he insists upon the rationality of the evangelists' inspiration, this rationality does not have any relation to the historical circumstances under which it was operative. The rationality Origen has in view is essentially timeless and unhistorical. He never speaks of John as a philosopher, but he is willing to quote the first verse of his gospel as a statement of "our philosophy" about the Son of God;[1] and if this statement is philosophical, presumably the evangelist was concerned with philosophical thought. It would be better to say that the evangelist, though no philosopher, was an instrument of a philosophical revelation.

Could we expect Origen to have considered the evangelists' purposes more fully? We might think so if we look at his discussion of "personification" in *Contra Celsum*. Here he attacks Celsus for putting non-Christian statements in Christians' mouths, and he argues that consistency of character is important in a literary work. Homer is admired because "he keeps the character of the heroes the same as they were when he started, such as that of Nestor, or Odysseus, or Diomedes, or Agamemnon, or Telemachus, or Penelope, or one of the others".

On the other hand, "Euripides is made a fool of by Aristophanes for writing inappropriate verses, because he often attributed to barbarian women or slave girls words containing ideas which he had learnt from Anaxagoras or some other wise man". Origen's statement is hardly original; just the same contrast is pointed out by Theon.[2]

[1] *C* 5, 24, p. 25.
[2] *C* 7, 36, p. 187; Chadwick, op cit., p. 424 (cf. p. 245); Theon 60, 27.

We praise Homer for putting appropriate words into the mouth of each of his characters, but we find fault with Euripides because he unsuitably makes Hecuba discuss philosophy.

In other words, rhetoricians were well aware of the function of an author as creator of the personages in his story.

Origen does recognize this function to some extent when he notes the difference between John and the synoptic evangelists. He cannot develop the idea further, however, since for him there is really no middle ground between history and fiction or myth. To lay more stress on the creativity of the evangelists as historians would have meant that he could not pass so easily from literal truth or untruth to allegory. He would have had to abandon the rhetorical foundation of the allegorical method.

INSPIRATION AND CONTRADICTION

The anti-Christian writer Celsus took pleasure in pointing out the fact that the various gospels contradict one another. "Some believers", he said, "as though from a drinking bout, go so far as to oppose themselves and alter the original text of the gospel three or four times over, and they change its character to enable them to deny difficulties in the face of criticism."[1] As we have seen, Origen did not need to be informed by non-Christians that the gospels disagree with one another. The controversies of the previous century had made all intelligent Christians aware of the fact. In the face of it he was willing to employ the traditional answer that though there are four gospels they are really one,[2] but he was not willing to rest in the comfort provided by this declaration. His own critical studies, and probably his awareness of those made earlier by Gaius of Rome, made it necessary for him to try to analyse the contradictions as sharply and precisely as possible. His advice to the reader of his *Commentary on Matthew* reflects the procedure he followed.[3] "By placing the gospels side by side at these passages and comparing them, you will find out what is said." (In passing we may suggest that this sentence implies that the gospels were available on scrolls as well

[1] *C* 2, 27, p. 156, tr. H. Chadwick. Celsus may be using Marcionite arguments.
[2] *J* 5, 7, p. 104.   [3] 16, 8, p. 490.

as in codex-form, for the work of comparison would surely be far easier for one working with scrolls than for one turning the leaves of a codex.) In any event, Origen firmly believed in the necessity of detailed critical comparison. He probably did not know the *Diatessaron* of Tatian, but if he knew it he did not accept it. Indeed, he brought difficulties to the attention of those who did not recognize their existence: he says that Celsus is probably unaware that in the gospels the genealogies of Jesus are inconsistent.[1]

In Origen's view some of the difficulties in the gospels were due to the way in which the text had been transmitted. In this process three kinds of errors could have been introduced: (1) those due to carelessness in copying; (2) those due to rashness in emendation of the text; and (3) those due to prejudiced correctors who made additions or deletions.[2] This last group of errors includes those intentionally made by enemies of the Church.[3] Origen says that his analysis has been confirmed by his experience in dealing with the variants to be found in the Greek Old Testament.

The particular passage with which he is dealing is that concerning Jesus' "counsel of perfection" (Matt. 19.19), where, as we have said, Matthew's sentence "Thou shalt love thy neighbour as thyself" is not found in either Mark (10.19) or Luke (18.20). Since Origen believes that Matthew was written first, he can argue that neither Mark nor Luke would have omitted the sentence had it actually been spoken by Jesus. And the extent of the textual variants in the gospels, he believes, justifies his treating it as a scribal addition.[4]

Not all, or even many, of the disagreements in the gospels can be accounted for on the basis of textual criticism. There are more serious difficulties, as Origen is aware, especially in regard to John and the synoptics. Indeed, says Origen, everything in the gospel story is a matter for controversy.[5] Christians say that Jesus had a virgin mother; Marcionites say he had no mother; Ebionites say he had a human father and mother. Some say his

[1] C 2, 32, p. 159.   [2] M 15, 14, pp. 387–8.   [3] M 134, p. 274.
[4] M 15, 14, p. 387.   [5] L 17, pp. 115–16.

body was from heaven; others say it was just like ours. After he rose, his body bore the marks of the nails, but it could pass through closed doors. Even the predictions of the prophets about him are subject to dispute.

The most striking differences, as earlier critics had pointed out, were to be found by comparing the sequences of events in the first few chapters of the synoptics and John. In the synoptics we find Jesus' baptism, his temptation in the wilderness, the beginning of his preaching in Galilee, and the call of his first disciples. In John we find the baptism, no temptation, the call of the first disciples, the first miracle at Cana, and the cleansing of the temple in Jerusalem (which the synoptists place toward the end of Jesus' ministry). Moreover, where the evangelists agree as to the sequence of events they describe the events somewhat differently. All this had already been pointed out by Gaius of Rome, and Tatian had tried to solve the difficulty by accepting the synoptists' order of events. But Origen was unwilling to agree that his favourite evangelist, "the most wise John", could have been wrong.[1]

Other people might suggest that the evangelists disagreed because the memories of some of them were inaccurate,[2] but in Origen's opinion, as we have seen, divine inspiration guaranteed correctness in remembering;[3] "none of the evangelists made an error or spoke falsely".[4] We may infer that this opinion of his was in part based upon his own phenomenal memory for scripture passages, clearly evident in his homilies and in his *Discussion with Heraclides and the other Bishops*, recently discovered on papyrus. If his own memory was so good, the memories of the inspired evangelists cannot have been less perfect. His opponents, he says, are really claiming that the gospels are not true, that they are not written by divine inspiration, that they are not recorded with a coherent arrangement.[5]

We shall presently discuss the way in which Origen endeavoured to solve the difficulties involved in these disagreements. Here, however, we wish simply to point out that some of

[1] J 10, 13, p. 183.   [2] J 6, 34, p. 143.   [3] M 16, 12, p. 510
[4] J 6, 34.   [5] J 10, 3, p. 172.

them arise from a confusion of inspiration with exact historical accuracy, as well as from an erroneous theory of the way in which the gospels were composed. It is possible that if Origen's own memory had not been so good he could have admitted that the evangelists were not always absolutely right. And had he been a less productive writer he might have seen that others sometimes copied from sources. In other words, his own genius stood in the way of his understanding the work of some, at least, of the evangelists.

When he himself copied from the writings of others, he usually did so either in order to use the documents as authorities (the Bible, Stoic definitions, etc.) or in order to refute them word by word (Heracleon, Celsus). The idea of taking a source and modifying it slightly (as in the case of Clement's use of Philo) was alien to him, and he was therefore unable to understand the method of the synoptic evangelists.

THE JOHANNINE-SYNOPTIC CONTRADICTIONS

Early Christian writers, as we have already seen, were well aware of the differences between John and the synoptic gospels; Hippolytus must have tried to explain them in his two works against Gaius. The importance of Origen's handling of the subject is due to his attempt to derive theological meaning from the differences. Analysis of the letter leads to insistence upon allegory.

Everyone was aware that John does not give a genealogy of Jesus or describe his temptation. How was this difference to be explained? Origen insists upon considering the purpose the fourth evangelist had in mind when he wrote. John began his gospel with God, and as a divine being Jesus had no genealogy. Moreover, John knew that God cannot be tempted; therefore he did not record the temptation.[1] That Jesus was tempted as a man is plain from Matt. 4.4: "Man shall not live by bread alone."[2] Here we seem to be on the edge of a neat explanation of this difference between the synoptics and John. The synoptics describe Jesus as a man; John describes him as God.

[1] *L* 29, p. 131; *M* 92, p. 210; 126, p, 262.
[2] *P* 3, 2, 1, pp. 245–6; *L* 29, p. 180.

The explanation is not really quite so neat, however, since Origen has already shown that the synoptic temptation narrative must be symbolical. In it we read that the devil took Jesus to a high mountain from which he saw the kingdoms of the whole world and their glory (Matt. 4.8; Luke 4.5). Only a "careless reader", says Origen, could imagine that with "the bodily eye" Jesus saw the kingdoms of Persia, Scythia, India, and Parthia.[1] The mode of action in the story is incredible, literally understood; therefore the story is an allegory. Origen therefore explains that the "kingdoms" must have meant a totality, i.e. the devil's rule over the whole world.[2] At another point he argues that it is "incredible" that the devil could have led or taken the Son of God anywhere; Jesus must have gone voluntarily, like an athlete going to a contest.[3] This argument is inconsistent with that by which he showed that the temptation story is an allegory, but we recall that it is used in a homily and that homilies sometimes express various aspects of a religious problem as treatises do not.

The basic point he has in mind is that the temptation story is primarily symbolical, whether it speaks of Jesus as a man or as the Son of God. Since both the synoptic gospels and that of John are dealing with symbols, they can be reconciled only by considering the symbols which lie behind their verbal expressions. The discord among the gospels is to be resolved by the use of allegorization (ἀναγωγή).[4]

An equally serious difficulty arises when we compare the place of the cleansing of the temple in John with that assigned it by the synoptic writers. Here there is a genuine "historical discord". And Origen proceeds to take the hypothetical case of four inspired writers—obviously the evangelists—who speak of God's presence "through an historical symbol". They will say that God appeared to a particular witness at a particular time in a particular place; that he performed a particular action, appeared in a particular form, and went away to another particular place. Since the writers are describing revelations given them individually, they will disagree. Literally understood, their accounts are false. They

[1] *P* 4, 3, 1, p. 324.   [2] *L* 30, pp. 184–5.   [3] *L* 31, p. 187.
[4] *J* 10, 3, p. 175.

are myths. They contain internal, not external, truth.[1] They can be recognized as myths because they disagree on just those points at which contemporary rhetoricians found myths and legends internally inconsistent. (See Chapter 2.)

Origen is now in a position to proceed to his criticism of the story of the cleansing of the temple. Taken as history, he says, the narrative is improbable (ἀπίθανος). The term he uses, as we have seen, is the one used by Greek analysts in criticizing narratives ordinarily regarded as historical. In his view the story of the cleansing of the temple not only is told differently by the various evangelists but also contains inherent improbabilities.[2] How could merchants have sold unclean animals in the temple? How could a person thought to be a carpenter's son have acted so boldly among "myriads" of people? To use a scourge of cords (supposing that someone prefers to refer the story to the Son of God rather than to Jesus) would hardly be characteristic of the Son. The story as told by John, then, is not literally historical.[3]

But the synoptic version is not historical either. Matthew cannot be writing history, for there is nothing worth recording in his statements about the two disciples who went to get an ass and a colt, or about Jesus' sitting upon them and entering the city.[4] If Matthew is writing for Jews and showing how prophecy was fulfilled, it is singular that the Jews themselves point out that the whole prophecy in Zechariah was not fulfilled. And as literal history his story is open to sharp criticism. A journey of fifteen stadia is hardly worth reporting. Again, how could Jesus ride on two animals at the same time?[5] And for the disciples to tell the ass's owner that "the Lord needs him" was unworthy of the Son of God.[6]

Once more, Origen's criticisms are not altogether consistent. Sometimes he speaks of what was suitable for the carpenter's son, sometimes of what the Son of God should have done or said. But they are intended to demolish the historicity of the narrative,

---

[1] J 10, 4, p. 174.   [2] J 10, 22, p. 194.
[3] J 10, 25, pp. 197–8.   [4] J 10, 26, pp. 198–9.
[5] Clement, Protr. 121, 1, had endeavoured to avoid the difficulty by stating that the two animals drew a chariot on which Jesus rode.
[6] J 10, 27, pp. 199–201.

one way or another, and details that could not be rejected as unworthy of Jesus could be rejected as unworthy of God's Son. The story must be taken symbolically. It is a story about the Logos, not about Jesus, and about the human soul, not about Jerusalem.[1]

Origen concludes, rather triumphantly, that there is "only one refuge" for those who wish to defend the story; this is the "more divine power of Jesus". By an appeal to this power they can support the historical character of the event—"if it took place".[2] But he has already pointed out that "when the four evangelists use many examples of deeds and words in relation to the marvellousness and paradoxical character of the power of Jesus, they have woven into the writing, describing it as perceptible to the senses, what was clear to them purely and through the mind alone".[3] This statement means that an appeal to the divine power of Jesus can be made only by a simple believer, not by a theologian.[4] For an Origenist will recognize that the work of "weaving in" is due to the divine author of scripture, who inspired the evangelists.

The way in which the weaving took place deserves a closer look. In Origen's systematic treatment of inspiration and exegesis he tells us that where spiritual truths did not correspond to historical events, "the scripture wove into the historical narrative what did not take place—at some points what cannot take place and at others what can take place but did not".[5] This is to say that scripture, like literature in general, contains a combination of various literary forms. Theon tells us that the well trained rhetorician will be able to create such combinations. He can combine one historical narrative with others (86.2; 92.24), or he can combine myth with historical narrative (74.3). For example, he can begin with a myth and can say that "a camel who wanted horns was deprived even of ears"; then he can state that "the experience of this camel seems to me to resemble what happened to Croesus the Lydian", and can go on to the narrative about

[1] *J* 10, 28, p. 201.   [2] *J* 10, 25, pp. 197–8.   [3] *J* 10, 5, p. 175.
[4] Cf. *L* fr. 15, p. 239 : simple believers are edified by considering the mighty works of God; others ought to go on to spiritual understanding.
[5] *P* 4, 2, 9, p. 322.

Croesus (75.9–16). Origen is pointing out that scripture is arranged in a similar fashion. It combines historical narrative with myth (what cannot take place) and fiction (what can take place but did not).

In his analysis of these forms, however, he does not use the prejudicial terms "myth" and "fiction". Instead, he substitutes the words "enigma" and "parable", since they are to be found in scripture itself. We know that these words are the equivalents of "myth" and "fiction" because Origen's definitions of them, provided in his *Commentary on Proverbs*, are identical with the Greek definitions of the ordinary Greek terms.[1] We might suppose that Origen's conception was different from that of the rhetoricians because he insists on the hidden meaning to be found in "enigma" and "parable", but the rhetoricians too claimed that "myth" contains an image of some truth.[2]

Under what circumstances did the evangelists, or the Logos or Spirit which inspired the evangelists, make use of enigmas and parables (to use Origen's terminology)? Origen says that usually the spiritual meaning and the literal expression of it coincide, but where spiritual truths cannot be expressed literally they are presented in symbolical form, indeed in what, literally considered, is practically false.[3] Once more his interpretation is close to what the rhetoricians said. "When will the orator speak falsely", asks Hermogenes, "if his audience is conscious that he speaks falsely?" The answer is that he will do so when the falsehood is of benefit to his hearers.[4] In other words, the rhetorician will make use of the beneficial or medicinal lie. According to Origen, God makes use of the same procedure, like a father dealing with an infant son or a physician treating a patient. "The whole of divine scripture is full of such medicines."[5]

At the time Origen wrote his tenth book on John he thus regarded the story of the cleansing of the temple as a medicinal

[1] E. Klostermann in *ZNW* 37 (1938), 58, 61, citing Lomatzsch 13, 220. 225–6. According to Tryphon (III, 193, 13) enigma includes something "impossible and impracticable".

[2] See the Glossary, p. 122.   [3] *J* 10, 5, p. 175.

[4] II, 441, 27 Spengel (435, 4 Rabe); cf. Sextus Empiricus, *Adv. math.* 7, 42–5.

[5] *Jerem. hom.* 20, 3, p. 180 Klostermann; cf. Hanson ,*Allegory and Event*, pp. 210–31.

myth. By using the method of ἀνασκευή he had shown that it was incredible. The place is wrongly described, for in the temple there were no unclean animals. The person, regarded either as the man Jesus or as the Son of God, would not have used a whip of cords; and therefore the mode of action is also incredible. The time ascribed to the action is improbable because there were so many people present. In addition, Origen had shown that the story was told inconsistently, since the Johannine version disagrees with that found in the synoptics.

To appeal to Jesus' miraculous power in defence of the story meant appealing to an authority to some extent outmoded. For Origen had pointed out that while the remarkable miracles were once able to evoke faith "they did not keep their impressive character with the passage of time, and are now supposed to be myths". This notion of the declining credibility of miracles is Stoic.[1] But who is the person who supposes them to be myths? It may be a non-Christian critic of the gospels. But it may also be, and in view of what we have said it probably is, Origen himself.

Origen certainly regretted having spoken so emphatically on this subject. By the time he wrote his thirteenth book on John he was ready to say that in dealing with the cleansing of the temple he had shown that Jesus was revealing his miraculous power—in spite of the fact that this is just what he had not shown.[2] Much later, in the *Commentary on Matthew*, he said that previously he had explained the Johannine narrative to the best of his ability; he had proved that the boldness and authority of one regarded as a carpenter's son was not inferior to the paradoxical miracles of the gospels. His allegorization of the narrative, he claims, was due to his "slavery to the letter".[3] Evidently his mind was changing.

But the extent to which it changed should not be exaggerated. In the same commentary Origen discusses the story of Jesus' anointing by a woman (Matt. 26.6–13; Mark 14.3–9; Luke 7.36–50; John 12.1–8).[4] Many, he says, suppose that the four evangelists are speaking of the same woman, and indeed there is a good

---

[1] *J* 2, 34, p. 92. Cf. Cicero, *De natura deorum*, 2, 5. Hanson, *Allegory and Event*, pp. 221–2.

[2] *J* 13, 56, p. 286.   [3] *M* 16, 20, pp. 543–4.   [4] *M* 77, pp. 178–86.

deal of material common to the four.[1] If one considers the details, however, it is clear that several women are involved. The ointment is poured on Jesus' head in Matthew and Mark but on his feet in Luke and John. In Luke she is a sinner, while in John she is Mary the sister of Martha; neither Matthew nor Mark calls her a sinner. In Luke she weeps, while in John she does not. In Matthew, Mark, and Luke the episode takes place in the house of a certain Simon, while in John it is in some other house. In Matthew the event occurs two days before the Passover, in John six days before it. In the synoptics nothing is said of the filling of the house with the odour of the ointment, as it is in John. Thus the stories contain descriptions of different circumstances, actions, places, times, and results, and on the grounds established in Greek rhetorical analysis, they are all incredible.

What conclusions can be drawn? Origen suggests three possibilities. (1) The evangelists may really contradict one another, and in this event some of them are speaking falsely. (2) They may be describing the actions of several women (but this possibility is excluded by the general resemblances in the stories). (3) "A little more boldly"—historically speaking, there were one, two, or even three women; but the main concern of the evangelists was with mysteries of faith, and they did not take sufficient pains (*non satis curaverunt*) to tell the story in accordance with the truth of history. Instead, they "wove in" spiritual truths—to which Origen turns.

It is obvious that in this passage, written late in his life, Origen was still adhering to the theory of "weaving in" which he had set forth in his treatise *De principiis* and had employed in the *Commentary on John*. His mind clearly did change in regard to the story of the cleansing of the temple, but it did not change so much that he abandoned his theory of the primacy of the spiritual. The truth of history remained secondary for him.

When he first dealt with the cleansing, Origen concluded that the only demonstrably historical items in the story were the existence of the temple itself and the presence of crowds at

---

[1] Tatian regarded the story as the same in Matthew, Mark, and John (39.7–17 Hill) but different in Luke (14.45—15.11).

festivals there. We may suspect that his notion of history is close to the content of Josephus's works, for in them we read of the temple and the crowds but not of Jesus' ministry.[1] In the story of the anointing, the historical items are the persons of Jesus and of one woman or more, and the act of anointing. Obviously there is a significant difference in Origen's treatment of the two stories, for in the exegesis we have just discussed he does not deny that Jesus was really present and was really anointed. Just as he has come to believe that there is more historical truth in the cleansing of the temple, so he finds that the anointing was a real event.

What is the meaning of Origen's change of mind, as far as his historical method is concerned? We are fortunate in possessing his exegesis of these two narratives which, in some respects, are remarkably similar. Both the cleansing and the anointing are placed near the beginning of the passion narrative by three of the evangelists but not by a fourth.[2] In both cases Origen feels that he must examine the details of the stories in order to find out what common elements they have and what differences are present. At points where differences exist, Origen claims in regard to both stories that spiritual truths have been "woven in". But in the story of the anointing, the weaving is confined to matters of detail. The principal reason for this difference seems to lie in Origen's diminishing confidence in the method of historical criticism set forth by the rhetoricians. By employing this method in order to assess the truth or falsity of the cleansing narrative he had reached the conclusion that it was literally, historically false. He could have used the same method in dealing with the story of the anointing, but he did not do so. Instead, he restricted himself to the comparison of the various accounts. Such a comparison led him to raise questions about various details and about the time of the event. It did not lead him to suggest that the event itself was unhistorical. In other words, Origen was no longer as sure as he once had been that he could differentiate myth and fiction from history.

[1] On Josephus see p. 115. In Origen's text of Josephus there was no description of the work of Jesus.

[2] Cleansing: Matthew, Mark, Luke against John; anointing Matthew, Mark, John against Luke.

It is therefore evident that, while Origen's mind did change as he considered the historical problems to be found in the gospels, it did not change simply because of theological presuppositions or a conservatism produced by age. It changed, at least in part, because he continued to apply the historical method taught by rhetoricians and used in his earlier works; he continued to apply it but he came to recognize its limitations. Indeed, as we have seen, he came to regard his earlier analysis of the incredibility of the cleansing story as "slavery to the letter", insistence upon the verbal details of the historical narrative at the expense of the reliability of the whole narrative.

We shall presently see that in his treatise *Contra Celsum* he pointed out that the method of κατασκευή, demonstration of the truth of a historical narrative, is exceedingly difficult to apply. We should add that he must have recognized that to demonstrate falsity was a task almost equally arduous. In his later works, then, he has come to realize that not all the problems of historical exegesis arise out of the texts. Some of them are provided by the method or methods involved.

A Different Approach—Contra Celsum

If new occasions teach new duties, we should expect to find Origen treating the gospel narratives differently when he came to write his reply to the *True Discourse* of the anti-Christian writer Celsus. In this reply he was no longer defending allegorical exegesis against simple believers and heretics who insisted on taking the gospel stories in a crudely literal way; he was defending the gospel stories themselves against an opponent whose way of looking at them was much like his own. And this opponent had said that the gospels contained a good many examples of fictions and myths.[1] What was Origen to do, when he himself, though using a different terminology, had expounded the same doctrine?

In the first place, he could insist upon the importance of exact scholarship and could criticize a few minor inaccuracies in Celsus'

[1] *C* 3, 27, p. 224.

account. "Those who practise avoiding mistakes take great pains to search and examine the statements on each subject and give their opinion rather slowly and carefully when they are deciding that one group of people is telling the truth and another telling falsehood in their narratives about miraculous happenings. For not all men give clear evidence of their credibility, nor do all men make it manifest that they have told men fictions and myths."[1] He could also insist upon the importance of philosophical presuppositions in dealing with such narratives. Naturalistic philosophers can criticize miracle stories; others should not do so.[2]

But while these arguments undoubtedly have their place in creating an atmosphere favourable to Origen's case, he recognizes that they do not answer the charges Celsus makes. The only answer, after all, to historical criticism is more historical criticism. A scorpion is no substitute for an egg. In the second place, therefore, he proceeds to discuss the nature of historical criticism itself, with a reference to the traditional rhetorical method of κατασκευή, "confirmation" of the truth of a story. "An attempt to substantiate (κατασκευάζειν) the truth of almost any story as historical fact, even if the story is true, and to produce complete certainty (καταληπτική φαντασία, a Stoic term) about it, is one of the most difficult tasks and in some cases is impossible."[3]

Here Origen is probably referring to the famous Eleventh Oration of the rhetorician Dio Chrysostom, who, as we have seen, argues on the basis of ἀνασκευή, "refutation", that neither *Iliad* nor *Odyssey* was true, and began with the words, "I know that to teach all men is difficult, while to deceive them is easy". But while Dio had rejected the historical character of the Homeric poems altogether, Origen followed another method of Homeric exegesis according to which the poems were partly true and partly false. Historical facts were to be found in them, but there were also "woven in" mythical and fictitious elements.[4] So he goes on to speak of the Trojan war, into which were "woven" impossible stories (i.e. myths) about sons of the gods and

[1] *C* 5, 57, p. 60; tr. H. Chadwick.
[2] Cf. *Miracle and Natural Law* (Amsterdam, 1952), pp. 199–200.
[3] *C* 1, 42, p. 92.
[4] Cf. Strabo, *Geog.* 1, 2, 9, c. 20; *The Letter and the Spirit*, pp. 95, 102.

fictitious stories (πλάσματα) about Oedipus and Jocasta, ficti-tious because of the mention of the Sphinx.[1] These references probably come from some Stoic manual on Homeric exegesis. But they cannot be discounted as simply taken over by Origen from a source he followed. The point he is making is completely dependent upon the analogy he has drawn between Greek mytho-logy and its analysis and the gospels and their analysis.

This fact becomes clear as he draws his conclusion. "Anyone who reads the stories with a fair mind who wants to keep himself from being deceived by them will decide what he will accept and what he will interpret allegorically, searching out the meaning of the authors who wrote such fictitious stories, and what he will disbelieve as having been written to gratify certain people. We have said this by way of introduction to the whole question of the narrative about Jesus in the gospels."[2] The authors, then, are the evangelists. The "certain people" who are being "gratified" by the gospel narratives, literally interpreted, must be simple be-lievers. And the fair-minded reader is the critic like Origen who is able to decide what is true and what is not.

What is true? Origen has already attacked Celsus' story that "the mother of Jesus was turned out by the carpenter who was betrothed to her, as she had been convicted of adultery and had a child by a certain soldier named Panthera".[3] Origen regards this story as a "myth", but uses it as proof that his opponent recog-nizes the fact that Joseph was not the father of Jesus. He then proceeds to argue that the story of virginal conception is ap-propriate in regard to Jesus. According to Pythagoras, Plato, and Empedocles, "there are certain secret principles by which each soul that enters a body does so in accordance with its merits and former character". Furthermore, according to the physiogno-mists such as Zopyrus, Loxus, and Polemon, "all bodies con-form to the habits of their souls".[4] These remarks show that the virginal conception was "necessary".

---

[1] The Sphinx is fictitious according to Palaephatus (*De incred.* 4, pp. 10–12 Festa), whose work was used by rhetoricians like Theon (p. 96, 4–6 Spengel); cf. Dio Chry-sostom (*Or.* 11, 8).

[2] *C* 1, 42, p. 93. [3] *C* 1, 32, p. 83. [4] 1, 33, p. 85.

But was the virginal conception possible? Celsus compared the story with Greek myths about Danae, Melanippe, Auge, and Antiope; Origen is willing to add the birth of Plato, son of Apollo and Amphictione, but says that all of them are mythological.[1] In order to prove the possibility he speaks of it as "credibility" of the virginal conception of Jesus, he mentions female animals which conceive spontaneously, such as the vulture, and the Greek notion that the first men came into existence from "generative principles" in the earth.[2]

It is after this discussion that he speaks of the dove at Jesus' baptism and explains the method of κατασκευή, which he is employing. Celsus thinks that the story about the dove (Luke 3.22) at Jesus' baptism is a fiction.[3] Here Origen really agrees with him. The descent of the dove and the opening of the heavens were certainly not perceptible to the senses.[4] But he has to insist that the story of the spiritual event is true, and he therefore suggests that Jesus probably told his disciples about his inner experience. Alternatively, one might say that "not all those who recorded the accounts of the form of the dove and the voice from heaven heard Jesus describing these things; but the Spirit that taught Moses the history before his time ... also taught the writers of the gospel about this miracle which occurred at the time of Jesus' baptism".[5] What this sentence means is that Luke's statement about the "corporeal form" of the Spirit probably does not come from Jesus himself but is a fictitious addition, inspired by the Spirit in order to point beyond corporeality.

Other points at which Celsus accuses the evangelists of writing fiction cause Origen less embarrassment. He is able to argue that hostile critics are more likely to write fiction than are the sincere disciples of Jesus,[6] and he can claim that when Celsus treats Judas' betrayal as fact but his repentance as fiction he is being inconsistent. Indeed, Celsus' own argument is "incredible".[7]

---

[1] 1, 37, p. 89.

[2] He probably speaks of credibility rather than of possibility because he does not wish to insist upon the factual nature of his parallels (he certainly does not himself accept the Greek story about the first men).

[3] *C* 1, 40, p. 90.   [4] *J* fr. 20. pp. 499–501.

[5] *C* 1, 44, p. 94.   [6] *C* 2, 10. p. 138.   [7] 2, 11, p. 139.

Again, Celsus claims that the disciples wrote fiction when they said that Jesus foreknew and foretold what was going to happen to him. Evidently he is referring to the passion-predictions often questioned by modern scholars. Origen replies that Jesus also predicted the persecution of his disciples; and such predictions are so unusual that they must be true. If these are true, Jesus' prediction of his own death is also true.[1] Moreover, if the evangelists were writing fiction they would hardly have recorded Jesus' predictions of the denial of Peter or the defection of the disciples.[2] Origen's basic point here is that since the disciples had no motive for reporting matters discreditable to themselves, their accounts of these matters must be true. As he says of the Gethsemane scene—which Celsus accepted but regarded as shameful[3]—"to conceal tales of this sort was easy, by not recording them at all".[4] In other words the Christian narratives are not "prejudicial".

Again, Celsus regarded the stories of Jesus' raising people from the dead as fictitious. Origen replies that "if it were fiction, many would have been described as rising, and those who had already spent more time in the tombs". Actually, however, there are only three such cases in the gospels: the daughter of the synagogue chief (Luke 8.49–56), the only son of the widow (Luke 7.11–17), and Lazarus, who had been in the tomb four days (John 11.1–44).[5] From Origen's other writings it is not altogether clear just how literally he took these stories. Of the first he says that while simple believers marvel at miracles, it is more important to consider that the girl symbolizes the synagogue of the Jews.[6] We do not possess his comments on the second. And Eustathius of Antioch bitterly criticizes Origen's exegesis of the story of Lazarus.[7] Origen, he says, should have glorified the great power of Christ and should have used it as proof of his deity; but he said nothing relevant to this purpose and instead treated Lazarus allegorically (ἀνήγαγεν) as a man who was sick and, indeed, dead in sins. Once more, we find that Origen's basic

---

[1] *C* 2, 13, pp. 141–2.   [2] *C* 2, 15, p. 144.   [3] 2, 24, p. 153.
[4] 2, 26, p. 155.   [5] *C* 2, 48, pp. 169–70.   [6] *L* fr. 15, pp. 239–40.
[7] Eustathius, *De engastr.* 21; Migne, *PG* 18, 656D; *J* fr. 63a, pp. 540–1.

concern is with what he considers the spirit, not the letter, of the miracle.

Moreover, in the very passage in which he lists the three raisings from the dead, he indicates that there is a hidden meaning in the words, "She is not dead but asleep" (Luke 8.52)[1], and he adds that the miracles took place in order to "lead many to the marvellousness of the doctrine of the gospel". In accordance with the promise of Jesus (John 14.12), however, the disciples later performed greater works than the sense-perceptible miracles which Jesus accomplished.[2]

Finally, we find that Celsus criticized the stories of the resurrection of Jesus himself. He began his attack by arguing that the resurrection resembled the tricks of ancient "divine men" who were trying "to convince simple hearers whom they exploit by deceit". He then suggested that no one "who really died ever rose again with the same body", and proceeded to criticize the Christian story. If other stories are myths, why should the Christian account be regarded as "noble and convincing"? What of Jesus' "cry from the cross when he expired, and the earthquake and the darkness"?

> While he was alive he did not help himself, but after death he rose again and showed the marks of his punishment and how his hands had been pierced. But who saw this? A hysterical female, as you say, and perhaps some other one of those who were deluded by the same sorcery, who either dreamt in a certain state of mind and through wishful thinking had a hallucination due to some mistaken notion (an experience which has happened to thousands), or, which is more likely wanted to impress the others by telling this fantastic tale, and so by this cock-and bull story to provide a chance for other beggars.[3]

Origen denies that the Greek stories are analogous, for Jesus was in fact crucified publicly; he really died—and rose. And for Jews and Christians alike resurrection is an unquestionable dogma. The earthquake and the darkness can be confirmed from the historical narrative of Phlegon of Tralles.[4]

[1] Christians do not die but sleep (*M* fr. 185–6, pp. 88–9).
[2] *C* 2, 48, p. 170. Cf. *Is. hom.* 6, 4, p. 274 Baehrens.
[3] *C* 2, 55, tr. Chadwick.
[4] *C* 2, 56–9, pp. 180–2. But elsewhere Origen denies that this is so; see p. 97.

As for the resurrection witnesses, they might have experienced hallucination had the event occurred at night. "But his idea of a vision in the daytime is not convincing when the people were in no way mentally unbalanced and were not suffering from delirium or melancholy." There is no evidence in the gospels to show that Mary Magdalene was hysterical.[1]

Unfortunately for Celsus' own consistency, he goes on to criticize the nature of the resurrection appearances by saying that "after his death, Jesus used to produce only a mental impression of the wounds he received on the cross, and did not really appear wounded in this way". Origen has no difficulty in pointing out that according to John 20.25–7, Jesus appeared and showed his wounds to Thomas, a disciple "who did not believe and thought the miracle to be impossible".[2]

Another objection was that "if Jesus really wanted to show forth divine power, he ought to have appeared to the very men who treated him despitefully and to the man who condemned him and to everyone everywhere". Origen replies by making use of his theory that Jesus did not always appear in the same way to everyone; he had several aspects, which differed in proportion to the spiritual levels of the witnesses.[3] Celsus also argued that "if he really was so great he ought, in order to display his divinity, to have disappeared suddenly from the cross". Origen's main answer to this objection is based on the question of fact. To be sure, Jesus could have disappeared in this way, but he did not do so. And if he had done so, Celsus would doubtless have asked, "Why did he disappear after arriving at the cross, when he did not do this before his passion?" And in Origen's view Celsus actually ends with absurdity. He says that "when he was punished he was seen by all, but by only one person after he rose again, whereas the opposite ought to have happened". The "opposite" would be for him to have been seen by one person at the crucifixion and by all after the resurrection. But this would be "impossible and irrational".[4]

[1] 2, 60, p. 183. Presumably Celsus recalls that according to Luke 8.2 seven demons had emerged from her.
[2] 2, 61, p. 183.   [3] See Chapter 4, pp. 80–1; C 2, 63–7, pp. 184–9.
[4] 2, 68–70, pp. 189–93.

At another point in his treatise Celsus discussed the angelic visitations recorded in the gospels and therefore touched upon the resurrection story once more.[1]

> They say that an angel came to the tomb of this very man (some say one angel, some two), who replied to the women that he was risen. The Son of God, it seems, was not able to open the tomb, but needed someone else to move the stone.

Origen replies that the gospels do not disagree as much as Celsus supposes. Matthew (28.2) and Mark (16.5) do have one angel, while Luke (24.4) and John (20.12) have two. But "the writers that have one angel say that this one was he who rolled back the stone from the sepulchre, whereas those that have two say they stood in shining raiment before the women who came to the tomb, or that they were seen 'sitting in white robes' within it".[2] The story is historically true. When Celsus speaks of the inability of the Son of God to roll away the stone, he is "like a young fellow at school who has been given the task of pulling some argument to pieces". In other words, he is using the method of ἀνασκευή at a point where Origen regards it as inappropriate. Origen replies that it is "more dignified" for an inferior servant to have moved the stone than for the rising Lord to have done so. Furthermore, the story contains a philosophical allegory.[3]

Obviously Origen is using the method of κατασκευή in all these instances, and he is trying to substantiate the historical truth of the narratives. In the last examples we have cited, he is evidently trying to prove that the physical body of Jesus was raised from the dead—or so it appears.

But as usual he is presenting only one aspect of his doctrine. Especially in his earlier works he was always anxious to avoid the errors both of heretics, who denied a bodily resurrection altogether (and he could see that Celsus' approach was similar to theirs) and of the simpler believers, who believed in the resurrection of the physical body.[4] In the early treatise *On the Resurrection* Origen carefully explained that human bodies are composed of the four elements: earth, water, air, and fire.[5] Then he went on to

---

[1] 5, 52, p. 56.　　[2] 5, 56, p. 59.　　[3] 5, 58, p. 61.
[4] Lommatzsch 17, 61–2.　　[5] Ibid., 62.

say that the body of Jesus was different from that of human beings, since it was not born of the seed of a man and the pleasure of the flesh. He did eat and drink after the resurrection, but he did not conceal the nature of the body which was made of air and was spiritual.[1] The form of his body remained the same, but the substance was different.[2] And such a doctrine was not abandoned by Origen in his old age. In *Contra Celsum* he says that Jesus' resurrection body was on the borderline between the density (παχύτης) it possessed before the passion and the way it would appear as a naked soul.[3] It is worth noting that Origen never refers to the words of Luke 24.39 about the flesh and bones of the risen Jesus, even though he does say that Jesus "evidently seems to have eaten some fish after his resurrection".[4]

How "positive" is Origen's historical treatment of the life of Jesus when he writes against Celsus? Certainly he defends the stories of the virginal conception, the descent of the dove, the resurrections of dead persons. Jesus predicted his own passion and the defection of his disciples; Judas really betrayed him, though later, like the other disciples, he repented. But when Origen speaks of miracles he betrays a certain hesitation—not so much in the case of virginal conception, for which he knows pagan parallels (thus he reverses the attitude of modern writers) as in the cases of the dove's descent and of resurrections. His position in regard to the resurrection of Jesus, the cardinal and undeniable miracle, is not ambiguous, though it seemed so to literalists in antiquity. There is reason to suppose that he did not regard the resurrection of Jesus as "physical"—but at the same time he undoubtedly regarded it as historical.

ORIGEN AND THE HISTORICAL METHOD
Summary

We have seen that Origen regarded the refutation of a narrative ostensibly historical as a task much easier than its confirmation. This view was based partly on the nature of the method he used,

[1] Ibid., 65.   [2] Epiphanius, *Haer.* 64, 14, 9—15, 1, p. 424, Holl.
[3] 2, 62, p. 184.   [4] *C* 1, 70, p. 124; John 21.13.

taken over from the schools of rhetoric, and partly on his theological purpose, which involved the refutation of a good deal of
"the letter" so that the "spirit" could be revealed. Origen was
not interested in what he called "mere" history. He was a
philosophical theologian who used history only where history
suited his theological purposes. Indeed, there is considerable
justification for claiming that he was primarily concerned not with
history but with the historical method; it was his misfortune
that the historical method he used was ultimately inadequate.

His use of the historical method of his time is most clearly
evident in those books of his *Commentary on John* which he
wrote just after leaving Alexandria for Caesarea. Presumably he
felt that he had been released from the pressures placed upon him
by the bishop and the simple literalists in Egypt; now he could
employ his method as thoroughly as possible and could search the
scriptures for their allegorical meaning. Over a period of time,
however, he came to regard his method somewhat less highly. He
had once come close to denying the historical nature of at least
the first four chapters of John; later he corrected his own interpretation, at least in regard to the cleansing of the temple, and
came to recognize, at least in part, the limitations of the method
he had been using.

4

ORIGEN AND THE LIFE OF JESUS

THE MINISTRY AND PERSON OF JESUS

GIVEN the existence of the synoptic and the Johannine portraits of Jesus, and the partial explanation of their differences as due to their emphases on the humanity and on the divinity of Jesus, it was still necessary for Origen to explain how it was that the portraits could be as different as they were. In the second century there had been many Christians, especially gnostics, who were unable to believe that a divine being could have become incarnate; they argued that the Christ had merely seemed to be born, to suffer, and to die. In their view the miracles proved Christ's divinity; nothing proved his humanity. And in writings fairly close to such speculation we find the idea that Jesus appeared in different forms at different times to different persons.[1] From "tradition" Clement informs us that sometimes, when the beloved disciple reclined in Jesus' bosom, there was nothing tangible on which he could rest.[2]

Origen was undoubtedly influenced by such traditional information, but the real point of departure for his thought lay in the gospels themselves, where he could find a link with John in the synoptic story of the transfiguration. This story shows that "the Logos has different forms".[3] And because Matthew (17.2) and Mark (9.2) say that Jesus was transfigured "in the presence of" the three disciples, while Luke (9.29) states only that "the form of his person became different", it is possible that he was transfigured before some but, at the same time, not before others.[4] The reason for this must be that the evangelists are describing a spiritual vision, not one perceptible to the senses.[5] Each witness saw Jesus in proportion to his spiritual comprehension.[6]

In Origen's view the transfiguration story was the key to the

---

[1] *Acta Iohannis* 93, pp. 195–6 Bonnet; W. Bauer, *Das Leben Jesu*, pp. 313–14.
[2] *Hypotyp.* frag. 24, p. 210 Stählin.   [3] *M* 12, 36, p. 152.   [4] *M* 12, 37, p. 153.
[5] *C* 4, 16, pp. 285–6.   [6] *C* 6, 77, pp. 146–9.

ways in which the disciples saw Jesus, not only at that time but always. As the Logos, Jesus was like the Old Testament manna which turned into whatever each person desired (here Origen follows Philo).[1] And such metamorphoses took place both corporeally and in relation to the nature of the Logos, which does not appear in the same way to all.[2] The notion that Jesus' physical appearance changed is, of course, based on the story of the transfiguration, as well as on Luke's story of the resurrection appearance on the road to Emmaus. The disciples did not recognize him at first (Luke 24.16)—for he was seen by them "as they were able to see".[3] Moreover, the theory explains why it was necessary for Judas to identify Jesus for the soldiers who arrested him; they could not tell who he was "because of his metamorphoses".[4]

Evidently this theory, in spite of its possible meaningfulness in relation to spiritual edification,[5] and its implicit insistence on the subjectivity of the evangelists (sometimes explicit),[6] leaves historical understanding in ruins. The Jesus of whom Origen speaks is finally neither God nor man but, in his phrase, "a sort of composite being".[7]

But Origen does not always adhere to this theory. Indeed, most of the time he treats the various gospels as records of historical events. And we must therefore turn to his analyses of the gospel stories in order to see what he makes of their account of the life of Jesus.

The different genealogies of Jesus in Matthew and Luke presented a problem. Julius Africanus had militantly rejected the notion that both were fictitious and were composed in praise of Jesus. False praise of God is false, and therefore the genealogies have to be reconciled. By using several ingenious hypotheses Africanus was able to reconcile them.[8] Origen, on the other hand, was content to point out that the persons mentioned in the

---

[1] Cf. the note of Klostermann on *M* 100, p. 218.   [2] *M* 100, pp. 218–19.
[3] *L* fr. 85, p. 274.   [4] *M* 100.
[5] F. Bertrand, *Mystique de Jésus chez Origène* (Paris, 1951), pp. 14–46.
[6] *J* 1, 6, p. 8.   [7] *C* 1, 66, p. 119.
[8] Cf. W. Reichardt, *Die Briefe des Sextus Julius Africanus an Aristides und Origenes* (*TU* 34, 3, Leipzig, 1909).

genealogies are different; that the genealogies are arranged in descending order in Matthew, in ascending order in Luke; and that Luke, who places the genealogy after Jesus' baptism, does not include any women in it.[1] He then turns to the allegorical meaning which must be sought because the gospels disagree.

A spiritual meaning could be found in Matthew's genealogy[2] as well as in Luke's, for Origen insists that the word γένησις in Matt. 1.1 is different from the word γέννησις in Matt. 1.18. The former refers to "the first formation from God"; the latter, to the "consecutive descent from condemnation to death because of the transgression".[3] This distinction is not very solidly based, since the best manuscripts read γένησις at both points; but the reading of Irenaeus was the same as that which Origen followed.

Origen insisted upon the historical actuality of the virginal conception, though at times he recognized it as a "mystery" of faith.[4] He was willing to accept the testimony of apocryphal gospels in order to defend the perpetual virginity of Mary; the so-called brothers of Jesus, he says, were sons of Joseph by a previous marriage.[5] They were called brothers by a legal fiction.[6] By providing two Old Testament examples (Isa. 46.4; Gen. 8.7) in which "until" could be translated as "constantly", Origen was able to explain Matt. 1.25 as meaning that Joseph "did not know" Mary—i.e., know the source of her conceiving—"at any time when she had given birth, and he saw the signs which took place".[7] This exegesis is rather strained.[8]

Origen gives no precise day for Jesus' birth, possibly because in his view only the unrighteous are described in scripture as observing their birthdays.[9] There is a fragment ascribed both to Origen and Eusebius[10] in which an attempt is made to reconcile the divergent chronological data about Jesus' infancy found in

---

[1] L 28, pp. 172–3.
[2] Matthew's genealogy must be taken spiritually since literally it disagrees with data given in 2 Kings (*Rom. comm., PG* 14, 850C–1C).
[3] M fr. 11, pp. 19–20.   [4] M fr. 281, p. 126.
[5] M 10, 17, pp. 21–2 (*Nativity of Mary* 9, 2, p. 19 Testuz).
[6] J fr. 31, p. 506.   [7] M fr. 22, p. 24.   [8] Cf. L 7, p. 49.
[9] M 10, 22, p. 30; from Philo, cf. Hanson, *Allegory and Event*, p. 249 n8.
[10] M fr. 23, p. 25.

Matthew and in Luke; but we may probably suppose that the information given in it does not come from Origen.[1]

As for the important question of the duration of Jesus' ministry, Origen changed his mind on this subject. In his earlier writings, when he inclined to regard historical information found in John as almost purely allegorical, he accepted the synoptic chronology and held that Jesus preached the gospel for a year and a few months[2] or, less precisely, for a year.[3] When he came to regard the historical value of John more highly he stated that the ministry lasted about three years[4] and Judas' discipleship not quite three years.[5] His reconciliation of John with the synoptics cannot be regarded very highly, since in his later period he implied that Jesus was crucified in the fifteenth year of Tiberius[6] and stated that he was in the world for thirty years.[7] Here he was giving information derived from the gospel of Luke (3.1,23) but neither examining it critically nor correlating it with the gospel of John.[8]

Origen was not really interested in chronology, as we shall see when we come to his remarks on the date of the crucifixion. He explains the star which led the Magi as "like a comet"; he refers to the treatise on comets by the Stoic Chaeremon to show that comets are sometimes portents of good events to come;[9] but he does not make any effort to state when the "comet" might have appeared.

When he deals with the story of the boy Jesus in the temple (Luke 2.41–52) he provides a kind of psychological analysis of it. Luke 2.48 has Mary say to Jesus, "Behold, your father and I have been looking for you anxiously." This saying cannot be taken literally. Mary knew about the virginal conception; Joseph too must have known in view of Matthew's story of the nativity. They knew that Jesus was divine. Therefore they must have been afraid that Jesus had returned to heaven. Moreover, the story

---

[1] The Magi visited Jesus when he was two years old; then he was taken to Egypt, and remained there until he was four, in the forty-fifth year of Augustus and the first year of Archelaus. The two years named are not identical.

[2] *P* 4, 1, 5, p. 299.   [3] *L* 32, p. 195.   [4] *M* 40, p. 79.
[5] *C* 2, 12, p. 141.   [6] *M* 40.   [7] *M* 78, p. 188.
[8] Cf. Bauer, op. cit., 287–8.   [9] *C* 1, 58–9, pp. 109–10.

shows that "the Father's house" (Luke 2.49) is the temple; therefore the Father of Jesus was God, not Joseph.[1] Elsewhere Origen has already explained that Joseph was called the father of Jesus because he was his guardian.[2]

We have already discussed Jesus' baptism and temptation when in dealing with the Johannine-synoptic contradictions. Here it should be added that Origen did not think that the three temptations described by Matthew and Luke took place during the forty days of fasting. What of the forty days' temptations in Mark? They were not described by the evangelists, probably because they were "greater than could be written".[3]

A severe chronological difficulty arises when one considers the sequence of events after the temptations. In John Jesus is not tempted but calls his disciples near Bethany, then goes via Cana to Capernaum, and finally cleanses the temple in Jerusalem (John 1.35—2.22). The Baptist has not yet been imprisoned (3.24). In Matthew and Luke Jesus goes first to Nazareth, then to Capernaum; in Matthew and Mark he begins his journey after John's imprisonment; by the sea of Galilee (Matthew, Mark) or the lake of Gennesaret (Luke) he calls his disciples.

First we should notice that Origen tries to clear up some of the minor topographical difficulties. The text of John 1.28, he says, should not read "Bethany" but "Bethabara". He himself has made a pilgrimage to the holy land, and he knows that Bethany is only fifteen stadia from Jerusalem, while the Jordan river is 180 stadia farther.[4] Again, one might suppose that the sea of Galilee is different from the lake of Gennesaret; actually they are the same, and one can also use the name "sea of Tiberias", as in John 6.1.[5]

But, literally understood, the texts still present difficulties. Origen rather tentatively suggests that the different accounts of the call of Simon Peter in John and the synoptics refer to different

[1] L 19, pp. 127–8.   [2] *nutricius*, L 16, p. 107; L 17, p. 111.

[3] L 29, p. 178; cf. John 21. 25. The same explanation is given in regard to the Lucan summary of the Baptist's proclamation (Luke 3.18; L 27, pp. 168–70) and the fact that not all parables are interpreted by the evangelists (M 14, 12, p. 304).

[4] J 6, 40, p. 149. He uses the distance from Bethany to Jerusalem (found in John 11.18) to prove that the triumphal entry must be allegorized (J 10, 27, p. 200).

[5] M 11, 18, p. 65; L fr. 3, p. 233.

persons,[1] but there are further "discords in relation to the letter". The synoptic—Johannine contradictions lead the reader to suppose that none of the stories can be taken literally.[2] And there are further difficulties within one of the synoptics. Luke has Jesus go first to Nazareth, then to Capernaum; but in Nazareth we find a reference to works already done in Capernaum. Therefore, the story contains a "mystery"; and the simplest solution, in Origen's view, is to regard Nazareth as equivalent to the Jews, Capernaum to the gentiles.[3]

Origen does not care for the old gnostic exegesis of Jesus' descent to Capernaum (Luke 4.31; John 2.12) as representing his coming down to the material world.[4] He insists that according to the synoptic gospels Jesus performed many real actions in the city.[5] But he also recommends the compilation from the four gospels of everything written about Capernaum—"the words and works of the Lord there, how often he stayed there, when he is said to have descended to it, when gone into it, and whence".[6] The allegorical meaning is about to make its appearance. Indeed, Daniélou has pointed out that Origen seems to take over Gnostic allegorization when he suggests that the "brothers" of Jesus in John 2.12 are actually "powers" which had come down with him.[7] Because of Origen's insistence upon the perpetual virginity of Mary, the "brothers" were obviously not really brothers.

We have seen that at the time he wrote his Commentary on John Origen accepted practically nothing in the second chapter as historical. Some geographical details remained valid: thus Capernaum and Jerusalem were certainly places, and Cana (though most of Origen's comments on John 2.1–11 are lost) was probably a place too. We do not know what Origen made of the historical setting provided in the third chapter of John, for the portions of his commentary which dealt with it have not survived; it is at least possible, however, that he treated it symbolically.

Origen's treatment of the fourth chapter of John reflects his

[1] *J* 10, 8, pp. 177–8.   [2] *J* 10, 3–5, pp. 172–6.   [3] *L* 33, p. 196.

[4] *J* 10, 11, p. 180. Marcion in A. v. Harnack, *Marcion: das Evangelium vom fremden Gott* (2nd ed., Leipzig, 1924), pp. 184*–5*; cf. *The Letter and the Spirit*, p. 64 n7.

[5] *J* 10, 11–12, pp. 180–2.   [6] *J* 10, 12, p. 182.

[7] *J* 10, 9, pp. 178–9; J. Daniélou, *Origène* (Paris, 1948), pp. 191–2.

determination to show that it is essentially unhistorical. He reads in John 4.1 that the Pharisees know about Jesus' work of baptizing; but in the synoptic gospels Jesus nowhere baptizes—and, in addition, John 4.2 states that Jesus himself did not baptize. Moreover, John disagrees with the synoptics as to the time of the Baptist's imprisonment.[1] Therefore, since the accounts differ in regard both to actions and to times, the Johannine account must be regarded as symbolical. Again, in John 4.35 Jesus asks, "Do you not say, There are yet four months, then comes the harvest?" Origen treats this quotation as a literal indication of time.[2] In Judaea the harvest begins either in Nisan or Iyar; in either case, when we subtract four months we get back to winter. Was John 4.35 spoken in the winter? No, it was not. The Passover mentioned in John 2.13–15 (and Passover was observed in Nisan) is mentioned in John 4.45 as having taken place quite recently; the Galilaeans have clear memories of it. Origen is insisting upon, and, indeed, exaggerating the importance of the sequence of historical events, so that he can take the text allegorically.[3] He is claiming that since the story is chronologically incoherent it cannot be taken literally. And, though he does not say so at this point, he apparently believed (as he was writing on John) that the ministry of Jesus lasted only about one year. Johannine chronology was therefore *a priori* unacceptable.

In dealing with Jesus' reception in Galilee Origen was impressed by the lack of logical continuity in John 4.43–5. There he read that Jesus went to Galilee, *for* he himself testified that a prophet has no honour in his own country; when he came to Galilee, the Galilaeans welcomed him. Since the sequence of ideas does not make sense, Origen concluded that both Judaea and Galilee must be symbols rather than names of real places.[4]

He also pointed out that there are historical difficulties in the story of the son of the royal officer (βασιλικός) in John 4.46–54. Here Origen's comments seem rather inconclusive, probably because it was difficult to provide much real evidence against the historicity of the account. He tries to show that it is difficult

---

[1] *J* 10, 8, p. 178.   [2] See also *Rom. Comm.* 3, 7 (*PG* 14, 943B).
[3] *J* 13, 39, pp. 264–5.   [4] *J* 13, 54, pp. 283–4.

to identify a βασιλικός. The more simple-minded reader, he says, may suppose that the βασιλικός served Herod, or perhaps that he was someone of Caesar's household. It is not clear whether he was a Jew or not. He did have high rank because his slaves are mentioned in the plural. Since in this context Origen also discusses the similar story (Matt. 8.5–13) of the centurion's son or servant, we assume that his basic purpose was to show how difficult it was to identify the centurion with the βασιλικός or, for that matter, to draw any historical conclusion at all. Actually both the βασιλικός and his son are symbols, and Origen agrees with Heracleon that the father is one of the "archons" of the "aeon".[1] Here Origen has provided exceedingly flimsy grounds for joining the Valentinians in their allegorization of the stories.[2]

But there is a difference between the gnostics and Origen. In the first place, the content of their exegesis is not simply identical with his. In the second place, he finds it necessary, as apparently they did not, to prove that the passages he deals with must be taken allegorically. The method he uses, as we have already seen, is that of ἀνασκευή. In the story of the Samaritan woman, the time is wrong; in that of Jesus' journey to Galilee, the reason assigned is incredible; and in that of the royal officer, the identity of the person involved is obscure. He has shown, at least to a reader acquainted with his method, that the narratives contained in the fourth chapter of John are at least improbable (fictions) or, at most, false (myths). To use his own terminology, we should say they are either parables or enigmas (cf. p. 66).

In Origen's view, then, the first four chapters of the gospel of John cannot be reconciled with the synoptics, and they contain internal inconsistencies which prove that they must be taken not literally but allegorically. The fact that the "Bethabara" of John 1.28 is a real place does not prove that the events located were perceptible to the senses, any more than the fact that there was a real temple in Jerusalem proves that it was cleansed. At least in the stage in his thinking represented by this part of the *Commentary on John*, Origen regarded the contents of its opening

[1] *J*13, 57, p. 288; 13, 62, p. 295; Daniélou, op cit., p. 192.
[2] Cf. Irenaeus, *Adv. haer.* 1, 7, 5, p. 64.

chapters as unhistorical. We may recall that Tatian felt free to rearrange the sequence of narratives in the first five chapters of John. (We do not know what Origen did with the fifth chapter since his commentary on it is lost.)

On the other hand, when all four gospels do agree he accepts their historical character. The feeding of the five thousand is recorded not only in the sixth chapter of John but also in the synoptic gospels. Origen points out that in some details the stories are not in agreement; thus the boy with five barley loaves and two fish (John 6.9) is not mentioned by the synoptists. But he has no doubts about the reality of the miracle, at least by the time he writes his *Commentary on Matthew*. (Once more, his comment on the Johannine version has not survived.) Why did Jesus "look up" to the heavens? "With the rays of his eyes he was, so to speak drawing down power from there which would be mixed with the loaves and the fish." Moreover, he "blesses" the food. By this word of blessing he was "increasing and multiplying" it, as in the account of God's blessing at creation in Gen. 1.28.[1]

Of course there are symbolical details in the Johannine discourse which follows the miracle. The verse about eating the flesh of the Son of Man and drinking his blood (John 6.53) is a New Testament example of the letter which kills (2 Cor. 3.6).[2] Origen insists upon a more spiritual interpretation of the Eucharist.[3]

There was not just one feeding, as in John and Luke, for in Origen's opinion the feeding of the four thousand (Matt. 15.32–9) is a separate and distinct narrative about another event. In the story of the five thousand, the disciples tell Jesus that it is evening, and he asks them about the food they have; it consists of five loaves and two fish. The crowds recline on the grass, and Jesus blesses the food. In the story of the four thousand, Jesus speaks to the disciples about the crowd that has been with him for three days; there are seven loaves and a few fish. The crowd falls down on the ground, and Jesus gives thanks.[4] Indeed, Origen

---

[1] *M* 11, 2, p. 36. [2] *Lev. hom.* 7, 5, p. 387 Baehrens. [3] *J* 32, 24, p. 468.
[4] *M* 11, 19, pp. 67–8.

hints that there may be three stories of feeding, for John describes the miracle as taking place in the mountains.[1] His final
conclusion, however, is that there were two.[2]

Another miracle which Origen discusses in considerable detail
is the healing of an epileptic child (Matt. 17.14–21; Mark 9.14–29;
Luke 9.37–43). In dealing with the story he points out that it
belongs to a class of healings in which people ask for others to be
aided; other examples are the centurion's servant (Matt. 8.5–13;
Luke 7.1–10); the royal officer's son (John 4.46–54); Jairus'
daughter (Matt. 9.18–26; Mark 5.21–43; Luke 8.40–56); and the
Canaanite's daughter (Matt. 15.21–8; Mark 7.24–30). In another
kind of story Jesus acts on his own initiative, as in the case of the
man who had been paralysed for thirty-eight years (John 5.2–9).
These stories show that the miracles are the result of divine
power, not of faith alone.[3] The miracle itself, in this instance, was
the expulsion of an evil spirit. To be sure, Matthew relates that
the child's father said he was "a lunatic" (σεληνιάζεται), and
medical men explain lunacy as due to waters in the head which
move with the phases of the moon. It is possible that the unclean
spirit observed these phases. But we "who believe the gospel"
must hold that the case was not simple lunacy, since that can
sometimes be cured by Egyptian incantations.[4]

Here Origen is combining insistence on the uniqueness of
Jesus' healing ministry with "scientific" acceptance of both
medicine and magic. The result is not especially fortunate. And
since to this story Matthew has appended Jesus' saying about
faith moving a mountain, indeed "this mountain" (17.20),
Origen is mistakenly moved to interpret the mountain as the
spirit which was in the lunatic.[5] Elsewhere he compares the
working of faith in the moving of mountains to the "natural
attraction" of a magnet to iron and of naphtha to fire.[6] At points
like this we have to recognize that Origen was capable of nodding.

A different kind of problem was to be found at the point
where Matthew (8.28) tells of two demoniacs who came out of
tombs to meet Jesus, while Mark (5.2) and Luke (8.27) tell the

---

[1] P. 68; John 6.3. [2] C 2, 46, p. 168. [3] M 13, 3, p. 187; cf. 10, 19, p. 26.
[4] M 13, 6, pp. 193–4. [5] M 13, 7 ·p. 197. [6] M 10, 19, p. 25.

story in greater detail but mention only one. Origen does not seem to recognize that it is characteristic of Matthew to describe pairs (9.27; 20.29). And at this point he does not make use of an allegorical explanation as he does in another instance where Matthew has two persons instead of the one found in Mark and Luke (see p. 93). Instead, he gives a purely literary interpretation. Matthew was writing "generically" about exorcisms and left out part of the story. Mark and Luke, concerned with an individual example, gave fuller details.[1]

The number of the demoniacs is not the only question which arises in relation to this story, which deals with demons which entered the bodies of swine and drove them from a cliff into the sea. Where was the cliff? At one point in his *Commentary on John* Origen tried to solve the geographical problem. The evangelists, who had accurate knowledge of Judaean geography, cannot have made a statement which was obviously false. Therefore when most of the manuscripts known to Origen located the miracle in "the country of the Gerasenes", their reading was corrupt; Gerasa is "a city of Arabia, in the vicinity of neither a sea nor a lake". Some manuscripts mentioned the "Gadarenes", but near Gadara there is neither a lake nor a cliff. Origen therefore felt free to substitute "Gergesenes", since Gergesa is a town by the lake of Tiberias (sea of Galilee). "Near it there is a cliff bordering on the lake, and from it one is shown that the swine were cast down by the demons." Since the name Gergesa means "habitation of those cast out", Origen feels that it must be substituted for either Gerasa or Gadara.[2]

By combining geographical information with symbolism Origen justifies a purely conjectural emendation of the gospel text.

PETER AND HIS CONFESSION

One of the crucial points in the synoptic gospels is the scene placed by Matthew and Mark near Caesarea Philippi, where the apostle Peter acknowledges Jesus as the Christ. Almost nothing is made of this scene by John, who alludes to the tradition only in

[1] *M* fr. 164, p. 81.   [2] *J* 6, 41, p. 150.

a couple of verses (6.68–9). We are therefore not surprised to find that Origen undertakes to minimize the importance of Peter in his treatment of the passage. According to Matt. 16.18–19 Jesus said to Peter, "on the rock (πέτρα) I will build my church". What is the rock? Origen carefully explains that the rock is "every imitator of Christ", and he goes on to argue that the rock cannot be identified as Peter. "If you think that on that one Peter alone the church is built, what of John the son of thunder, or each of the apostles? Did the gates of Hades prevail against the others?" Moreover, it is clear from John 20.22 that the Holy Spirit was given to all the disciples, not to Peter alone. Origen has to admit that according to the literal meaning of Matthew, the rock was Peter; but according to the spirit, it means everyone who becomes what Peter was.[1] He points out that both Mark and Luke "do not add" the words "Son of the living God" to "you are the Christ"; they do not add the blessing and the promise given by Jesus to Peter.[2] He may wish to say that something has been interpolated in Matthew's account. But his theory of the composition of the gospels prevents him from doing so, and in the absence of any textual variants of importance he cannot provide a more definite statement.

He is aware, however, of Peter's rebuke of Jesus, and he explains it as due to the apostle's imperfect knowledge. Peter had just begun to learn about Jesus' future suffering, which he regarded as unworthy of the Son of the living God; the prediction of suffering had not been revealed to him.[3] Actually this doctrine was absolutely essential, for it is necessary to preach "Jesus Christ crucified" (1 Cor. 2.2), and it is useless to preach him and to be silent about the cross. Indeed, it is more important to proclaim the crucifixion than to speak of the nativity, the star of Bethlehem, the angels, or the other miracles.[4] This remark seems to be directed against those who upheld the primacy of Peter and relied on the gospel of Matthew to prove it, for nativity, star, and angels are to be found in Matthew but not in John.

On the other hand, when Origen is not concerned with the

[1] *M* 12, 10–11, pp. 86–8. [2] 12, 15, p. 105.
[3] *M* 12, 21, p. 116. [4] 12, 19, pp. 111–12. Contrast *J* 32, 16, p. 452.

question of primacy he can treat Peter in quite a different way. In Matt. 18.18 Jesus speaks to the disciples about binding and loosing on earth and in heaven (ἐν οὐρανῷ). Is this the same as his similar statement to Peter in Matt. 16.19? No, it is not, says Origen. Peter received the keys of the kingdom "of the heavens" and what he bound or loosed on earth was to be bound or loosed "in the heavens" (ἐν τοῖς οὐρανοῖς). Therefore to him was given authority in more than one heaven—indeed, in all heavens.[1] Here Origen is minimizing the authority of the Church and maximizing that of Peter. He either forgets or, more probably, disregards what he has said earlier. Yet we must recall that in his view Peter was by no means as perfect as the disciple who reclined in the bosom of Jesus.

FROM GALILEE TO JERUSALEM

Because of his detailed studies of the synoptic parallels, Origen was well aware that the sequence of events in Matt. 18.10ff differs from that in Luke 9.51ff. To-day we explain this divergence as due to Luke's insertion of a collection of "travel-teachings" or "peripatetic teachings" between Mark 9.50 and Mark 10.1. Origen, as we have seen, did not believe that Luke used Mark and therefore could not explain the divergence. He was aware that Matt. 19.1–12 parallels Mark 10.1–12 (question of divorce) and that the blessing of the children (Matt. 19.13–15; Mark 10.13–16) has a Lucan parallel (Luke 18.15–17). And he knows that when the journey to Jerusalem really begins, Matthew and Mark agree as to the sequence of events, and Luke concurs in part. "As in most other cases, Matthew and Mark have the same order."[2] But even where the order is approximately the same, one must remember that there is a hidden meaning. Even if the story about Jesus' passage through Jericho is historically true, we should remember what Jericho and Jerusalem mean in the parable of the Good Samaritan; here, therefore, Jesus is depicted as passing from this world to the celestial Jerusalem.[3] Moreover, there are differences. Is Matt. 20.29–34 the equivalent of Mark 10.46–52

[1] M 13, 31, p. 270.   [2] M 16, 8, pp. 490–1.   [3] M 16, 9, pp. 501–3.

and Luke 18.35–43? If one considers "mere history" he will say there were three visits to Jericho because the details are so different. But there is a hidden meaning. The two blind men in Matthew are Israel and Judah; Mark alone mentions Bartimaeus and explains his name as "son of Timaeus" because of the merit (τίμιον) of the patriarch Jacob-Israel.[1] Moreover, Luke has Jesus draw near to Jericho; Mark has him go into it and come out of it; Matthew mentions only the going out. This has a mystical significance, since Jericho means the world. So in Luke the blind man asks who Jesus is; in Mark he hears that it is Jesus the Nazarene; in Matthew two hear that Jesus is passing by.

Since this story has a mystical significance, it was all the easier for Origen to insist that the story of the triumphal entry was allegorical too. As we have seen in his earlier work he was convinced that it was entirely allegorical. Later he came to believe that it was both literal and allegorical. He still insisted that conflicting details had to be taken symbolically.[2]

THE PASSION NARRATIVE

We have also seen that Origen insisted that the story of the anointing of Jesus was more mystical than historical—once more because of the disagreements of the evangelists. When he came to consider the last supper, however, he firmly held that it was a historical event to which a date could be given. To be sure, in the *Commentary on John* Origen said that Jesus died "on the Passover".[3] But in the *Commentary on Matthew* he seems to have changed his mind.[4] He feels free to say that while Jesus did actually eat the Passover on the fourteenth of Nisan, there is no reason for Christians to do so; they celebrate a new and spiritual Passover—Christ.[5] The disciples were eating "in accordance with the commandment of the law".[6]

The Gethsemane story is omitted by John, who is concerned more with Jesus' divinity than with his humanity and knows that

<hr>

[1] *M* 16, 12, pp. 511–12. [2] *M* 16, 14, pp. 520, 522. [3] *J* 28, 25, p. 423.

[4] Bauer, op. cit., p. 162 n1, argues that in *J* 28, 25 *pascha* refers to the whole feast including the αϙyma; to me it seems more likely that Origen's mind changed.

[5] *M* 75, pp. 175–6; 76, p. 178; 79, pp. 188–9. [6] *M* 80, p. 191. Cf. C 1, 70, p. 124.

God the Logos cannot be tempted and that God, who is impassible, cannot want to escape suffering.[1] Historically the scene was real, however. Only three disciples witnessed it because they were firmer in their faith than the others; and it was this scene that they witnessed so that they would not become over-confident about their own fidelity.[2]

Celsus, a generation earlier, had ridiculed the story of Gethsemane.[3]

> If these things had been decreed for him and if he was punished in obedience to his Father, it is obvious that since he was a god and acted intentionally, what was done of deliberate purpose was neither painful nor grievous to him. Why then does he utter loud laments and wailings, and pray that he may avoid the fear of death, saying something like this, "O Father, if this cup could pass by me"?

Origen replies that Jesus "assumed with the body also its pains and griefs". The story, therefore, is not inconsistent, logically or theologically. But what of Celsus' carping criticism of Jesus' actions and words? First, the gospels do not say that Jesus "uttered wailings".[4] Second, Celsus does not quote Jesus' words accurately; Jesus said, "Father, if it be possible, let this cup pass from me" (Matt. 26.39). Third, he quotes only the words which reflect the weakness of Jesus' human flesh, not those which refer to the willingness of his human spirit: "nevertheless, not as I will, but as thou wilt"—a sentiment expressed not once but twice (Matt. 26.39,42).

It could also be said that when Jesus was praying for the cup to pass from him he was not praying for himself but for the Jewish people, whom he wanted to save from their fate.[5] But Origen's main line of approach, at this point, is based upon the doctrine that Jesus really suffered human agonies; he did not merely seem to do so.

Origen draws moral implications from the actions of the chief personages related to the passion narrative. For instance, only

---

[1] *M* 92, p. 210.   [2] *M* 91, p. 207.   [3] *C* 2, 23-4, pp. 152-3.

[4] But cf. Heb. 5.7: "in the days of his flesh, he offered up prayers and supplications, with loud cries and tears, to him who was able to save him from death".

[5] *C* 2, 25, p. 155; *M* 92, p. 209.

Matthew (26.22) and Mark (14.19) represent the disciples as asking about the betrayer, "Is it I?" These evangelists, "being men", were mentioning the fact of the changeable will of those who are still making progress.[1] Judas is the prime example of the man who has such a changeable will. There were contrary feelings in his heart,[2] and his later repentance proves their existence.[3] Caiaphas is obviously evil. Matthew explicitly mentions him (26.3,57); Luke mentions not only Satan and Judas but also the high priests (22.3–4); and similarly Mark mentions Judas (14.10) and the hostile high priest as well (14.60–3). Origen is placing the responsibility for the crucifixion on Caiaphas.[4] Herod was partly responsible for Jesus' death, for he could have released him and prevented his death;[5] Herod's wife too may have plotted against Jesus, as she did against John the Baptist.[6] On the other hand, Pilate was not responsible at all. His attitude toward Jesus was favourable, and he recognized him as the real king of the Jews;[7] indeed, he recognized him as the Christ,[8] though he was not actually an "eyewitness of the Logos".[9]

THE CRUCIFIXION

In 1 Cor. 1.23 the apostle Paul states that the apostolic preaching of Christ crucified was a stumbling-block to Jews and folly to gentiles. To a considerable extent the exegesis of Origen represents an attempt to remove these difficulties from the accounts of the crucifixion. Gnostic teachers had already argued that the spiritual Christ could not really have been crucified. Origen comes very close to their view when he explains to Celsus that no Christian really believes that the Life could have died; it was the human Jesus who was crucified.[10] In the synoptic gospels he reads that Simon of Cyrene carried Jesus' cross (Matt. 27.32; Mark 15.21; Luke 23.26); but in John 19.17 the cross is carried by Jesus himself. He gives two explanations of this difference. First he

[1] *J* 32, 19, p. 459.   [2] *C* 2, 11, pp. 138–9.
[3] *J* 32, 19, p. 458; *M* 117, pp. 246–7. Other citations in Bauer, op cit., p. 174. The other disciples fled because they had not made enough progress; ibid., pp. 179–80.
[4] *J* 28, 13–14, pp. 405–8.   [5] *M* 10, 21, pp. 28–9.   [6] *M* 13, 2, p. 185.
[7] *M* 118–19, pp. 251–2.   [8] *M* 124, p. 258.   [9] Cf. Bertrand, op. cit., p. 25.
[10] *C* 7, 16, p. 168.

points out that John is speaking of the spiritual nature of Jesus; in relation to this nature Jesus carried his own cross. He is unwilling to give up the lesson taught by the synoptics, however; they show that we should carry the cross too;[1] and therefore he suggests that perhaps Simon and Jesus took turns in carrying the cross. Perhaps, as some say, Simon means "obedience".[2]

Another difficulty occurs in the story of the two thieves crucified with Jesus. According to all four gospels Jesus was crucified between them (Matt. 27.38; Mark 15.27; Luke 23.33; John 19.18). Nothing more is said of them in John, but according to Matthew and Mark both of them reviled him (Matt. 27.44; Mark 15.32), while in Luke 23.39–43 one reviled him while the other was penitent. Origen does not usually favour Luke against the other evangelists, but here he suggests that Luke, "as he announced (1.3), is giving a more accurate account". One thief was converted because he had heard of Jesus' miracles or saw the darkness which was "already" present according to Luke 23.44. On the other hand, Origen is unwilling to abandon entirely an explanation he has provided in the *Commentary on John* (in a part now lost). There he has suggested that there were really four thieves, the two of Matthew and Mark and the two of Luke.[3]

According to Luke 23.43 Jesus said to the penitent thief, "To-day you will be with me in Paradise." Since in the Church's view Jesus did not go immediately to Paradise but descended "to the so-called heart of the earth", the text presented a difficulty. As Origen states, some critics proceeded to remove the verse, treating it as an interpolation.[4] He prefers a simpler explanation: Jesus set the believing thief in Paradise before descending.[5] In any event, the words contain a deeper meaning. "To-day" refers not to an earthly day but to the whole new age now beginning.[6]

In describing the darkness "over the whole earth" or "over the whole land" from the sixth to the ninth hour (Matt. 27.45; Mark 15.33), Luke (23.44–5) added the words "while the sun's light failed" or "while the sun was eclipsed" (τοῦ ἡλίου

---

[1] Cf. also *M* 12, 24, p. 125.   [2] *M* 126, pp. 262–4.
[3] *M* 133, pp. 270–1. Marcion omitted the story of the penitent thief.
[4] Marcion deleted not only this verse but the whole pericope.
[5] *L* fr. 81, p. 273.   [6] *J* 32, 32, pp. 479–80.

ἐκλιπόντος; according to some manuscripts, "and the sun was darkened", καὶ ἐσκοτίσθη ὁ ἥλιος). A certain historian named Thallus identified the darkness with an eclipse, but Julius Africanus pointed out that since an eclipse was impossible at the time of the full moon (Passover), the darkness must have been "made by God".[1] Origen follows a similar line of reasoning. He knows that the anecdotal historian Phlegon has mentioned an eclipse in the reign of Tiberius—though not at the time of the full moon,[2] when an eclipse would be impossible. He proceeds to show that neither Matthew nor Mark mentions an eclipse, and that it is absent from most manuscripts of Luke.[3] How did it get into the text? Perhaps it was due to a mistaken conjecture by someone who wanted to explain the darkness; more probably it was inserted by enemies of the Church. In any case, it is an unnecessary addition, for the "darkness" mentioned by Matthew is clearly limited to Jerusalem or to Judaea, since the events described in what follows (Matt. 27.51–3) are related to those places. The darkness was probably due to very dark clouds.[4]

Another difficulty was to be found in Matt. 27.46 (Mark 15.34; no parallels in Luke or John), where Jesus cries out, "My God, my God, why hast thou forsaken me?" It might be supposed—as it is by most New Testament critics—that this cry of dereliction expresses the fullness of the human suffering of Jesus. Origen is anxious to avoid this interpretation, and he therefore insists that when Matthew and Mark speak of a "loud" or "great" voice, they are referring to the "divine voice" by which the cry was uttered.[5]

The sequence of the events accompanying the death of Jesus is given differently by the three synoptists. Matthew describes an earthquake and the opening of tombs; a centurion and others,

---

[1] M. J. Routh, *Reliquiae Sacrae* II (2nd ed., Oxford, 1846), pp. 297–8.

[2] Perhaps the solar eclipse of 24, Nov. 29, or the lunar eclipse of 3, Apr. 33 (P. de Labriolle, *La réaction païenne*, Paris, 1934, p. 218). In writing against Celsus, Origen is not so critical: see p. 75.

[3] Sun darkened, K θ, many others, Latin, Syriac, Marcion; sun eclipsed, B S C.

[4] *M* 134, pp. 272–5.

[5] *M* 135, p. 280. In *C* 3, 32 (p. 229) Origen simply refers this verse to Jesus' power to lay down his life. For the idea that a divine voice should be unique cf. Celsus in *C* 6, 75, p. 144.

seeing the miracles, acknowledge Jesus as the Son of God (Matt. 27.51–4). Mark has none of the miracles; the centurion's confession is based on the way in which Jesus died (Mark 15.44–5). In Luke 23.47 the centurion speaks of him as a "righteous" or "innocent" man. Origen is not much impressed by the story in Matthew, which refers to the "fear" of the witnesses and makes their faith depend on miracles. He finds more meaningful the account in Mark, where the centurion understood the events in proportion to his ability to understand (for Origen the κεντυρίων of Mark was different from the ἑκατοντάρχης of Matthew and Luke). He understood the real miracle, which was the quick death of Jesus, the one who had power to lay down his life.[1]

THE TEACHING OF JESUS

From the opening chapters of the four gospels, Origen was aware that there was almost as much diversity in their accounts of the teaching of John the Baptist and of Jesus as there was in their stories of Jesus' ministry. He usually treats this kind of diversity, however, as complementary rather than contradictory. The different evangelists, inspired by the Spirit, draw different lessons from what John or Jesus taught. For example, the four evangelists say that John came to baptize in water; only Matthew (3.11) added "for repentance" or "with repentance in view". He was teaching that the utility of baptism depends on the predisposition of the person who is baptized.[2] But when Origen encounters the word "repent" again, in Matthew's account of the proclamation of Jesus (4.17), he notes that it has already been spoken by John the Baptist (Matt. 3.2) and that it is lacking at this point in some manuscripts.[3] He therefore deletes it and says that since Jesus was receiving "a people prepared" (Luke 1.17) and no longer in need of repentance, he did not urge them to repent.[4]

When he deals with the aphoristic, "gnomic" teaching of

---

[1] John 10.18; M 140, pp. 290–1.   [2] J 6, 33, p. 142.

[3] The word is omitted in the old Latin k, in the Sinaitic and Curetonian Syriac, and by Clement and Eusebius.

[4] M fr. 74, p. 45.

Jesus in the synoptic gospels, he cannot believe that it is as simple as it appears to be. Thus in the treatise *De principiis* he cites synoptic sayings as examples of irrational or impossible commands. "Carry no purse, no bag, no sandals; and salute no one on the road" (Luke 10.4). "If anyone strikes you on the right cheek, turn to him the other also" (Matt. 5.39; you would be struck on the left cheek, not the right!). "If your right eye causes you to sin, pluck it out and throw it away" (Matt. 5.29; how could you tell which eye was responsible?). These commandments cannot be taken literally.[1]

As we have already seen, early Christians were accustomed to classify the gospels as ἀπομνημονεύματα which contained χρεῖαι and γνῶμαι. Origen is no exception to this rule; he uses the verb ἀπομνημονεύειν in speaking of the work of the evangelists.[2] Moreover, when the elder John dealt with the χρεῖαι contained in Mark, he made use of conventional rhetorical analysis of such materials. It is on the foundation laid by his predecessors in gospel criticism and in Graeco-Roman rhetoric that Origen builds when he discusses the teachings handed down from Jesus. Among rhetoricians the χρεία could be criticized on the grounds that it was obscure, that it added unnecessary details or omitted what was necessary, that it was impossible, that it was improbable or incredible, that it was false, that it was prejudicial, that it was useless, or that it was shameful.[3] Similar criticisms could be made of legislation.[4] And on either basis Origen could analyse the teaching of Jesus as reported in the synoptics, and could declare it "irrational" or "impossible". The teaching of Jesus could thus be analysed from a rhetorical point of view; so could the prayer which he taught his disciples.

The rhetorician Theon provided an elaborate classification of different kinds of χρεῖαι (97.11—101.2), and in dealing with the Lord's Prayer Origen seems to be making use of something like it. Theon divides his "verbal χρεῖαι" into two kinds, those which are declarative (ἀποφαντικόν) and those which are responsive (ἀποκρίτικον). One kind of responsive verbal χρεία is that given

---

[1] *P* 4, 3, 3, pp. 327–8. Cf. *M* 13, 24, p. 244.   [2] See the Glossary, p. 120.
[3] Theon, p. 104, 15–18 (examples, 104.18—105.18).   [4] *P.* 129, 7–10.

in answer to a request (κατὰ πύσμα) which requires a relatively long answer. It would appear that Origen has something like this in mind when he analyses the Lord's Prayer as reported by Matthew (6.9–13) and by Luke (11.2–4). He lists three possible explanations of the differences. (1) The prayer might be the same; but according to Matthew it was delivered on a mountain and without a prior request, while in Luke it was set forth "in a certain place" after a request had been made. (2) The prayer might be the same, expressed on two different occasions. (3) Perhaps there were two different, but partly similar, prayers, delivered on different occasions.[1]

Origen obviously rejects the first two solutions because of the differences between the prayers and their circumstances.[2] By looking at the circumstances he is able to bring the prayers into some relationship with Greek rhetoric. He therefore explains that the prayer in Matthew was given "without any previous request, in a declarative manner", or "in a declarative discourse".[3] This statement seems to imply that for Origen the Matthaean version is a declarative verbal χρεία uttered in circumstances not clearly defined (cf. Theon 97.16–22), while the Lucan version is of the kind given in answer to a request. Because the prayers have to be given different formal classifications they cannot be simply identified, even though Origen is willing to consider the possibility that the Lucan form is an abbreviation of that found in Matthew. His own solution, expressed in a fragment on Luke, is that there are two prayers which contain some common materials.[4]

Naturally Origen considers the detailed differences. Matthew uses the invocation, "Our Father in the heavens", since "in the heavens" is frequently found in his gospel; on the other hand, by omitting the expression Luke shows that "the divine" is transcendent.[5] "Hallowed be thy name" is imperative in form, but

[1] O 18, 3, pp. 341–1.

[2] Cf. E. G. Jay, *Origen's Treatise on Prayer* (London, 1954), p. 138 n1.

[3] I translate "declarative" from ἀποφαντικός, my own emendation (based on Theon) of the manuscript's ἀποτακτικός, which does not make sense. Jay (op. cit., p. 137 n3) emends, following Bentley and Delarue, to ἀποτατικός; he then translates "in an extended manner" and "in an extended discourse".

[4] L fr. 41, p. 253; cf. O 30, 1, p. 393 (Luke's version esoteric, Matthew's exoteric).

[5] L fr. 42. p. 253; cf. O 23, 1, pp. 349–50.

optative in meaning, just as in the Greek of the Septuagint.[1] As for ἐπιούσιος (translated "daily" in English versions), Origen is eager to show that it cannot be used of ordinary bread of any kind. It is a word not found in Greek, either among "the wise" or among the unlearned. This statement suggests that Origen has been unable to find it in the lexicons in use at Alexandria or Caesarea in his time. He thinks that it was probably made up by the evangelists; in the Septuagint too there are examples of peculiar Greek words or forms. And he proceeds to derive it from ἐπί "upon" in the sense of "beyond", and οὐσία, "being" in the sense of "actuality" or "perceptibility to sense". This analysis,[2] as Cadiou has observed, is in large measure based on research in lexicons.[3] "Deliver us from evil" or "the evil one" is omitted in the Lucan version because Jesus is giving private instruction to his disciples who had already been delivered. Matthew's prayer, then, is for public use; that in Luke, for theologically-minded Christians.[4]

When Origen turned from prayers to parables he found himself on firmer rhetorical ground. As we have already seen, he sometimes used "parable" to include anything which a rhetorician might have classified as "fiction". But he was of course aware that the parables of Jesus were more than ordinary fictions; they were fictions which contained a special point, "metaphorically" indicated "by transference".[5] Rhetoricians gave similar definitions. Herodian tells us that a "parable" is a comparison with something which happens or is like what happens,[6] and Trypho's doctrine is similar.[7]

Now Origen knew that in the synoptic gospels there are many parables told by Jesus. Mark provides a collection of them in his fourth chapter, and he also explains why they were used and gives an allegorical explanation of one of them. "With many such parables he spoke the word to them, as they were able to bear it; but apart from parables he did not speak to them, and privately

---

[1] *O* 24, 5, pp. 355–6. [2] *O* 27, 7–8, pp. 366–8.

[3] R. Cadiou in *Revue des études grecques* 45 (1932), pp. 275–6; actually on one lexicon, the doxography edited by H. Diels (*Doxographi Graeci*, Berlin, 1879 and 1929, pp. 457–8) in its Stobaean form.

[4] *L* fr. 42, p. 254. [5] Lommatzsch 13, 220, 226.

[6] III, 104, 1 Spengel. [7] III, 201, 12.

he explained everything to his own disciples" (Mark 4.33–4). Both Matthew and Luke closely followed Mark, though both omitted the notion of secret explanation, perhaps because it was being exploited by heterodox opponents.

Origen was delighted with the Marcan theory of private explanation. "One must consider, in regard to every parable whose explanation (διήγησις) is not recorded by the evangelists, that he explained everything to his own disciples in private, and therefore those who wrote the gospels concealed the interpretation (σαφήνεια) of the parables, since the matters revealed in them were greater than the nature of writing, and the world itself could not contain the books written (John 21.25) on such parables."[1] Therefore the private teaching of Jesus to his disciples (Mark 4.34) has not been recorded,[2] and Origen can say that "we confess that we do not reach the full depth of the meaning of the parables".[3]

There are those who suppose that the gospel writings have only one meaning, but actually God's plan provided that they should be understood simply by the simple. For those who have the desire and the ability to hear them more acutely, there lie concealed wise matters, worthy of the Word of God.[4]

To Mark's collection of parables, Matthew added the parable of the tares (Matt. 13.24–30) and an explanation of it (13.36–43), given by Jesus when he had left the crowds and had gone into "the house". Origen took advantage of this expression to compare other gospel passages in which the "house of Jesus" was mentioned, and he reached the conclusion that it has a symbolical meaning.[5] "To approach Jesus in his house is to be introduced to a higher revelation and to close intimacy with the Son of God."[6]

For this reason a careful allegorical interpretation of the parables is not only defensible but necessary. In the parable of the sower all three evangelists wrote that some of the seed fell "by the way"; they did not write "in the way" because according to John 14.6 Jesus himself is "the way". But Matthew and Mark

---

[1] *M* 14, 12, p. 304.   [2] *C* 6, 6, p. 76.   [3] *M* p. 305.
[4] *M* 10, 1, p. 2.   [5] *M* 10, 1, pp. 1–2.
[6] F. Bertrand, *Mystique de Jésus chez Origène* (Paris, 1951), p. 81.

paid more attention to symbolism than Luke did. They wrote
that some of the seed fell "on rocky ground", while Luke wrote
"on the rock". He should not have done so, since either Christ or
Peter was the rock.[1] In the explanation of this parable, Matthew
mentioned "the evil one", Mark "Satan", and Luke "the devil".
Origen points out the fact, but his explanation has not been preserved; presumably he identified the three. Some hearers receive
the Word "immediately" with joy, but have no root in themselves. Luke omits the word "immediately" but it is necessary in
order to define the class of believers being described.[2] Finally,
both Matthew and Mark speak of the falling away of these believers in "tribulation or persecution"; Luke mentions only "temptation" or "trial"—he is generalizing.[3]

Here we have an explanation of an explanation. Origen adheres
fairly closely to the literal meaning of the text. But he cannot
refrain from trying to create a rather systematic interpretation of
Jesus' use of parables, especially in the light of Mark's remarks
about the privacy of the true exegesis. Parables are for outsiders,
or for disciples who will later be given private instruction.[4]
But according to Matthew (13.44–50) Jesus addressed three
parables, those about the treasure, the pearl, and the net, to his
disciples in the house. Origen's explanation of this difficulty is
based on rhetorical analysis. These three parables are not parables but comparisons (ὁμοιώσεις). When Mark 4.30 has Jesus
say, "With what can we compare the kingdom of God, or what
parable shall we use for it?" the difference between a comparison
and a parable is indicated (M 10, 4, pp. 4–5).[5]

Not all rhetoricians differentiated these forms in just this way.
For example, Trypho treats the comparison (simile) as the genus
which includes three species, one of them being the "parable".[6]
On the other hand, Herodian agrees with Origen that a parable
and a simile are different. A simile is shorter than a parable and
does not end with a general conclusion.[7]

[1] M fr. 291, pp. 129–30.   [2] M fr. 293, p. 131.   [3] M fr. 292, p. 130.
[4] L fr. 26, p. 245.   [5] Actually it is not indicated; this is Semitic parallelism.
[6] III, 200, 4–6 Spengel; so also Polybius of Sardis, III, 106, 16–18; and (more elabor-
ately) Cocondrius, III, 239, 25–9.
[7] III, 104, 1–7. The three Matthaean parables which Origen treats as similes have no
conclusions.

Therefore Origen did have good rhetorical precedent for his analysis. The only difficulty with it is that the distinction he makes does not seem to have occurred to the evangelist whose work he is discussing.

The evangelist Matthew (13.53) refers back to the whole preceding section and says that "when Jesus had finished these parables, he went away from there". It would appear that the inspired Matthew did not understand the distinction Origen has been making. All is not lost, however, for the allegorist. When Jesus went away, he came to his own country (Matt. 13.54). Therefore he was not in his own country at the time he was speaking in parables. His disciples had to follow him to his own country—literally Nazareth or Bethlehem, mystically Judaea.[1] Since they were in an alien land, he spoke to them in parables, says Origen. We might ask how, if they were in an alien land, they could be in "the house of Jesus". The allegorical explanation does not fit the text it is supposed to explain. Origen would have been better advised had he abandoned the notion that parables were addressed only to outsiders.

In any event, he feels free to interpret the parables as allegories, and in explaining the deeper meaning of the parable of the unmerciful servant (Matt. 18.23–35) he explicitly says that he is doing so in a manner analogous to that of the explanations given by the evangelists.[2] The expositor needs the spirit of Christ in producing his exegesis,[3] for the only real exegete of the parables is Jesus, who privately explained everything to his own disciples.[4] For this reason, heretical exegetes, who find the wrathful Demiurge in the parable, are wrong—though in Origen's view the "tormentors" are those (presumably angels) in charge of punishments,[5] and the "accounting" which takes place in the parable refers to the Last Judgement. This point is confirmed by exegesis of other synoptic parables, and we find it strikingly paralleled in gnostic (Carpocratian) interpretations of similar passages.[6]

[1] M 10, 16, pp. 20–1. On the necessity for leaving alien lands to come to Jesus cf. Bertrand, op. cit., pp. 72–4.
[2] M 14, 6, p. 287   [3] P. 288.   [4] M 14, 11, p. 302.
[5] 14, 13, p. 313.
[6] 14, 12, pp. 305–8. Irenaeus, Adv. haer. 1, 25, 4, pp. 208–9. Cf. also L 23, pp. 154–5.

In dealing with this parable Origen comes close to providing a systematic treatment of it. First he gives a moral application of it; he calls this the περίνοια. Then he mentions the fact that there is a simpler and more literal meaning. But he is eager to press onward to the higher and more mystical explanation, analogous to the explanations given by the evangelists themselves.[1] He has no real exegetical system, however. When he comes to the parable of the labourers in the vineyard (Matt. 20.1–16), he gives four different explanations. First comes an allegorical explanation like that of the parable of the Good Samaritan, with which we shall presently deal. Second, the five groups of labourers are identified with five stages of the spiritual life, related to five spiritual senses. Third, the parable contains a secret doctrine relating to the creation of the soul. And finally, Origen provides simpler, "more useful" exegesis for those who are shocked by the more secret doctrines.[2] As Daniélou has pointed out, this treatment is gnostic in tendency and (partly) in content.[3]

The parable of the Good Samaritan in Luke (10.29–37) had already been taken allegorically by Origen's predecessors.[4] For them the man in the story was Adam, who went down from paradise (Jerusalem) to the world (Jericho) and was mistreated by hostile powers (robbers). The law (the priest) and the prophets (the Levite) passed him by, but Christ (the Samaritan) cured his disobedience (his wounds) and set him on his own body (the beast) and brought him to the church (the inn)—and so on. Origen accepts this exegesis, simply adding refinements of his own. The man is not only Adam but also Jesus; the Samaritan is the Son of God.[5] Similarly the parable of the Prodigal Son has an allegorical meaning, for the repentant youth says, "I have sinned against heaven and before thee" (Luke 15.21). He could not have said "against heaven" had heaven not been his native country.[6]

Origen was not favourably impressed by the efforts of others

[1] 14, 6. pp. 286–7.
[2] 15, 32–37, pp. 446–61. For "secret doctrines" cf. *P* 4, 2, 8, p. 320, etc.
[3] *Origène*, pp. 196–8.
[4] Irenaeus, *Adv. haer.* 3, 17, 3, p. 93.
[5] *L* 34, pp. 201–2. For the Samaritan as Saviour cf. *J* 20, 35, p. 374, and Daniélou, op. cit., p. 195; so Clement, *Quis div. salv.?* 29, 2.
[6] *L* fr. 72, p. 269.

to provide equally subtle analysis. Some critic wanted to reject the parable of Dives and Lazarus. He argued that if Lazarus lay in Abraham's bosom (Luke 16.22–3), others must have lain there earlier. When another righteous man came to the place, Lazarus would have to be removed to make room for him. Origen points out that this critic was not aware that "myriads" could be in Abraham's bosom at the same time. After all, in the gospel of John we read that John "historically" lay in Jesus' bosom; but the Son of God was in the bosom of the Father.[1]

Given the allegorical meaning of parables, it was obvious that difficult sayings of Jesus had to be interpreted allegorically too. According to Matt. 18.2–3, Jesus set a child in the midst of the disciples and said, "Truly I say to you, unless you turn and become like children, you will not enter into the kingdom of heaven". Why "like children"? Origen explains that infants (παιδία) do not possess any of the passions, including fear; therefore to be like children means being free from emotion.[2] This is his "simpler" explanation, but he can give another, "either for the sake of doctrine or for the sake of exegetical exercise" (εἴτε ὡς δόγματος εἴτε ὡς γυμνασίου ἕνεκεν). According to this interpretation the child is the Holy Spirit, which Jesus placed in the midst of his disciples, and we should be like the apostles![3]

Another difficult saying of Jesus is found in Matt. 19.12, which speaks of three classes of eunuchs: (1) "from their mother's womb"; (2) made so by men; and (3) self-made on account of the kingdom of heaven. Origen divides exegetes of this verse into two groups. The first group takes the first two classes of eunuchs literally and "corporeally", treats the third class as analogues, and proceeds to act upon this exegesis. These people are "friends of the gospel letter" and they "do not understand that Jesus also spoke of these matters in parables and that they were said in spirit". They cite the *Sentences* of Sextus in defence of their view, and quote Philo at his most literal-minded point.[4]

[1] *J* 32, 20, p. 462; *L* fr. 77, p. 271. For the symbolical meaning cf. Bertrand, op. cit., pp. 36–7; 137–9.
[2] *M* 13, 16, p. 221.   [3] 13, 18, pp. 226–7.
[4] *M* 15, 1, pp. 348–50; 15, 3, p. 354. *Quod det. pot. insid. soleat* 176, cf. H. Chadwick, *The Sentences of Sextus* (Cambridge, 1959), pp. 109–12.

The second group, including Origen himself, recognizes that the first two classes are "somatic" but that the third is not.[1]

Similarly in expounding verses in Luke Origen treats them as allegorical. "Let the dead bury their own dead" (Luke 9.60) is mystical because it cannot be taken literally.[2] "Greet no one by the way" (Luke 10.4) is clearly irrational if taken as a literal command.[3] The saying about five sparrows in Luke 12.6 is like and unlike the saying about two sparrows in Matthew, they can be referred to the five spiritual senses of the righteous.[4] Jesus' counsel not to invite friends to a banquet (Luke 14.12) cannot be meant literally, "for it is not characteristic of a wise man to invite the poor who are not believers, or not to invite his friends who are poor and believers".[5]

The method is always the same. If a saying, taken in a crudely literal way, seems impossible or irrational, the exegete is free to treat it in an allegorical, "mystical" way and use this treatment as part of his theological construction.

ESCHATOLOGICAL ELEMENTS

Since in Origen's view the most profound of the gospels was that according to John, and since in John the eschatological emphasis of the synoptic gospels is largely lacking, it is not surprising that he was concerned with the reinterpretation of eschatology. He knows that it is present in the synoptics. But "those who hear the gospel more deeply, and do everything they can so that the gospel may not be veiled in any part of it, do not pay much attention (*non multum curant*) to the universal end of the age and the question whether it will be sudden and universal or by degrees; they pay attention only to this point, that the end of each individual takes place when he does not know the day or the hour of his departure, and that upon each one of us 'the day of the Lord will come like a thief' " (1 Thess. 5.2). So when Mark 13.35 speaks

[1] On the exegesis of this verse cf. W. Bauer in *Neutestamentliche Studien G. Heinrici* (Leipzig, 1914), pp. 235–44. The saying about plucking out an eye or cutting off a hand (Matt. 5.29–30) must also be understood allegorically (*P* 4, 3, 3, p. 328; *M* 13, 24, p. 244; 15, 2, p. 353).
[2] *L* fr. 29, p. 246.
[3] *P* 4, 3, 3, p. 327; *M* 15, 2, p. 352.
[4] *L* fr. 57, p. 260.
[5] *L* fr. 68, p. 266.

of the master's coming "in the evening, or at midnight, or at cockcrow, or in the morning", Origen explains that these moments refer to youth, middle age, more advanced age, and old age.[1]

What then of such sayings as Matt. 19.29, which seems to say that believers will receive a hundredfold the houses, brothers, sisters, father, mother, children, and lands they have left for Jesus' name's sake? Origen says that the literal meaning of this verse is "not despicable"; believers actually are hated by their relatives and receive innumerable spiritual gifts. They gain Christian brothers and sisters, Christian parents who are the bishops and the presbyters, and Christian children who are the children in the Church. But "lands" and "houses" cannot be taken literally except by a "forced" interpretation. And if they are allegorical, then the other items must also be allegorical. The "brothers and sisters" must be angels as well as human beings; the "lands and houses" are to be found in the divine paradise and in the city of God.[2]

When the mother of the sons of Zebedee (Matt. 20.20) or the sons themselves (Mark 10.35) ask for seats beside Jesus in his glory, they are expressing a false corporeal understanding. If the mother asks, her request reflects "womanish simplicity"; if they ask, they are "men who are still imperfect and know nothing".[3]

The language of the "little apocalypse", therefore, must obviously be taken allegorically. For example, it says in Matt. 24.29 that "the sun will be darkened, and the moon will not give its light". No doubt such darkness can be explained as due to smoke from a cosmic conflagration. But the world will not come to an end in this manner; instead, we read in the same verse of Matthew that "the stars will fall from heaven". Moreover, taken literally the verse contradicts Isa. 30.26, which speaks of the light of the moon being as the light of the sun, and the light of the sun being "sevenfold". Origen knows literalists who may say that something "by nature impossible" is possible, but his own conclusion is that the darkened sun is the devil, while the moon is the congregation of the wicked, and the stars are hostile powers in

[1] *M* 56, p. 130.　　[2] *M* 15, 25, pp. 422–5.　　[3] *M* 16, 4, p. 473.

heaven.[1] Therefore the "clouds" on which the Son of Man will come (Matt. 24.30) must be "animate and rational clouds".[2] Matt. 24.31 says that the angels will gather the elect "from one end of heaven to the other"; but Mark 13.27 mentions the gathering "from the end of the earth to the end of the heaven". This disagreement proves that both expressions are allegorical.[3]

What Origen feels about all this eschatological material is clearly shown in his comment on Matt. 25.34, where the evangelist speaks of "the foundation (καταβολή) of the world". There is a deeper meaning to this expression (etymologically it could be related to "casting down"), but Origen says he will not entrust it to writing. To do so would be like casting pearls before swine![4] In the early treatise *De principiis* he was not so reticent. There he said that it referred to the descent of souls into the world.[5]

In other words, behind the simple and inadequate literal meaning of eschatological sayings in the gospels there lies a deep hidden mystery, one which has meaning not only in relation to the future of individuals but also in relation to Origen's own mythological understanding of the origin of the souls and of the world.

One might suppose that the saying, "There are some standing here who will not taste death before they see the Son of Man coming in his kingdom" (Matt. 16.28), would present some difficulties. But Origen is able to face them. We have already seen that in dealing with the question of the perpetual virginity of Mary, seemingly contradicted in Matt. 1.25, he insists that in scripture the words for "before" (ἕως οὖ, or ἕως ἄν) do not necessarily set a limit for the action described. So here he makes the same point, comparing Matt. 28.20; "I am with you always, before (ἕως) the end of the age." No limit is set in either case.[6] But since the problem of dying remains, he then goes on to explain that to "taste death" does not literally mean to die.[7] Here his exegesis seems no more reliable than it often is.

[1] *M* 48–9, pp. 99–103.   [2] *M* 50, p. 109. So also on I Thess. 4.17 (*PG* 14, 1302D).
[3] *M* 51, p. 115.   [4] *M* 71, p. 168.
[5] 3, 5, 4, pp. 273–5 (citing Matt. 25.34; John 17.24; Eph. 1.4; and Heb. 4.3); cf. *J* 19, 22 (p. 324).
[6] *M* 12, 34, pp. 146–7.   [7] *M* 12, 35, pp. 149–50; cf. *J* 20, 43, p. 386.

It is significant that when Origen is dealing with an eschatological passage in Matthew he reveals the nature of his method. In Matt. 19.27 Peter says to Jesus, "Lo, we have left everything and followed you; what then shall we have?" Origen cannot believe that even Peter could have asked a question so crudely literal in appearance. "One reader will retain these words in accordance with the literal meaning, but another, having refuted them (ἀνασκευάσας), will allegorize the content of the letter because of its insignificance."[1] Once more the method of ἀνασκευή is to be applied at a point where the literal meaning is offensive to a symbolist. By making use of it, the teaching of Jesus and the apostles can be freed from its eschatological framework, and the true spiritual content can be restored.

[1] *hos ou megalophues*, M 15, 21, p. 409.

5

THE ENIGMA OF JESUS

As FRÉDÉRIC BERTRAND points out, in his valuable *Mystique de Jésus* to which we have already referred one of Origen's principal concerns was to "internalize" Jesus.[1] Sometimes Origen retains the historical letter of the gospels; sometimes he does not; but always he is concerned with the inner, spiritual meaning of the text. And it is in relation to the life of Jesus that he develops a whole system of symbolism, and refers it to the Christian's spiritual development.

> What the evangelists report is oriented toward a reality of a profound and mysterious order. All the external facts which they described portray the inner life of the Christian and of the Church. In other words, it is in the soul of the believer and in the Church that the mysteries denoted in these pages are now reproduced.[2]

This fact means that the rôle of literary and historical criticism, important though it is, is always subsidiary to Origen's main concern with the soul.

Yet it is obvious that Origen did make use of the techniques of criticism and that at significant points they indicated to him the direction of his thought. Along with his conception of development in the spiritual life of the believer he held a conception of development in the life and thought of the apostles; it was John who, because he reclined on the Lord's bosom, most fully understood his divine nature. Therefore when comparison with the other gospels shows that John disagrees with them, one must believe that the disagreement is intentional and that the spiritual meaning is that set forth by John.

This kind of analysis is most fully utilized in the books of the *Commentary on John* written soon after Origen's departure from Alexandria for Caesarea; but it recurs in books which he wrote at a much later date. He never abandoned it, even though over a period of time he came to value more highly the historical

[1] *Mystique de Jésus chez Origène* (Paris, 1951), p. 146.   [2] Ibid., p. 41.

elements in all four gospels. In general, however, he did not value them simply because they were historical but because he realized that they had meaning for the edification of simpler believers and because they could be used as stepping stones toward symbolism.

What lies behind Origen's understanding of the gospels, and indeed of the Christian religion, in this manner? We should surely agree with Bertrand that to a considerable extent Origen is building upon his own religious experience.[1] But the reality of this experience is not denied if one goes rather more deeply into both the personal and the philosophical roots of Origen's "pedagogical idealism" and recognizes with Hal Koch the close ties between Origen's thought and that of some of his contemporaries.[2] In Origen's view of the inspiration of various biblical writers there is a strong emphasis on the pedagogical work of the Logos. We have already seen that he believed that Paul made progress toward perfection, and that the greatest of the evangelists was John, who reclined on the Lord's bosom. But he was willing to express the view even more plainly, as he does in the *Selecta in Ieremiam*: Paul laid the foundation, while Luke and Timothy built the upper story.[3] The illumination possessed by Timothy, however, was inferior to that of Paul.[4] In Origen's opinion the universe was a great school room. The Logos was the master of the school; he appeared in various guises to various pupils. His best pupils were the apostles, but best of all were the apostles Paul and John.[5]

It is easy enough to see that a scheme like this is closely related to Greek philosophical conceptions of Origen's time. Koch has traced the parallels in considerable detail. We should add that it corresponds with the course of education provided in the Greek philosophical school. The curriculum of God is remarkably

---

[1] Ibid., pp. 148–52; cf. also the work he cites, W. Völker, *Das Vollkommenheitsideal des Origenes* (Tübingen, 1931).

[2] *Pronoia und Paideusis: Studien über Origenes und sein Verhältnis zum Platonismus* (Berlin-Leipzig, 1932).

[3] Lommatzsch 15, 445; A. Zöllig, *Die Inspirationslehre des Origenes* (Freiburg, 1903), pp. 73–6.

[4] *M* 12, 15, p. 104.   [5] *C* 3, 76, p. 268.

similar to the curriculum with which Origen himself had been acquainted. Brought up at first with encyclical studies such as grammar and rhetoric, he passed through and beyond these to philosophy and the exegesis of scripture. He came to realize that the study of literature, in which for him history was apparently included, was merely preliminary to the true philosophy which lay in and behind the words of scripture. As we have repeatedly seen, he did not abandon the study of rhetoric. At any rate, he did not stop using its methods. But he used them in the service of philosophical theology.

Does Origen's idea of revelation as education come altogether from his own experience and his own education? We must allow for the influence of another factor in his thought. This factor is based on the data he possessed about the development of Pauline spirituality as reflected in the epistles. But he was also aware that the other apostles advanced in their apprehension of the meaning of Christ, and that they proclaimed a more perfect doctrine after the resurrection.[1] Peter's early rebuke of Jesus shows how little he understood.[2] Neither Peter nor any other apostle was perfect before the Passion.[3]

Now since in Origen's opinion the true meaning of Jesus' teaching was not eschatological, he encountered a difficulty when he found John the son of Zebedee, traditionally the author of the "spiritual" gospel, asking for a seat at Jesus' side in his kingdom (Mark 10.35). Two explanations were possible. Either John did not write the fourth gospel (but Origen had no reason to question the tradition that he did) or else his understanding of Jesus' teaching was considerably modified by later events. Origen took the latter alternative and stated that at this point John and his brother were "still imperfect and completely ignorant".[4]

In other words, the theory of development was made necessary by a combination of evidence from the gospels and evidence from tradition about the evangelists. The consequence of the theory must be, though Origen does not explicitly say so, that John has radically rewritten the life of Jesus from the standpoint of his later

---

[1] *M* 12, 15, p. 108, 12, 18, pp. 109–10.   [2] *M* 12, 21, p. 116. Cf. *M* 13, 9, p. 206.
[3] *M* 12, 40, p. 158.   [4] *M* 16, 4, p. 473.

knowledge while the other three evangelists have often been content to relate historical facts. Origen really does state this consequence, though in different language, when he says that John emphasized the divine nature of Jesus while the other evangelists laid stress on his humanity. This is to say that the gospels disagree because John wrote a theological treatise unlike the less explicitly theological synoptics.

So much for the general theory of development. What of the specific differences to be found in the gospels? Here we have found a remarkable use of the rhetorical method of ἀνασκευή, which constantly comes to light all the way from the early treatise *De principiis* to the late *Commentary on Matthew*. In the late apologetic treatise *Contra Celsum* Origen puts ἀνασκευή in reverse and tries to prove the historical reliability of some of the gospel narratives, but he himself admits the difficulty of his new task. His results are rather less convincing than those reached in a more negative direction. His heart does not seem to be in his work, for the confirmation of historicity does not lead to the immediate possibility of allegorizing.

Perhaps it should be said that he is really interested not in history as such but in the use of historical methods. Even with all his insistence—some of the time—that the events described in the Bible really occurred, "certain passages", as H.–C. Puech has observed, "remain alarming".[1] Puech cites *J* 10, 18 (p. 189):

> You must not suppose that historical realities are figures for other historical realities and corporeal things for other corporeal realities; instead, corporeal things are figures for spiritual realities and historical realities for intelligible realities.

If Origen really means what he says, he is definitely abandoning typology in favour of allegory and emptying events of their historical meaning.[2]

The element of alarm in regard to Origen's viewpoint is not diminished if we consider his use of the word *historia* in dealing with the New Testament. He is aware that Greek historians tell

---

[1] *Man and Time (Papers from the Eranos Yearbooks* 3, New York, 1957), p. 53 n19.
[2] See the definitions by Hanson, *Allegory and Event*, p 7.

true stories about voluntary self-sacrifice, about scholars in exile, about the work of evil spirits, and about the life of the Cynic philosopher Crates.[1] Origen is really interested in their work not as history but as a quarry for moral examples. He thus resembles, and is, a rhetorician or a philosopher rather than a historian. To be sure, he finds history valuable when it confirms the Bible. In this regard his most useful source was the work of Josephus, whose writings he employs more fully than those of any other historian.[2] Indeed, it would appear that sometimes when Origen speaks of history in a rather vague way he has Josephus in mind. Probably this is the case when he says that history tells us nothing about a forty-six year period in which the temple was being built, and almost nothing about the office held by the "royal officer" of John 4.46.[3] It is not clear, however, how he can say that it is clear from history that after the coming of Jesus there was no king of the Jews;[4] he is obviously neglecting the reign of Agrippa I (A.D. 37–44).

A special case is provided by his statement that there is no historical record of anyone's having encountered a "griffin".[5] Certainly Herodotus thought the griffin was mythical, but Origen's mind changed on the subject. In writing against Celsus he finally accepted its existence. Here as elsewhere, when Origen wanted to insist upon allegorization he could claim that something mentioned in scripture was not a historical phenomenon; if he was not concerned with allegory he could admit historicity. In the latter sense the gospels and Acts, in his view, do contain history.[6]

His main concern, however, is with the non-historical meaning. The unhistorical parts of scripture point beyond themselves to a spiritual meaning; indeed, everywhere the true meaning lies "beyond the history".[7] The exegete's mind must be "released

[1] J 6, 54, p. 163; J 13, 13, p. 285; J 28, 19, p. 413; M 15, 15, p. 391.
[2] Cf. G. Bardy, "Le souvenir de Josèphe chez les Pères". Revue d'histoire ecclésiastique, 43 (1948), p. 181.
[3] J 10, 28, p. 213; J 13, 58, p. 288.   [4] P 4, 1, 3, p. 296.
[5] P 4, 3, 2, p. 326; cf. Miracle and Natural Law (Amsterdam, 1952), p. 202.
[6] P 4, 3, 4, p. 329; J 6, 33, p. 143; M 15, 15, p. 392.
[7] P 4, 2.8—3.5, pp. 320–1; J 10, 22, p. 194; 10, 26, p. 199; 10, 40, p. 217.

from historical materials", for these provide nothing but a "stepping-stone".[1] Examples found in the commentaries on John and on Matthew alike reflect Origen's latent contempt for what he sometimes calls "mere history".[2] In view of this attitude, it is hard to see how he can criticize "the heterodox" for "rejoicing in allegories and referring the history about the healings to therapies of the soul".[3] Their method, and some of their results, are his own.

A sentence in the *Commentary on John* reveals one of the contemporary consequences of Origen's allegorization. "People marvel at Jesus", he says, "when they look into the history about him, but they no longer believe when the deeper meaning is disclosed to them; instead, they suppose it to be false."[4] Origen is obviously criticizing the literal-minded believer who cannot see any justification for allegorization or the consequent allegory. And if we consider the passages which Origen allegorizes in the gospels we are likely to share the literalist's view. As Hanson says, "Origen approached the Bible . . . with a series of presuppositions in his mind which had nothing particular to do with the thought of the Bible itself."[5] Because of this fact, it was necessary for him to insist that the texts often meant what they did not say.

To some extent Origen's position can be defended on the ground that there is a considerable element of ambiguity in language, even in the language of historians, and that many biblical texts are susceptible of more than one interpretation. To say this, however, is to miss the point that Origen was insisting not upon ambiguity as such but upon the correctness of his own spiritual interpretation. The method he employed meant that first he took a text with overwhelming literalness and then, having found some difficulty, proceeded in the direction of an equally overwhelming allegorization. The result was that while verbally he retained an outline (though not a very clear one) of the life and

---

[1] *J* 10, 5, p. 175; 20, 3, p. 329.
[2] In the late *M* 16, 12, p. 510; for the "mereness" of history cf. the rhetorician Theodore of Gadara, cited above, p. 73.
[3] *J* 20, 20, p. 352.   [4] *J* 20, 30, p. 368.   [5] *Allegory and Event*, p. 369.

teaching of Jesus, his central concern was with the "spiritual meaning" he found in it.

To assess the significance of his analysis is exceedingly difficult, since (1) he obviously valued John most highly among the apostolic writers, and (2) John himself points toward the appropriation of theological truth as a post-resurrection process. The gospels were written by men who were both remembering Jesus and discovering what he meant. Thus after Peter's vision (Acts 10.9–15), "the Spirit of Truth who was leading Peter into 'all the truth' (John 16.13) told him the 'many things' which he could not bear while Jesus was still with him according to the flesh".[1] Origen found that the tradition of the Church, as he understood it, pointed away from primitive misunderstandings of Jesus through John's more symbolical interpretation to his own exegesis. The basic ground on which Origen's view can be criticized is that he treated both John and himself as somehow exempt from the conditions of space and time or, in brief, of history. Origen confuses his own understanding of John not only with what the evangelist himself may have intended but also, on the other hand, with Truth itself. While his understanding is partly justified by John's love of symbolism and double meanings, it is a question whether the symbols point beyond themselves in the direction in which Origen was looking; and the gospel itself must be interpreted in relation to its own historical environment, which is not Platonic but Jewish (whether Palestinian or Hellenistic).

In the work of Origen and his predecessors we find an attempt to solve the problem presented to the Church by the existence of the four gospels. In varying ways, as we have seen, they tried to use the best literary and historical methods of their time. It cannot be said that they solved the problem or that they were able to write a life of Jesus. What remains significant in their work is not any solution. It is the fact that they did face the problem and tried to solve it. In this respect, and perhaps in this respect alone, their work has lasting significance.

At one point it is clear that Origen, at least, could perhaps have gone on beyond his rather formal literary and historical

[1] *C* 2, 2, p. 129.

methods. We have already seen that he was aware, in a rather literalistic way, that Jesus revealed himself in different ways to different persons, and that he correlated this variety with the different witnesses' levels of spiritual apprehension. But Origen was also aware of differences on a more simply human level. He could speak of the generic likeness of men as men and then go on to suggest that there are specific differences not only external but also mental. Paul was Paul; Peter was Peter and not Paul. Such differences extended even to the ways in which Peter and Paul would write the letter Alpha. And the specific content of various Christian virtues varied in relation to the person who wrote of them.[1] Had Origen further considered this point, and had he related it to the nature of the various books of the New Testament and their historical background, he would have gone far in the direction of modern critical and theological study.

He did not take this step, however, and we must therefore be content to see in his thought—as in that of the early Church generally—not final conclusions but elements which, combined in new ways and supplemented by other considerations, can be used in creating a more adequate understanding of the life of Jesus.

[1] *Num. hom.* 2, 2, pp. 10–12 Baehrens; cf. *O* 24, 2, pp. 353–4.

GLOSSARY

This section deals with four of the principal terms used by Graeco-Roman writers in analysing narratives: ἀπομνημόνευμα, ἱστορία, μῦθος, and πλάσμα (for some of these terms, and others, cf. *The Letter and the Spirit*, pp. 120–42). For the method of citation cf. p. vii.

1. Ἀπομνημόνευμα, ἀπομνημονεύειν

According to the rhetorician Theon, an ἀπομνημόνευμα is ⟨the record of⟩ an action or a subject with practical significance (βιοφελής, 96, 23). In other words, it is chiefly a longer χρεία (K. von Fritz in Pauly-Wissowa, *RE* Suppl. VI, pp. 87–9). The word implies an emphasis on the reliability of the record, since it is often used of "memoirs" written by witnesses (e.g., Xenophon on Socrates; cf. E. Schwartz in *RE* II, pp. 170–1; J. Weiss, *Das älteste Evangelium*, Göttingen, 1903, pp. 6–22). The genitive with the noun usually, though not always, refers to the subject of the memoirs rather than to their author. Justin, speaking of the gospels, classifies them as ἀπομνημονεύματα "of the apostles" or "composed by the apostles and their followers" (*Dial.* 103; also, *passim* in *Dial.* 100–7; *Apol.* 1, 66, 3, cf. 33, 5). The ἀπομνημόνευματα of Peter (*Dial.* 106) are probably the gospel of Mark, according to tradition composed by the apostle's disciple. Justin's follower Tatian apparently used the word in the same way (*Or.* 21, p. 23, 18 Schwartz; cf. 23, 7–8). The noun is not found frequently in early Christian literature; it occurs in Clement, *Str.* 2, 118, 3, in the singular to refer to the "memorial", a gnomic command, which Nicolaitan gnostics had received from their founder, and in Origen, *C* 7, 54, p. 204, in the plural to indicate what, in relation to the words of Heracles, his admirers cannot supply. In these instances the noun undoubtedly points toward the aspect of reminiscence.

The use of the verb is somewhat different. It occurs in Papias' defence of Mark, who "was not wrong when he wrote down single items ὡς ἀπομνημόνευσεν—as he remembered them, or in the form in which he recorded them?" The meaning of Papias' sentence (Eusebius, *H.E.* 3. 39, 15) seems unclear. When Justin (*Apol.* 1, 33, 5) says that the apostles were οἱ ἀπομνημονεύσαντες everything about the Saviour, he probably has in mind both recalling and recording. Similarly in two passages in Clement (*Protr.* 79, 3; *Str.* 5, 82, 4) both meanings are to be found, the first in regard to Clement himself, the second in regard to Luke's work in Acts (Paul at Athens). Two other passages, however, use the word primarily to mean "record"; speaking of his gnostic knowledge, Clement says that "there are some things not recorded by us" (*Str.* 1, 14, 2); and he says that Aristotle "records that Zaleukos . . . received the laws from Athena" (*Str.* 1, 170, 3). In neither case can the primary meaning be that of remembering.

Similarly the passages cited by Weiss (op. cit., p. 8 n1) from Irenaeus do not prove his contention that ἀπομνημονεύειν indicates remembering. Its Latin equivalent *meminit* is used twice of the evangelist John and his gospel (*Adv. haer.* 2, 22, 3, p. 328; 4, 10, 1, p. 172; cf. *commemoratus est*, 4, 2, 3, p. 148), but it is also used of Luke (5, 21, 2, p. 383). Of course Luke could have remembered Paul's teaching, in Irenaeus' view, but it would seem more likely that what is emphasized is recording. On the other hand, Weiss also cites Irenaeus' *Epistle to Florinus* (Eusebius, *H.E.* 5, 20, 6), and there ἀπομνημόνευεν means both recall and relate but not record.

Origen uses the verb of the author of Hebrews (Eusebius, *H.E.* 6, 25, 13) and of the evangelists (*J* 6, 34, p. 143; 10, 3, p. 172; *M* 16, 12, p. 510). In each instance the verb is related to remembering, but the aspect of remembering is explicitly stated separately. Therefore the primary meaning of ἀπομνημονεύειν for Origen is to record, not to recall.

2. Ἱστορία

Ἱστορία, according to Theon, is a systematically constructed narration (60, 6), and a narrative is an account which sets forth events which took place or as if they took place (78, 15). Most grammarians and rhetoricians distinguished history from both myth and πλάσμα (q. v.). But in Theon's definition all are treated as forms of history. A similar treatment is given by the grammarian Asclepiades (Sextus Empiricus, *Adv. math.* 1, 252–3). There are three kinds of history: true (factual), false (πλάσματα and myths), and like the true (as in comedy and mimes). True history deals with (1) the persons of gods, heroes, and famous men, (2) places and times, and (3) actions. (For the rhetorical analysis based on such subjects cf. pp. 39–44.)

The noun does not occur in the New Testament or the apostolic fathers, though the verb ἱστορεῖν, in the sense of "make acquaintance" is found in Gal. 1.18 and perhaps in Ignatius, *Eph.* 1, 2. The apologist Aristides (13, 7) raises the question of whether the Greek histories are mythical, "natural", or allegorical. Justin uses the verb to mean "relate" or "recount", in regard to Greek stories of the gods (*Apol.* 1, 21, 4; 22, 4; *Dial.* 69, 2), to a narrative by Moses (*Apol.* 1, 53, 8), and to his own statements (*Dial.* 62, 2). Tatian uses the noun of Greek and oriental writings (*Or.* 1, p. 1, 11 Schwartz; 31, p. 32, 21 [correct chronology required for truth in history]; 36, p. 38, 6 and 14; 37, p. 38, 20; 39, p. 40, 1) and of Hebrew-Christian history (40, p. 41, 11). Athenagoras uses the noun of Greek histories (*Leg.* 20, 3; 26, 1; 29, 1; 30, 4). The same use is found in Theophilus (*Ad Autol.* 2, 1–2.6; 3, 2 [useless histories of Herodotus and Thucydides]).

Their contemporary Lucian wrote a treatise on *How History is to be Written*; in it he stated that history must not contain an invocation of the Muses (10) and must avoid the myth and the encomium, as well as the hyperboles contained in both (8). Its "only goal is utility, which comes from truth alone" (9).

For Origen's use of history cf. pp. 114–16 above.

3. Μῦθος

The rhetoricians ordinarily differentiated history (no. 2), myth, and πλάσμα or fiction (no. 4). History is an account of what did take place; myth is an account of what could not take place; fiction is an account of what did not take place (Sextus Empiricus, *Adv. math.* 1, 263–4; cf. P. de Lacy in *American Journal of Philology* 69, 1948, pp. 267–8). Sometimes, however, myth and fiction were treated together and regarded as consisting of the genealogies of gods and heroes (Asclepiades in Sextus Empiricus 1, 252–3); such an analysis meant that stories of the gods could be treated as history. "Fictioned myth" or "to fiction a myth" (μῦθον πλάσσειν) is a common expression after Plato (*Tim.* 26 e); cf. Palaephatus, *Incred., passim*; Philo, *Exsecr.* 162; Theon 75, 11 and 32; Hippolytus, *Ref.* 6, 19, 4; Origen, *M* 17, 30, p. 670. In any event, myths were not true, even though they might "portray truth" (Theon 59, 21; 72, 28; Aphthonius, II, 21, 2; cf. Nicolaus, III, 453.19—455.5) or provide guidance for the conduct of life (Hermogenes 3, 11 Spengel, 2, 4 Rabe). In the opinion of some analysts, myth was characteristic of tragedy, fiction, or comedy (Quintilian, *Inst. Or.* 2, 4, 2; cf. Dio Chrysostom, *Or.* 11, 7; Diogenes Laertius 5, 88; "tragic myth" of Valentinus, Hippolytus, *Ref.* 6, 42, 2).

The falsity of myths is emphasized in the Pastoral Epistles (1 Tim. 4.7; 2 Tim. 4.4; Tit. 1.14, "Jewish"; 1 Tim. 1.4, associated with genealogies, as above) and in 2 Peter (1.16; "follow" as in Josephus, *Ant.* 1, 22). The word "myth" does not occur in the apostolic fathers, but in Ignatius, *Magn.* 8, 1, we find "the ancient useless μυθεύματα"; the ending of the word implies the artificiality of the myths' origin. (Clement could hardly be expected to use the word when he treats the story of the phoenix as historical, 25, 1 and 5.) Among the apologists myths are uniformly regarded as false, and both Aristides and Tatian complain about allegorical exegesis of them (cf. W. den Boer in *VC* 1, 1947, pp. 156–8). Similarly Hippolytus, in his *Refutatio*, always uses the word in relation to the false stories told by Greeks, barbarians, and gnostics.

For Origen cf. pp. 65–6. Note that the object of heterodox worship is "a fiction (πλάσμα) and not truth, a myth and not mysteries" (*J* 13, 17, p. 241). Cf. also the note of Hanson, *Allegory and Event*, p. 276 n3.

4. Πλάσμα

In rhetoric the word means "fiction", a narrative which is lifelike but untrue, though as we have seen (no. 3) it was not always sharply differentiated from myth. One man's myth was another man's πλάσμα. In its rhetorical sense it does not occur in the New Testament, the apostolic fathers, or the apologists. Origen regards the Sadducees' story of the woman with seven husbands (Matt. 22.25–8) as either a myth (*L* 39, p. 226; *M* 17, 30, p. 670, 22) or a fiction (*M* p. 670, 28; 17, 33, p. 688). In writing against Celsus, who had said (*C* 3, 27, p. 224) that the gospels contained myths and πλάσματα, Origen argues only that the gospel stories are not πλάσματα (1, 40, p. 90; 2, 10–11, pp. 138–9; 2, 13, p. 141; 2, 15, p. 144; 2, 26, p. 155; 2, 48, p. 169; 2, 56, pp. 180–1; 3, 33, p. 229, possibly because his allegorical method still requires him to treat some of them as myths, but more probably because he is combining myth with fiction (cf. 1, 42, pp. 92–3, where "impossible" stories are called πλάσματα).

APPENDIX

ORIGEN'S EXEGETICAL WRITINGS ON THE GOSPELS

Six of Origen's works are especially significant for his exegesis of the gospels.

(1) His treatise *De principiis* (*P*) is extant in some Greek fragments, which include most of the fourth book (on inspiration and exegesis), in a Latin translation (and edition) made by Rufinus in 397, and in Latin fragments of a more literal translation made by Jerome in 398. The text was edited (along with passages from the anathematisms of the council of Constantinople in 553) by Paul Koetschau in 1913 (*Die griechischen christlichen Schriftsteller der drei ersten Jahrhunderten, Origenes Werke* V, Berlin). There is an English translation by G. Butterworth, *Origen on First Principles* (London, 1936).

(2) His *Commentary on John* (*J*) has largely been preserved in two manuscripts of the thirteenth and fourteenth centuries, edited with Greek fragments by Erwin Preuschen in 1903 (*GCS* IV). The contents of the books are as follows:

Book I on John 1.1 (pp. 3–51)
- II   John 1.1–7 (pp. 52–97)
- III   (lost)
- IV   fragments (pp. 98–9)
- V   fragments (pp. 100–5)
- VI   John 1.19–29 (pp. 106–69; end lost)
- VII–IX (lost)
- X   John 2.12–25 (pp. 170–225)
- XI–XII (lost)
- XIII   John 4.13–54 (pp. 226–97)
- XIV–XVIII (lost)
- XIX   John 8.19–25 (pp. 298–326; beginning and end lost)

XX	John 8.37–53 (pp. 327–88)
XXI–XXVII	(lost)
XXVIII	John 11.39–57 (pp. 389–424)
XXIX–XXXI	(lost)
XXXII	John 13.2–33 (pp. 425–80)

The average number of *GCS* pages for complete books is about 50, and it thus appears that the whole work would have contained about 1600 pages. Not all of it was equally significant. Origen naturally expounded the prologue more fully than he did later sections of John; the first ten books, indeed, average about $6\frac{1}{2}$ pages of exegesis per verse. But the last twenty-two books cannot have contained more than about two pages of exegesis per verse. It is highly probable that Origen never wrote more than thirty-two books.

(3) *The Homilies on Luke* (*L*) are preserved in a Latin translation made by Jerome and in Greek fragments. The oldest manuscript of the Latin version comes from the ninth century. M. Rauer edited the text in 1930 (*GCS* IX).

(4) The treatise *De oratione* (*O*) survives in one Greek manuscript of the fourteenth century, which was edited by Koetschau in 1899 (*GCS* II). It contains, among other things, exegesis of the Lord's Prayer.

(5) The *Commentary on Matthew* (*M*) is preserved in two ways. (a) In Greek, in addition to fragments, we possess books X–XVII (on Matt. 13.36—22.33) in three manuscripts of the thirteenth and fourteenth centuries; these were edited by Erich Klostermann in 1935 (*GCS* X). (b) There is also a Latin version of the sixth or seventh century; it begins with XII 9 (Matt. 16.12) and continues to the end of the gospel. The oldest manuscripts of this version come from the ninth and tenth centuries; it was edited by Klostermann in 1933 (*GCS* XI). The edition was completed with fragments, indices, and essays by Klostermann, E. Benz, and L. Früchtel in 1941–55 (*GCS* XII). The exegesis is disposed as follows:

Book X on Matt. 13.36—14.15 (pp. 1–34 Klostermann)
XI Matt. 14.15—15.39 (pp. 34–69)

XII	Matt. 16.1—17.9 (pp. 69–170)
XIII	Matt. 17.10—18.18 (pp. 170–271)
XIV	Matt. 18.19—19.11 (pp. 271–348)
XV	Matt. 19.12—20.16 (pp. 348–461)
XVI	Matt. 20.17—21.22 (pp. 461–574)
XVII	Matt. 21.23—22.33 (pp. 575–703)

It will be seen that Books X and XI are considerably shorter than the others, and by comparing the formulas with which Origen concluded books of the early *Commentary on John* and Book VI of the late *Contra Celsum*, Klostermann was able to show that the *Commentary on Matthew* has been abbreviated. The Latin translation begins at Comm. XII, 9 (on Matt. 16.13), p. 80, and continues after the Greek ends.

| Ser. comm. 1–23 on Matt. 22.34–23.39 (pp. 1–54) |
29–62	Matt. 24.1–51 (pp. 55–145)
63–73	Matt. 25.1–46 (pp. 145–74)
74–114	Matt. 26.1–75 (pp. 174–241)
115–145	Matt. 27.1–66 (pp. 241–99)

(6) The Greek text of *Contra Celsum* (*C*) was edited from two fourteenth-century manuscripts by Paul Koetschau in 1899 (*GCS* I–II). Recent papyrological discoveries have not contributed as much as had been expected; see J. Scherer, *Extraits des livres I et II du Contre Celse d'Origène* (Cairo, 1956). There is an excellent English translation by H. Chadwick, *Origen: Contra Celsum* (Cambridge, 1953).

BIBLIOGRAPHY

Since full bibliographies on ancient exegesis can be found in *The Letter and the Spirit* (London, 1957) and in J. Pépin, *Mythe et allégorie* (Paris, 1958), this list includes only works fairly closely related to the work of Origen.

GENERAL

DE FAYE, E. *Clément d'Alexandrie*, Paris, 1898.

PRAT, F. *Origène le théologue et l'exégète*, Paris, 1907.

BAUER, W. *Das Leben Jesu im Zeitalter der neutestamentlichen Apokryphen*, Tübingen, 1909.

BIGG, C. *The Christian Platonists of Alexandria*, 2nd ed., Oxford, 1913.

TOLLINTON, R. B. *Clement of Alexandria*, London, 1914.

DE FAYE, E. *Origène, sa vie, son œuvre, sa pensée*, Paris, 1923–8.

SMITH, H. *Ante-Nicene Exegesis of the Gospels*, London, 1925–9.

CADIOU, R. *La jeunesse d'Origène*, Paris, 1935.

MOLLAND, E. *The Conception of the Gospel in the Alexandrian Theology*, Oslo, 1938.

DEN BOER, W. *De allegorese in het werk van Clemens Alexandrinus*, Leiden, 1940.

MONDÉSERT, C. *Clément d'Alexandrie*, Paris, 1944.

CAMELOT, T. *Foi et gnose . . . chez Clément d'Alexandrie*, Paris, 1945.

DANIÉLOU, J. *Origène*, Paris, 1948.

DE LUBAC, H. *Histoire et Esprit*, Paris, 1950.

CHADWICK, H. *Origen: Contra Celsum*, Cambridge, 1953.

HANSON, R. P. C. *Allegory and Event*, London, 1959.

WILES, M. F. *The Spiritual Gospel*, Cambridge, 1960.

SPECIAL

BORST, J. *Beiträge zur sprachlich-stilistischen und rhetorischen Würdigung des Origenes*, Freising, 1913.

HARNACK, A. *Der kirchengeschichtliche Ertrag der exegetischen Arbeiten des Origenes, Texte und Untersuchungen* 42, 3–4 (Leipzig, 1918–19).

STREIBER, E. "Einiges zur Schriftauslegung des Origenes", *Internationale kirchliche Zeitschrift* 13 (1923), pp. 145–69.

BARDY, G. "Les traditions juives dans l'œuvre d'Origène", *Revue biblique* 34 (1925), pp. 217–52.

CADIOU, R. "Dictionnaires antiques dans l'œuvre d'Origène", *Revue des études grecques* 45 (1932), pp. 271–85.

KLOSTERMANN, E. "Ueberkommene Definitionen im Werke des Origenes", *Zeitschrift für die neutestamentliche Wissenschaft* 37 (1938), pp. 54–61.

KLOSTERMANN, E. "Formen der exegetischen Arbeiten des Origenes", *Theologische Literatur-Zeitung* 72 (1947), pp. 203–8.

BERTRAND, F. *Mystique de Jésus chez Origène*, Paris, 1951.

LÄUCHLI, S. "The Polarity of the Gospels in the Exegesis of Origen", *Church History* 21 (1952), pp. 215–4.

LÄUCHLI, S. "Die Frage nach der Objektivität der Exegese des Origenes", *Theologische Zeitschrift* 10 (1954), pp. 178–97.

DANIÉLOU, J. "Origène comme exégète de la Bible", *Texte und Untersuchungen* 63 (Berlin, 1957), pp. 280–90.

PÉPIN, J. "A propos de l'histoire de l'exégèse allégorique: l'absurdité, signe d'allégorie", *Texte und Untersuchungen* 63 (Berlin, 1957), pp. 395–413.

INDEXES

EXEGETICAL TERMS

BIBLICAL PASSAGES INTERPRETED BY ANCIENT
AUTHORS BEFORE ORIGEN

BIBLICAL PASSAGES INTERPRETED BY ORIGEN

ANCIENT AUTHORS OR LITERATURE

A. PAGAN
Aphthonius, 45–6, 122
Aristaenetus, 50n
Arrian, 48–9
Asclepiades, 121
Celsus, 59–60, 70–8, 94, 123
Chaeremon, 83
Cicero, 67n
Cocondrius, 103n
Dio Chrysostom, 44–5, 71–2, 122
Diogenes Laertius, 122
Hermogenes, 14n, 15, 17n, 19, 40, 45, 66, 122
Lucian, 39, 121
Nicolaus, 122
Orphic literature, 47
Palaephatus, 72n, 122
Plato, 122
Polybius of Sardis, 103n
Porphyry, 51
Quintilian, 15, 40, 122
Sextus Empiricus, 47–8, 66n, 121
Strabo, 71n
Theodore of Gadara, 40, 116n
Theon (Aelius), 14n, 15, 17n, 18n, 40–5, 58–9, 65–6, 72n, 99–100, 119–22
Trypho, 101, 103
Xenophon, 20, 119

B. JEWISH
Josephus, 69, 115, 122
Philo, 56n, 62, 81n, 106, 122

C. CHRISTIAN*
Alogi, 28
Apollinaris of Hierapolis, 30

Aristides, 121–2
Athenagoras, 121
Clement of Alexandria, 23, 30, 35–7, 47, 50, 57, 62, 64n, 80, 119–20
Clement of Rome, 122
Epiphanius, 28
Eustathius, 74
Gaius of Rome, 28–9, 59, 61
Gregory Thaumaturgus, 51–2
Hippolytus, 29, 62, 122
Ignatius, 121–2
Irenaeus, 13n, 21n, 23, 32–5, 82, 87n, 104n, 105n, 120
Julius Africanus, 39, 81
Justin, 14, 16, 19–22, 119–21
Melito, 29–30
Muratorian fragment, 30–2
Papias, 14–19, 21–2, 32, 36
Sextus, 106
Tatian, 22–8, 37n, 47, 60–1, 68n, 88, 119, 121–2
Theophilus of Antioch, 30, 121

D. GNOSTIC/SECTARIAN
Basilides, 10
Carpocratians, 104
Cerinthus, 33
Ebionites, 55n, 60
Heracleon, 13, 62, 87
Marcion, Marcionites, 10–12, 34, 39, 59n, 60
Montanists, 28–9
Quartadecimans, 29–30, 37
Theodotus, 12–13
Valentinians, 12–13, 34, 87

* Eusebius and Origen are omitted because their names occur so frequently.

133

MODERN SCHOLARS

INTRODUCTION TO THE SERIES

As business life becomes more complex, so the field of industrial economics grows increasingly important. Though the problems in the micro-world of the firm and the influence of its behaviour on society as a whole are studied extensively there still exists a lack of that collaboration between students of different nationalities which has proved to be so fruitful in other sciences and even in other parts of economics.

Another obstacle to the development of this field of our science is the relatively few contacts in many countries between economists and business men.

The principal aim of this present series is to stimulate study and research in this part of economics and to further an interchange of ideas and results on an international basis. In general it is expected that contributors will not only give the present state of informed opinion in their respective countries on the subjects treated but also include the results of their own study and research. Although this may sometimes lead to some overlapping the editors feel that this may not be undesirable, in so far as it serves to link together the parts of the subject.

As the reader will see, the level of treatment is that appropriate to an audience of graduate academic standard. Nevertheless, the volumes are not addressed to academic scholars only but also to those engaged in management. A knowledge of basic economic principles is assumed.

If the publishing of this series gives an impulse to the fostering of international collaboration in this important section of economics and focuses attention on the necessity for further development of industrial economics and on the mutual benefit economics as well as practical business life may derive from it, the goal of the editors will be achieved.

THE EDITORS

BIOGRAPHICAL NOTES

J. L. BOUMA: Institute of Industrial Economics, State University of Groningen, The Netherlands.

EDGAR O. EDWARDS: Professor of Economics at the Rice University, Houston, Texas, U.S.A.; formerly of Princeton University, Princeton, N. Jersey, U.S.A.

Author of: *Theory and Measurement of Business Income* (with P. W. BELL); "Classical and Keynesian Employment Theories, A Reconciliation", *Quarterly Journal of Economics*; "The Effect of Depreciation on the Output-Capital Coefficient of a Firm", *Economic Journal*.

L. H. KLAASSEN: Professor of Regional and Social Economic Research at the Netherlands School of Economics in Rotterdam, The Netherlands.

Author of: *Observations on the Planned Provision of Nitrogen Fertilizer for the World* (with J. TINBERGEN and E. H. MULDER).

L. M. KOYCK: Professor of Economics at the Netherlands School of Economics in Rotterdam, The Netherlands.

Author of: *Distributed Lags and Investment Analysis; The Prices of Investment Goods and the Volume of Production in the United States* (with HENDRIEKE GORIS).

W. ARTHUR LEWIS: Principal of the University College of the West Indies, British West Indies; formerly Stanley Jevons Professor of Political Economy in the University of Manchester (1948–1958).

Author of: *Overhead Costs, The Theory of Economic Growth, Economic Survey 1918–1939, The Principles of Planning.*

J. L. MEIJ: Professor of Industrial Economics, State University of Groningen, The Netherlands.

Author of: *Weerstandsvermogen en Financiële Reorganisatie van Ondernemingen* (Financial Stability and Financial Reconstruction of Enterprises); *Leerboek der Bedrijfshuishoudkunde I en II* (Principles of Industrial Economics, Vol I & II).

DAVID WALKER: Professor of Economics at Makerere College, The University College of East Africa, Uganda.

Author of: *Some Economic Aspects of the Taxation of Companies*, The Manchester School, 1954; *The Direct – Indirect Tax Controversy, Fifteen Years of Controversy*, Public Finance, 1955.

CONTENTS

INTRODUCTORY

J. L. MEIJ *(Editor)*.

There are but few fields in managerial economics where the gap between theory and practice is so wide as in that of depreciation of durable assets.

It is not the aim of this book to fill that gap wholly. It takes a good deal of work to achieve such an objective. A volume like this, however, may be supposed to further scientific thinking in this area as well as the application of its results to practical business life.

According to the objective of these Studies, viz. the interchange of ideas and findings in the field of industrial economics, first of all an attempt has been made to compare different viewpoints on this subject developed in different countries. Nevertheless, it seemed worthwhile not only to collect different theoretical approaches and scrutinize them, but also to try to confront them with practical entrepreneurial behaviour.

Seen from a managerial point of view depreciation taken in a wider sense, also including obsolescence, has different aspects. Therefore, management is confronted with the depreciation problem in various ways.

First, there is the problem of valuation of the services rendered by machines and other fixed assets used in production for costing purposes. We need not refer to controversial concepts such as marginal costing, full costing, direct costing and the like to conclude that the valuation of the services of fixed assets may be necessary when applying all these concepts.

There is yet another problem of valuation with regard to durable assets. Seen from the viewpoint of costing, depreciation gives rise to evaluating the used services of the assets. For the balance-sheet it is necessary to evaluate their non-used services. Every time we have to determine our periodical profit and set up the balance-sheet, in general at the end of the year, we have to evaluate the services still available in our assets. The profit figure, too, is affected by the way in which these services are evaluated.

Often there is a deviation between the value of the non-used services according to the applied system of depreciation and the amount figuring on the balance-sheet. This can be the case for three reasons. First, management may have the impression that the amount computed by the depreciation system is not adequate compared with the real value of the assets at the end of the year, the latter being supposed in general to have a lower value because of unforeseen causes. Thus, there is an extra loss that must be covered by gross profits.

The second reason for evaluating assets at a lower amount lies in the desire to make reservations against unforeseen losses in the future.

Finally, depreciation is often used as a means of making secret reservations in order to be able to expand the business without the consent of share-holders.

A third aspect of the depreciation problem is the determination of the moment when the asset must be replaced. Though there will always be a moment when the total value of the asset eventually deducted by the value of the residuum, its scrap value, is totally written off, it is clear that it is not sure that replacement has to take place at that very moment. Thus, this problem is not automatically solved by application of a depreciation system that seems to be adequate at the moment it was chosen.

Finally, by calculating depreciation costs and by selling the product at a price which includes an allowance for depreciation an amount for replacement is gradually earned. We can only hope, however, that at the moment the asset must be put out of use an amount necessary to finance replacement is at our disposal. In practice this is not often realised. Therefore, depreciation gives rise to the problem how to get the means for re-investment.

It is clear that those different problems only arise in a dynamic economy, an economy with changing prices and production techniques. If prices were stable and production techniques remained the same, all problems were solved automatically by calculating the value of the services of the assets in the price of the product. Then assets were put out of use at the moment their productive capacity was exhausted and would be replaced by exactly the same ones and at the same price.

Under these circumstances that moment could be predicted in advance. Moreover, at that moment we would have received the amount necessary to finance replacement. Replacement under such conditions does not give rise to any problem except that of choosing the adequate depreciation system. The asset is to be replaced as it is written off and the necessary means for re-investment will then be available. The dynamic character of our economic life forces us to consider the problems around the depreciation phenomenon separately. We are inclined to forget their correlation. It is just in management, however, that they are linked together. We must state, nevertheless, that in business practice the problem of evaluation of used and non-used services and the problem of actual replacement are often treated as two different subjects.

Whether or not there is a more or less close connection between depreciation and replacement policy depends on our ability to predict the moment of replacement and to determine in advance the decrease in value of the assets and their services during their life-time.

[At first sight depreciation might be considered as a purely technological question and not as an economic one. Replacement follows depreciation automatically. At the moment its capacity is fully exhausted the asset must be replaced.

Economic problems arise from the fact that it might be rational to put aside means of production whose stock of services is not totally exhausted and, moreover, that there are different alternatives of replacement of an instrument that has become obsolete. It need not always be replaced by an identical one. To state this in another way we can say that the economic problems of depreciation and replacement are caused by the fact that economic life-time is shorter than technical and further that we are concerned with economic replacement, i.e. replacement by an instrument that fulfils the same function in the business, though it need not be a purely identical item.

It is not justified, however, to say that all depreciation systems must be based on economic life-time and that an instrument can never be replaced by an identical one.

We may distinguish two concepts of technical life-time. First, the absolute technical life-time, being the period from the moment the instrument is put into use until it can no longer render any sort of service, in other words, is totally useless. It can only be sold as scrap. There is also a relative technical life-time. In this case we must relate life-time with the special function the instrument has to perform in a particular process of production. This concept of life-time we may call relative technical life-time. We can define this relative technical life-time as the period during which the asset can deliver services that are useful in that particular process.

For every individual business only the last concept, not the first, is relevant. For a particular process of production it does not matter whether any sort of equipment can render some valuable service when it cannot be used in that process. There are a lot of cases in which a means of production cannot be used any longer in a particular process of production though it is still worthwhile to use it in another.

Railway equipment no longer to be used on the main lines might be used during a considerable amount of years on branch lines. Old machines can be used as reserve equipment or to fabricate products of lower quality. Even if there are no possibilities to use the instrument in the original business, another one may possibly have a use for it. For some equipment as ships, autobuses and other means of transportation there is a largely developed second-hand market. Other equipment, however, can also be sold to other companies. We may say that for several instruments there exists a functional degradation. When the necessity of functional degradation arises, the technical life in the original function has come to an end. The means of production are beginning a new life on a lower level.

The causes of this degradation are different. They are qualitative or quantitative in character. In some cases the means of production can no longer deliver their products or their services in the quality required by the process of production as it is executed in the particular enterprise. When the number of products delivered or of services rendered diminishes, though the quality remains the same, the maintenance of the equipment in its original function may also become impossible. From an organizational point of view it might then prove difficult to maintain the instrument in its original position. For, if it does not last the same quantity of services, how are we to get the rest ? As the means of production are indivisible, there is no other solution but to buy a new instrument and to put the old out of use. In this case, too, we can say that the technical life-time of the asset in the function wherein it is used has expired. But a new life can now begin whether in another function in the same enterprise or in another business.

In all these cases, and we might suppose there are many, putting out of use is a technical necessity, whether it may be a question of diminished quality or of organizational difficulties. Thus, this relative technical life-time, as we have called it, is of far more importance than is often supposed. This fact makes the depreciation problem much easier in a certain respect. The moment of replacement does not give any difficulty, but also the life-time of the instrument in its function can be foreseen more easily. The only difficulty lies in the determination of the value of the instrument at the moment of degradation. If the instruments are sold and there is a large second-hand market, more or less exact estimates of the second-hand value can be made. The degradation within the enterprise gives rise to more uncertainty, but here, too, the difficulties do not seem to be insurmountable.

Not always, however, will the relative technical life-time be decisive. There are many cases wherein the equipment must be put out of use before its relative technical life-time is over. When its products of services remain the same quantitatively and qualitatively, this can only be because of the increasing complementary costs, the expenses by which the use of the equipment is attended. Increasing complementary costs may go with diminishing capacity from a quantitative or qualitative angle, but this need not be the case. When increasing maintenance and repair work can be done in periods the equipment is not used, e.g. in the evening or on Saturday afternoon, complementary costs are still increasing but neither the number nor the quality of services need diminish.

In such cases, before relative technical life has expired, a moment can be reached where the value of the products or the services rendered is equalled by the necessary complementary expenses. At this moment the economic life-time is over, for the nett value of the services rendered has become zero or even negative.

What is said here can be easily illustrated by the following simple graphs, (see page 6).

In both graphs the value of the services rendered or the products made by the equipment are indicated by the dotted line BDC. After point D corresponding with A on the x-axis this value goes down, maybe by declining number or by declining quality. The curve Ps indicates the complementary costs. In Fig. 1, however, at A they still have a nett value, the latter having dropped to zero at E. The nett value of the services is indicated by the dotted line QE. For reasons explained before, however, often the equipment cannot be maintained after A is reached.

In Fig. 2 the same case is illustrated, with the only difference that the point of intersection of the complementary costs now lies before A. Now the equipment is to be put out of use before the service value declines.

Thus, we can say whether the relative technical life-time or the economic life-time is decisive depends on which is shorter. The shorter of the two is always decisive.

We can now answer the question what is the meaning of economic life-time for the calculation of the amount of depreciation. There are two cases in which economic life-time, being the shorter, is decisive viz. (a) if the machine can be kept in use notwithstanding the declining

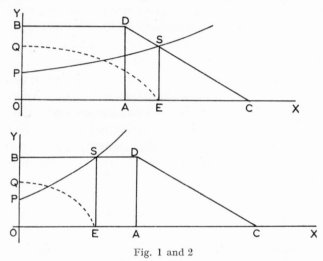

Fig. 1 and 2

of the number or the quality of its services; (b) if the complementary costs are increasing so rapidly that they become equal to the value of the services rendered before that value declines because of their declining quality or quantity.

The first case is not very realistic in modern business. There always seems to be a lack of elasticity as to number and quality of the services. In industry deviations in quality will often be prohibitive for selling especially when the products are sold under brand. Selling under brand as is more and more the practice in industry requires a standardized quality. In transportation also a standardized quality of the services is necessary for safety, comfort and similar purposes.

For organizational reasons a fixed number of services is required. A decline in capacity because of depreciation of the machines cannot easily be handled. It is difficult to adapt the organization to a declining capacity of some machines. If the machines are not able to render the number of services necessary to keep up the capacity of the whole plant, there is no alternative but to put them out of use. Perhaps they can only remain in the plant as reserve capacity. This is, as we have seen, only one of the forms of functional degradation.

More realistic, therefore, is the second case. In many cases even the declining of number and quality of the services can be kept up by more expensive maintenance.

Thus, not only the establishment of the moment of actual replacement becomes a question of comparing the value of the services of the equipment with the complementary costs, but also the determination of economic life-time only consists in estimating those costs in the successive years.

In many cases of practical life the complex problem of depreciation can often be simplified as it consists only in estimating complementary costs.

Can those complementary costs be determined in advance ? Insofar as the increase is caused by technological factors such as wear and tear, we may concede this if we can pre-suppose normal employment. Complementary costs can rise, however, because of unforeseen influences as increased wage rates, higher prices of raw material, means of maintenance etc. If the prices of the product or the service of the machines cannot be increased, economic life-time is shortened. These events cannot be foreseen.

On the other hand the value of the services of the existing equipment may decline as a consequence of technical progress by which new equipment delivers more products or services at the same time and the same complementary costs or services of better quality. This development is also inpredictable to a large extent.

We may therefore distinguish between endogenous and exogenous depreciation factors. The first can be foreseen in a certain respect. They are a consequence of the special qualities of the instrument itself, of its innate gifts, so to say. The constructor of the machine can inform us about these qualities and what their consequences are. In our opinion it is only on the base of these endogenous factors that we can make estimates as to future depreciation and that we are able to build up a depreciation system.

The exogenous factors are as far as they show no measurable trend unforeseeable. We, therefore, can only adapt our system to the new factors if they come into being. The exogenous factors are also those that make the asset obsolete after a shorter or longer time. We must reckon with those factors in particular if we wish to replace our equipment at the best moment.

In conclusion we can say that, apart from exogenous factors, we can predict relative technical as well as economic life-time. Which of the two will be shorter and therefore decisive for the depreciation system to be chosen will depend upon:

a) the moment the services rendered are declining in quantity or quality;

b) the consequence of this declining for the business, whether the equipment can or cannot remain in use unless this declining;

c) the degree of increasing of the complementary costs.

These three factors, being determined by endogenous factors, can be predicted to a sufficient degree to set up a depreciation system.

Not to be foreseen are the influences on the value of the products made or of the services rendered and the influences on complementary costs caused by exogenous factors. They cannot be used in constructing a depreciation system, but they must be taken into account by determining the moment of replacement.

Thus, the determination of the moment of replacement does not follow immediately from the system of depreciation chosen. It presents in itself a separate problem, though not totally independent from the depreciation system.

It may seem as if the real life-time in many cases, or practically always, will be shorter than the predicted one. In practical business life, however, we do not always mention it. Often we may find the reserve equipment already written off, but still remaining in use.

There are two reasons for this situation.

First, there is the practice to write off extra amounts to cover the unforeseen depreciation. When the latter does not appear, the machine can be written off while it is not put out of use. Moreover, unforeseen factors may also have a tendency to lengthen the life-time in certain circumstances. The services of the equipment or the product fabricated with it may increase in value by exogenous causes so that the moment of replacement can be rationally postponed notwithstanding the fact that the machine is totally written off. This fact in itself, it is clear, can never be a reason to put the instruments out of use.

We have given here a more or less personal view on the depreciation problem. The reader will see from the following contributions, however, that this problem can be approached in a different way.

The present volume does not cover all the aspects of the depreciation problem explicitly and wholly but implicitly and in a certain degree they are all covered.

Professor Lewis' contribution deals with depreciation and obsolescence as factors in costing.

Though he starts with considering different purposes for measuring depreciation, his main assignment is "to define depreciation for the purpose of calculating costs". In this respect he makes a very important distinction, viz. depreciation to maintain general command over goods and services and depreciation to maintain the production capacity of the firm, a distinction which is important whenever the price of the particular assets of the enterprise moves differently from the general price level. The first objective may be indicated as keeping capital intact.

In a competitive market depreciation to maintain the productive capacity of the firm intact enters into cost, but in a non-competitive one the concept of a fair price may play a considerable rôle in price-determination. The fair price is more connected with maintaining capital intact *.

A fruitful condition that brings in a certain sense the controversy between marginal costing and full costing to a synthesis is his concept of escapable costs. It is not only necessary that marginal price equals marginal cost, but that to the total paid for the goods or services produced by a durable asset equals total escapable costs.

When considering price policy from an angle of continuity we can say that all costs come under the category of escapable costs, that is to say that there is always a moment when we can decide to make the decision to replace or not. In fact, that is another way of saying that all goods and services used in production must be replaced in the end. A further point of value for the analysis of the depreciation costs is the concept of retainer costs, i.e. the costs of holding assets unused. This concept makes it easy, as Lewis says, "to tie together the analysis of the cost of using surplus capacity and the analysis of the cost of using assets at full capacity".

In the second chapter Professor Edwards deals principally with the financial side of the depreciation problem. If we view the problem

---

* In my own opinion a synthesis between two objectives could perhaps be found by saying that the aim of the enterprise is not maintaining capital or productive capacity intact but maintaining its income in the sense of its gross revenue or turnover.

in that way, we must divide the gross-revenue we receive from the goods or services produced with the aid of durable assets into quasi-rent and complementary costs. The problem then becomes one of splitting up quasi-rent into income and depreciation.

In principle three different ways to solve this problem are indicated by the author viz. subjective-depreciation, market-depreciation, and internal rate-depreciation.

Subjective-depreciation considers as income the interest on the sub-jective value of the machine, subjective value being the discounted sum of all quasi-rents plus scrap-value. The rest of the quasi-rent is depreciation.

Market-depreciation considers the decrease in market-value of the asset as depreciation; the rest is income.

Internal rate-depreciation is based on the idea that the enterprise in each period should earn income at an internal rate of return. Here too income is given and depreciation is a residual, but the internal rate is selected in such a way that depreciation just equals the original costs. In contrast with market-depreciation, subjective depreciation as well as internal rate-depreciation are of an arbitrary character depending as they do on expectations.

It is clear that these methods of depreciation are essentially different ways of dividing quasi-rent into income and depreciation. In practice, however, this division is not often considered as a criterion for selecting a depreciation method. So called arbitrary methods such as the straight line- and declining balance-methods are used, but their effect on the distribution of the quasi-rent of the machine is usually not an important factor in the decision.

Given an even-age distribution of machines, all of the depreciation techniques will give the same results in each period for the stock of machines as a whole, though not for each machine separately. From the sum-total of all machines every year one or more but always the same number must be replaced. Whatever method is used every year we must have an amount to replace the number of machines exhausted, and the even-age distribution of the machines makes total depreciation independent of the pattern applied to each machine.

If there is no growth, an even- or stable-age distribution is one in which the number of available machine-years in stock is just one-half of those available if all the machines were totally new. This proportion differs, however, as the rate of growth (and the life-time of the machines) changes.

An interesting part of Professor Edward's contribution consists in the analysis of the influence of various rates of growth in various other directions, as for instance the ratio of depreciation to the cost of running physical replacement and the ratio of the first to the cost of new acquisitions.

ʻThese concepts help him to predict the extent to which firms with different constant rates of growth will be able to finance their total machine acquisitions as well as their replacements (variously defined) out of internally generated funds. This is demonstrated by several tables and, more generally, in the mathematical appendix.

ʻThe influence of deviations of the depreciation techniques allowable for tax purposes from the internally consistent methods is then discussed. These deviations exert their influence in various way as for instance on the rate of profit, the rate of growth, and on the choice of machine-types.

Finally, the author considers the adjustment of depreciation charges for price changes. An important though often forgotten distinction is drawn between the case in which the prices of depreciable assets move in harmony with the general price-level and where they move differently. It is worthwhile to compare this consideration with those of Professor Lewis in the first chapter.

ʻRegarding the first case Professor Edwards rejects "the idea that depreciation should supply sufficient funds to finance the ultimate replacement of that machine." This idea, he claims, is based on the assumption that depreciation funds are held in the form of cash until the machine is actually replaced, an assumption that is not realistic. It is more likely that such funds will be invested in assets which, like the machines, rise in price in proportion to the price-level. Therefore, not by ultimate replacement, but by current cost depreciation the firm will be placed in a position that enables it to maintain its real capital. There is, in our opinion, still another aspect to this question. If we look at the whole complex of capital goods of a business and not at a single machine or machine-group we will always find a diversity of life-time of those goods. That means, that in existing firms and in particular in large companies there will always be a tendency to an even-age distribution. The funds to replace the old machines are furnished then by the actual current cost depreciation. In that case we do not need the condition that the price of the depreciable assets move in harmony with the general price level. Every year the same amount of assets is to be renewed. The money needed therefore is furnished by depreciation at current costs. The problem of ultimate replacement does no longer exist in that case.

Whereas in the first case there is no difference between current cost and price-level depreciation because both sets of prices are moving in the same way, in the second case they seem to be alternatives. The author's opinion, however, is that the two kinds of adjustment are complementary. The current cost of assets indicates depreciation charges (and thus affects operating profit) and the current value of unused assets. The price level adjustment divides the capital gains (or losses) so disclosed into real and fictional elements and is also necessary to compare the operating profits and capital gains of different periods.

Though in Professor Edwards' contribution it was inevitable to pay attention to taxation allowances regarding depreciation, as they influence the ability of the firm to finance replacement out of its internally-generated funds, nevertheless it seemed worthwhile to dedicate a separate chapter to the problem arising from the way the system of taxation regards depreciation charges as costs subtractable from business profits. The third chapter contributed by Professor Walker deals with that side of the depreciation problem.

As a matter of fact, there is a real chance that both chapters are overlapping one another on this point. The different ways in which both authors have approached their problem, however, makes this overlapping more an advantage than a drawback.

Professor Walker occupies himself principally with taxes on nett income. Though he based his reflections on the tax-system of the United Kingdom with whose problems he is most familiar, his contribution is worthwhile also to scholars of most other countries since they largely meet with similar tax laws and, consequently, similar problems.

The author underlines the necessity for the government to give rules in how far expenditures are subtractable costs of production. In his opinion the distinction often made between current and capital expenditure does not seem important.

Nevertheless, it has taken much time in many countries before depreciation was considered as a cost of production for tax purposes. The effects of discrepancies between the permissible depreciation for tax purposes and the depreciation the tax-payer thinks necessary and those of accelerated depreciation are discussed and demonstrated by simple examples and easily readable tables. The influence of rising prices with different systems of calculating depreciation allowances are dealt with at great length.

In the last chapter the results are summarized of a study made by two Dutch institutions, the "Nederlandsch Economisch Instituut" at Rotterdam and the "Bedrijfseconomisch Instituut" of the State University of Groningen. The study was done by R. Iwema and A. Tabak of the "Nederlandsch Economisch Instituut" and J. L. Bouma of the "Bedrijfseconomisch Instituut" under direction of Professors L. M. Koyck and L. H. Klaassen of the Netherlands School of Economics and myself of the State University of Groningen.

Based on a study in the Dutch language by myself, first a critical survey is given of a number of theoretical approaches of the depreciation problem. They are confronted with my own one that may be considered as indicative of the way the problem is often treated in Dutch literature. An objection against the goodwill theory defended by many authors is that profits cannot be imputed to single means of production. They are always the result of the combination of more sorts of means of production. Moreover, even if it were possible to do so, the service life of the machine is taken too long, viz. so long that the whole profit of the business will be consumed before the means of production is put out of use. The business would have had more profit if it had replaced the old machine when the replacement costs of its produce, i.e. the costs by producing with a new machine, were equal to the complementary costs by using the old one.

In a synthesis it is tried to bring Taylor and Hotellings views in line with my own, notwithstanding the fact that these authors had concentrated their attention primarily on the moment of replacement, whereas I had stressed more the problem of the evaluation of the nett services rendered by the machine.

More important perhaps for the practice of business life than these theoretical considerations were the findings on entrepreneurial behaviour with regard to replacement. One of the most remarkable statements is without doubt that there is often a time-lag between scrapping and re-investment, so that it can be said that there is no definite replacement of assets that are worn out. There are moments of putting machines out of use and other moments of buying new ones. In doing so the firm reaches a certain elasticity in its production capacity and a possibility to adapt it to fluctuating business conditions. From this point of view this behaviour can be considered rational.

It is clear, however, that this time-lag between scrapping and re-investment can only occur if there is a pretty large number of machines lasting the same work, so that a more or less even age distribution of durable goods is reached. In the case of one or a little number of durable goods this policy cannot be followed.

Though this book cannot be considered to give a final solution of the problems concerning depreciation and replacement policy it is hoped that it may outline the different aspects of these problems and the different ways in which they are tackled. The editor hopes that it will be a stimulus to those who contributed to this volume as well as to others for further analysis. Then the goal of the series will be reached.

He wishes to thank all those who helped in composing this book. Apart from the authors, he would like to mention Mr. H. Willems who made very fruitful remarks as to chapter IV and Mr. W. A. Nijenhuis who composed the index.

Last but not least he feels grateful to the "Nederlandse Organisatie voor Zuiver Wetenschappelijk Onderzoek", which made a grant to do some research work on entrepreneurial behaviour in this field.

CHAPTER 1

DEPRECIATION AND OBSOLESCENCE
AS FACTORS IN COSTING*

W. ARTHUR LEWIS

University of Manchester, England

I. THE MEANING OF DEPRECIATION

The value of an asset usually changes with time. In some cases the asset becomes more valuable as time passes. For example, wine matures with time. Favoured sites in a rapidly growing city become more valuable as population grows. The assets used to produce a new commodity become more valuable as the commodity becomes more popular. And most assets increase in monetary value in an inflationary situation, though the "real" value of some, corrected for changes in the general price level, may actually be falling.

Inflation apart, most physical assets decline in value after a time, even though there may be passages in their life when they are appreciating in value. In some cases the decline in value can be prevented by continually reinvesting in the asset, to replace what is lost. For example, the farmer maintains the value of his land by investing fertilisers, and by spending money on soil practices which conserve fertility. Buildings and bridges can be kept going for a very long time in the same way. Even some machinery can be kept going; one can still find in some factories steam boilers which were first installed eighty years ago. But most man-made assets eventually give out altogether.

Depreciation measures the amount by which the value of an asset falls through time. This depends partly on how well the asset is maintained—whether the buildings are painted regularly, whether leaks in the boiler are fixed at once, whether broken parts are immediately replaced, and so on. The cost of maintenance and repair is not usually included in depreciation. The cost of keeping the asset "in a good state of repair" is usually calculated separately, and treated as an

---

* I am indebted to Professors Robert Eisner, A. D. Scott, and David Solomons for helpful comments on the manuscript.

operating expense on the same footing as wages and raw materials. Depreciation therefore measures the extent to which the value of the asset has deteriorated although it is being kept in a good state of repair. What constitutes a good state of repair is a matter for the judgement of the management, or, if the management wishes to sell the asset, it is a matter for the consensus of the second-hand market.

There are half-a-dozen reasons why an asset may deteriorate in value even though it is well maintained. First, portions of the asset may be consumed in process of use; for example, rubber tyres are worn away. Secondly, the physical yield of the asset may decline; for example the physical output of most radio valves declines with use. Thirdly the asset may become more costly to operate, either because it uses more labour or materials per unit of output, or because it breaks down more often and maintenance costs rise. Fourthly, a new machine may be invented which is cheaper than the existing machine ever was, whether because it is cheaper to build and instal, or because it requires a smaller input of labour or materials per unit of output. And fifthly, the asset may lose value because new products come on the market which the buyers prefer.

We can group these reasons so as to distinguish between depreciation and obsolescence. Obsolescence is that loss in value which is due to the competition of new inventions. It corresponds therefore to the fourth and fifth reasons listed above. Depreciation is all that other loss in value which would occur even if the asset did not have to compete with new inventions.

Depreciation itself may further be analysed according to whether it occurs only in so far as the asset is used, or whether the asset falls in value whether it is used or not. This distinction is important to economic analysis because economic analysis is concerned with the effect of decisions to produce. If the asset will deteriorate in value equally whether it is used or not, the deterioration in value does not enter into the decision whether to use or not, except in so far as it affects the prior decision whether to retain the asset or to dispose of it.

In what follows we shall make no use of the distinction between depreciation and obsolescence. We shall use the term "depreciation" to cover all deterioration in the value of an asset which is maintained in good repair, whether this deterioration is due to the emergence of competing assets or products or not. The distinction we shall be using is between deterioration which is due to use and deterioration which is independent of use.

II. THE PURPOSE OF MEASURING DEPRECIATION

All the problems of measuring depreciation which this chapter discusses arise out of the fact that "the value of an asset" is not a unique quantity. An asset has different values for different purposes, so we get different amounts of depreciation according to the purpose of our measurement. In practice, depreciation is measured for four different purposes, which may well yield answers.

(A) In order to compute tax liability.
(B) In order to decide for how much to buy or sell the asset in the second-hand market.
(C) In order to decide what part of the gross profit to distribute to the owners of the business.
(D) In order to decide how much to charge the consumers of the product.

A. TAX LIABILITY

Within the framework of legislation, the income tax authorities make their own rules for the calculation of depreciation. These rules are based more or less upon current business practice, but they do not coincide with business practice. This subject is discussed in a separate chapter by Professor David Walker.

B. VALUATION OF ASSETS

The second occasion for measuring depreciation is when the asset is valued for purchase or sale in the second-hand market. The difference between the original cost of the asset and its present value measures the amount of depreciation which has occurred.

In estimating present value the original cost of the asset is irrelevant. What the asset is worth now depends on its earning power in the future, irrespective of what price may have been paid for it in the past, or of how much it may have earned in the past. In formal terms its present value is the sum of expected future benefits (including final scrap value) discounted at the appropriate rate of interest. This is a subjective rather than an objective quantity, since it depends upon guessing what the future benefits may be, and on choosing a rate of interest appropriate to this type of investment.

There are several obstacles in the way of giving quantitative expression to this concept of value.

First the future life of the asset is not predictable, even if one

assumes that potential yield in each year is known. This is because
the asset may cease to exist for unpredictable physical reasons, no
less than for economic reasons. If one buys one hundred of a particular
type of asset, and subjects each item to roughly the same use, it is
improbable that all hundred will give out at the same time. Some will
break down immediately, some will last almost indefinitely, and the
life span of the rest will be distributed, with a marked bunching around
one particular length of life. In other words, the life table of a hundred
machines somewhat resembles the life table of a hundred men. Engi-
neers try to meet this situation by calculating mortality tables for
each important class of asset. Thus, the best one can do in valuing
an asset is to assume that it will have an average life, in the sense
determined by such a table, while recognising that actual life may be
greater or less.

Secondly, there is not one potential pattern of yield, but several.
If the asset is used heavily at the beginning, operating costs may be
higher and yield may be lower in later years than if the asset is used
less intensively at the start. Length of physical or of economic life may
also be affected. Hence the problem is not simply to discount back
future benefits, but also to pick that pattern of use which yields the
highest discounted value. The problem raises no theoretical difficulty,
but in practice it depends on making an enormous number of inter-
related guesses.

Thirdly, much of the guessing about future yields is so uncertain
as hardly to be worth while. One way out is to assume that future
yields will be the same as current or as past yields. Another way out
is to assume that yields in later years will be so small as not to be worth
taking into account. Either way the calculation is hazardous.

Fourthly and most fundamentally, for a great many assets the
concept of the net yield of the particular asset is meaningless, because
this asset collaborates with so many other assets in producing the final
product that it is not feasible to isolate even its marginal contribution.
What is the marginal contribution of the office chairs, or of the parking
lot for staff cars, or of the boiler which raises steam for the works?
One can think of the assets as a whole yielding a stream of future
benefits which can be estimated, but for many individual assets it is
useless to ask what the future stream of benefits will be.

Given these objections, the most practicable way to value some
assets is not to estimate their future yields but to compare them with
the cost of replacing them new. If an asset would not be worth replacing

if it were suddenly destroyed, this escape is barred. But if the asset would be worth replacing, then its present value is equal to the cost of replacing it minus some allowance for expired service, minus also some allowance for the superior efficiency of the replacement (more product, or more attractive product, or lower operating costs). Here too some guesswork is involved, but it is not so formidable as is the guessing of the stream of future yields.

Whichever method of valuation one uses, a wide margin may exist between the value of an asset to its owner and the value to the most favourable prospective purchaser. We shall call the value to the owner "the inside value", and the price which the asset would fetch second-hand "the scrap value". The inside value depends upon the use the owner is making of the asset, and on the discount rate be uses. The prospective buyer may take a very different view of the future, or may work with a different discount rate. He may also not have such good opportunities open to him for using the asset profitably, so that the use to which he would put it may be quite different. Even if his calculations were exactly the same as those of the owner, he would still have to take into account the cost of removing the asset and installing it in a new place, plus any commissions payable to the brokers in the second-hand market.

The theory of asset replacement is treated in another chapter. All we need to note at this point is the fact that when the purpose of valuation is to decide whether to scrap the asset or to keep it, the relevant calculations have to be made not in terms of the sum originally paid for the asset, but in terms of present costs and future yields.

In this context, as in any other, depreciation measures the extent to which the value of an asset has deteriorated in the course of a year (or other time period). If we seek to quantify it, however, we get two different answers, one showing the deterioration in scrap value, and the other showing the deterioration in inside value to the owner.

C. CALCULATING NET PROFIT

The third purpose of calculating depreciation is to prevent the asset's owner from consuming his capital; i.e., to ensure that he will have in a depreciation fund at the end of the asset's life a sum equal to the amount originally paid for the asset. The law imposes this requirement upon most public companies ("dividends must not be paid out of capital") though not on all. And in any case "good business practice" requires the owners of a business to set aside from their gross profits what is required to maintain their capital intact, before deciding what part of the profits may be currently consumed.

But what is meant by maintaining capital intact? This concept has no unique meaning.

(1) In current accounting practice the meaning is usually to maintain constant the original money value of the investment; and this is also most often the meaning sanctioned by law. This means that there should be deducted from gross profits during the life of the asset sums which will amount at the end of the asset's life to its original cost. We leave for later discussion the question how these sums should be spread over the asset's life, noting for the moment only that, when dealing with fixed assets (as distinct from liquid assets) current practice takes no account of year to year changes either in the scrap value or in the owner's inside value. For the moment we confine ourselves to discussing how much depreciation should be set aside in total over the whole life of the asset.

(2) Suppose that the price of the particular asset is unchanged, and that the general price level is unchanged, but that a new model of the asset is invented which costs the same but yields a much greater output. Then when the asset is replaced by the new model, the owner's capital is unchanged in general purchasing power, and in relation to other people's capital. But the real productive capacity of his firm is increased, and therefore in terms of real output his real capital is increased. Here we meet the distinction between maintaining real capital intact in terms of general purchasing power, and maintaining real capital constant in terms of the real productive capacity of a particular firm. This distinction becomes important and troublesome when the asset's price moves in different proportions from the general price level.

(3) If the price of the asset changes proportionately with changes in the general price level, the problem is as simple as in the case where all prices are unchanged. The competitive price of the product rises, and so does gross profit. Hence if depreciation is charged at replacement cost enough can be saved in the fund to replace the asset without bringing fresh finance into the business; while at the same time real consumption can be maintained nearly intact (intact if the price rise occurs immediately after the asset has been bought; but if it occurs later in the life of the asset, heavy additions need to be made to the depreciation fund in later years to make up for the deficiency in earlier years, unless the fund has been invested in assets whose value has risen

correspondingly, e.g., in equities, in real estate or in inventories). The distinction between maintaining intact the individual's command over goods in general and maintaining intact the capital in terms of real output capacity does not arise.

(4) Now suppose that at the end of the asset's life the cost of replacing it has risen, though the general level of prices remains the same as when the investment was first made. If the depreciation fund contains only the original money cost, the sum saved thereby will not be sufficient to replace the asset. Should the amount set aside for depreciation therefore rise as the cost of replacing the asset rises, in order to maintain *real* capital intact? In a competitive market the price of the product will have risen, because the cost of maintaining or expanding output has risen, and owners of assets purchased at the old price will have been earning higher gross profits out of which they could set aside larger amounts for depreciation, while maintaining consumption nearly intact. On the other hand, since the average level of prices is assumed to be constant, the relative position of the owners of these assets vis-a-vis other members of the community remains unchanged in real terms if depreciation is set aside equal only to original cost. The extra profit is a windfall gain, which can be consumed while maintaining real capital (in the sense of command over goods and services in general) intact.

Conversely, one may assume that the money cost of replacing the particular asset falls, while the general price level remains unchanged. Owners will then in competitive conditions earn lower gross profits, and be able to replace the asset with smaller sums of money, while maintaining consumption more or less. If they do this, however, their capital will fall relatively to other people's, and they will not be maintaining it in terms of command over goods and services in general.

Here we see the conflict between depreciation for the purpose of price formation in competitive conditions and depreciation for the purpose of maintaining intact the real spending power of owners. From the moment the asset's price changes, the asset-cost which will enter into competitive pricing is the cost of replacing the asset; but the asset-cost which is relevant to maintaining the individual's capital intact is the original cost of the old asset, adjusted only for changes in the general price level. There is the same conflict between price formation in competitive conditions and price fixing in monopolistic or other conditions where pricing is based on what is considered fair; i.e. on recompensing producers in accordance with their past expenditure; in competition the product's price will be based on new asset cost, whereas in "fair" pricing the product's price will be based on old asset cost.

This distinction between depreciation to maintain general command over goods and services intact, and depreciation to maintain productive capacity of the firm intact, is important whenever the price of the asset moves differently from the general price level. Some writers claim to be able to prove that in these cases it is more "scientific" to base depreciation upon the asset price than upon the general price level; but this is not so. Their claim is based upon a confusion between depreciation for price determination and depreciation for maintaining capital intact. If the firm wishes to maximise its profits, it should relate the price of its product to marginal cost. Then, insofar as the price of the asset is reflected in marginal cost, marginal cost will rise as the asset's price rises, even if the general price level is constant. It can also be shown, on the general assumptions of welfare economics, that the price of the product should rise as the replacement cost of the asset rises.

However, this does not throw light upon depreciation for maintaining capital intact. Given the price rise, the asset's owner will make a windfall profit, which he may legitimately consume if he so desires; it cannot be proved that he ought to save it by writing it off as depreciation. Conversely, if the asset's price falls, he should lower his prices, and will make a windfall loss. If he decides to reduce depreciation accordingly he will be able to maintain his consumption intact temporarily and his productive capacity intact permanently, but he will end up a poorer man in comparison with other citizens, since his capital will not be maintaned intact in terms of general purchasing power; and his consumption will therefore also in due course fall. Very few of the accountants who recommend writing up depreciation when the asset's price rises, would also recommend writing it down when the asset's price falls relatively to the general price level; indeed, in the case of public companies, the law would not allow them to do so, since this would be "paying dividends out of capital".

The conclusion seems to be that the asset price is relevant to price determination, but it is the general price level which is relevant to maintaining capital intact, in the usual meaning of this phrase. Thus, when one speaks of maintaining capital intact it must be clear whether one means

(i) in terms of money or in real terms, so that the original money investment is multiplied by an index number of prices; and

(ii) if in real terms, whether one means to maintain the owner's capital intact in terms of real output capacity of the particular asset, or in terms of general command over goods and services. If the former, the relevant price index is the price index of the particular asset; if the latter, it is an index of the general purchasing power of money.

D. PRICE POLICY

A firm cannot always make its own price. If it has to accept the market price, or to follow a lead given by some other firm, it does not need to measure depreciation for the purpose of setting prices, thought it will need some measure of depreciation for other purposes, such as for taxation, or as a guide to dividend policy, or as an element in deciding how much to produce. A firm can set its own price only if its market is less than perfectly competitive, and if, given market imperfection, it has some freedom of manoeuvre vis-a-vis rival firms.

In a competitive market price is set by marginal cost, which is the difference made to total cost by producing one unit of output more or less (though the concept of a "unit" of output raises difficulties to which we shall revert later). Given the market price, each firm finds it profitable to produce the quantity whose marginal cost equals price; and given the demand, the market process determines a price such that the marginal firm finds it just worth while to remain in the particular line of business.

Now the element of depreciation which enters into marginal cost is "user cost", which may be defined briefly for the present as the difference made to the value of the firm's assets by the decision to produce one unit of output more or less. If the firm has surplus capacity, (i.e. spare, excess, or idle capacity) and if the value of assets does not vary with use, user cost may be (but is not necessarily) zero. Whereas, if the firm is working at full capacity, the expansion of output requires the installation of extra capacity, and so user cost may be very high. In neither case is user cost a function of the original cost of the assets already installed, unless it happens in the full capacity case that the cost per unit of output of installing new assets is the same as the cost per unit of output of existing assets.

In a non-competitive market, price is not tied in the same way to marginal cost, and so the depreciation concept used in price determination is not necessarily user cost. Usually marginal cost sets a lower limit to price, but even this is not necessarily so. Sometimes a firm will sell below marginal cost, temporarily, as for example in order to retain important customers during an economic blizzard, or permanently, in order to promote the sale of some other product which yields a more than compensating profit, or, as in the case of some public utilities, because law or custom requires that certain unremunerative services be maintained. More usually the firm will charge something more than marginal cost, according to the quantities it thinks it can sell at different prices. In many cases, if market conditions permit, the firm will set prices at what it considers to be a "fair" level, fair both to itself and to its customers.

The concept of a "fair" price plays a considerable part in price determination in practice. It is applied to all public utilities regulated by law or by public commission. It is used also by many other firms, whether on moral grounds, or whether because they are afraid to attract hostile comment or public investigation or regulation if they charge more, or whether because they are afraid that if they charge more than is fair, new competition will be stimulated.

Almost invariably the depreciation concept which is used in determining a "fair" price is not user cost, but depreciation for the purpose of maintaining capital intact, using one of the several meanings of this term. This depreciation is therefore measured with reference to the past cost of assets already installed (usually not even corrected by a price index), and bears no relation to user cost, which is measured with reference to the future. The two concepts may by accident coincide. But they will certainly coincide only in the special case where there is no surplus capacity, and the price of assets is unchanged, and output is directly proportional to input (that is, there are no economies or diseconomies of scale). Given all three of these conditions, or some accidentally appropriate combination, depreciation for calculating marginal cost and depreciation for determining a "fair" price will coincide; but otherwise, and more usually, the concepts yield different results.

Many economists have argued that user cost, as calculated for marginal cost, is the only legitimate concept to use for price determination, but the argument cannot be sustained without exceeding the confines of economic analysis. It rests on the proposition that the national output is maximised if the output of each commodity is such as would obtain if every commodity were sold at a price equal to its marginal cost; provided that at the same time the consumers of each commodity derive from it, in total, satisfactions which they value more highly than its total escapable cost. This proposition is valid, given the usual restrictive assumptions of welfare economics. On the other hand, maximising the national output is not the only objective of social policy. Many people also consider that social policy should be fair, and if a policy which would maximise the national output would also be unfair, economics cannot prove that output maximisation is more important than the fairness.

It is not even possible to deduce from the conditions for output maximisation that price should equal marginal cost. There are two conditions, not one; a marginal condition and a total condition. There is no more reason to translate the marginal condition into "price must equal marginal cost" than there is to translate the total condition into "total revenue must equal total escapable cost". The very act of translation into price terms moves us on to a different plane, where we have to think in terms of what is a practicable method of pricing, and have also to remember that the act of levying a price serves not only to determine outputs, but also to redistribute incomes from one set of persons to another. If we nevertheless perform this illegitimate act of translation, a better rendering would seem to be "marginal price must equal marginal cost *and* the total paid must equal total escapable cost". Thus in those cases where, because of an indivisible item of cost, average cost exceeds marginal cost, the right policy would be not to charge marginal cost, but to use some such system as the two-part tariff, the block quantity discount tariff, or some other form of price discrimination, with the object both of having a marginal price equal to marginal cost and also of raising in total a sum equal to total cost.

This discussion, however, has taken us beyond the limits of our present subject matter. This chapter is not concerned with determining what the relation between price and cost ought to be, or even with establishing what the relation is currently in the real world. Our assignment is simply to define depreciation for the purpose of calculating cost. The definition has yielded two different concepts: depreciation as measured for cost where cost relates to past expenditure, and depreciation as measured for user cost. The two succeeding sections examine these concepts in greater detail.

III. DEPRECIATION AS CAPITAL MAINTENANCE

In this section we are concerned with the depreciation concept which springs from the desire to maintain capital intact. When we considered this concept in the preceding section we confined ourselves to discussing what sum should be raised in total over the whole life of an asset; now we address ourselves to the question how this sum should be spread over the life from one year to another. In this context life must be interpreted in accordance with average expectations, such as are yielded by the engineer's asset mortality tables.

The most common practice in the United States of America has been to charge a constant sum each year as depreciation. Usually this sum is the total required divided by the number of years over which it is to be levied. Thus, if an asset is expected to have a life of ten years, and a scrap value at the end of the tenth year of £100, and if the total sum required to be maintained is £1,500, then £1,400 must be raised in depreciation over ten years, and therefore £140 will be written off each year. This is known as the "straight line" method of depreciation.

Since the sums which are written off each year can be invested inside or outside the business, they are capable of earning interest. If this interest is credited to the depreciation fund, the total sum available at the end of ten years will be more than £1,400. Thus, if compound interest is credited at 5 per cent annum, the total sum will be not £1,400 but £1,761. Accordingly it has been argued that the correct sum to raise annually is that sum which reinvested annually at compound interest will aggregate to the required total. This is known as the "sinking fund" method. In this case the annual write-off would be £111.3, which invested annually at compound interest will be worth £1,400 at the end of ten years. Obviously the validity of the argument depends upon whether the depreciation quotas actually are reinvested profitably, or are invested at a loss (e.g. a capital loss), or are held in liquid form. It also depends on whether one thinks it matters whether interest earned on depreciation quotas goes into the depreciation fund or into general revenue. As we shall see in the next section, if we assume perfect competition, full capacity and static conditions, the depreciation which enters into price will have to take account of the compound interest element. But depreciation for price determination and depreciation for maintaining capital intact are two different concepts. If the sole purpose of writing depreciation off in the books is to maintain capital intact, and not to determine prices or to value assets for scrapping, it does not seem to matter much into what fund one pays the interest earned on depreciation quotas.

It is convenient to approach the question how depreciation should be spread over the life of an asset from one year to another by considering possible disadvantages of writing-off the same amount in each year. These may be listed as follows:

(A) The fact that the price of the asset may change during its lifetime.

(B) The fact that the earning power of the asset fluctuates.

(C) The fact that the value of the asset does not decline by a constant amount each year.

(D) The fact that depreciation measured in this way may mislead those who determine the firm's price and output policy.

A. PRICE CHANGES

We have seen that if capital is to be maintained in a real sense, and not just in terms of money, accumulated depreciation must equal the original cost of the asset multiplied by the appropriate price index number—what is appropriate depending upon whether what we are maintaining intact is the firm's productive power or the value of the shareholders' capital in general purchasing power. It follows that writing off a constant sum each year is not consistent with maintaining real capital if prices change.

If one determines that total depreciation must equal original cost multiplied by an index number, the write-off from year to year may assume a queer pattern. For example, if the price index number halves when the depreciation fund already contains two-thirds of the original cost, depreciation in the remaining years is negative. Or, if the price index number doubles when three quarters of its life has already expired, the sum to be levied as depreciation in the remaining quarter of life becomes enormous. If the depreciation fund has been invested in assets which have also appreciated in value, the extra depreciation can be met simply by bringing the capital appreciation into the books; but in other cases it has to be written off against profits. Of course, if the price of the asset doubles, gross profit will probably also sharply increase, so that it is possible both to keep net profit constant and also to levy more as depreciation; but in extreme cases it may be impossible to make up the whole deficit without sharply reducing net profits in the last years of life, or even showing a net loss. This is one reason why accountants and income tax authorities are reluctant to give up basing depreciation on original money cost only, and shift to index number calculations only in periods of sharp and persistent inflation. Needless to say, this results in evading one set of problems at the cost of being entangled in another—the fact that the depreciation fund is not serving to maintain real capital intact.

B. FLUCTUATIONS IN EARNINGS

Insofar as the purpose of measuring depreciation is to withhold from dividend distribution over the whole life of an asset a sum equal to its cost, there is no particular reason to withhold the same sum in each year; the only guide is convenience. If one were trying to measure by how much the assets had declined in value during the year, there might be a unique answer, but this is not the purpose of those who write off a constant sum in each year, and the sum they write off is not based on measuring the decline in asset values, whether conceived as scrap or as inside values. Again, if one were measuring user cost for price determination the answer might be unique, but this is neither the purpose of the constant write-off, nor the solution it yields. One is therefore left with no guide but convenience.

Now, if the yield of the asset fluctuates sharply, it may be most convenient to write off very large sums during profitable years, and very small sums during lean years. This introduces greater stability into dividend distributions, and into consumption. Indeed, from the national point of view, it would help to mitigate cyclical fluctuations if firms would distribute rather less during booms and rather more during recessions. This would come about automatically if the rule of thumb for calculating depreciation were to relate the annual sum to the gross profit ratio. (If replacement policy followed the same principle the effect on the economy would be destabilising; but we are here discussing not replacement but depreciation.)

Many accountants would be unhappy if the depreciation write-off fluctuated with earnings, since this might open the door to abuses by business managements. So long as the accountant has a rule of thumb, the amount written off in depreciation is not open to managerial manipulation; whereas, if a discretionary element enters, the result may be that the errors are in the direction of writing off too little. On the other hand, there are already some discretionary elements, under various guises. Directors do have special write-offs at convenient moments, and they do create special reserves from time to time. Accountants continue to base their calculations on original cost, while directors take account of inflation by creating special funds, not on a constant annual basis, but as is convenient from time to time, having regard to profit fluctuations from year to year.

Indeed, nowadays when in most prosperous businesses dividends are but a small proportion of gross profits, and are kept more or less stable irrespective of annual fluctuations in profits, it does not matter much whether dividends are kept stable by putting a fluctuating amount into the dividend reserve fund, or by putting a fluctuating amount into the depreciation fund. The point has significance only in those other firms which live from hand to mouth, and in these firms it may well be the best practical policy for those concerned to pretend that it would be scientifically incorrect to reduce depreciation quotas in years of low profits. Otherwise it becomes harder to ensure that dividends are not paid out of capital.

C. Asset Valuation

If a constant amount is written off in each year the value of the asset as shown in the books will bear no relationship to its real value. The value of most assets deteriorates very sharply in the early years of life, and more slowly thereafter. The main reason for this is that the early years are the most productive, and the most trouble-free. Hence net yield is highest in the first four or five years, and may then fall rapidly. In addition, the scrap value of an asset falls as soon sa it is bought and installed, since, even if it is sold immediately in perfect condition, the cost of selling it and of dismantling any fixtures in which it has been embodied, has to be substracted from the price which it could fetch if it were in the maker's warehouse.

Therefore, still sticking to rule of thumb methods, if one wanted the book value of an asset to be a truer reflection of its real value (whether its scrap or its inside value) the "diminishing balance" method of depreciation, which is widely used in the United Kingdom, would be superior both to the straight-line method, which has been general in the U.S.A., and also to the sinking-fund method, which is the favourite of the mathematically inclined. The diminishing balance method writes off each year not a constant amount but a constant proportion of the amount still standing in the books. For example, if one wants to write an asset down to 5 per cent of its value in 12 years (i.e. allowing 5 per cent for ultimate scrap value), one should write off 22.1 per cent of the amount on the books at the end of each year (ignoring interest on the depreciation fund). Thus by the end of three years (the first 25 per cent of its life) the asset has been written down by 53 per cent of its value; and at the end of six years (the first half of its life) it has been written down by 77 per cent. This is much more realistic than it would be to value the asset at three-quarters of its original price when it was three years old.

It may be objected that nobody expects the balance sheet value of a fixed asset to be its true value; neither its scrap value nor its inside value is relevant since the asset is not normally for sale. If any question of selling it arises, a special investigation can be made for the purpose of valuation. Indeed, to emphasise that depreciation in this context is not linked to the value of the assets, some writers refer to the writing off as "amortisation", a term which more properly applies to the provision made for repaying a loan.

The same answer can be made to the comment that if the asset appears in the books at a false valuation, the owner will be misled in deciding whether or not to replace it by a new asset; delaying replacement if book value is too high, and replacing too soon if book value is too low. It is often alleged that some businessmen base their replacement decisions on the book value of their assets, so that accelerated depreciation encourages early replacement, while straight-line depreciation causes assets to be replaced less frequently. As we saw in the preceding section, replacement policy should be based upon the discounted future revenue of the asset, which we have been calling its "inside value", so decisions made on any other basis are erroneous. But since replacement happens only once in an asset's lifetime, a special investigation can be made for the purpose when necessary.

The argument that the books need not show the real value of the assets (in the sense of discounted future yield) is founded upon the proposition that the sole purpose of writing off depreciation annually is to keep funds within the business. Even on this basis, however, the constant annual write-off can be criticised. In the first place, if the assets lose half their value within the first quarter of their life, but only a quarter of their value is retained within the business, then capital has not been maintained intact. The gap will be closed in the later years of life by retaining funds in excess of real depreciation. This leads to the second criticism, which is that it may be dangerous to fix for depreciation a time-pattern which differs from the yield pattern of the asset. If the asset is going to yield disproportionately in its earlier years, it is unsafe to distribute dividends disproportionately in earlier years, relying on cutting dividends in later years even more than is necessary because of high depreciation levies which have been postponed. It seems both safer and more convenient to write down substantially when profits are substantial, and to leave little to be written off in later years when profits are low. Such a policy has also the advantage, shared by the policy of allowing depreciation to fluctuate with fluctuations in yields, that it makes more stable the sum shown as net profit in each year, and so helps to stabilise personal consumption and saving.

Some businessmen are disposed to go even further: to write off the asset not over the whole course of its life, but completely within four or five years, or even in extreme cases completely within the first year. The main argument for this is caution. Since what an asset will yield after five years from now is even less predictable than what it will earn in the next five years, it is thought prudent to provide for the possibility that it may be completely out-moded in five years. At the same time, the early write-off forces the owner to restrain his consumption until he has got his money back, after which it is safe to enjoy his profits to the full. Depreciation could not be calculated on this basis for determining prices in a market where the firm had several rivals, since the business would then go mainly to the firms which had already written down their assets and no firm would get business in the first year of its assets' life. But the purpose of accelerated depreciation is to influence not price policy but dividend policy. Quite different calculations are made for determining prices.

The difference which the method of depreciation makes to the amount written off annually is much greater in the case of a single asset than it is when all the assets of the firm are considered together, some of which are nearer the end of their life than others. There is a limiting case where the method makes no difference to aggregate depreciation. This is the case where (i) the stock of capital is constant, with asset prices unchanged, and (ii) the average age of the assets is constant because all assets are of the same type, and one is scrapped and replaced every year. On these assumptions, the total sum levied in depreciation in each year is the same whether one uses the straight line method, or the diminishing balance method, or whether one writes off each asset completely in the first year. This limiting case, however, must be very rare, if it is ever found, and the slightest relaxation of the assumptions will alter the result. For example, if gross investment is assumed not to be constant, but to be growing by a constant percentage each year, then the stock of capital ceases to be constant, and grows in each year. Methods involving an earlier write-off then bring in more depreciation in each year than does the straight line method. Adoption of these methods then also affects the financial position of the firm. For example, on these assumptions less income tax is payable so long as the business continues to grow, provided that the tax authorities permit use of the diminishing balance or other accelerated methods than if they insist on the straight line method. Also the business saves more, and needs less external money to finance its expansion.

In most firms the stock of capital is constant most of the time, since expansion takes place in spurts and not at a regular rate each year. The average age, however, is not constant, since a lot of equipment is installed together at one time, and average age increases every year until it is replaced. In these circumstances the earlier write-off methods make a substantial difference to the time-pattern of aggregate depreciation. The firm also accumulates funds which it will not need for some time, since most of the cost of plant is written off long before it falls due for replacement. These funds can safely be used for expanding the business.

The proposition that more is saved with accelerated depreciation so long as the business is expanding but not otherwise is easily illustrated by an arithmetical example. Take a new business just coming into existence, and assume that it invests £100 a year gross. Assume that the assets are identical, that they have a life of four years, and that their price is constant. Then the stock of capital will increase every year for four years, after which it will be constant, the gross investment of subsequent years serving merely to replace the asset scrapped in each year. If the firm uses the straight line method, depreciation in successive years will be

      25   50   75   100   100   100   . . .

and the new money brought into the business will be

    100   75   50   25   0   0   . . .

But if the firm writes each asset off completely in its first year, depreciation will be

    100   100   100   100   100   100   . . .

and the new money brought into the business will be

    100   0   0   0   0   0   . . .

Once the stock of capital becomes constant, in the fifth year and after, the two methods yield the same results, but in the earlier period, while the stock of capital is still growing, the results are substantially different. The second method raises 400 in depreciation in the first four years, and keeps new money down to 100; whereas the straight line method raises only 250 in depreciation in the same period, and involves raising 250 in new money. Of course, if the owner puts up all the money, his total income, saving and consumption over the first four years will be the same by either method; the difference is significant only where it is not necessarily the original owners who put up new money when it is required.

Since limiting cases are seldom relevant, it is for most firms significant to decide whether to write off a constant amount each year, or whether to accelerate depreciation. If the firm's assets grow less productive with age, balance sheet values will be significantly greater than real values in the earlier years if it writes off the same amount each year. Also, if it is expanding, accelerated depreciation will contribute more funds in each year than straight-line depreciation. To write off each asset completely in the first year is an extreme decision, which goes to the other extreme of depressing balance sheet values significantly below real values, and which also results in substantial saving if the business is expanding. However, where to draw the line between a constant and an immediate write-off is a matter for business decision; it is not a question to which there is a "scientific" answer.

D. PRICE DETERMINATION

The final objection to calculating depreciation by writing off the same amount each year is that a pricing policy based on this method of depreciation might lead to undesirable loss of business if competition is keen. In a competitive market the element of depreciation which enters into prices is user cost, which may fluctuate widely from one year to the next, in accordance with the extent of surplus capacity. Indeed this objection holds not only against the straight line method, but also against any other method of depreciation which is not based on assessing user cost whenever a pricing decision has to be made. Apart from the fact that these are rule of thumb methods, whereas the assessment of user cost requires assessment of the particular conditions of the moment, there is the even more fundamental obstacle that, whereas the purpose of these methods is the maintenance of capital intact, actual market conditions may be such that appropriate pricing is not consistent with maintaining capital intact. Strictly, depreciation for maintaining capital intact measures the difference in the value of an asset from one moment to another, whereas user cost measures only that part of the difference which is due to use. Even in the full capacity case, depreciation for pricing is based on the cost of replacing the asset, whereas depreciation for maintaining capital intact should presumably be based on the original cost of the asset, adjusted for changes in the general price level.

These objections are met by asserting that the purpose of writing off depreciation in the accounts is not to determine price policy, any more than it is to determine replacement policy, or to show the scrap value of the assets. The purpose is simply to retain within the business enough funds to replace the owners' capital when the asset's life expires. All these other objectives are valid objectives, but they call for special calculations as required.

The truth is that each purpose for which depreciation is measured requires a different concept. Nothing but confusion would flow from deciding that one of these concepts is more "scientific" than all the others, and from trying to make it serve all purposes.

E. CONCLUSION

The conclusions of this section may be stated briefly as follows:

(1) Depreciation for the purpose of maintaining capital intact is different from other depreciation concepts, and calculations made for this purpose are not necessarily appropriate for other purposes.

(2) If capital maintenance is defined in real rather than in money terms, changes in prices may call for considerable variation in the amounts written off from year to year.

(3) If profits fluctuate, it is more convenient for the shareholder to write off depreciation in years of high profits rather than to write off a constant amount in each year, but this point is not significant in firms which maintain a dividend stabilisation reserve or its equivalent.

(4) If the yield of the assets declines rapidly in the early years, it is more appropriate to write off most of the depreciation in the early years than to spread depreciation evenly over the life of the assets. But the significance of this point depends not only on the time pattern of yields, but also on whether the stock of capital and its average age are constant, on the degree of caution in managerial estimates of future yields, and on the extent to which depreciation is used as a source of saving for expanding the firm.

IV. DEPRECIATION AS USER COST

In this section cost means differential cost: the difference which is made to total cost by changes in the level of output. This is the cost concept which is relevant in those situations where price is determined not by charging what is "fair", but by calculating the minimum which could be charged without out-of-pocket expense, and by adding something (which may be zero or negative) to this minimum.

For this purpose the test which must be applied to an item of expenditure is whether it is "escapable", i.e., whether it varies with changes in output. If an item of expense cannot be escaped by reducing output, it does not enter into the calculation of user cost.

We have avoided the term "marginal" cost, and used the term "escapable", because the term marginal relates to a change of output by one unit only. But the concept of a unit is ambiguous wherever there are indivisible items of expenditure. For example, a railway company may calculate the cost of carrying one more passenger, or of adding one more carriage to the train, or of running one more train, or of working one more station. What is escapable at one of these levels of decisions may be inescapable at a different level, but at each level all that is escapable is relevant. The term "marginal" is therefore not appropriately indentified with the cost concept we need, unless it is defined in such a way that the term "unit of output" is an elastic concept, stretched to suit the relevant level of decision. This ties in with the comment made earlier to the effect that it is erroneous to say that price should equal marginal cost; for, if what is involved is a comparison between the consumer's valuation of the product and the escapable cost of production, the term "marginal" is misleading unless it is stretched to include changes in the scale of output at the relevant level of decision.

The concept of escapability has not only a quantity dimension, but also a time dimension. Costs which are inescapable today may yet be escapable next week. For example, at any time a firm is committed by its contracts. It may be hiring resources (buildings, staff, machinery, etc.) at a level surplus to its current requirements. If the firm is calculating the escapable cost of making an addition to output, it must know not only the size of the addition (whether it is within the capacity already on hand) but also for how long this addition will last. If the addition will be completed within the lifetime of existing contracts, and if the firm has no other use for the surplus capacity, then the cost of these contracts is not escapable, and does not enter into the calculation of differential costs. But if contracts would expire while the additional output is still wanted, the cost of renewing these contracts will then have become escapable, and will be a part of differential cost. The same applies to the fixed assets of the firm. Decisions which will be fully executed within the lifetime of all existing assets are not in the same category as decisions of longer term, which embrace periods during which the question of replacing some assets will arise.

We must also remember that assets fall due for replacement at different times. Expiry of an asset may put the firm into the position that it is at full capacity with respect to that type of asset, while it has surplus capacity in others. Assets which fall due for replacement have to be considered in terms of full capacity user cost. What is more, some of these assets bring complicated decisions in their train. Asset A may expire in year n, and assets B and C may be due to expire in years $(n + 4)$ and $(n + 6)$ respectively. A may be an expensive asset with a long life, such that there is no point in replacing A in year n unless one has already decided to replace B and C when their turn comes. Hence the expiry of A in year n may make year n the year of decision for B and C also. In this year of decision all relevant assets will be reviewed, and unless the group as a whole is expected to pay (e.g., unless it may pay to renew B in year $(n + 4)$ and C in year $(n + 6)$), A will not now be renewed.

Thus, in calculating user cost one must distinguish between commitments which have already been made, and commitments which have not yet been entered into; and even within the category of existing commitments, one must distinguish between those which expire within the relevant period, and those which do not. The analysis which follows is accordingly separated in accordance with this distinction. We consider first the case where the firm is already committed to assets, with surplus capacity; and then the case where, because it is working at full capacity, the analysis of the cost of expanding output can be made without reference to existing commitments.

A. SURPLUS CAPACITY COST

In this part of the analysis we assume that the firm has surplus capacity, such that it can produce additional output without any additional investment. The problem is to define user cost, meaning the difference made to asset values by the decision to increase output.

First, we must be certain that surplus capacity exists in all the relevant senses. The quantity dimension must be right. That is to say, the additional output under consideration must not be so large that if it were taken on there would no longer be surplus capacity. New business of this magnitude, even though it merely eliminated surplus capacity without requiring new investment, would put the firm into the full capacity category. To take on such an order would prevent the firm from taking on some other order which might come along, so calculations would have to be made in terms of the potential yield from orders which this one eliminates; thus we would no longer be assuming surplus capacity.

Also in the quantity dimension one must remember the existence of indivisibilities. There may be surplus capacity for some types of assets but not for others; surplus capacity in railway tracks, for example, but not surplus engines or carriages. Then we get a mixture of two user costs; one for the assets which would have to be installed, or which would now be fully occupied, and another for those which would continue to have surplus capacity even if this order were accepted.

Then there is the time dimension. We must be certain that the order fits wholly into a period of surplus capacity, since an order which overlaps a period of full capacity imposes a need for additional investment, and must be treated accordingly. Any replacements which fall due during the relevant period, and any later replacements which these in turn may bring in their train, must be treated as full capacity items.

If we are certain that surplus capacity will exist for all the relevant time, the problem becomes simple. We have to isolate what difference is made to the cost or value of the assets by taking on additional business.

First it may be that some of the assets the firm is using have merely been hired, on contracts which permit the firm to return them during the period under consideration. Thus the cost, or some part of the cost, of these assets is escapable if the firm chooses not to produce, and must be included in user cost. On the other hand, though the firm may have the right to return the assets, it may find it more convenient or more profitable to keep them, in the interest of expected future output. Then their current rental belongs not to the user cost of this period but to the user cost of the periods for which they are being kept.

Similarly, the firm is in a position to scrap its surplus assets instead of using them. The decision whether to use them therefore involves both the question whether to keep them, and also the question whether to use them or to keep them unused. The first question involves measuring what Professor David Solomons has called "the retainer cost", while the second involves measuring "wear and tear".

The retainer cost is the cost of holding the assets unused. This is the interest on the sum the assets would fetch if they were sold, plus any deterioration in their value during the period for which they are held. For the purpose of measuring this deterioration, the value of the assets at the beginning of the period is their scrap value, but the value at the end of the period depends on whether the assets will be sold at the end of the period (in which case it is the scrap value), or will continue to be held by the firm (in which case it is the inside value). Thus, writing S for scrap value and V for inside value, r for the relevant rate of interest, the subscripts 0 and 1 for the beginning and end of the period, and the subscripts u and n to indicate whether the asset is used or not used during the period, the retainer cost is

$$(S_0 - S_{n1}) + rS_0 \tag{1a}$$

if the asset will be sold at the end of the period, or

$$(S_0 - V_{n1}) + rS_0 \tag{1b}$$

if the asset will not be sold at the end of the period,
    Using the same symbols, wear and tear is

$$S_{n1} - S_{u1} \tag{2a}$$

if the asset will be sold at the end of the period, or

$$V_{n1} - V_{u1} \tag{2b}$$

if the asset will not be sold at the end of the period.

In deciding whether to use the asset or not, the firm has to consider both the retainer cost and the wear and tear. However, retainer cost is relevant only if it is positive. For if the asset will rise in value by more than the interest cost it will be held whether it is used or not, and the amount by which it will rise in value is not relevant in determining whether to use it or not. It is only if the asset will fall in value, or will rise in value by less than the interest cost, that the question arises whether the asset should be held; and so it is only in this case that retainer cost enters into the cost of using the asset.

Thus, we may write user cost as

$$(S_0 - S_{n1} + rS_0) + (S_{n1} - S_{u1}) \qquad (3a)$$

if the asset will be sold at the end of the period, or

$$(S_0 - V_{n1} + rS_0) + (V_{n1} - V_{u1}) \qquad (3b)$$

if the asset will not be sold at the end of the period, with the further proviso that in either case the first term is taken into account only if it is positive.

It is a matter of the choice of words whether to define user cost so that it includes retainer cost, or is confined to wear and tear only. Retainer cost, if positive, is part of the cost of use; it enters into marginal cost, and is relevant to profit maximisation. It differs from Marshall's supplementary cost, which is the sum required to maintain capital intact. Retainer cost was neglected by Lord Keynes in his definition of user cost in *The General Theory of Employment, Interest and Money*, because he assumed that the assets are retained whether they are used or not; i.e., he assumed that retainer cost is zero or negative. Keynes's chief interest was in the economy considered as a whole). However, since retainer cost may be positive, and since retention is necessary to use, it seems better to define user cost to include retainer cost as well as wear and tear. Moreover, as we shall see, this formulation makes it easier to tie together the analysis of the cost of using surplus capacity and the analysis of the cost of using assets at full capacity.

If the first term of equations 3a or 3b is zero or negative, and is therefore irrelevant, the equation becomes equivalent to saying that user cost is equal to the value of wear and tear caused by use. This second term may be positive or negative. It is negative if use helps to maintain value. It is positive only in those cases where economic life is shortened by use, and is not determined by obsolescence or by physical deterioration due to the elements. In these circumstances the cost of present use is that some future use of the asset is thereby eliminated, and the value of this cost is the discounted present value of the gross profit which will thus be lost. Thus, we may assume the asset to be still capable of yielding m years of output, its actual life n years being greater than m if there are some intervals during which production is unprofitable. The owner chooses the m most profitable years, and the user cost is the discounted present value of the profit which could be earned in the marginally profitable year which is just included or just excluded from the list. (From the standpoint of years which are included it is the $(m + 1)$ th most profitable year, which is the year that they displace; whereas from the standpoint of the excluded years, it is the mth most profitable year, which has displaced them. For convenience we shall refer to the marginally most profitable year as the mth). This mth year may be any year $1, 2, \ldots, n$ in the sequence of n years.

The position of the mth year in the sequence does not affect decisions. After this year has passed, calculations continue to be based on the fact that each remaining output-year of the asset's capacity has already been booked for some output at least as valuable as the mth, if not also more valuable. Wear and tear now becomes equal to the least valuable output which still remains. But if expectations of yield remain unchanged, this makes no difference to what is included or excluded.

The preceding paragraphs have calculated user cost in terms of output years, but this is easily translated into terms of the cost of marginal output. If the asset is capable of producing m units of output through its life, the owner chooses the m most profitable; (when allowance is made for periods of asset idleness, the actual life of the asset, n years, exceeds the equivalent period which it would take to produce m units of output without interruption). Marginal wear and tear is then the discounted present value of the marginally included m th unit of output. In every year the asset will be used intensively up to the point where the discounted yield on the marginal unit of output equals the discounted value of the mth unit of output.

The case where fluctuations in output are expected is especially interesting, since these involve periods of surplus capacity lying between periods of full capacity. It is necessary to be certain that additional work taken on in periods of temporary surplus capacity will not spread over into periods of full capacity. An order for continuous supply "until further notice" must be treated as an order requiring additional assets of its own if it will extend over periods of full capacity.

If additional output is demanded which is limited to a period of surplus capacity, with retainer cost zero or negative, user cost is zero if the asset's life does not depend on use, and is wear and tear (i.e. discounted value of use in the displaced $(m + 1)$th period) if life depends upon use. Many kinds of business have regular fluctuations in output, due to the coincidence of regular fluctuations in demand with the impossibility or the high cost of storing the product or service; and in many such businesses the user cost of assets in the surplus periods is zero or nearly zero. Examples are transportation, electricity, hotels, places of entertainment, and so on. Such businesses usually recognise that user cost in slack periods is zero or rather small, and they adjust their prices so that virtually the whole cost of their assets is raised in periods of full capacity. One well known exception is the British electricity supply industry, which has traditionally charged the same price at all times, and which is only slowly and in marginal traffic experimenting with charging lower prices for off-peak supplies.

B. Full Capacity Cost

We now assume that the firm is operating at full capacity, and is calculating the cost of taking on new business. This involves installing additional capacity. How is the cost of this capacity to be allocated between different outputs or different years?

At this stage we need hardly reiterate that the cost of existing capacity throws no light on the problem. It cannot be assumed that the cost of additional output will be proportionately the same as the cost of existing output. Neither is the answer to be found by adding the cost of the addition to existing cost, and dividing the whole by the new level of output. The additional output must be costed separately.

Given the cost of the new asset and its potential capacity over the whole of its lifetime, an average cost per unit of capacity could be calculated. Better still, if the asset is expected to be worked below capacity for part of the time, total cost could be divided by expected total output instead of by full capacity output. But these averages would be irrelevant. Suppose that the yield of the asset is expected to fluctuate, in accordance with fluctuations in demand, which will show up as fluctuations in price or in output. If we arrived at user cost simply by averaging total cost we should find some periods in which yield would not cover user cost so defined, and in which production should therefore not take place. But this result would be incorrect, since cost arbitrarily determined in this way does not really tell us what difference, if any, production makes to costs in that or any subsequent period.

There are only two cases where user cost may be deduced directly from the original cost of the asset, and neither of these occurs frequently.

The first is the case where the asset will yield the same amount in each year. User cost may then be interpreted as the minimum sum which the annual yield must be if the investment is to be worth while. This sum is given by the formula

$$S_0 \cdot \frac{r(1 + r)^m}{(1 + r)^m - 1} \qquad (4)$$

where S_0 is the original cost of the asset, and m the number of years of useful life.

In the other case we have to assume that the inside value of the asset and its scrap value (or purchase price) are always the same, presumably because the market is perfect in every sense. Then, applying the formula derived in the preceding section, the user cost of the first year reduces to

$$S_0 (1 + r) - S_{u1} \qquad (5a)$$

which is the interest on the purchase price plus the decline in the market value of the asset during the year. Each succeeding year has a corresponding cost. When these are summed, the total equals the original cost of the asset, plus interest on the sum outstanding in each year. The result is possible, however, only because we have assumed that scrap value is at all times the measure of cost; we then get the same sort of answer that we would get if we assumed the firm to be hiring the asset instead of buying it.

In the normal case scrap value is not the same as inside value, and yield is not constant from year to year. User cost cannot then be computed with reference to original cost.

An asset must be thought of as yielding a series of different services through its life, the difference consisting in the timing. Once installed, it yields a number of services in unalterable proportions, each service being the capacity to produce at a particular time. These capacities are a "joint product," and the appropriate analysis is that of joint supply in fixed proportions.

The solution to the joint supply case with fixed proportions is that the total cost cannot be allocated between the products other than by the market process. Mere averaging will not do. The products taken together must yield the total cost, but some will yield a larger portion and others a smaller portion or nothing, in accordance with what the market will bear. At some times during its life the asset will have a high yield, while at other times it will have a low yield. The firm must get what it can at different times, subject only to the condition that the asset should not be installed unless the firm expects to earn its total cost over the lifetime of the asset.

Let us take a concrete example. The firm is already working at full capacity. It makes a new contact, and is asked to quote for a new order. An additional asset would have to be installed, and we assume that the life of the asset is known, and is not determined by wear and tear. If the order is for a quantity equal to full capacity of the asset throughout its life, the answer is simple: cost per unit is total cost divided by total quantity, if interest is excluded when calculating cost, or is in accordance with the formula (4) given on page 42, which includes interest in cost. More probably the order is for a short period only, leaving open the question whether it will be renewed, and if it is renewed, whether demand will be steady or fluctuating. The firm has then to make its best guess as to what other business will be available to supplement this order at times when it is not keeping the asset fully occupied; and to replace the order altogether if it should not be repeated, or if it should be repeated with intervals of less than full capacity. In this way the firm makes its best guess as to the projected time pattern of use of the asset. As already mentioned in Section II, this guessing has many complications—isolating the yield of the particular asset, choosing the best time pattern of use, and so on—but some such guessing cannot be avoided when deciding whether an asset is worth buying or not. If the firm regards the future as very uncertain, once the original order is completed, it will want to recoup the major part of the asset's cost from this first order, even though this order may be completed very early in the life of the asset. Alternatively it may think that prospects will grow better with time. It may be anxious to take on this order as a gateway to better things; to a connection with a prized and long desired customer, or to a foothold in what is considered to be an expanding market. Then it will deliberately add very little for depreciation to the prices of earlier outputs, in the expectation of a fuller harvest later. (How much it will retain from profits in each year as depreciation, if it wishes to maintain the value of its capital intact, is a separate question, to which, as we have already seen in Section III of this chapter, it may decide to give a different answer).

It should be noted that the analysis applies whenever some fluctuation in the asset's yield is foreseen, even though the asset is expected to work at full capacity throughout its life. Yield may vary at full capacity because the price of output varies, or because of variations in operating costs. Thus yield may be expected to decline progressively throughout the asset's life, or it may be expected to fluctuate. The case where surplus capacity is expected at some periods is merely the limiting case in which expected yield is zero.

These results can be tested against the formulae for user cost which were given above in discussing the surplus capacity case. In terms of these formulae, the cost of purchasing an additional asset is identified with S_0, since this is the sum that can be saved by not purchasing.

Let us calculate user cost in the first year. If the asset will be sold at the end of the first year the problem of allocating costs between years does not arise. If the asset will not be sold, the relevant formula is

$$(S_0 + rS_0 - V_{n1}) + (V_{n1} - V_{u1}). \tag{3b}$$

If the inside value of the asset substantially exceeds its original cost, V_{n1} may exceed S_0 by more than the interest cost. Then the first term (the retainer cost) will be negative, and only the second term will count. In the limiting case $S_0 = V_0$, since, if the inside value exceeds the cost of buying and installing the asset, investment will be pushed to the point where these two are marginally equal. In this case user cost reduces to

$$rV_0 + (V_0 - V_{u1}) \tag{5b}$$

where the second term is the depreciation in the inside value of the asset during the year. Since the value of the asset is the sum of the discounted yields in each year, the main element in this depreciation is the yield of the first year (the rest is due to the fact that the yield of subsequent years is discounted back one year less in V_{u1} than in V_0). We deduce, therefore, that the main element in the user cost of the first year is the yield of that year, provided that originally the asset is not marginally profitable. If we can further identify S_1 with V_{u1}, we will get a series of user costs which when added together will just exhaust the total cost, each year being represented by its expected yield. However, if the inside value and the scrap value ever diverge, summation no longer gives this simple result.

Normally retainer cost is zero or negative, at least after the first year, and user cost consists only of wear and tear. This is zero if life is determined by obsolescence or by mere passage of time, in which case the cost of the asset has again to be allocated in accordance with yields. If life is determined by wear and tear, user cost will be the discounted yield of the marginally excluded $(m + 1)^{\text{th}}$ year. In the limiting case where yields are the same in each year user cost can be determined by the formula already given,

$$\frac{r(1 + r)^m}{(1 + r)^m - 1} \tag{4}$$

related either to S_0, if the investment is marginally profitable, or to V_0, if V_0 exceeds S_0. The limiting case, however, is unusual. Where yields vary from one year to the next, the marginally excluded yield will be below the average of the included yields, and will bear no fixed relationship to S_0 or to V_0. There is a minimum below which the yield must not fall if the asset is to be used, but if we wish to allocate the full cost of the asset between the years, we are still thrown back on the proposition that each year must yield what it can above user cost, so that the sum of the discounted yields is not less than original cost.

C. Conclusion

User cost is an unsatisfactory concept in practice because it turns upon estimates of the future yield of an asset in each period of its life. Accordingly, except in simple cases where user cost is zero or negative, the estimates are highly speculative and subjective, and are of the sort which change easily between breakfast and lunch. These uncertainties are inherent in the problem. Moreover, they separate this calculation in degree but not in kind from other business calculations, since most business decisions have in the last analysis to be based upon guesses about the future. The main practical result of this uncertainty is that in estimating user cost, business men tend to attach small value to distant yields, and tend to require an asset to pay for itself in a very short time. Some firms in the United States of America are reported not to embark upon new investment inless they expect the investment to pay for itself within four years of coming into full production. No doubt there is wide variation in this respect between individuals, between industries, and between countries; but in view of the uncertainties we need not be surprised that most business men tend to take only rather roughly a concept to which economists have tried to bring so much precision.

CHAPTER 2

DEPRECIATION AND THE MAINTENANCE OF REAL CAPITAL

EDGAR O. EDWARDS *

Rice University, Houston (Texas) U.S.A.

A perplexing problem, common to economic and accounting theory, is the division of a firm's net annual receipts between depreciation on the one hand and income on the other. The first is usually related, in one sense or another, to the maintenance of capital and, it is argued, its careful identification is necessary as a prerequisite to equitable tax and dividend policies. This "division problem" has been discussed often in the literature, much basic theory has been developed and the difficulties entailed in making such a division have been well exposed.[1]

In practice rather arbitrary definitions of depreciation have been adopted (e.g., straight-line depreciation based on historic cost) and these have usually taken little if any account of the characteristics of a dynamic economy—price movements, growth, and technological change. It is not surprising then that businessmen everywhere, in periods of generally rising prices, express strong demands for more sophisticated techniques. These demands are most vigorous in those countries where production is capital intensive (depreciation represents a high proportion of total cost), and as capital intensity increases over time the demand for improved techniques will likely grow apace.

Two noteworthy developments have accompanied the post World War II revival of the demand for more equitable depreciation policies. The first, discussed more thoroughly in other contributions to this volume, is the growing awareness on the part of economists and other architects of government policies that depreciation may be a useful device for achieving various policy objectives. The manipulation of tax-deductible depreciation charges as a means of smoothing business fluctuations, preventing inflation, and stimulating growth has become

* The author is grateful for Ford Foundation funds administered by Princeton University which financed research during the summer of 1957.

an almost common consideration. The difficulties inherent in determining depreciation on the basis of "internal equity" (the maintenance of real capital) have undoubtedly contributed to the willingness of many to modify depreciation charges in order to attain these other ends.

The second, which is very much a concern of ours, is the attempt to incorporate a growth variable into depreciation theory. The hypothesis has been advanced that growth alone will alter the relationship between depreciation and replacement.[2] This suggestion is an intriguing one partly because much of the earlier income and depreciation theory did not suggest this result, but also because it implies that the unadjusted depreciation charges of growing firms may be sufficient to finance replacement even in the face of inflation.

These developments suggest that a review of depreciation theory in terms of internal equity would not be out of order. In this context we shall be concerned with depreciation as a measure of replacement and as a device for maintaining capital intact. Other criteria, such as promoting growth or stability, will be given only incidental consideration. We shall explore the adequacy of depreciation charges in terms of the replacement criterion under both stationary and dynamic conditions, and will attempt to reconcile recent growth-depreciation hypotheses with the earlier body of depreciation theory.

It will come as no surprise, I am sure, that the task develops essentially into that of identifying various conceptual ambiguities under a variety of conditions. Neither depreciation nor replacement is an unambiguous concept. Depreciation may be measured subjectively or objectively; it may be based on historic cost or current cost. Replacement has been used to mean, among other things, physical replacement of machines, replacement of value (subjective and market), and replacement of output capacity. Communication is bound to be difficult so long as these shades of meaning persist.

I. CAPITAL MAINTENANCE UNDER STATIONARY CONDITIONS

A. The Single Machine Enterprise[3]

The "single machine enterprise" operates under the restriction that it can own but one machine at a time which it can employ in only one way. Initially, we shall impose other restrictions on the hypothetical entrepreneur, namely:

1) he holds single-valued expectations with certainty for the span of time stretching to his horizon;

2) there are no changes in technology; and

3) there are no changes in prices or price levels.

Even under these stringent conditions depreciation and replacement are ambiguous concepts. To point up these ambiguities we shall treat each in turn.

Depreciation can be resolved into three elements:

1) *asset life*—the time period over which depreciation charges are made,

2) *the depreciable amount*—the sum to which a machine's depreciation charges are designed to total, and

3) *the depreciation pattern*—the division of the depreciable amount among the short periods making up asset life.

It will be convenient to discuss the determinants of asset life first and to treat the depreciable amount and the depreciation pattern together.

1. *The Determination of Asset Life*

a. *The General Principle.* When an entrepreneur contemplates the purchase of a machine he must compare the expected value of the services the machine will render to the costs he must incur in acquiring the machine. The value of the machine's services in any period is a *quasi-rent* and is determined (in his expectations) by deducting from the proceeds he realizes from selling the machine's output all costs incurred in producing and selling that output (raw material, labor, etc.) *except* depreciation on the machine and any interest costs related to the acquisition of the machine. These costs are excluded because he wants to know if the quasi-rents attributable to the machine will in fact cover the cost of the machine and the interest payments made (or the interest receipts sacrificed) in order to finance that cost.

If each quasi-rent is independent of every other one, a unique quasi-rent pattern emerges. If not, many different quasi-rent patterns are possible in which case each can be treated as though it were a different machine. The entrepreneur discounts each quasi-rent in the given pattern; i.e., he adjusts the amounts to compensate for differences in their dates of collection. This makes them properly additive and the sum of any number of consecutive quasi-rents can be determined. The length of the stream of quasi-rents that yields the maximum sum (or subjective value) determines in principle the life of the machine.

As the occasion will arise where simple mathematics will prove helpful, a restatement of these considerations in mathematical terms is in order. Designating the series of quasi-rents, R_1, R_2, $\ldots R_n$ where n indicates the last dated quasi-rent whose inclusion makes the subjective value of the machine a maximum, the interest rate, i, and subjective value, V, we have

$$V = \frac{R_1}{(1+i)} + \frac{R_2}{(1+i)^2} + \frac{R_3}{(1+i)^3} \cdots \frac{R_n}{(1+i)^n}.$$

If the subjective value of the machine, V, exceeds its market or objective value, C, the purchase of the machine promises to be profitable if operated with a life of n years.

This general principle can be made a bit more explicit by considering some of the particular factors which determine the life of a machine.

b. *Maximum Economic Life.* The *maximum technical lifetime* of a given durable good ends at the moment when its repair is physically impossible (the lead in an automatic pencil). If this were the only limitation on lifetime, however, it is likely that most durable goods would live forever. Too often this technical limitation is confused with an economic limitation—the high cost of repair. It may be that a durable good breaks down and the cost of repairing it is so high relative to the cost of replacing it that the repair alternative is never seriously considered. Electric light bulbs, fence posts and railway ties are examples of items whose lifetimes are usually regarded as being technically determined though the high cost of repair may be a more sensible explanation. In general then the *maximum economic lifetime* of a durable good terminates at that point where repair cost (the cost necessary to enable the item to produce at least one additional unit of output) exceeds replacement cost.*

The *economic lifetime* of a capital good will usually be shorter than maximum but under some circumstances the two may coincide. The so-called "constant efficiency type" of capital good is usually alleged to have this characteristic, but the meaning of efficiency in this context merits investigation.

---

* The maximum lifetime of a durable good cannot always be defined in calendar time independent of the way in which it is used. For some goods, such as telephone lines, maximum lifetime is independent of the time pattern of use. For others, such as electric light bulbs, the maximum lifetime is a function of the pattern of use. In this case the best we can do is to treat the pattern of use as an integral part of the definition of the good; a good having several possible patterns of use is really several goods.

If *technical efficiency* is meant, the capital good must be one that emits a constant output stream in the process of which it utilizes a constant input stream. If, on the other hand, *economic efficiency* is meant, the capital good must yield a constant series of quasi-rents. In addition to a constant flow of output, the rate at which that output is *sold* and the prices of both outputs and inputs must be constant over time. Thus, constant technical efficiency combined with a constant sales and input volume and constant input and output prices is sufficient to make the asset's economic lifetime coincide with its maximum lifetime.

On the other hand, constant economic efficiency is not a necessary condition for the identity of economic and maximum lifetimes. A durable good characterized by diminishing economic efficiency (declining quasi-rents whether caused by falling revenues, rising operating costs or a combination of the two) may yet yield in its later years sufficient net receipts to warrant its use until its maximum lifetime is reached.*

c. *The Quasi-Rent Pattern.* More interesting problems are encountered when we consider those factors that may cause economic life to be shorter than maximum. A necessary condition for a shortened economic life is diminishing economic efficiency, at least toward the end of asset life. If our entrepreneur has a durable good whose market value is zero and he does not contemplate replacement, he will plan to keep the asset so long as its quasi-rents are positive *or* the present value of the remaining stream of quasi-rents is positive. In other words the asset's expected life will not expire until a period is reached when the machine's quasi-rent *and* the present value of any number of consecutive future quasi-rents is zero or negative. Its market value being zero the entrepreneur has nothing to gain by selling the good. It will pay

* Increasing economic efficiency is another case in point but it is often regarded as unrealistic. The usual ground given is the casual observation of the *technical* efficiencies of goods. It is clearly possible, however, for a good having a *diminishing* technical efficiency to be characterized by *increasing* economic efficiency. A good turning out output for which demand is increasing rapidly may have both of these characteristics, for example. This violates static assumptions, of course.

Observation suggests, however, that even technical efficiency need not decline steadily over a good's lifetime. The period required to put new automobiles and trucks into first class operating condition is usually one of increasing efficiency if only because of the lay-up time involved, a factor not usually covered by guarantees. Examples of increasing efficiency throughout a lifetime are more difficult to find, but the tables in a tavern in Princeton apparently improve in direct proportion to the number of students' initials carved on them.

him, therefore, to keep the good (1) if any net gain is currently obtainable or (2) if the present value of contemplated gains for any number of consecutive periods exceeds the present value of the additional costs necessary to procure those gains.

If a good yields a continuously declining stream of quasi-rents, the first condition is sufficient because the second then follows from it— the present value of any number of future quasi-rents must be negative when any single quasi-rent is zero or negative. We shall assume a diminishing quasi-rent stream throughout the remainder of this section.

d. *Disposal Values*. Let us introduce the notion of a disposal value—the value obtainable if the machine were to be sold as scrap or as a going machine, whichever is highest. If this value is constant over time the entrepreneur has a perpetual opportunity to dispose of the machine at that price and to invest the proceeds at the market rate of interest. It will no longer pay the entrepreneur to hold the machine beyond the point where its quasi-rent becomes equal to the interest he can obtain on that scrap value. As the quasi-rents may be positive (though smaller) beyond this point, the existence of a constant disposal value has shortened the expected life of the machine.*

But disposal value is likely to decline over time. Granting this, it is no longer safe to say that the good's economic life will terminate when the quasi-rent falls to equality with the disposal value. By using the good for an additional period the entrepreneur is not simply sacrificing the interest for one period on the good's immediate disposal value; he is also sacrificing interest *forever* on the amount by which disposal value is expected to decline over the period.** The present value of this foregone interest stream, given the interest rate, is the amount of the decline in disposal value itself. The entrepreneur should not plan, therefore, to keep his durable good beyond the point where

---

* If the stream of quasi-rents is not a continuously declining one, the entrepreneur may not dispose of the machine the first time the quasi-rent becomes equal to or less than interest on the disposal value. He must compare the present value of the remaining quasi-rents (the pattern and length of the stream of quasi-rents to be discounted being determined as that which yields the highest present value) with the disposal value. If, however, there are no costs involved in disposing of and acquiring a machine at the disposal value, he will dispense with the machine in every period in which the quasi-rent is less than interest on the scrap value and reacquire it in every period in which the quasi-rent is greater.

** In other words, the cost of using the machine for another period is the difference between interest on present market value from now on and interest on the reduced market value from the end of the period on.

its quasi-rent falls to equality with interest on disposal value *plus* the expected decline in disposal value over the period.*

e. *The Entrepreneur's Horizon: No Replacement Contemplated.* So long as replacement is excluded, the introduction of a horizon for the entrepreneur results in modifications that are quite straightforward. It is only necessary to distinguish between *planned life* and *actual life* where the former represents the entrepreneur's view at the time the machine is purchased and the latter is the view of the omnipotent economist observer who is not limited by the horizon.

An entrepreneur will not purchase the good unless the observable quasi-rents, those that fall within his horizon, have a present value in excess of the cost of the good. Obviously, many long-lived assets will not be acquired though a longer horizon might make them profitable. Thus the originally planned life of a good cannot exceed the time period included within the horizon.** The actual life of a machine may well extend beyond the original horizon date because as time passes subsequent periods fall within the entrepreneur's horizon and these quasi-rents may warrant the extension of asset life. Life will be extended an additional period so long as the new distant quasi-rent exceeds (1) interest on the new distant disposal value and (2) the expected decline in disposal value over the new distant period. The entrepreneur will continue using the machine so long as the present value of (a) any number of successive (and foreseen) quasi-rents and (b) the related end disposal value exceeds the machine's immediate disposal value.***

f. *The Entrepreneur's Horizon: Replacement Contemplated.* If we permit our hypothetical entrepreneur to contemplate replacement, another

---

* It should be noted that an increasing disposal value would tend to *lengthen* planned asset life as compared to life with a constant disposal value. If we permit rising quasi-rents also, our criterion must be changed. The machine will be kept so long as the present value of the stream of quasi-rents and end market value (the length of the stream defined to yield the largest present value) is greater than present market value.

** This factor may account in part for the heavy reliance by businessmen on the "payout period" (the period over which a machine's quasi-rents equal the initial investment) as a means of weighing alternative investments. If the minimum payout period imposed by management corresponds with its horizon, the objective observer cannot criticize too harshly. Expectations are not entertained about post-horizon events.

*** It should be noted as the Lutzes have pointed out (*op. cit.*, pp. 104–5), that in all cases discussed so far (i.e., cases involving no replacement) the cost of a machine is not a determinant of its lifetime.

factor is introduced that will tend to shorten the economic life of the durable good. The entrepreneur will undertake replacement sometime if he expects the present value of the successive quasi-rents and disposal value associated with the new machine to exceed the cost of the machine at the time of its purchase. The amount of this excess we call "goodwill" following Preinreich.[4] Interest on this goodwill represents an addition to the possible earnings of the entrepreneur should he dispose of his existing machine—by buying the new machine he will enhance his income by the amount of interest on its present value but he will sacrifice interest earnings on its cost whether he borrows the funds or obtains them by selling interest-earning securities. Thus the entrepreneur will find replacement worthwhile (and will conclude the life of the existing machine) as soon as the quasi-rent on the existing machine falls below the sum of (1) interest on its scrap value, (2) the decline in disposal value over the period, and (3) interest on the goodwill of the replacement machine.*

If the entrepreneur anticipates a chain of replacements, the life of the durable good is shortened even more. Each machine in the chain has a positive goodwill and the goodwill of the chain, being the present value of all the machine goodwills, must exceed the goodwill of the first machine in the chain. The existing machine must now compete with a chain of machines whose goodwill exceeds the goodwill of the first replacement. The entrepreneur will plan to replace the existing machine just before its quasi-rent is expected to fall below the sum of (1) interest on its scrap value, (2) the decline in its scrap value and (3) interest on the goodwill of the chain that replaces it.

If all of the machines in the chain have identical (diminishing) quasi-rent and disposal value patterns, the entrepreneur's plans *at any moment* will entail the shortest life for the first machine and a longer life for each succeeding machine as the present value of the goodwills on the following (fewer) machines becomes smaller. The last machine in the chain will have a presently planned life that is independent of replacement. Intriguing as this escalator effect, discovered by Preinreich,[5] may be, it is of academic interest only. The actual life of each machine in the chain does depend upon the entrepreneur's horizon but each machine will have the same actual life. As time passes the entre-

---

* This rule is valid if quasi-rents on the existing machine are monotonically decreasing over time, disposal value is constant or falling, and the goodwill of the new machine is independent of the timing of its introduction. Then we can be sure that the deficiency of a single quasi-rent implies the deficiency of all subsequent ones.

preneur's given horizon will extend to a later calendar date so that when replacement occurs an additional replacement will be planned at the end of the chain giving what is now the first machine in the chain a life equal to the life of the machine replaced. Preinreich's result will hold for a machine's actual life only if the entrepreneur's horizon is fixed on a particular calendar date and the time encompassed by it diminishes as the present moves toward it.

We can say, however, that the more distant the horizon, the shorter the (equal) lives of durable goods in the chain. From this it follows that if the entrepreneur's horizon lengthens (shortens) with the passage of time, the lives of identical durable goods will shorten (lengthen).

In what follows we shall assume that the entrepreneur has determined the life of his existing machine by considering all of the rational factors which may affect its life, including those we have discussed: the machine's maximum life, its declining quasi-rents, its disposal value and any decline in that, the possibility of replacement, and the length of the entrepreneur's horizon. When the life of the durable good is so determined the stage is set for a consideration of depreciation itself. It should be clear, however, that asset life determined in this way is a purely subjective matter.

2. *Determining the Depreciation Charge*

The facts we have at our disposal about the durable good include:
(1) its life as determined by the entrepreneur,
(2) its quasi-rent pattern (assumed to be monotonically decreasing),
(3) the interest rate (which is assumed constant over time),
(4) its present value and the present value of the chain, if one is involved,
(5) its cost, and
(6) its disposal values over time.
The problem is to divide each quasi-rent into depreciation and income elements. Several approaches are possible depending upon the depreciation base selected and the method used to allocate this amount among different periods.

The principal alternative depreciable amounts are cost and subjective value, but within the confines of each of these concepts lie additional choices. Should depreciation be based upon original cost or on an estimate of ultimate replacement cost? Should we depreciate the subjective value of the machine or the subjective value of the chain of machines? As events unfold the current cost of replacement becomes objective information as does the disposal value of the machine and its past quasi-rents; in the light of this new information estimates of ultimate replacement cost may be changed and subjective values may be revised. Clearly the periodic depreciation charge is subject to considerable variation depending upon the nature of the base selected and whether or not this base is variable over time. In addition, the equivocal nature of the time pattern to be applied to the base expands further the range of values that the depreciation charge could assume.

Whether funds equal in amount to these depreciation charges are adequate for replacement depends also on the concept of replacement employed. For the single machine enterprise it is useful to distinguish four such concepts: (1) the replacement or maintenance of subjective value, (2) the replacement of original cost, (3) the physical replacement of the machine when its economic life has been exhausted—ultimate replacement, and (4) the replacement or maintenance of some form of market value. We shall find that different theories of depreciation have implicit in them one or another of these concepts of replacement. It will become possible as we delve into the subject to identify other concepts as well.

a. *"Subjective" Depreciation.* It has been pointed out that depreciation is intimately related to income, the two being the only components into which quasi-rent is usually divided. Several authors have chosen to define income and then to investigate what meaning can be assigned to the residual, depreciation.[6]

Income is for these people the maximum value that could be consumed during a period and leave the consumer feeling as well off at the end of the period as he felt at the beginning. This concept of income rests on subjective valuations and any consumption during a period which reduces subjective value represents consumption of capital not of income. That part of each quasi-rent which is not income will, if appropriately invested, just maintain subjective value at its level at the beginning of the period. Thus depreciation is defined as the amount necessary to permit the maintenance of subjective value, i.e., to permit the maintenance of a constant stream of income should the owner of capital so desire. Should an entrepreneur increase his capital (invest a part of his income) or decrease his capital (disinvest or consume a part of his capital), income and depreciation for the next period must be recomputed on the assumption that the new level of subjective value is to be maintained.

So long as expectations are realized, the income of each period is equal to interest, at the external rate, on the subjective value of capital at the beginning of the period, and the remaining amount of each quasi-rent is depreciation. The theory of this is not very complicated. Subjective value is the present value of the stream of quasi-rents expected over the machine's life. If each quasi-rent is received at the end of each period, the subjective value of the machine at the beginning of a period, V_0, is simply the subjective value at the end of the period, V_1, plus consumption, C_1, both discounted one period. Thus

$$V_0 = \frac{V_1 + C_1}{(1 + i)},$$

and income, Y, is

$$Y = iV_0 = C_1 + (V_1 - V_0), \tag{1}$$

i.e., income is either consumed, C_1, or invested net, $(V_1 - V_0)$. Making the special assumption that the entire quasi-rent, Q_1, is consumed, and denoting by V_I the subjective value that would obtain in that case at the end of the period, it can be shown by substituting Q_1 for C_1 and V_I for V_1 in expression (1) that

$$Q_1 = iV_0 + (V_0 - V_I). \tag{2}$$

The quasi-rent is divided into income, iV_0, and depreciation, $D_1 (= V_0 - V_I)$, elements.

As in fact income is either consumed, C_1, or invested, I_1, it follows that

$$Q_1 = C_1 + I_1 + D_1, \tag{3}$$

i.e., each quasi-rent can be divided into consumption (C_1) and gross investment ($I_1 + D_1$) or alternatively into income ($C_1 + I_1$) and depreciation (D_1).

This simple theory disguises much of the meaning of the depreciation method it involves. A concrete example may promote understanding with only a nominal sacrifice of rigor. We shall assume that a single machine enterprise has a horizon equal to the economic life of its machine, that the economic plan of the firm anticipates quasi-rents from the use of the machine of $2000, $1000 and $900 at the end of each of the first three periods of operation and a scrap value of $200 at the end of that time. The market rate of interest being 6%, the machine has a subjective value to the enterprise of $3700; its cost is $2998 (a typical quotation in the United States!).

The economic plan of the firm is depicted in Table 1.

TABLE 1

THE ECONOMIC PLAN OF A HYPOTHETICAL FIRM

Subjective Depreciation

	Period				
	1	*2*	*3*		*Total*
1. Quasi-rents	$2000	$1000	$900		$3900
2. Scrap value				$200	200
3. Total machine receipts	2000	1000	900	200	4100
4. Income from machine (6% of its subjective value)	222	115	63	—	400
5. Depreciation and scrap value	1778	885	837	200	3700
6. Interest on securities at 6% (Invested depreciation)	—	107	159		266
7. Total Income (Item 4 plus item 6)	222	222	222		666

If the plan operates according to expectations, the enterprise will earn total income in each period of $222. As time passes an increasing proportion of this income will be earned by investment in securities at the external rate of return (6%) and a decreasing proportion will be earned from the machine. In the fourth period the enterprise will be in a position to earn all of its periodic income of $222 from securities and this income should continue to be receveid at this rate through all subsequent periods.

Subjective depreciation permits the firm to recover enough in each period to replace the decline in the subjective value of the machine with the market value of securities. In this way the subjective value of the firm's total assets, machine plus securities, can be just maintained from one period to the next and yet the entrepreneur can withdraw an income of $222 per period. At the end of the machine's life the subjective value of the firm's assets, now entirely securities, is supported completely by market values whereas at the outset of the plan subjective value exceeded market value of the machine by $702. The plan has operated to convert this goodwill into *bona fide* market values. But this is precisely what every profit-seeking plan attempts— the conversion of purely subjective values, which are not exchangeable, into market values that are generally recognized and readily transferable.

The information we have is not sufficient, however, to depict the time pattern of the conversion of goodwill into market value. While we know the market value of the firm's securities over time, we know the market value of the machine at only two points, at the beginning of the plan when it was purchased and at the end of the plan when it will presumably be sold for scrap. Yet it has been shown that some knowledge of the time pattern of market values was necessary in order to determine carefully the economic life of the machine.*

Let us assume that the market values of the machine at the end of the first and second periods are $1500 and $1000 respectively. We can now depict, as in Fig. 1, the time pattern of the firm's plan on the

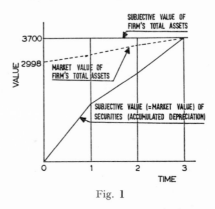

Fig. 1

assumption that all income is withdrawn by the entrepreneur. As the subjective value of the firm's machine shrinks it is replaced by securities having a market value (and presumably a subjective value as well) equal to the shrinkage. Thus the subjective value of the firm's total assets is maintained over time, but because the firm's plan is finite this requires that the market value of the firm's assets rise to equality with subjective value at the termination of the plan. What was originally goodwill is transformed over time into explicit market values. The possibility of such conversion is characteristic of any finite economic plan. The entrepreneur is free, of course, to withdraw

* See above, p. 51.

amounts in excess of his income but in that event he is knowingly reducing his (subjective) capital by the amount of the excess.

The time path of this tranformation may vary considerably between the origin and termination of the plan and yet be consistent with the retention of the machine over its specified lifetime. The range of values the machine may take on will be larger, (1) the larger the gap between the profitability of the machine and the profitability of the firm's next best alternative, (2) the greater the costs of transfer, and (3) the larger the fixed costs entailed in putting the machine into operation. If the market value of the machine falls by too much over its first period of life, it will pay the firm to buy a machine one year old rather than a new one; on the other hand, if its market value does not decline sufficiently, the firm will find it profitable to sell the machine before the specified terminal date. That the market values are expected to fall within the relevant range is established by the adoption of the specified plan.

If the firm has no alternative to the purchase of the machine except the purchase of securities and there are no transfer or fixed organization or installation costs, the range of consistent market values can be specified. The market value of the machine can at no point prior to the termination of the plan exceed its subjective value; on the other hand, the market value of second-hand machines can not be so low that the purchase of one will yield a goodwill in excess of that of a new machine. Because subjective depreciation is based on subjective value only, the various market values that might consistently attach to the machine will not affect in any way the amount of subjective depreciation taken in each period.

b. *"Market" Depreciation.* Another method of depreciating is to trace over time via depreciation charges the market value of the machine instead of its subjective value. This method is one for which accountants have expressed a preference. It permits the firm to maintain the market value of its assets as opposed to their subjective value.

By market value is meant a constellation of market values, one for the new machine, one for a machine one period old, another for a machine two periods old, etc. The assumptions of constant prices and an unchanging technology are not being violated. The prices of machines of the various ages are still constant over time but as each period passes a new market value is assigned to the aging machine.

"Market depreciation" relates then to changes in the market value of a machine as it ages. That is not to say that its market value is unambiguous nor that it can always be easily determined. For the purpose of developing the theory, however, we shall assume the necessary conditions, namely, that markets exist for machines of all ages, that these markets are perfect particularly in the sense that anyone has equal access to both the buying and selling sides, and that there are no transport or installation costs. A unique market value being determined for a machine of each age, market depreciation for a period is simply the change in market value over the period in question, where no factor except age and use affects that market value.

We shall also assume that the machine is used by many firms not all of which are equally efficient. As the market value of a machine of any age is determined by the composite of all demands for it in conjunction with supply conditions, the subjective value assigned to the machine by our enterprise may differ from its market value. The stage is set for a more detailed examination of market depreciation. The example used previously to illustrate subjective depreciation can be reinterpreted on the basis of market depreciation. Table 2 contains the necessary data.

TABLE 2

THE ECONOMIC PLAN OF A HYPOTHETICAL FIRM

Market Depreciation

	Period				
	1	*2*	*3*		*Total*
1. Quasi-rents	$2000	$1000	$900		$3900
2. Scrap value				$200	200
3. Total Machine Receipts	2000	1000	900	200	4100
4. Depreciation and Scrap Value	1498	680	620	200	2998
5. Income from Machine	502	320	280	—	1102
6. Interest on Securities at 6% (Invested Depreciation)	—	90	131		221
Total Income (Item 5 plus 6)	502	410	411		1323

This method, designed to make book value of the machine adhere carefully to its market value, abandons in the process the concept of income as a stream constant in size. Depreciation is based on market values determined outside the firm and the income residual would not likely be a constant. If it is assumed with this method that the entrepreneur withdraws the reported income from the enterprise, the effects of market depreciation on the progress of the firm's plan over time would be as depicted in Fig. 2.

The amount of depreciation taken in each period permits the enterprise to maintain the market value of its total assets from period to period. Unless some "income" as well as depreciation is reinvested subjective value is bound to decline until at the end of the machine's life goodwill has entirely disappeared. As goodwill materializes in market values it is withdrawn under the label of income. The objective observer, who is likely to judge a firm's welfare by the market value of its assets, would pronounce the firm as well off at the end of the

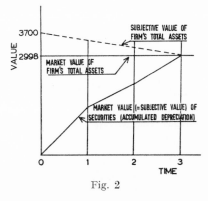

Fig. 2

plan as it was at the beginning or for that matter at any point in between. The concept of replacement implicit in the market depreciation approach is then the replacement of market values as they disappear over time and with use.

c. *"Internal Rate" Depreciation.* A third theoretical view of depreciation which merits discussion rests on the assumption that the enterprise should earn income in each period at the internal rate of return applied to the investment in the machine. Like subjective depreciation, income is defined and depreciation is a residual, but the internal rate is selected in such a way that by the end of the machine's life, the total depreciation (plus scrap value) is just equal to the original cost of the machine, an end situation similar to that attained under market depreciation.[7] The data on the hypothetical company are reconstructed in Table 3 to reflect "internal rate" depreciation.

According to the internal rate method, income from use of the machine

TABLE 3

THE ECONOMIC PLAN OF A HYPOTHETICAL FIRM

Internal Rate Depreciation

		Period			
	1	2	3		Total
1. Quasi-rents	$2000	$1000	$900		$3900
2. Scrap value				$200	200
3. Total Machine Receipts	2000	1000	900	200	4100
4. Income from machine (20% of book investment)	600	319	183	—	1102
5. Depreciation and scrap value	1400	681	717	200	2998
6. Interest on securities (Invested Depreciation) at 6%	—	84	125		209
Total Income (Item 4 plus 6)	600	403	308		1311

is computed by applying the internal rate to the remaining investment in the machine. The book investment in any period is determined by subtracting the residual quasi-rent (depreciation) from the book investment of the preceding period. Clearly at any date other than the beginning and end of machine life the computed investment may differ substantially from actual market value because no market value data for such a date are incorporated in the computation of book investment. If the machine had a single use and all single enterprise firms who employ the machine were equally efficient, arbitrage between the new machine and used machine markets would tend to bring market values into conformity with the computed investment figures. Under these circumstances market depreciation and internal rate depreciation would yield the same pattern over time. Under more usual circumstances, however, the two theories would yield different time patterns of value and depreciation. We shall continue to treat them as separate theories.

Income from the machine and depreciation on it will accumulate over the life of the machine to the same totals under both market and internal rate methods. If reported income is withdrawn in each case, however, the market value of the enterprise's total assets, machine and securities, will differ in the two cases because the timing of securities purchases under the internal rate method will differ from the time pattern specified by the market depreciation method. As another consequence of this, income from securities, and therefore total enterprise income, will differ from one method to the other both in each period and over the machine's total life (compare the total income figures in Table 3 with data in Table 2). When prices and technology are constant, internal rate depreciation is consistent with the ultimate replacement concept, that is, it permits the accumulation of sufficient funds to replace market value (and the machine) at the end of the existing machine's lifetime. The method does not permit the period-to-period replacement of either subjective value (as does the subjective depreciation method) or market value (as does market depreciation). Its essential characteristic is the maintenance of a constant internal rate of return, and the base on which it is to be earned is usually specified as depreciated original cost. When prices are changing, therefore, it is not likely to supply the appropriate funds for even ultimate replacement of market value. It is the theory which most probably underlies the various arbitrary techniques based on original cost, but we suggest below an alternative view.

d. *The Methods Compared.* Subjective depreciation differs from the other two methods in another important respect—it is not independent of contemplated replacement. If the entrepreneur's horizon encompasses the life span of two machines and the replacement of the first machine is expected to be profitable, the subjective value of the new plan will exceed the subjective value of one machine by the present value of the goodwill on its replacement. The more extensive the horizon, the larger the subjective value of the firm's plan is likely to be. This larger subjective value will affect the division of each quasi-rent into income and depreciation elements. The external rate of interest applied against the larger subjective value raises income in each period at the expense of depreciation. The size of the transfer within each (given) quasi-rent from the depreciation category to the income category depends not only on the extension of the horizon but also on the size of the subsequent goodwills brought within the extended horizon.

Stationary conditions combined with an infinite horizon produce an interesting case which can also serve as a standard for comparison. Under these circumstances the firm expects to operate an infinite chain of machines all of which will yield the same series of quasi-rents.* This set of very special circumstances is significant because it yields

---

* We assume also that the quasi-rent pattern of each machine is such that replacement does not affect machine life.

the intriguing result that over the life of each machine subjective depreciation will equal market (and internal rate) depreciation.[8] *Standard subjective depreciation*, as we shall call it, is illustrated in Table 4 on the assumption that the machine of earlier examples is but the first of an infinite chain of machines. The subjective value of the chain is computed to be $7380.

TABLE 4

THE ECONOMIC PLAN OF A HYPOTHETICAL FIRM

Subjective Depreciation for an Infinite Chain

	Period			
	1	2	3	Total
1. Total Machine Receipts	$2000	$1000	$1100	$4100
2. Income from machine	443	349	310	1102
3. Depreciation and Scrap Value	1557	651	790	2998
4. Income from Securities	—	94	133	227
Total Income (Item 2 plus 4)	443	443	443	1329

Total depreciation ($2998) and total machine income ($1102) are identical to the respective amounts obtained under the other two methods. The reason for this is not hard to find. The infinite horizon and the constancy of the expected stream of goodwills means that subjective value can be maintained simply by maintaining market value. Purchasing a new machine at its market price automatically maintains the subjective value of the chain of machines. When the horizon of the entrepreneur was limited to one machine he could only anticipate the investment of depreciation funds at the external rate of interest. To maintain a constant stream of subjective income the amount so invested had to be large. With an infinite horizon the entrepreneur can expect to continue earning at the higher (constant) internal rate.

The effect can be viewed in another way. The higher subjective value of the chain of machines as compared to the single machine is reflected in higher subjective income, the external rate of interest being constant. But the periodic quasi-rent on each machine is not affected by the extension of the entrepreneur's horizon. Therefore the amount of each quasi-rent that can be labelled depreciation is reduced by exactly the amount that income is increased. When subjective depreciation is standard the total amount transferred from depreciation to income over the life of one machine brings total machine income and total depreciation into equality with the comparable figures for market and internal rate depreciation. Under these circumstances the granting of market depreciation for tax purposes works no hardship on the firm. The firm cannot argue that market depreciation is insufficient to maintain subjective value.

But any factor which raises or lowers the subjective value (and therefore the subjective income) of the firm's plan of operation relative to the standard subjective value without affecting the cost of machines in the chain or the quasi-rent pattern of the first machine will lower or raise the depreciation charge computed in each period for that machine relative to standard subjective depreciation. Thus if the firm expects that each machine in the chain will be more profitable than the preceding one, the subjective value of the plan will exceed the standard subjective value, subjective income will rise and the total depreciation taken over the life of each machine will be less than the cost of replacing it, and market depreciation would exceed subjective depreciation. Depreciation charges on the subjective basis will be high enough to maintain subjective value but because each machine is more profitable than the preceding one, the reinvestment of market depreciation would raise the subjective value of the chain. Such an increase is net investment, according to the subjective theory, not replacement.

If the machine is not divisible, however, the entrepreneur must replace it with another identical machine in order to stay in business. A financing problem exists. Subjective depreciation is deficient as a means of financing physical replacement and the entrepreneur must seek funds in the market or invest some of his income in order to make up the deficiency.

Similarly, if it is expected that each machine in the chain will be less profitable than the one it replaces, the subjective value of the chain will be less than the subjective value of the standard chain. Subjective income will be less also and total depreciation taken over the life of each machine will exceed its cost of replacement (and market depreciation) though not by so much as in the single machine horizon case.

The standard chain yields subjective depreciation charges which, over the life of each machine, total to the same amount as market and internal rate depreciation charges, but it does not follow that the machine income and depreciation charges *per period* must be identical. The differences will be reflected in the different amounts earned from securities under the three methods. There are circumstances, however, under which even the period-to-period pattern of depreciation charges will be identical for all methods, but these circumstances are not entirely realistic. If the internal rate of return is equal to the external rate of return, subjective value will equal cost and internal rate depreciation will be identical over time to subjective depreciation. More plausibly, if we assume continuous replacement (so that no excess funds are invested at the external rate), the two techniques will yield identical results. If in addition the machine has a single use and the firms employing it are in perfect competition and are equally efficient, the market depreciation pattern will tend toward equality with that of the other methods.

In the absence of taxes management can always arrange its dividend and investment policies in such a way that essentially the same results are achieved under all three methods. If subjective depreciation exceeds market depreciation, for example, management need only "reinvest" an appropriate part of its reported income under the market or internal rate methods. These compensating adjustments will have the effect of making these methods comparable to subjective depreciation. If taxes are levied on reported income, however, this possibility vanishes.

e. *Objectivity of the Methods.* The subjective value of a machine or a chain of machines depends upon expectations of future events and the time span for which expectations are held. Even if, as events unfold, these expectations are gradually realized, the division of each quasi-rent into income and depreciation elements continues to rest on subjective factors—the entrepreneur's expectations of still future events. While the entrepreneur is free to make the division in estimating his own welfare, it is not likely that this method will be accepted as a basis for tax computation or even for reports to other interested parties.

A further complication exists in the modern corporation where the locus of expectations cannot be clearly identified. While subjective estimates of one kind or another lie at the root of corporate decisions, nevertheless the evaluation of these decisions is more likely to rest on the unfolding of actual events. The diffusion of managerial decisions is likely to elevate the importance of objective depreciation methods simply because subjective depreciation is difficult to identify even internally.

Internal rate depreciation is no more objective, however, than subjective depreciation. It, too, rests for its determination on expectations of future events but these expectations are coalesced in the internal rate of return instead of in subjective value.

Though neither of these methods is objectively applicable, the principal distinction between them, namely, the difference between cost and subjective value as a depreciation base, is of at least theoretical significance for tax purposes. Should depreciation allowable for tax purposes permit the recovery of subjective value or of market value over the life of the machine? One maintains the well-being of the entrepreneur given his expectations. The other permits the maintenance of his purchasing power in the market, not necessarily on a day-to-day basis in the case of the internal rate method but over the life of the machine. Depreciation under the latter method may exceed, equal or fall short of subjective depreciation. If we measure optimism and pessimism of the entrepreneur in terms of deviations from the standard subjective depreciation pattern, then internal rate depreciation rewards the optimistic by granting depreciation charges that are larger than he would demand subjectively and penalizes the pessimistic by granting charges that are less than he deems necessary.

The merit of the internal rate method lies in the fact that by the end of the life of the machine it permits the firm to replace exhausted market value. But the technique employed for doing this depends upon expectations, and is therefore subjective in nature; it disregards market value at every point in time except at the beginning and end of the machine's life. Market depreciation, on the other hand, permits the same end result but has two theoretical advantages over internal rate depreciation. It permits the maintenance of market value at every point in time and is theoretically measurable objectively. The determination of depreciation by this method depends for any period on events that have already transpired. A knowledge of asset life, which we have seen depends on expectations, is not necessary; neither is a knowledge of subjective value nor of the internal rate of return an essential feature of the method. It has also been pointed out in criticism of the internal rate method that the assumption of a constant internal rate of return over the life of the machine is itself wholly arbitrary.[9]

f. *Arbitrary Depreciation Techniques.* The depreciation techniques that are used in practice may be regarded as means of approximating either internal rate or market depreciation. Professor Jones interprets them as approximations to internal rate depreciation.[10] These methods, which include the straight-line technique, the declining balance technique, the sum-of-the-years-digits method, the compound interest method and various production unit techniques, involve either (1) constant periodic charges for depreciation, (2) charges which decline in size as machine life progresses or (3) charges which increase over time. They all have the characteristic that total charges over machine life are equal to original cost less scrap value, though the same techniques could be applied to other depreciation bases. The choice of one technique over another is apparently to be made, however, on the basis of the time pattern of the charges, not on the amount to be depreciated.[11] In any event under the stationary conditions we are assuming the time pattern is the relevant consideration.

Each arbitrary technique will yield a pattern of charges that is compatible with internal rate depreciation only for machines having a specifiable quasi-rent pattern. For example, if quasi-rents are constant over time, an unusual situation, a system of rising depreciation charges is necessary. As the value of the machine diminishes over time, machine income, computed on this diminishing value at a given internal rate, must also be declining and the depreciation charges, the residual part of constant quasi-rents, must be rising. They must be higher in each period by the decline in income, i.e., by the income sacrificed at the internal rate on the amount by which the value of the machine has been reduced.*

If depreciation charges are constant over time (as with the straight-line technique) and income is a constant percentage (the internal rate) of machine value, which is declining, the sum of the constant charge and the declining income will yield a series of quasi-rents which also declines. Thus a mildly declining quasi-rent pattern is necessary if straight-line depreciation is to represent a good approximation of internal rate depreciation. Obviously more rapidly declining quasi-rents are necessary if diminishing charge methods are to be rationalized in terms of the internal rate theory.

Those who explore the relevance of arbitrary depreciation techniques by comparing the results so achieved with market value patterns are testing them as approximations of market depreciation.[12] The market values of given machines of different ages (and degrees of use) are used to estimate the pattern. The percentage decline in value from machines of one age to machines of another yields a pattern of depreciation rates which can serve as a means of estimating the value of a

---

* Such a series of charges is characteristic of the compound interest method for computing depreciation.

particular machine at different points in time. It should be clear, however, that such a rate pattern could be applied to any base, a point which will attain added significance when price changes are admitted to the analysis. Applying the rate pattern to original cost is but one possibility, namely, the possibility suggested by internal rate depreciation.

Under the stationary conditions we have assumed, however, all of the methods considered, except subjective depreciation, yield total depreciation funds over the life of the machine which with scrap value are just sufficient to replace it even though the charges per unit of time may differ substantially.

Before turning to the multiple machine enterprise let us summarize briefly the relationship between the three theoretical depreciation methods discussed and the four replacement criteria previously identified. Subjective depreciation provides for the continuous replacement of subjective value, market depreciation provides for the continuous replacement of market value, and internal rate depreciation provides for the replacement of original cost. As no price changes have been admitted to the analysis, the latter two methods also meet the ultimate physical replacement criterion. Neither the original cost nor the ultimate replacement criterion requires any particular time pattern of depreciation charges so long as the total conforms to original cost in the one case and to the cost of ultimate physical replacement in the other.

B. The Multiple Machine Enterprise and the Achievement of an Even Age Distribution of Machines

Both the periodic depreciation charge and the amount of new machine acquisitions which can be called replacement depend in part on the amount and rate of new acquisitions in the past. When the amount and rate of new acquisitions is variable, as it is in the multiple machine enterprise, the dimensions of the depreciation-replacement relationship are enlarged. This enlargement is not to be attributed to changing prices or changing technology (these we shall deal with later) but rather to the rate of growth of the enterprise.

As a prelude to the explicit recognition of the growth variable, it will be useful to reexamine our concepts of replacement in terms of the non-growing multiple machine enterprise and to introduce another concept of replacement which has captured considerable attention in recent years. A review of the factors which determine a new firm's initial stock of machines given stationary demand and supply conditions is the first order of business. Starting with this initial stock composed entirely of new machines other factors will induce the firm to vary its rate of new acquisitions of machines over time so that eventually the machine stock assumes an *even* age distribution, i.e., the machines in the stock will be divided equally among all possible age groups.

1. *The Optimum Initial Stock*

The number of new machines a new firm should acquire initially and the rate at which it should plan to add to its stock should together represent a course of action whose goodwill is greater than any alternative course of action. The size of the initial stock of machines the firm will acquire is subject to several limitations not all of which need apply in a particular case. These are (1) monopsony in the machine market, (2) imperfect competition, (3) monopsony in the markets for related factors of production, (4) diseconomies of scale, (5) a rising supply curve for funds, and (6) the planned rate of subsequent acquisitions.[13]

If the enterprise's demand for machines affects the price the enterprise must pay for them a point will be reached where an additional machine will not increase the goodwill of the enterprise. The effect on marginal goodwill is in this case a result of the higher machine cost. The second and third factors affect marginal goodwill also but they do so by reducing the quasi-rents on all machines. If the firm operates in an imperfectly competitive atmosphere, an increase in the size of the initial stock of machines will reduce the quasi-rents on the other machines in the stock by reducing the selling price that can be obtained for their outputs. This interdependence among machines may be reflected also on the cost side if factors of production complementary to the machine rise in price as the enterprise increases its demand for them. As the marginal quasi-rents decline the marginal goodwill also declines and further increases in the initial machine stock become less and less profitable. The existence of diseconomies of scale has essentially the same effect but through higher managerial and administrative costs rather than through higher direct operating costs.

The fifth factor, the availability of funds, is usually reflected in a rising borrowing rate of interest or in rationing. As the marginal borrowing rate rises the present value of the marginal quasi-rents attributable to an additional machine declines and another limit is imposed on the size of the initial machine stock. If capital is rationed, the firm will purchase the initial stock of machines this fund permits provided none of the other conditions are violated.

The interdependence among machines is matched by an interdependence among periods. Thus if capital is rationed in total, a firm faced with a rising supply price of machines may find it profitable to postpone the purchase of some marginal machines to a later period when their cost will be less. The present value of their goodwill when purchased later may be greater than their goodwill when purchased initially. Perhaps of greater importance is the planned addition of machines during the lifetime of the initial stock. This factor will tend to reduce the quasi-rents expected from the initial stock and will therefore tend to reduce the size of the initial stock which is optimum.

2. The Timing of New Acquisitions

Under certain rather special sets of circumstances the rate of acquisition of new machines may be zero until the initial stock of machines is due for replacement. If the machines that compose the initial stock are of the constant (technical and economic) efficiency type and the only limitation on the size of the initial stock is imperfect competition or diseconomies of scale (in conjunction with perfect or imperfect competition) and the demand and cost conditions are constant over time, there will be no incentive for the firm to add new machines to its initial stock. The addition of a machine at any time will have the same effect on profit that it would have had if added to the initial stock. If this effect is favorable, the machine would be included in the initial stock, not added at a later date.

If the machines are of the diminishing efficiency type, as appears more likely, the chances that a firm will not add new machines before the initial stock is worn out seem remote. If the demand for the firm's product is constant over time, the factors causing the quasi-rents on the initial machine stock to decline over time can be classified as affecting variable costs or fixed costs, most probably both. If it is fixed costs alone that are affected (costs of supervision, minimum maintenance costs and the like) the output per period, so long as it pays to produce at all, will not be affected by the reduced quasi-rents—marginal costs and demand conditions are invariant from one period to another. If monopsonistic effects in the machine market are negligible and the supply of funds is perfectly elastic to the firm, there is no reason for adding new machines during the lifetime of the initial stock.

Undoubtedly other, probably equally bizarre, sets of circumstances can be specified under which the size of the machine stock will remain constant over time but these should be sufficient to illustrate the improbability of such behavior on the part of the firm. When such circumstances do exist the behavior of the multiple machine enterprise can be interpreted in terms of the principles set forth for the single machine enterprise—the stock of machine has all of the essential characteristics of a single machine.[14]

Circumstances which appear to be more usual suggest that a firm will find it profitable to acquire some new machines during the lifetime of the initial stock. A firm in imperfect competition, for example, that operates machines of the diminishing efficiency type will find such acquisitions profitable so long as marginal costs are affected at all by the diminished efficiency of the machines in the initial stock. Fig. 3

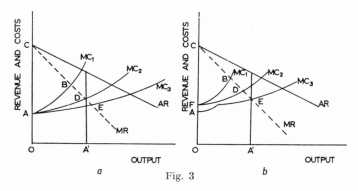

Fig. 3

illustrates this possibility.[15] In Fig. 3a the marginal cost curve of the firm is depicted as the horizontal sum of the marginal cost curves of the individual machines it employs. Thus the firm's marginal cost is MC_1 if it employs one machine, MC_2 if it employs two, and MC_3 if it employs three. The marginal quasi-rent of one machine is ABC, of two machines, ABD, and of three machines, ADE.* We assume that the present value of the marginal quasi-rents of three machines is not high enough to warrant the initial purchase of a third machine.

Fig. 3b depicts the firm's situation in the next period. Because of diminishing efficiency the marginal cost curves on the first two machines have shifted upward and to the left. As a consequence adding a third new machine may now be profitable because its initial marginal quasi-

---

* This follows from the fact that the total quasi-rent of the firm is the area between the marginal revenue curve and the relevant marginal cost curve.

rent is now higher than before, namely, FDEA, and presumably each subsequent marginal quasi-rent will also be higher. As more time passes, causing the marginal cost curves of the three machines to shift further upward and to the left, it may become profitable to acquire other machines as well. In fact, as Professor Lutz has pointed out, if the number of machines is a continuous variable and static conditions prevail, enough machines will be acquired in each period to just maintain the aggregate marginal cost curve that was optimum in the first period; prices and outputs will be constant over time.[16] The number of machines in stock and the rate of new acquisitions will, of course, vary from period to period until an even age distribution is achieved, i.e., until the machines in stock are distributed equally among all possible ages. Henceforward the machine stock and the rate of new acquisitions (all physical replacements) will be constant.

3. *Replacement Criteria Reexamined*

Once an even age distribution of machines is achieved, the aggregate quasi-rents of the machine stock will be constant from one period to another so long as static conditions continue. The market value of the machine stock will also be invariant over time and replacement expenditures, too, will be unchanging from one period to the next. If the entrepreneur's horizon is unlimited, we can properly treat the machine stock as a machine of infinite life although its components are constantly changing.

Under these circumstances all of the depreciation techniques developed for the single machine enterprise come to the same thing. Let us distinguish between *gross quasi-rents*, gross receipts less all expenditures except interest and replacement, and *net quasi-rents*, gross receipts less all expenditures except interest but including replacement. The constant, perpetual stream represented by the latter when discounted to the present yields the subjective value of the machine stock. Interest on this amount, subjective income (it is also the net quasi-rent), when subtracted from the gross quasi-rent leaves as depreciation an amount just sufficient to maintain subjective value by replacing the machines retired during the period.

The internal rate method yields identical results if the infinite horizon is recognized in the computation. Then the net quasi-rents, when discounted by the internal rate, yield the market value of the machine stock at any time. This rate applied to that market value yields the net quasi-rent as income and the difference between gross and net quasi-rents as depreciation, the amount needed for replacement. It is evident that the market value method yields the same result.

It is also true that under these circumstances any of the arbitrary depreciation techniques based on original cost will yield identical aggregate depreciation charges per period so long as the same technique is applied to all of the machines in the stock. The machines in the stock are divided equally among all of the possible age groups. However irregular the time pattern of depreciation charges appears when applied to an individual machine, the total of the charges on all machines in any one period will be constant period after period and equal to the aggregate charges yielded by any other arbitrary technique.

But a new concept of replacement can now be isolated. Is the periodic depreciation charge on the entire machine stock adequate to finance the purchase of the physical replacements needed in the period to preserve the size of machine population? This criterion, we shall call it *running physical replacement*, is met in the case now under discussion—a firm operating a machine stock of even age distribution under static conditions. Regardless of depreciation technique, total depreciation charges per period should equal

$$\frac{1}{n}(C - S),$$

where n is the lifetime of each machine, C is the original cost of the machine stock and S is the scrap value of the machine stock. The even-age distribution of the machine stock means that the cost of running physical replacement must be

$$\frac{1}{n}C.$$

The funds available for this purpose include depreciation,

$$\frac{1}{n}(C - S),$$

and the scrap value realized on the machines retired from stock in this period,

$$\frac{1}{n}S.$$

These funds are just equal to the cost of running physical replacement.*

We have then five replacement criteria by which to judge the adequacy of depreciation charges: (1) *the continuous replacement of subjective value* criterion rests on the premise that subjective value should be maintained from period to period; (2) *the continuous replacement of market value* criterion suggests that each period's depreciation charge should be sufficient to maintain the market value of the firm's assets in that period; (3) *the replacement of historic cost* requires that, by the end of a machine's life, depreciation accumulate to its original cost; (4) *the ultimate physical replacement* criterion suggests that depreciation charges on a particular machine should be sufficient to provide for its ultimate replacement; (5) *the running physical replacement* criterion requires that each period's depreciation charge be just sufficient to maintain a constant physical stock of machines. Given static conditions, an infinite horizon, accurate expectations and a machine stock evenly distributed by age, *all* of these criteria are satisfied by *all* of the depreciation methods we have discussed (subjective value, internal rate, market value, and original-cost-based arbitrary methods). When these conditions are violated, however, and many of them are likely to be in the real world, the convenient identities of replacement criteria and of depreciation methods vanish. It becomes necessary to choose from among the alternatives. What these alternatives are and what they mean under various sets of dynamic conditions including growth, price and price level changes, and changes in technology are the subject of the succeeding section.

II. CAPITAL MAINTENANCE UNDER DYNAMIC CONDITIONS

A. GROWTH

In developing replacement criteria it was convenient to treat the rate of new machine acquisitions as a function of the various demand and cost conditions which the firm expected to prevail in the present and future. Under the static conditions we assumed it was shown that a new firm would be likely to achieve eventually an even age distribution of machines and that henceforth the amount of new acquisitions

---

* It should be pointed out, however, that this equality does not hold for the single machine enterprise. According to the running physical replacement criterion each period's depreciation charge is excessive except in the period when physical replacement actually occurs. In that period, under static conditions, the charge is deficient by the sum of the prior excesses.

would be constant and equal to the firm's periodic depreciation charges. Under these conditions the rates of growth of demand, of the stock of machines, of new acquisitions, of depreciation charges, and of profits would be equal to each other and to zero. In the interim period, before an even age distribution of machines was achieved, the rates of growth of the stock of machines, of new acquisitions, and of depreciation charges would be positive although the rate of growth of demand was zero. The diminished efficiency of the aging machines had to be compensated for by the addition of new machines in order to meet the same demand.

Similar interim differentials in the rates of growth of these variables would exist if a new firm commenced business in a state in which demand was growing steadily. Beyond this interim period, however, the rates of growth in all of the variables would be equal to each other, the machine-related variables (machine stock, new acquisitions, and depreciation charges) having been brought into conformity with the steady growth in demand. The manner in which growth tends to affect depreciation-replacement relationships can be most constructively examined in the later period when a stable age distribution of assets has been achieved. Having adopted this approach it is a matter of indifference whether we assume a constant rate of growth in demand or a constant rate of growth in new machine acquisitions at the outset because beyond the interim period the two rates will be equal. It is convenient to deal with a constant rate of growth in new machine acquisitions but one should be aware that if such a growth rate is economical for a new firm from its beginning, it implies an uneven growth in the demand for the firm's product until the interim period has elapsed.[17]

1. *The Achievement of a Stable Age Distribution of Machines*

If a firm expands its acquisition of new machines at a constant rate and the machines acquired are identical having a life of n years, a life which we can assume has been determined on economic grounds, the machine stock of a new firm will have reached a stable age distribution after the passage of n years. The initial stock will then have been scrapped and the machine stock will be composed of those machines acquired in the last n years. Given a positive rate of growth, the amounts spent on the more recent acquisitions will exceed the amounts spent on earlier acquisitions and the average age of the machines in stock will be dominated by the newer machines. On the other hand, if the growth rate is negative (the amount of new acquisitions declines from period to period), the older assets will dominate the average machine age.

A convenient way of expressing the stable age distribution of machines is through the proportion, z, of the actual machine-years of service remaining in the machine stock to the machine-years such a stock would represent if all machines in it were new. This proportion is indicated for several values of machine life, n, and rates of growth of new acquisitions, k, in Table 5.

TABLE 5

THE STABLE PROPORTION OF LIFE REMAINING IN A MACHINE STOCK
FULLY ADJUSTED TO THE RATE OF GROWTH, k*

(Each machine has a life of n years)

k \ n	5	10	20	30	50
—.10	.46	.42	.34	.28	.19
—.05	.48	.46	.42	.38	.31
—.02	.49	.48	.47	.45	.42
0	.50	.50	.50	.50	.50
.02	.51	.52	.53	.55	.58
.05	.52	.54	.58	.62	.69
.10	.54	.58	.66	.72	.81

* The proportion, z, is determined from the following formula: $z = 1 - 1/kn + 1/(e^{kn}-1)$. Its derivation is indicated in the Mathematical Appendix, Expressions (1) through (6). (Proportion of Life Expired $= 1 - z$.)

It will be noted that when the rate of growth is zero the stable age distribution is one in which the machine-years remaining in the stock represent exactly one-half of the machine-years in a new stock of the same size. When the firm is growing or declining, however, the stable age distribution is relatively newer or older. In the extreme case of fifty-year assets, a firm growing at a rate of 10% would be operating on a year-to-year basis with 81% of its machine-years still in stock while a firm that is declining at a rate of 10% would be operating steadily with a machine stock that has only 19% of its original machine-years left. A rate of growth of 5% in machines having a thirty-year life yields a stable proportion of 62%*.

* The figures which appear to be most relevant for the United States are enclosed in the small box which encompasses machine (and construction) lives of 20 to 30 years

2. *Depreciation and the Replacement Criteria*

a. *Running Physical Replacement.* The fact that growth or decline throws the stable age distribution of a machine stock to either side of the even age distribution typical of a non-growing firm lies at the root of the depreciation-replacement problem as discussed in recent years.[18] When a firm is growing machines are being added to the stock at a greater rate than machines are being withdrawn. Depreciation taken by any method that spreads original cost over the whole life of a machine must now be larger than the cost of replacing machines withdrawn from the stock. Whatever the depreciation technique, it is applied to a larger machine stock than n times the number of machines withdrawn. But the non-growth case is one in which the technique is applied to a stock *equal* to n times the number of machines withdrawn, and in that case depreciation charges are just equal to running physical replacement. When a firm is declining, on the other hand, the size of the machine stock on which depreciation is taken is smaller than n times retirements and depreciation charges will fall short of the cost of replacing physical retirements.*

Any of the popular arbitrary depreciation techniques can be used to illustrate this principle. The straight-line technique, still widely used in the United States, is convenient and simple. We shall assume that scrap value is zero in which case annual depreciation is simply $1/n$ times the original cost of the machine stock. This method implies that each machine-year of service has the same value as every other machine-year of service. When prices are constant, it follows that the proportions in Table 5 indicate the ratio of the book value of machines to the original cost of machines, the machine-years in the numerator (those remaining in stock) and the machine-years in the denominator (the number if the stock were new) both being multiplied by the same price per machine-year to put them on a value basis.[19] As one would

---

and rates of growth of two and five percent. These averages have some meaning for the economy as a whole but other figures in the table may be more relevant for particular industries and firms.

  * This should not be construed as saying that, of two firms of equal size, the one which has been growing must have depreciation charges that are currently larger than those for a non-growing firm. A depreciation technique yielding charges that increase with the age of the machine disproves this statement. The depreciation charges for the growing firm would in that case be weighted heavily by new machines on which charges are low. But the same firm will have substantially smaller retirements than the non-growing firm and the *ratio* of its depreciation to its cost of running replacement will exceed one, the ratio applicable to the non-growing firm.

expect the rapidly growing firm with long-lived machines has a high proportion of the original cost of its machines reflected in book value. The firm simply has not had time, nor will it ever have time if it continues to grow, to depreciate substantially the bulk of its assets.

But while the growing firm never has time to accumulate a high reserve for depreciation relative to the original cost of its machine stock, it's growth creates annual depreciation charges that are well in excess of the cost of physical replacement. The ratios of depreciation when scrap value is zero, D_0, to the cost of running physical replacement, R, are presented in Table 6 for various rates of growth, k, and for various asset lives, n.

TABLE 6

STABLE RATIOS OF D_0/R^* FOR VARIOUS ASSET LIVES, n, AND RATES OF GROWTH, k

(Expressed as percentages)
(Straight-line depreciation, zero scrap value)

k \ n	5	10	20	30	50
—.10	79	63	43	32	20
—.05	89	79	63	52	37
—.02	95	91	82	75	63
0	100	100	100	100	100
.02	105	111	123	137	172
.05	114	130	172	232	447
.10	130	172	320	618	2948

* Based on the formula, $D_0/R = \dfrac{(e^{kn} - 1)}{kn}$.

See Mathematical Appendix, Expression (10) and its derivation.

It is apparent that growth (or decline) upsets the equality between depreciation and the running physical replacement criterion. A growth rate as modest as 5% coupled with an asset-life of 30 years yields annual depreciation charges that are over 2.3 times the amount needed for replacement in this sense. A 10% growth rate with fifty-year assets would yield depreciation charges over 29 times replacement requirements. Even a growth rate of 2% with twenty-year assets yields depreciation charges that are excessive by nearly 25%.

A firm that is declining in size is faced with a deficiency of depreciation charges according to the running physical replacement criterion, but the deficiency is not as great percentagewise as is the excess for

growing firms. Thus a firm that is declining steadily at the rate of 5%
with twenty-year assets finds its depreciation charges falling short of
the cost to replace retired machines by 37% (100%–63%) while a firm
growing at 5% has an excess of 72%. This is because when two firms
are of the same size at the start the one declining at a given rate has
successively *smaller* absolute changes from period to period in its
amount of acquisitions than has a firm growing at the same rate. If
the *amounts* of growth and decline were constant instead of the *rates*
the respective excesses and deficiencies would be equal.

It is the departure, because of growth and decline, of depreciation
charges from running replacement requirements that has captured so
much attention of late in the journals.[20] That such a departure is
economically significant assumes, of course, that replacement requirements can be properly defined as the very special criterion we have
just explored. As the argument has been advanced, it has overlooked
the possibility or desirability of defining replacement in any of the
other ways explored earlier in this paper. According to the replacement
criterion selected, the conclusion is unshakable—growth destroys the
equality between depreciation and replacement. It remains to explore
briefly whether or not growth alone alters the adequacy of depreciation
charges according to other replacement criteria.

b. *Ultimate Replacement and the Replacement of Historic Cost.* The two
replacement concepts, ultimate replacement and replacement of original
cost, can be easily disposed of. As prices are assumed constant the
satisfaction of one criterion is sufficient to satisfy the other. Depreciation by any of the arbitrary methods we have discussed provides
for each machine just enough funds, if income is sufficient, to recover
with scrap value the original cost of that machine. The fact of growth
or decline of the firm does not alter the sufficiency of depreciation
charges according to these replacement criteria.

c. *Continuous Replacement of Market Value.* Any of the arbitrary depreciation techniques that were discussed earlier in the paper yields
excess funds according to the running replacement criteria. To assess
each of the two criteria remaining to be discussed (continuous replacement of market value and continuous replacement of subjective value),
we must first make the assumption that whatever arbitrary technique
we select is consistent under stationary conditions with the replacement concept being examined. Given this consistency we can then

proceed to investigate the effect growth may have on the adequacy of depreciation charges according to the selected criterion.

Let us investigate the continuous replacement of market value first. For the single machine enterprise this concept exhibited the greatest potential as an objectively equitable concept. Does growth destroy this characteristic? Let us assume that the market value pattern of the machines purchased by our firm accords with the straight-line depreciation technique. For the stationary firm confronted on all sides by constant prices the depreciation charges it computes will record the decline in market value of the machines it holds during each period. To maintain market value this is also the amount the firm must retain *in whatever form.**

We shall now argue that neither growth nor decline alters this general principle. The existence of growth does not alter the fact that depreciation measures the decline in market value of the firm's machines. If some other amount were retained by the firm, its market value would change. Of course, if a firm is growing or declining, its market value is changing in response to the growth or decline. But the fact of growth or decline does not affect the amount of funds the firm should be permitted to keep in order to *maintain* market value at the same level. The fact that a firm *chooses* to enhance or to dissipate its market value does not affect the size of the market value that depreciation charges, when covered by income, are designed to sustain. Depreciation charges, according to this replacement concept, indicate the amount of market value that should be added back (from whatever source) *if* market value is to be maintained. The reasoning applies when any technique, straight-line or not, is the appropriate one. Growth *per se* does not affect the validity of the replacement concept.

d. *Continuous Replacement of Subjective Value.* The continuous replacement of subjective value is more difficult to evaluate as a replacement concept under growth conditions because it depends upon the expectations of the particular entrepreneur. It will be recalled that under anticipated stationary conditions and an infinite horizon depreciation for the firm would be constant from one period to another and equal in amount to that determined by other techniques. Under reasonable conditions consistent with constant growth it would appear that subjective depreciation should grow at the same rate as the other

* The stationary assumption suggests that the form chosen will be new machines of the same type.

growth variables. One set of reasonable conditions would be the following:

(1) The firm faces a demand curve which shifts iso-elastically and at the given growth rate. In the absence of technological change and changes in productivity this would appear to be a reasonable assumption and one which sets the stage for constant prices. Population and income grow, of course, but the distribution of neither changes.
(2) There are no monopsonistic effects on factor prices (including machine prices) and the larger quantities demanded each period can be and are supplied at constant prices.
(3) There are no diseconomies of scale or if there are, the limit set by them expands at the given growth rate, say through improvements in managerial organization and better trained executives.
(4) Borrowing conditions are constant period after period so that the growth rate can be maintained at the same marginal borrowing rate and the ratio of external to internal funds is constant.

If these conditions exist and are expected, subjective value depreciation charges should grow at the given growth rate. But this is not sufficient to show that for growing firms these depreciation charges should *exceed* running replacement requirements at every point in time because running replacement requirements are also growing at the same rate. It is clear, however, that prices, costs, and the firm's gross quasi-rents per dollar of invested capital are constant over time. It follows that to buy an additional amount of subjective value in the future the firm must plan to increase its invested capital in the same proportion. To maintain the subjective value that can be associated with the current capital investment (the market value of the machines) i.e., excluding the present value of subjective values to be acquired in the future with planned additional investments (as opposed to the reinvestment of depreciation), the firm must simply maintain its current capital investment. In this sense market depreciation will permit the maintenance of subjective value as well as market value and we have already shown that for growing firms market depreciation exceeds running physical replacement. Therefore subjective depreciation will exceed it, too.*

* This is a brief summary of a difficult problem. For the single machine enterprise we were able to show, for example, that growth reduced subjective depreciation below market depreciation. That was a situation, however, where *larger* future goodwills were associated with an *unchanged* capital investment. In the case in the text every increase in subjective value requires a proportionate increase in cost. It would not make sense to relate the present value of all future goodwills to *currently* invested capital alone, nor to relate interest on subjective value so computed to the quasi-rent now produced by the currently invested capital alone. To do so might conceivably show depreciation to be negative, a nonsensical result. We have dealt, therefore, with

e. *An Assessment of the Running Physical Replacement Criterion.* We can conclude that running physical replacement is not replacement in any relevant sense. Replacement in this context is a misnomer. Satisfying the running physical replacement criterion maintains a constant machine stock but not a constant *stock of machine-years* with the single exception of stationary firms. For the stationary firm with constant prices, the running physical replacement criterion is equivalent to the others. Growth destroys its usefulness as a concept of replacement while growth leaves the value of the other replacement criteria unaffected. This is because *the amount of running physical replacement at any moment is completely unaffected by and entirely independent of growth.* Given the cost of new acquisitions made *n* years ago and constant prices since, the cost today of financing running physical replacement is determined. The amount is the same whether the firm has remained stationary, grown at a fantastic rate or wasted away. If it is replacement in any meaningful sense in which we are interested in a growing economy, we must look elsewhere.[21]

If this view is correct Eisner has criticized unjustly so-called "replacement cost" depreciation proposals by evaluating them in terms of a replacement criterion which is itself inadequate. He has written:[22]

"Those urging 'replacement cost' would not be satisfied with charging *the cost of replacing those assets currently requiring replacement,* although it is in terms of this cost that they make their appeal. They offer proposals to adjust currently allowable depreciation charges by price indices or to revalue assets in accordance with current market price, which indicate clearly that they would really like to base depreciation charges on *the cost of replacing all assets on the books....* It is a bit difficult to see the justification for these critics in using 'replacement' as a cost basis and then discarding it as an allocation basis."

We would be inclined to interpret the authors Eisner criticizes as suggesting that depreciation in any period should permit the replacement of the *value* of all asset services used during the period as opposed to the number of physical machines. If this is so, their position should be the easier one to defend.

3. *Depreciation and New Acquisitions*

In order to maintain the *value* of a firm's stock of machines as opposed to its physical count, the replacement criterion selected must

the subjective value that can be associated with a given capital investment, recognized that this is going to grow over time, but do not include the discounted values of these increases in the figure that is to serve as the subjective value to be maintained by depreciation.

correspond to a value concept, the choice of which becomes difficult when growth rates are uneven or prices and technology are changing. In a steadily growing firm there remains, nevertheless, the problem of financing its new acquisitions in each period.

If depreciation is taken in accord with the straight-line technique and scrap value is zero, the ratio of depreciation charges, D_0, to the cost of new acquisitions, A, can be determined under an assumed steady rate of growth, k, and given asset life, n. Such ratios are presented in Table 7. It will be noted that while rapid growth and a long asset life tend to make depreciation charges a large multiple of running replacement requirements (Table 6), the same factors make depreciation charges a small fraction of the cost of new acquisitions. This relationship is reversed when growth rates are negative.*

TABLE 7

STABLE RATIOS OF D_0/A * FOR VARIOUS ASSET LIVES, n, AND RATES OF GROWTH, k

(Expressed as percentages)
(Straight-line depreciation, zero scrap value)

n \ k	5	10	20	30	50
—.10	130	172	320	618	2948
—.05	114	130	172	232	447
—.02	105	111	123	137	172
0	100	100	100	100	100
.02	95	91	82	75	63
.05	89	79	63	52	37
.10	79	63	43	32	20

* Based on the formula $D_0/A = \dfrac{(1 - e^{-kn})}{kn}$.

See Mathematical Appendix, Expression (11).

The relationship between the two ratios has an economic significance. For a growing firm to maintain a high ratio of depreciation to running replacement requirements the firm must succeed in financing and maintaining the related rate of new machine acquisitions. As its depreciation charges represent only a fraction of the required funds, the firm must be prepared to make up the deficit through the retention of earnings or the use of external funds or both. On the other hand,

* A comparison of Tables 6 and 7 reveals that the ratio, D/A, for a positive growth rate and a given asset life is exactly equal to the ratio, D/R, for a negative growth rate.

the declining firm finds that while its depreciation is insufficient to finance running physical replacement should it desire to do so, the charges are well in excess of the actual machine purchases it makes.

4. *Total Machine Funds and Acquisitions*

a. *Straight-Line Depreciation.* But the simplification employed of a zero scrap value has the effect of underestimating the amount of profits and external funds that the growing firm must obtain in order to finance its new acquisitions. Machines usually have a scrap value and its existence, if it is used in depreciation computations, will reduce the total machine funds (depreciation plus scrap value of retirements) made available to growing firms. This is because scrap value represents a source of funds only when machines are retired but it has the effect of reducing depreciation charges on all machines in (the growing) stock. The stable ratios of total machine funds, M, to acquisitions, A, for various scrap values (as percentages of machine cost), u, are presented in Table 8. We have taken advantage in this table of the fact that depreciation is such a function of asset life, n, and the rate of growth, k, that we can treat their product, kn, as a single variable.

The data reveal that for growing firms (positive kn's) the higher the

TABLE 8

STABLE RATIOS OF TOTAL MACHINE FUNDS TO NEW AQUISITIONS FOR VARIOUS kn's AND SALVAGE VALUE PERCENTAGES, u's

(Expressed as percentages)
(Straight-line depreciation)

u \ kn	—3.0	—2.0	—1.5	—1.0	—.5	—.2	0	.2	.5	1.0	1.5	2.0	3.0
0	618	320	232	172	130	111	100	91	79	63	52	43	32
.02	645	328	236	174	131	111	100	91	79	63	51	43	31
.05	688	341	243	177	132	111	100	91	78	62	50	42	30
.10	757	362	254	182	133	112	100	90	77	61	49	40	29
.20	896	403	275	192	137	113	100	89	75	58	46	37	26
.30	1035	445	297	202	140	114	100	88	73	55	43	34	24
1.00	2009	739	448	272	165	122	100	82	61	37	22	14	5

Based on the formula $M_s/A = \dfrac{(1 - e^{-kn})(1 - u)}{kn} + u\,e^{-kn}$, which, when $u = 0$ becomes $M_s/A = D_0/A = \dfrac{1 - e^{-kn}}{kn}$.

When $u = 1$, $M_s/A = R/A = e^{-kn}$.

See Mathematical Appendix, Expressions (12) to (15).

scrap value the smaller the percentage of the cost of new acquisitions covered by machine funds (depreciation plus salvage value). A larger salvage value, therefore, forces a growing firm to procure more funds from either retained earnings, external markets, or both.

The reduction in machine funds caused by the existence of scrap value is not sizable, however, unless both the scrap value percentage and the rate of growth are high. For a kn of 1, which Domar has suggested is a reasonable average for the United States[23], a scrap value percentage of 10% would reduce machine funds to only 96% of the amount computed on a zero scrap value basis. But the growth rates of individual firms may vary greatly from this average. A firm growing at a 10% rate with thirty year assets (a kn of 3) would find that a scrap value of 20% would reduce machine funds from 32% of acquisition cost to 26%.[24]

b. *Accelerated Depreciation.* When the depreciation technique utilized is accelerated or decelerated *relative to the straight-line technique,* the proportion of the cost of new acquisitions covered by depreciation charges is, for growing firms, increased or decreased respectively. An accelerated technique yields larger charges in the early years of asset life and lower charges in the later years.* As the machine stock of a growing firm is relatively newer than for a stationary firm, its depreciation is taken at an average rate in excess of the straight-line rate. The principle can be illustrated by any of several techniques. We have selected the true declining balance technique for this purpose.**

* As a rigorous definition of acceleration we offer the following: of two techniques giving rise to machine funds, M_2 and M_1, respectively, the first (M_2) is more accelerated than the second (M_1) of in the relevant range $\dfrac{d(M_2 - M_1)}{dk}$ is positive.

** By the true declining balance technique we mean the application of a percentage, a, to the net book value of assets to determine each period's depreciation charge where the percentage is selected in such a way that at the end of asset life, n, net book value is just equal to salvage value, S. The usual formula is

$$a = 1 - \sqrt[n]{\frac{S}{C}}$$

where C is cost. The continuous rate formula is

$$e^{-an} = S/C.$$

In our notation $S/C = u$.

The diminishing balance percentages permitted for tax purposes in the United States as well as those permitted in England are determined more on policy grounds than on the basis of internal consistency and need not yield expected salvage value as a residual book value.

The total machine funds supplied by declining balance depreciation plus scrap value are expressed in Table 9 as percentages of the cost of new acquisitions. The effect of growth on the M/A ratio is similar to that indicated in Table 8 but less pronounced, i.e., growth reduces the M/A ratio less when depreciation is accelerated.* Higher salvage values again act to reduce (increase) the M/A ratio for growing (declining) firms.

TABLE 9

STABLE RATIOS OF TOTAL MACHINE FUNDS TO NEW ACQUISITIONS
FOR VARIOUS kn's AND u's

(Expressed as percentages)
(Declining balance depreciation)

u \ kn	—3.0	—2.0	—1.5	—1.0	—.5	—.2	0	.2	.5	1.0	1.5	2.0	3.0
.02	300	190	157	133	115	105	100	95	89	80	72	66	55
.05	360	226	177	143	120	107	100	94	86	75	67	60	50
.10	533	274	203	156	123	108	100	93	83	71	61	54	44
.20	747	334	240	178	131	111	100	91	79	65	54	46	36
.30	938	404	271	191	136	113	100	90	76	60	48	40	30
1.00	2009	739	448	272	165	122	100	82	61	37	22	14	5

Based on the formula $M_d/A = \dfrac{a + k\,e^{-n\,(a + k)}}{a + k}$.

See Mathematical Appendix, Expressions (16) to (19).

A comparison of Tables 8 and 9 reveals that for low scrap values the diminishing balance technique yields substantially more machine funds for growing firms than does the straight-line technique, while for declining firms it yields substantially less. As salvage value becomes a larger percentage of cost, however, (i.e., as u increases) these differentials are quickly eroded. For firms employing thirty-year assets and growing at a 5% rate ($kn = 1.5$), the accelerated technique with a 2% salvage value finances 20% more of new acquisitions than does the straight-line technique, but only 8% more when salvage is as high as 20% of cost. In terms of machine funds the accelerated technique is

* It follows that, given a rate of growth, accelerated depreciation will bring about larger departures of the M/R ratio from its value under stationary conditions than would straight-line depreciation. Machine funds will exceed running replacement requirements by more (less) the more accelerated (decelerated) those charges are. It is this effect to which Eisner and Domar have drawn attention.

supplying 40% more than is the straight-line technique when salvage is 2% but only 12% more when salvage is 20%. The advantage of employing an accelerated method of depreciation is clearly much greater for those growing firms that employ assets whose salvage value percentage is low.

5. Total Internal Financing

a. *Depreciation Techniques Internally Consistent.* The percentage of new acquisitions that can be financed with depreciation charges depends upon the adequacy of gross income in providing funds equal to those charges. If depreciation charges aren't earned the actual ratio of internally generated funds to acquisitions will be reduced. On the other hand, the existence of a positive rate of retained profit (profit after taxes, interest and dividends) will raise the ratio.

It is convenient in introducing the profit rate to deal with internal rate depreciation and to assume that whatever arbitrary depreciation technique we choose to employ the depreciation pattern it discloses fits the quasi-rent pattern of the machines employed in that a constant rate of return is earned in each period on the remaining book investment. In this sense the depreciation technique can be termed, "internally consistent". We have seen that such a time pattern need not conform to either the subjective or the market value depreciation criterion, but it may conform to both under constant growth conditions if replacement is continuous, as we are assuming, and the machines are single use and used by equally efficient, competitive firms.* We shall assume that these conditions hold so that any internally consistent depreciation pattern is consistent with all three criteria.

We can now show that the amount of external funds a firm needs in order to maintain a given rate of growth depends upon the depreciation method that is internally consistent and ultimately, therefore, upon the quasi-rent pattern associated with the machine and the way in which it is used. The stable ratios of internally generated funds (machine funds plus retained profit) to the cost of new acquisitions are presented in Table 10 for (1) machines that are properly subjected to straight-line depreciation zero salvage value, (2) machines depreciated on a straight-line basis with 10% salvage and (3) machines subject to true diminishing balance depreciation with 10% salvage. The term, *bcr*, in the table is simply the rate of retained profit and can be treated as one variable here. In Table 10A, for example, a firm employing

* See above pp. 63–66.

TABLE 10

INTERNALLY GENERATED FUNDS (RETAINED EARNINGS PLUS MACHINE
FUNDS) AS A PERCENTAGE OF THE COST OF NEW MACHINE ACQUISITIONS*

A
Straight-line Depreciation, Zero Salvage

bcr/k \\ kn	—.2	.2	.5	1	1.5	2.0	3.0
—.5	116	86	69	45	28	15	—2
0	111	91	79	63	51	43	31
.2	109	92	83	71	61	55	45
.5	105	95	90	82	76	72	66
.8	102	98	96	93	90	89	86
1	100	100	100	100	100	100	100
2	89	109	121	137	148	157	168

B
Straight-line Depreciation, Salvage = 10%

bcr/k \\ kn	—.2	.2	.5	1	1.5	2.0	3.0
—.5	118	85	66	42	24	10	—7
0	112	90	77	61	49	40	29
.2	110	92	82	69	59	52	43
.5	106	95	89	81	75	70	65
.8	102	98	95	92	90	88	86
1	100	100	100	100	100	100	100
2	88	110	123	139	151	160	171

C
Diminishing Balance Depreciation, Salvage = 10%

bcr/k \\ kn	—.2	.2	.5	1	1.5	2.0	3.0
—.5	112	90	75	57	42	31	16
0	108	93	83	71	61	54	44
.2	106	94	86	77	69	63	55
.5	104	97	92	86	81	77	72
.8	102	99	97	94	92	91	89
1	100	100	100	100	100	100	100
2	92	107	117	129	139	146	156

* The percentages, 100 F/A, are determined from the formula,

$$\frac{F}{A} = \frac{bcr}{k} + \left(1 - \frac{bcr}{k}\right)\frac{M}{A} \ . \quad (M/A \text{ values from Tables 8 and 9.})$$

See Mathematical Appendix, Expressions (22) to (25).

thirty-year assets and growing at the rate of 5% has a kn of 1.5. If its rate of retained profits is $2\frac{1}{2}\%$, its ratio bcr/k is .5. Such a firm will be able to finance 76% of its machine acquisitions out of internally generated funds and must seek external funds to the extent of 24%. A higher salvage value tends to reduce the amount of internally generated funds (compare values in Table 10B with those in 10A) for growing firms (but to increase them for declining firms) so long as the rate of retention is less than the rate of growth (more accurately, so long as $bcr/k < 1$). This is because salvage values supply funds only on those assets actually retired and what is taken as salvage is taken at the expense of depreciation. From a given starting point n years ago growth has a multiplier effect on depreciation charges but not on salvage values currently realized. For this reason an increase in the depreciable amount at the expense of salvage value will increase machine funds available to the growing firm. But a higher salvage value per machine means that the stock of machines will at any time have a higher book value than if salvage value were lower and it is on this book value that the firm earns its profit. As the rate of retention increases, therefore, the salvage value effect on machine funds is increasingly offset by the rise in retained profit. When the rate of retention equals the rate of growth the net effect of the salvage value percentage is zero. If the rate of retention exceeds the rate of growth the effect of salvage value on retention exceeds its effect on machine funds and a higher salvage value will *raise* (lower) the ratio of internally generated funds to acquisitions for growing (declining) firms.

The comparison of diminishing balance depreciation with straight-line depreciation (Table 10B and 10C) reveals that the former has a similar dual effect on internally generated funds. Because depreciation charges are accelerated the growing firm has larger machine funds than with straightline depreciation, but for the growing firm the value of a machine stock composed of diminishing-balance-type machines will be less than the value of a machine stock composed of straight-line-type machines. At any retention rate, therefore, the diminishing-balance machines supply *less* retained profits than straight-line machines so that the full superiority of the accelerated technique as a provider of machine funds is not reflected in its superiority as a supplier of total internally generated funds. As the retention rate rises the inferiority of the accelerated-technique machines as suppliers of retained earnings increases offsetting to a greater extent their superiority as suppliers of machine funds. As the retention rate rises therefore, the overall superiority of the diminishing-balance machines as suppliers of internally generated funds is diminished until, when the retention rate is equal to the growth rate, it has disappeared. For retention rates higher than the growth rate the diminishing-balance machines are an inferior provider of internally generated funds for growing firms.

If the rate of retention equals the rate of growth, however, the firm is in a position to finance all of its growth from internal funds regardless of the type of machines employed and the depreciation method that is internally consistent. The firm is earning retained profits on book value at precisely the rate at which that book value is growing. This conclusion holds for any internally consistent depreciation method.* There will be a significant difference between methods, however. The proportion of internally generated funds that is machine funds will be larger and the proportion that is retained earnings will be smaller the more accelerated is the internally consistent depreciation method.

b. *Arbitrary Depreciation Techniques.* The depreciation technique allowable for tax purposes may differ from the internally consistent method. One could argue on equitable grounds that each firm, indeed, that each asset, should be granted the depreciation charge that is internally consistent, no more and no less. When tax allowable charges are limited to a range of possibilities, however, we can conclude on the basis of the argument so far that each growing firm should, in order to maximize true after-tax profit (internally consistent profit less actual taxes), select the technique that is most accelerated, while declining firms should select the least accelerated technique. The precise effect of an arbitrary technique on internally generated funds will differ depending upon (1) the internally consistent technique it is substituted for, (2) the tax rate $(1 - b)$, (3) the dividend or interest rate $(1 - c)$, and, of course, the sufficiency of income with respect to both the internally consistent and the tax allowable depreciation methods. Management's view of any saving or dissaving enters also. Three cases are discernible: Case 1: the saving or dissaving accrues entirely to the firm; Case 2: the firm divides any saving or dissaving with the owners; and

---

* This can be demonstrated as follows: When stable relationships have been achieved, the rate of growth, k, must equal the increment in value of the machine stock, A — M (i.e., new acquisitions less loss in value of the old machine stock), divided by the value of the machine stock N. The deficiency of machine funds with respect to A is (A — M), which is equal to kN. When $bcr = k$ the gap is just closed, i.e., retained earnings, bcrN, equals the deficiency, kN.

Case 3: the firm treats new reported after-tax income as real and retains $100\,c\%$ of it as before. We shall treat Case 1 only.*

The effect of permitting for tax purposes a more accelerated depreciation charge than is internally consistent is to raise total computed machine funds, M, at the expense of computed before-tax profits, rN. This converts computed taxable income from rN_1 to $(rN_1 + M_1 - M_2)$ and computed machine funds from M_1 to M_2 (the subscript, 2, indicates new book figures, the subscript, 1, old book figures which are also the internally consistent figures). Total internal funds before tax and dividend payments are unaffected and are equal to $(rN_1 + M_1)$. Use of a depreciation method that is accelerated relative to the internally consistent method increases fund retention by reducing taxes and, perhaps, dividend payments.

As the reduction in book profit is $(M_2 - M_1)$, the reduction in taxes (the tax saving) is $(1 - b)\,(M_2 - M_1)$. If the firm retains the entire tax saving, it will represent

$$100\,(1 - b)\,\frac{(M_2 - M_1)}{A}\,\%$$

of its current cost of new acquisitions. The M/A ratios in Tables 8 and 9 can be used to estimate the saving, as a percentage of acquisition cost, that would accrue to a firm employing straight-line assets having a 10% salvage value if such a firm is premitted to use the declining balance method instead. Table 11 contains these data for various kn's and $(1 - b)$'s. The size of the savings varies directly with the tax rate, the rate of growth, and the life of assets. A firm operating thirty-year assets and growing at the rate of 5% ($kn = 1.5$) would save 6% of acquisition cost per year at a tax rate of 50%. Savings would be proportionately higher at higher tax rates. If the tax allowable technique was computed for a lower (fictitious) salvage value, the saving would be enhanced. Computation of diminishing value depreciation on a 2% salvage value basis, for example, would increase the saving from 6% to 11.5%.

6. *Some Policy Implications of Arbitrary Depreciation Techniques*

a. *The Impact on Profit Rates.* The amount of tax savings can be stated as a percentage of the internally consistent value of the machine

---

* Formulae for the savings accruing to the firm under all three cases are presented in the Mathematical Appendix, Expressions (26) to (36). The savings to the firm are largest for Case 3 and smallest for Case 2. Case 1 appears to be a reasonable compromise.

TABLE 11

TAX SAVINGS AS A PERCENTAGE OF NEW ACQUISITIONS WHEN DECLINING BALANCE DEPRECIATION (SALVAGE VALUE = 10%) IS PERMITTED INSTEAD OF INTERNALLY CONSISTENT STRAIGHT-LINE DEPRECIATION (SALVAGE VALUE = 10%)

$(1-b)$ $\diagdown$ kn	—.5	0	.2	.5	1.0	1.5	2.0	3.0
.10	—1.0	0	.3	.6	1.0	1.2	1.4	1.5
.30	—3.0	0	.9	1.8	3.0	3.6	4.2	4.5
.50	—5.0	0	1.5	3.0	5.0	6.0	7.0	7.5
.70	—7.0	0	2.1	4.2	7.0	8.4	9.8	10.5
.90	—9.0	0	2.7	5.4	9.0	10.8	12.6	13.5
1.00	—10.0	0	3.0	6.0	10.0	12.0	14.0	15.0

Based on the formula, $\dfrac{X}{A} = (1-b)\dfrac{(M_d - M_s)}{A}$.

See Mathematical Appendix, Expressions (26) to (28).

stock. Thus stated it represents the impact of a specified arbitrary depreciation technique on the after-tax profit rate of a firm using machines requiring a specified internally consistent depreciation technique. Some sample percentages are presented in Table 12 for a growth rate of 5% and a tax rate of 50%. The arbitrary technique has the characteristic, M_2/A, while the internally consistent method has the characteristic, M_1/A. These characteristics can be read from Tables 8 and 9 for the straight-line and diminishing balance depreciation methods or computed for others. An example may clarify the use of the table. Suppose a firm growing at a 5% rate utilizes machines having a life of 30 years subject to internally consistent depreciation equivalent to the straight-line technique with a 5% salvage value. These factors yield an M_1/A ratio of .50 (Table 8). Suppose such a firm is permitted to depreciate according to the diminishing balance method with a fictitious salvage value of about 3%. This yields an M_2/A ratio of .70 (interpolated from Table 9). Table 12 reveals that the after-tax profit rate of this firm will tend to be one percentage point higher than if only its internally consistent depreciation charges were deductible for tax purposes. The more accelerated method is therefore equivalent to an increase of two percentage points in its pretax profit rate when the tax rate is 50%. On the other hand, a firm growing at the same rate but employing machines having the diminishing balance characteristic while it is forced to use the straight-line technique for tax purposes would find its after-tax profit rate reduced by 1.7 percentage points.

TABLE 12

THE CHANGE IN PERCENTAGE AFTER-TAX PROFIT RATE EFFECTED BY USE OF AN
ARBITRARY DEPRECIATION TECHNIQUE YIELDING M_2/A INSTEAD OF AN INTERNALLY
CONSISTENT TECHNIQUE YIELDING M_1/A

$(k = .05, \ b = .50)$

M_1/A \ M_2/A	.30	.40	.50	.60	.70	.80	.90	1	1.1
.30	0	.4	.7	1.1	1.4	1.8	2.1	2.5	2.9
.40	—.4	0	.4	.8	1.3	1.7	2.1	2.5	2.9
.50	—1.0	—.5	0	.5	1.0	1.5	2.0	2.5	3.0
.60	—1.9	—1.3	—.6	0	.6	1.3	1.9	2.5	3.1
.70	—3.3	—2.5	—1.7	—.8	0	.8	1.7	2.5	3.3
.80	—6.3	—5.0	—3.8	—2.5	—1.3	0	1.3	2.5	3.8
.90	—15.0	—12.5	—10.0	—7.5	—5.0	—2.5	0	2.5	5.0

Based on the formula,
$$\frac{\Delta F}{N_1} = \frac{k\,(1-b)\left(\dfrac{M_2 - M_1}{A}\right)}{1 - M_1/A}.$$

See Mathematical Appendix, Expression (29).

The depreciation penalty is equivalent to a reduction of 3.4 percentage points in its pre-tax profit rate (say from 10% to 6.4% or from 5% to 1.6%).

Table 12 has the advantage of considerable generality with respect to depreciation techniques (as these are reflected in different M/A ratios) but it is deficient in that the rate of growth is held constant. In Table 13 this defect has been remedied. Further, instead of typifying various depreciation techniques by the M/A ratio (which is itself a function of asset life, the rate of growth and the technique) a few particular techniques are specified—two that are assumed to be internally consistent (the distinction between the A and B sections is drawn on this basis), and six that are assumed to be tax allowable techniques. Of the six tax allowable techniques five can be termed *amortization* policies (numbered 1 through 5) in that they are based on the idea of limiting total amortization over the life of a machine to the cost of the machine. The other tax allowable technique (#6) is more appropriately termed a subsidy policy because it explicitly permits deductions in excess of machine cost. We see that only the subsidy policy affects the profit rate of the stationary firm. The table illustrates some conclusions concerning the effect of various policy techniques on (1) the rate of growth and (2) the allocation of resources among machines (or industries) of different types (i.e., machines having different quasi-rent patterns and therefore different internally consistent depreciation patterns).

b. *The Impact on Rates of Growth.*[25] The effect of tax allowable depreciation techniques on the incentive to grow can be summarized in the

TABLE 13

THE EFFECT OF GROWTH ON THE AFTER-TAX PROFIT RATE GIVEN VARIOUS COMBINATIONS OF INTERNALLY CONSISTENT AND TAX ALLOWABLE DEPRECIATION PATTERNS
$(n = 20; \ b = .50)$

A

Internally Consistent Technique: Diminishing Balance Depreciation
(2% salvage salue)

Tax Allowable Depreciation	k —.025	—.01	0	.01	.025	.05	.10
1. S. L.* (2%)	1.2	.5	0	—.5	—1.2	—2.1	—3.4
2. D. B.** (10%)	.6	.3	0	—.2	—.6	—1.1	—1.8
3. D. B.** (2%)	0	0	0	0	0	0	0
4. 20% I. A.*** + D. B.** (2%) on remainder	—.3	—.1	0	.1	.3	.5	1.0
5. 100% of cost of acquisitions	—1.3	—.5	0	.5	1.3	2.5	5.0
6. 20% I. A.*** + D. B.** (2%) on cost	1.7	1.9	2.0	2.1	2.3	2.5	3.0

B

Internally Consistent Technique: Straight Line Depreciation (2% valvage value)

Tax Allowable Depreciation	k —.025	—.01	0	.01	.025	.05	.10
1. S. L.* (2%)	0	0	0	0	0	0	0
2. D. B.** (10%)	—.3	—.1	0	.1	.3	.5	1.0
3. D. B.** (2%)	—.6	—.3	0	.3	.6	1.2	2.0
4. 20% I. A.*** + D. B.** (2%) on remainder	—.8	—.4	0	.3	.7	1.4	2.6
5. 100% of cost of acquisitions	—1.3	—.5	0	.5	1.3	2.5	5.0
6. 20% I. A.*** + D. B.** (2%) on cost	.2	.6	1.0	1.3	1.8	2.5	3.8

* Straight line depreciation, salvage percentage in parentheses.
** Diminishing balance depreciation, salvage percentage in parentheses.
*** Initial Allowance.

form of four theorems. These apply to the posttransition period, to firms whose machine variables have assumed stable relationships given the rate of growth. If amortization policy is changed, we assume the new technique to be applied to the firm's existing machine stock as well as to its new acquisitions so that relationships among machine variables immediately stabilize at the ratios consistent with the new policy. We assume also a tendency toward equality among the profit rates of different firms and industries. A neutral amortization policy we shall define as one that does not create differentials in the profit rates of growing and declining firms. Any depreciation policy which raises the after-tax profit rates of growing firms relative to less rapidly growing (or declining) firms is considered to provide a positive incentive in favor of growth. The size of the differential created is treated as an index of the size of the resulting incentive.

(1) *If the allowable technique is identical to the internally consistent one, there exists no incentive toward growth or decline.* The tax allowable method is completely neutral in this case. To achieve this result in practice, however, each firm should be permitted to use the techniques internally consistent with its use of its machines; a difficult administrative policy is posed.

(2) *If the allowable technique is more (less) accelerated than the internally consistent technique, there exists a positive (negative) incentive toward growth.*[26] In Table 13, for example, every allowable technique that is more accelerated than the internally consistent one (techniques 4, 5, and 6 when the diminishing balance technique is internally consistent and techniques 2, 3, 4, 5, and 6 when the straight-line method is consistent) has the effect of raising the profit rate more the higher the rate of growth. And unless the allowable technique involves a subsidy, declining firms are penalized by the employment for tax purposes of the more accelerated techniques. The more accelerated the allowable amortization technique relative to the internally consistent one, the greater the differential effect on the after-tax profit rates of growing and non-growing firms. Note, however, that a subsidy policy need not involve a greater differential than an accelerated amortization policy. In fact, the use of a subsidy policy to provide an incentive for growth may be *less* effective than some acceleration policies.

It can now be demonstrated that for growing firms an amortization policy geared to the running physical replacement criterion places a penalty on the use of all depreciable equipment. Any amortization policy must yield an M/A ratio for growing firms that can be as low as R/A and as high as one. The policy must yield total machine funds at least equal to the cost of running physical replacement and no higher than the cost of new acquisitions. (A subsidy policy must yield an M/A ratio in excess of R/A but has no upper limit.) On the other hand, no internally consistent depreciation technique can yield for growing firms an M/A ratio as low as R/A (this would require a machine to have a constant value over time until the very moment of its death) nor as high as one (such a machine would not be subject to depreciation). But an amortization policy designed to yield just enough funds to meet running physical requirements has an M/A ratio just equal to R/A. It follows that such a technique must be less accelerated than any internally consistent technique and must, if used for tax purposes, reduce the after-tax profit rates of all firms that use depreciable equipment. The size of the penalty is greater the greater the rate of growth and the more accelerated the internally consistent technique.

(3) *If a range of amortization techniques are available for tax purposes, growing firms will select the most accelerated one, declining firms will select the least accelerated one, and stationary firms will be indifferent.*

(4) *If a more accelerated amortization technique is substituted for a less accelerated one, the size of the incentive (discentive) toward growth is increased (decreased).* A new, more accelerated technique may therefore be favorable to growth as compared to the previous situation even though the differential it establishes between the profit rates of growing and non-growing firms is itself unfavorable.[27]

If an incentive toward growth is created for one firm, there is little reason to question its effectiveness. If similar incentives are extended to all firms simultaneously, however, it is not so clear that the rate of growth of the economy as a whole will be increased over the long run. In the short run the higher after-tax profit rates should encourage growth because additional borrowing and investment should appear to be profitable to each firm. The reduction in the real demand for non-investment goods that would follow from increased investment demand in a fully employed, stable economy, would tend to reduce the profit rates of all firms producing those goods. Whether this effect would just offset the amortization incentive is problematical.[28]

c. *The Impact on the Composition of Capital.* Unless an amortization policy affects machines of different types in precisely the same way, the policy is likely to stimulate the use of some kinds of machines at the expense of others. We identify type of machine in terms of the depreciation technique that is consistent with its quasi-rent pattern. As this is dependent on its use as well as its physical characteristics we could as well say that the patterns of use may be influenced by amortization policy. And as industry characteristics may limit the flexibility of a particular machine the relative profitability of different industries may also depend partly on amortization policy. We shall advance six theorems on this point in terms of more and less accelerated types of machines.* The translation to different uses or different industries is left to the reader. We again assume a tendency toward equality of profit rates and deal only with the situation in which the relationships among machine-related variables are stable.

(1) *If the allowable amortization technique varies with the internally consistent one, the policy is neutral with respect to choice of machine.* This point is illustrated for growing firms in Table 12 where it can be seen that the profit rate is unaffected if the M/A ratios for the two techniques are identical. Table 13 shows, that the profit rates for declining and stationary firms are also unaffected by such a policy. Such a policy is therefore neutral with respect to (a) rate of growth and (b) the composition of capital.

(2) *For stationary firms, any given amortization technique has a neutral effect on choice of machine but a subsidy policy will stimulate the use of more accelerated type machines.* Any amortization policy yields for stationary firms an M/A ratio equal to one as does any internally consistent technique. There is therefore no reason to prefer one type of machine over another on account of the allowable amortization technique. When a subsidy policy is instituted, however, a differential effect is introduced in favor of those machines whose quasi-rents are largest in the early years of machine life. The amount of the subsidy, some percentage of the cost of new acquisitions, is the same for all stationary firms but those stationary firms employing accelerated-type machines have a lower valued machine stock. Their after-tax profit *rate* is therefore raised by more than the profit rate of firms employing less accelerated types of machines.

(3) *For declining firms, any given amortization or subsidy technique, except that specified in Theorem (5), establishes an incentive in favor of more accelerated type machines.* This is the result of two forces. The

---

* The mathematical basis for these theorems is given in the Appendix, especially Expression (30).

more accelerated the machines employed by the firm the less the machine funds provided by its internally consistent depreciation technique. Therefore, the funds provided by any given arbitrary technique appear more favorable (tend to increase the profit rate more), the more accelerated the machines used by the firm. But the accelerated-type machines yield at the same time a lower value for the machine stock of the firm, which also tends to increase the profit rate.* For both reasons the profit rate of the declining firm will be more favorably affected the more accelerated the type of machine it employs.

(4) *For growing firms any given amortization technique, except that specified in theorem (5), will induce the firm to favor the less accelerated type of machine; a strong subsidy technique may reverse the incentive.* For the growing firm the two forces referred to in the preceding paragraph are opposed to each other. The less accelerated the type of machine employed the *lower* the amount of machine funds it provides to the growing firm. Therefore, any given arbitrary technique appears more favorable, i.e. tends to raise the profit rate more, the *less* accelerated the type of machine employed. But the employment of less accelerated machines *raises* the value of the firm's machine stock, which tends to reduce the profit rate.** It can be shown that the change in the profit rate obtained from a given arbitrary technique is completely unaffected by the type of machine employed when the arbitrary technique yields an M_2/A ratio equal to one.*** With any lesser ratio, an incentive exists for the growing firm in favor of less accelerated type machines; the use of less accelerated machines has a greater relative effect on machine funds than on the value of the machine stock. When the arbitrary technique yields a ratio greater than one, the effect of utilizing less accelerated machines on the value of the machine stock outweighs its effect on machine funds and the employment of such machines will *reduce* the advantage obtained from the allowable technique.

Any amortization technique, except the immediate deduction of the

* As
$$k = \frac{A - M_1}{N}, \qquad N = \frac{A - M_1}{k}.$$

When k is negative, $(A - M_1)$ is negative. For declining firms, therefore, the lower M_1, given k, the lower N, the value of the machine stock.

** For growing firms $(A - M_1)$ in the equation in the preceding footnote is positive. Therefore, the lower M_1 (the less accelerated the machines), the higher the value of the machine stock.

*** See Mathematical Appendix, Expressions (29) and (30) and the discussion of Theorem (5) below.

full cost of acquisitions, yields for growing firms an M/A ratio that is less than one. The use of such a technique for tax purposes favors, therefore, the use of less accelerated types of machines. Firms are encouraged to employ machines whose quasi-rents decline very slowly and to undertake maintenance expenditures that would not otherwise be profitable in order to raise later quasi-rents. The high level of machine maintenance in the United States until 1954 may be partly attributable to this effect.

A subsidy technique yields an M/A ratio that is reduced as the growth rate increases. At low growth rates it will yield an M/A ratio in excess of one. The heavier the subsidy involved, the higher the growth rate must be before the M/A ratio becomes less than one.* So long as the resulting ratio is greater than one, the growing firm is given an incentive to employ machines whose value deteriorates rapidly or to reduce their maintenance expenditures on existing machines. A subsidy policy that encourages growth may have the undesirable side effect, therefore, of encouraging the more rapid consumption of capital. An amortization policy providing the same growth incentive will nevertheless leave some incentive to preserve existing capital.

(5) *An amortization technique that requires the immediate deduction from income for tax purposes of the total cost of new acquisitions has a neutral effect on the choice of machine.* Sweden's experience with so-called "free depreciation" would be a case in point for those firms who utilized it in the fashion prescribed above. One must note, however, that while such a policy is neutral with respect to type of machine, as is a policy that equates the allowable technique to the internally consistent one, it offers a positive incentive toward growth. Its neutrality with respect to type of machine may appear a bit surprising at first if we view the type of machine in terms of asset life. Why should the immediate deduction of the cost of a long-lived machine be no more stimulating than the immediate deduction of the cost of a short-lived one? Yet it is not, because the profit rate for both is raised by a constant, given the rate of growth in new acquisitions.** The amount of the reduction

---

* The critical growth rate is that which makes $M/A + q = 1$ where M/A is the ratio obtainable with the amortization technique excluding the subsidy and q is the percentage of acquisition cost that can be deducted immediately without affecting the depreciation base. When q is zero, the critical k must be zero; when q is positive, k must be positive; and when q is negative, k must be negative. The tax on investment that has been used occasionally in Sweden can be treated as a negative q.

** The profit rate is raised by $k(1 - b)$. See Appendix, Expression (29) or the equation at the foot of Table 12. M_2/A for such a policy is, by definition of the policy, equal to one.

in reported profit, $A - M_1$, is clearly smaller for the firm employing shorter-lived assets (see, for example, data in Table 8, keeping in mind that kn is smaller for such a firm). But so, too, is the value of its machine stock because at any time its stock is composed of the acquisitions made over a shorter period of time than is the case for the machine stock of the firm employing longer-lived assets. The two effects are such that the reduction in reported profit as a percentage of machine value is precisely the same for machines of any life.*

(6) *If one amortization technique is supplanted by another relatively more accelerated one, the differential favoring less accelerated type machines for growing firms is reduced, and some shift of resources toward more accelerated types should follow.* In Table 13, for example, for firms growing at a 5% rate, a switch from the straight-line technique to a diminishing balance technique (10% salvage value) reduces the differential favoring straight-line machines from 2.1 percentage points to 1.6 percentage points. Thus any acceleration of allowable amortization, while encouraging growth, will tend to discourage as high a degree of capital maintenance as existed before.

We have presented these theorems in terms of more or less accelerated types of machines given machine life. Effective acceleration can also be obtained by shortening asset life itself or by purchasing machines having a shorter life.** The above analysis can be interpreted in terms of asset life by equating "longer life" to "less accelerated type." Some

---

* The rate of growth is given and equal for the firms. It can be defined as

$$\frac{A - M_1}{N}.$$

But this is precisely the definition of the reduction in reported profit as a percentage of machine value, $(M_2 - M_1)/N$ ($M_2 = A$ by definition of the policy.)

One might be inclined to argue that investments having only a one-year life or less must be discriminated against. In theory, however, every investment is depreciable on a continuous basis unless it is instantaneously recovered in which case investment is zero. If in practice the amortization technique is not permitted for any particular class of machines, be it the one-year or twenty-year class, that class is discriminated against.

** Given k, kn is reduced when n is decreased. For growing firms this will tend to increase M_1/A and M_2/A in the equation,

$$\frac{\Delta F}{N} = \frac{k(1-b)\left(\dfrac{M_2}{A} - \dfrac{M_1}{A}\right)}{1 - \dfrac{M_1}{A}},$$

which will reduce $\Delta F/N$ unless $M_2/A \geqslant 1$. Growing firms should tend to favor longer-lived assets.

of the principle conclusions can be summarized in this form. Given any amortization policy, except the immediate amortization of the cost of acquisitions, growing firms should favor long-lived assets and declining firms should favor short-lived assets. If this policy applies to all investments, however short their duration, growing firms should favor fixed capital investment over working capital and should tend to have a higher capital-labor ratio on this account than would a declining firm. If a strong subsidy policy is followed, however, growing firms would shift their preference to match that of declining firms.

These conclusions must be modified somewhat if short-lived investments (say under one year) are not subjected to the same amortization policy as longer-lived investments. If we assume, for example, that the short-lived expenditures can be deducted as expenses when made, the effective amortization policy for them yields an M/A ratio of one. There is no reason to prefer one short-lived investment to another because of the amortization policy. If the amortization policy applicable to long-lived assets is not so generous, however, growing firms will tend to favor short-term over long-term investments but will continue to prefer long-term over medium-term investments.*

d. *Other Policy Considerations*. The effects of different tax allowable depreciation techniques on rates of growth and types of assets purchased should not be exaggerated for policy-making purposes. The tendencies indicated in preceding sections may be considerably weakened and perhaps nullified when a more realistic view of expectations is taken. The uniformity of growth, the infinite entrepreneurial horizon, and the stability of governmental policy, are all matters subject to enormous reservation. The impact of these reservations on the theoretical effects of various depreciation policies remains largely a matter of judgment.

The large corporation with a long, successful history may well anticipate a relatively uniform rate of growth in the future. It seems less likely, given modern views of economic success, that a firm would anticipate a uniform decline. A more important reservation, however, is the span of time over which growth or decline is anticipated. The entrepreneurial horizon may not extend into the distant future. The emphasis in business corporations on pay out periods, which outside observers often regard as relatively short, is but one piece of evidence.[29] But even if horizons extend some distance into the future it

* To develop the full implications of these theorems for policy would carry us too far afield.

is likely that the rate of discount utilized is so high, (and perhaps rising) that the more immediate effects of business planning receive heavy preference. In either case the period between the establishment of a policy and the achievement of stable relationships consistent with it is likely to be most influential in determining business reaction to the policy. This transition period has a duration equal to asset life if the policy is applicable only to assets acquired subsequent to the effective date of the policy. This suggests that the principal impact of such a policy can be studied without great error by examining business expectations related to this period.*

If the horizon is shorter than an objective estimate of asset life or if the rate of discount is extremely high, those amortization techniques which offer a quick realization of benefits are likely to be more effective than other techniques which promise larger, but later, rewards. Domar has suggested, for example, that "an initial allowance of 40 or 50 per cent (in lieu of that amount of subsequent depreciation charges) should be... more effective than is the 5 year amortization allowed on American defense plants; yet in the long run it yields a smaller tax concession than does the other method."[30] Though he offers no reason for this conclusion it could reasonably be based on the assumption that business firms operate with a shorter horizon and/or a higher rate of discount than does the government.

An important factor in encouraging businessmen to prefer early policy benefits to later ones is the instability of government policy itself. Many policies are admittedly undertaken on a trial basis and the promise of later benefits may never be realized. Further, the exigencies of policy-making often require a policy to be announced as permanent when it is actually expected by the policy makers to be temporary. Thus a liberal amortization technique made available in a depression may be reversed when business activity has picked up; the later benefits which encouraged investment may be withdrawn. Finally, *bona fide* permanent policies are themselves subject to change when economic and political circumstances dictate. These matters suggest that businessmen are quite right in exhibiting a strong preference for immediate as opposed to future benefits when these benefits are awarded by policy decision.

* The transition period can, however, be reduced to zero by requiring the depreciation technique to be applied, as of the effective date, to assets already in stock as well as to new acquisitions.

B. PRICE CHANGES

The adjustment of depreciation charges for price changes has been a favorite subject of accountants for many years.[31] We have no intention of summarizing the extensive literature on the matter nor of exploring the many ramifications such an adjustment may involve. Our concern is limited to the adjustment as a means of bringing depreciation charges into line with one or another of the various concepts of replacement.

Unfortunately price changes themselves are not unambiguous. It will be useful to distinguish three sets of prices that are subject to differential changes—the price level, the prices of depreciable assets, and the expected prices and costs of the firm's future output. The first two of these are most important for the discussion to follow. Sections are devoted to depreciation when these two sets of prices move together and when they move differentially.

The determination of an appropriate depreciation charge under these different conditions involves (1) the selection of a depreciation technique, (2) the choice of a base to which to apply the technique and (3) an evaluation of the various possible results. The technique determines the proportion of the base which is applicable to a particular period of asset life. The technique may provide for a different proportion in different periods. The selection of an appropriate technique is not peculiar to a situation involving price changes, however. We shall eliminate it as a complicating variable by assuming for the most part that the straight-line technique is appropriate. We shall also assume unless otherwise specified that salvage value is zero.

1. *Proportionate Price Changes*

Among the possible bases for depreciation are historic cost, current cost, ultimate replacement cost, purchasing power cost (historic cost adjusted for subsequent changes in the price level), and subjective value. Once an acquisition has been made its historic cost is given and is unaffected by subsequent price changes. The current cost of an asset is the present cost of a new but otherwise identical asset. As we assume in this section that all prices move together, an asset's current cost and its purchasing power cost are the same.* Ultimate replacement cost is the cost of a new but otherwise identical asset at the time physical replacement in fact occurs.

---

* The controversy over these two bases is considered in a later section.

a. *The Replacement of Historic Cost.* Given a zero salvage value, a specified rate of inflation will, in the absence of real growth, act to raise historic cost depreciation charges by precisely the same amount that would result from an equal rate of real growth without price changes. The same pattern of money expenditures is necessary—in the one case to maintain a constant stock of machines, in the other case to finance the given real rate of growth.

When prices are rising the historic cost of each machine exceeds the cost of the last previous purchase. Thus the total stock of machines at any time has a historic cost in excess of what it would have been in the absence of price changes, and depreciation on this historic cost will be proportionately higher. Nevertheless the historic cost dictum that *each* machine should generate total depreciation charges during its lifetime just equal to the historic cost of the machine is not violated. Price changes subsequent to the purchase of a machine have no effect whatsoever on the computation of depreciation charges.

Such a concept of replacement ensures, if income is sufficient, a recovery of the same number of original money units expended. The fact that current money units may have a value different from the original money units has no place in the computation. This limitation of the replacement-of-historic-cost concept has long been recognized and has led to the search for a more realistic yet workable concept.

b. *Running Physical Replacement.* It is possible to judge the adequacy of depreciation charges as a means of financing replacement in terms of the maintenance of the given physical stock of machines.[32] This involves as we have seen a comparison of the depreciation on the total stock of machines with the cost of replacing those just retired. It is the *number* of identical machines that is to be maintained.

It will be recalled that historic cost depreciation just provided for running physical replacement when prices and the size of the machine stock were constant. Growth, on the other hand, tended to raise aggregate depreciation charges above the amount needed to make running physical replacement because the machine stock would then exceed n times the initial acquisition now being replaced.

When prices are rising, however, the cost to replace the initial acquisition must exceed the original expenditure—the replacement is made at *current* prices, not at the prices that prevailed n years ago. If growth is zero, historic cost depreciation on the entire machine stock must fall short of financing running physical replacement. The replacement is made at current prices whereas the machine stock is depreciated on the basis of its historic cost which represents a conglomerate collection of all (lower) prices since the initial acquisition. Assuming an even rate of inflation, historic cost depreciation yields an amount midway between the historic cost of the initial acquisition and the current cost of its replacement. The stationary firm will be unable to finance running physical replacement by retaining funds just equal to historic cost depreciation.* The larger the rate of inflation the greater the deficiency.

We have seen however, that growth by itself tends to make historic cost depreciation excessive with respect to running physical replacement. It stands to reason, then, that given some rate of inflation there is some real rate of growth which will just compensate for the inflation-induced deficiency. A more rapid rate of growth would yield excess funds. Some of these critical rates of growth are given in Table 14 for specified rates of inflation and asset lives.[33]

TABLE 14

THE PERCENTAGE RATE OF GROWTH WHICH EQUATES MACHINE FUNDS TO
THE COST OF RUNNING PHYSICAL REPLACEMENT FOR SPECIFIED p'S AND n'S
(Straight-line depreciation, zero salvage value)

n \ p (%)	1.0	2.0	3.0	4.0	5.0	10.0	20.0
5	0.96	1.9	2.8	3.8	4.6	8.6	15.0
10	0.96	1.9	2.7	3.5	4.3	7.5	12.1
20	0.94	1.8	2.5	3.2	3.8	6.0	8.8
30	0.91	1.7	2.3	2.9	3.3	5.1	7.0
40	0.88	1.6	2.1	2.6	3.0	4.4	5.8
50	0.86	1.5	2.0	2.4	2.8	3.9	5.1

Based on the formula, $e^{kn} - kn = pn + e^{-pn}$, determined by solving the expression for M_s/R (in historic cost prices) when it is placed equal to one. See summary of growth equations in the Mathematical Appendix.

The critical rate of growth is in every case less than the rate of inflation. The differential is small for short-lived assets and low rates of inflation and increases as these variables increase. A 3% real rate

---

* The values in Table 7 can be read to indicate the proportion of replacement cost covered by depreciation charges when prices are rising and real growth is zero. R in current prices is Re^{pn}, which has the same value as A in Table 7 ($A = Re^{kn}$). The k's in that table should simply be read as p's.

of growth with forty-year assets will permit a firm to finance running physical replacement with historic cost depreciation in the face of a 5% inflation. A 5.1% rate of growth with fifty-year assets will offset a 20% inflation so far as financing running physical replacement is concerned.

It is tempting to push even further on the basis of the running physical replacement criterion, perhaps because there appears to be something innately real about a constant stock of machines. During each year of production, however, the growing firm is using up one year of the service life of each machine in its stock. As the firm has been growing the number of machines in its stock must now exceed n times the size of the acquisition made n years ago. If the initial acquisition is set equal to one, its replacement now will add only n years of service life to the firm's machine stock while it has used up more than that amount during the year. Even if each year of service life has the same value, as is the case when straight-line depreciation is accurate, running physical replacement is insufficient to maintain the *value* of the machine stock. It replenishes fewer machine-years than are retired. In searching for a more significant definition of replacement we must also recognize that each machine-year may have a different value—the second year of service may be less valuable than the first and so on.

If the running physical replacement criterion has little to recommend it as a concept of replacement perhaps it can be regarded as meaningful in a financing sense. But even this is not usually the case. A growing firm demands more finance than the cost of running physical replacement while a declining firm requires less. Only for stationary firms can one argue that provision for running physical replacement will meet all financing needs. But then other replacement criteria can serve equally well.

c. *Historic Cost Depreciation As a Source of Funds.* The financing needs of a firm growing in an inflationary economy are represented by the cost of new acquisitions in each period. We have seen that growth tends to reduce the percentage of new acquisitions that can be financed by depreciation funds while decline increases it. The figures in Table 15 reflect this effect and show also how the percentage is modified by rising or falling prices.

For each rate of inflation there is a rate of growth which will permit a firm to equalize its depreciation charges and its cost of new acquisitions (the M/A percentage equals 100). The two rates must be equal

TABLE 15

THE EFFECT OF INFLATION AND GROWTH ON THE M/A PERCENTAGE
COMPUTED ON HISTORIC COST

(Straight-line depreciation, zero salvage value)

pn \ kn	−2.0	−1.0	−0.5	0	0.5	1.0	2.0	3.0
−2.0	1340	618	447	320	232	172	100	63
−1.0	618	320	232	172	130	100	63	43
−0.5	447	232	172	130	100	79	52	37
0	320	172	130	100	79	63	43	32
0.5	232	130	100	79	63	52	37	28
1.0	172	100	79	63	52	43	32	25
2.0	100	63	52	43	37	32	25	20
3.0	63	43	37	32	28	25	20	17
4.0	43	32	28	25	22	20	17	14

Based on the formula, $\dfrac{M_s}{A} = \dfrac{1 - e^{-n(p+k)}}{n(p+k)}$.

See summary of growth equations in Mathematical Appendix.

in absolute value but opposite in sign. Thus a real rate of growth of 3% can be financed entirely by depreciation charges if a rate of deflation of 3% prevails. The effect of growth, to increase current expenditures by more than historic cost depreciation, is just offset by the effect of deflation, to decrease current cost by more than historic cost. If inflation is characteristic of an economy, however, new acquisitions cannot be financed entirely by depreciation charges unless the firm is declining at the same rate that prices are rising.

As all prices in the economy are assumed to be rising at the same rate, there is no obvious reason to suppose that what was the optimum real growth rate in the absence of price change should be modified by the fact of inflation. Yet the tradition of historic cost depreciation introduces just such a factor. Whatever the growth rate of the firm the use of historic cost depreciation in the computation of taxes and dividends forces the firm to lean more heavily on external sources of funds when prices are rising than when they are constant. Table 15 indicates, for example, that a firm growing at a rate of 5% with twenty-year assets (a kn of 1) can finance only 43% of its current acquisitions with depreciation charges in a 5% inflation whereas constant prices would permit it to finance 63%. When all prices are rising in proportion one would expect external and internal financing to rise proportionately. But if all firms are forced by the historic cost convention to demand a more than proportionate amount of external funds in order to finance the same real rate of growth, the average real rate of growth of the economy may well be retarded. The supply of external funds is not likely to match the increased demand except at a higher real rate of interest. Of course, the lower rate of growth and the higher interest rate may ultimately have the effect of reducing the rate of inflation, presenting thereby a possible argument in favor of retaining historic cost as a basis for depreciation charges. But this argument extends beyond our present task.

d. *Continuous Replacement of Exhausted Service Values.* The distorted proportions induced by historic cost depreciation in the face of pro-portionate price changes affords a clue by which to test any replace-ment concept under the specified circumstances. An appropriate depre-ciation policy should leave unaltered by price changes the proportions that exist in their absence between all relevant asset variables, such as depreciation (and total machine funds), value of the machine stock, cost of new acquisitions, cost of running physical replacement, and cost of the stock of machines if all were new. Obviously, multiplying the values of these variables (as they would exist in the absence of price change) by any constant would leave the proportions among them unaffected. The appropriate constant is the current price index divided by the price index used to compute the constant price values. If acquisition cost n years ago is used as the constant price and that is set equal to 100, current values can be determined by multiplying by the current price index. The intervening history of price change is completely irrelevant, so long as the real rate of growth has been unaffected by it. And as we have assumed that all prices change in proportion, the index we use, whether of machine prices or of the price level, is a matter of indifference. But replacement considerations sug-gest that an index of machine prices is the theoretically correct procedure.

To determine replacement one must ask what it is that is being exhausted. During a particular year the firm uses one year of the ser-vice life of every machine in stock; if there are x machines, x machine years of service have been exhausted. The problem remains to value the x machine years. With straight-line depreciation the matter is simple—each machine year has the same value. The value today of any machine year is simply the current cost of a new machine divided by the number of machine years such a machine represents. The value exhausted by the firm, x times the current value of each machine year, represents the value that should be replaced. This amount is simply the straight-line rate, $1/n$, applied against the current cost of x machines; it is current cost depreciation.

If the applicable pattern of depreciation charges in not straight-line, each machine year used has a different value depending upon the age of the machine supplying it. For each stable age distribution of the machine stock there will be a unique average rate which can be applied to the current cost base (or the depreciated current cost base in the case of declining balance depreciation). What we are measuring in any event is the decline in the value of the machine stock due to the aging and use processes, the dissipation of asset services.

But a significantly different concept of replacement has crept up on us—the replacement of the current value of exhausted machine services. It is related to the replacement-of-market-value concept but is more narrowly defined. If the market value concept were strictly applied, we would measure depreciation as the change in the value of the machine stock from one point of time to another.[34] But this change in value is composed of two elements—(1) the value of exhausted services and (2) the change in the value of the unused machine services remaining in stock. It is useful, however, to distinguish between depreciation on the one hand and capital gains and losses on the other. The former is an operating expense, an expense related to *operating* a business; the latter is the sole result of *holding* machine services while their value increases. Most authors are agreed, I think, that the distinction is a necessary one. In any case the assumption under which we are now operating, that machine prices and the price level move together, means that no *real* gains can arise.

The computation of current cost depreciation requires no knowledge of historic cost depreciation. If, however, such figures are available and have been computed by the internally consistent technique they can be converted to current cost by applying an appropriate index number.* This index number, which is simply the ratio of current cost depreciation to historic cost depreciation given the growth rate of the firm and the rate of inflation, indicates also the degree to which historic cost depreciation is deficient or excessive. Such ratios are presented as percentages in Table 16.

---

* See Mathematical Appendix, Expression (41) and the various summaries of expressions.

TABLE 16

THE PERCENTAGE OF CURRENT COST DEPRECIATION TO HISTORIC COST
DEPRECIATION FOR GIVEN kn's AND pn's

(Straight-line depreciation, zero salvage value)

pn \ kn	—2.0	—1.0	—0.5	0	0.5	1.0	2.0	3.0
—2.0	24	28	29	31	34	37	43	51
—1.0	52	54	56	58	61	63	68	74
—0.5	72	74	76	77	79	80	83	86
0	100	100	100	100	100	100	100	100
0.5	138	132	130	127	125	121	116	114
1.0	186	172	165	159	152	147	134	128
2.0	320	273	250	233	214	197	172	160
3.0	508	400	351	313	282	252	215	188
4.0	744	538	464	400	359	315	253	229

Based on the formula $\dfrac{D_s{}^c}{D_s{}^h} = \dfrac{(p+k)(e^{kn}-1)}{k(e^{kn}-e^{-pn})}$.

These percentages indicate the amount by which historic cost depreciation charges should be raised (if prices are rising) or lowered (if prices are falling) to permit the firm to replace the values of the machine services exhausted during the period. A firm growing at a real rate of $3\frac{1}{2}\%$ with thirty-year assets ($kn = 1$) would have to retain 47% more funds than historic cost depreciation would indicate in order to replace exhausted values in a $3\frac{1}{2}\%$ inflation ($pn = 1$). To replace currently expired values in a 10% inflation ($pn = 3$) such a firm should be permitted to retain 252% of its historic cost depreciation charge. A non-growing firm is penalized even more severely. In a 10% inflation such a firm operating with thirty-year assets ($pn = 3$) should be permitted to retain 313% of its historic cost depreciation. Falling prices, however, tend to make historic cost depreciation excessive in relation to the replacement of the current value of expired asset services.

The deficiency of historic cost depreciation in an inflationary situation tends to be less the more accelerated is the internally consistent technique applied to the historic cost base. This can be seen most clearly in the nongrowth situation. In this case current cost depreciation (plus scrap value if any) is the same for all techniques; the acquisition of a new machine just replaces the years of asset services exhausted by using the even-age machine stock one year; any differential between the values of different machine years is immaterial.

Current cost depreciation (plus scrap) is just equal to the cost of new acquisitions regardless of technique. But historic cost depreciation differs according to technique if prices are changing. The more accelerated method takes a larger proportion of higher priced (newer) machines and a smaller proportion of the lower priced (older) machines than does straight-line depreciation. Thus, because the more accelerated technique supplies larger historic cost depreciation charges, these need not be raised by so much to equal current cost depreciation.*

Table 16 also reveals that the impact of changing prices is greater, percentage-wise, for declining firms than for growing ones. This result stems from the fact that declining firms carry the bulk of their machine stock at old historic cost prices while growing firms carry a preponderant share at relatively recent historic cost prices. The necessary adjustment of depreciation to a current cost basis is clearly not so great for the growing firm.

Whether such a depreciation adjustment should be permitted or required for tax purposes is a moot question because it turns on matters other than internal equity. Internal equity hinges essentially on the appropriate replacement criterion and current cost depreciation has many arguments in its favor. External equity considerations are not so clear,—it may not be feasible to apply the same principle to the tax status of non-business entities who nevertheless own depreciable property. Permitting current cost depreciation for one group but not for others might alter considerably the relative burden of taxes.[35]

e. *The Replacement of Subjective Values.* Subjective value, the value of an asset derived by management from its prospective stream of net receipts, is not likely to be affected by proportionate price changes. Each net receipt, higher because of price increases, is discounted by a higher monetary rate of interest. Each net receipt, say R_j when prices are constant, is raised by $(1 + p)^j$, where p is the annual rate of increase in all prices, including costs. But the general rate of increase in prices should be reflected in a higher monetary rate of interest such that the real rate of interest is unchanged. Thus the old rate, i, should adjust upward to a new rate, r, such that $(1 + r) = (1 + i)(1 + p)$.

---

* Diminishing balance depreciation with a correctly anticipated scrap value of 5% and a kn of zero must be raised by 16% when $pn = 0.5$, by 33% when $pn = 1.0$, by 67% when $pn = 2$, and by 100% when $pn = 3$. (See Mathematical Appendix, the summary of growth equations.) The relevant values for straight-line depreciation (zero salvage value) are 27%, 59%, 133% and 213%.

The discounted value of R_j becomes

$$\frac{R_j (1 + p)^j}{(1 + i)^j (1 + p)^j},$$

which equals

$$\frac{R_j}{(1 + i)^j},$$

its value when prices were constant.

This value is stated in constant monetary units bearing the date of the computation. If subjective value depreciation in these units was W without price changes it is W under the new circumstances also. In j prices, however, subjective value depreciation becomes $W(1 + p)^j$. On the other hand, let us suppose that in the absence of price changes, historic cost depreciation (equals current cost depreciation) was D. Translated into j prices this would be $D(1 + p)^j$ which would be current cost depreciation but not historic cost depreciation if prices have been rising. It follows that the ratio of current cost depreciation to subjective value depreciation is unaffected by proportionate price changes. If the two were equal in the absence of price changes, they should also be equal when all prices are changing at a uniform rate.

f. *The Ultimate Replacement Concept.* The idea that depreciation on a particular machine should supply sufficient funds to finance the ultimate replacement of that machine is essentially a red herring. It is based on a showing that when prices are rising historic cost depreciation funds held in the form of cash will be insufficient to finance the replacement machine. One cannot deny the proposition as stated but the adjustment implied, to base charges on ultimate replacement cost (i.e., to adjust every year all *past* charges as well as the current charge to conform to current prices), has been successfully challenged by many.[36]

The assumption attacked is that firms hold depreciation funds in the form of cash until the machine being depreciated is actually replaced. How a firm disposes of these funds is a matter of managerial decision that ranks with the disposition of any funds from whatever source. Presumably the firm attempts to maximize profits and few business men are so remiss in this regard as to hold increasing amounts of idle cash when prices are rising. It can be shown that funds equal to depreciation computed on a current cost basis, when invested in assets whose prices rise in proportion to machine prices, will maintain the real value of the firm's initial investment. The investment of funds in like machines is one way of accomplishing this result. When prices change disproportionately, the actual decisions of the firm may prove better or worse than this alternative but current cost depreciation places the firm *in a position* to maintain its real capital. Whether it makes the best use of these funds or not is a matter of managerial efficiency. Certainly depreciation policy should not be designed to maintain capital in the face of uneconomic decisions.

2. *Disproportionate Price Changes*. The introduction of differentials in price movements complicates the replacement problem by bringing to the fore certain difficulties that are dormant under other circumstances. We shall discuss briefly two such difficulties, namely whether depreciation should be adjusted by changes in machine prices or changes in the price level and the distinction between capital gains and losses and price-adjusted depreciation, and shall make some concluding remarks on subjective depreciation. It will be useful to distinguish three sets of prices—the price level, machine prices, and the prices expected to adhere to future inputs and outputs. We shall assume that the values of different machine years of service move proportionately to machine prices, i.e., that price changes do not affect the appropriate depreciation technique.*

a. *Current Cost vs Price Level Depreciation*. Once the need to adjust historic cost depreciation to an amount having some current significance had been recognized a controversy developed over whether this adjustment should be based on movements in the general price level or on changes in the particular prices of the assets subject to depreciation. Those who have advocated the price level adjustment have argued that adjusting historic cost depreciation upward by the percentage increase in a general price index (usually the Index of Consumers' Prices in the United States) indicates to the firm the amount that must be recovered in current monetary units in order to replace the purchasing power originally expended.[37] There is no real basis for quibbling with this position as stated. Some opponents have argued, however, that such an adjustment does not represent the current value of exhausted

---

* The appropriate depreciation technique need not be the internally consistent one. Rather it is the technique that yields a pattern of machine values that corresponds to the pattern of market values. This pattern may differ from firm to firm, however, if the rate and intensity of use varies from firm to firm.

services but only historic cost adjusted to a real rather than a monetary basis.[38] The current value of exhausted services can be determined only by reference to the prices of the assets that furnish these services. This is the basis for current cost depreciation.

The argument that one must choose between the two indexes is, however, misleading.[39] The two adjustments are not competitive but rather are complementary. Particular prices are necessary to determine the depreciation charge in a replacement context and the monetary amount of capital gains and losses; a knowledge of price level movements is necessary to determine real gains and losses and to compare in real terms the results of business operations in different periods. Each is important to a particular set of problems but the sets are quite distinct. A consideration of the relationship between capital gains and depreciation may clarify the distinction.

b. *Capital Gains and Depreciation Charges.* An example will best serve our purpose here. Let us assume that a particular kind of single purpose machine is used by several firms that are equally efficient and that entertain the same expectations regarding the future. Let the cost of this machine be $3636.00, the life of the machine 40 years, and its salvage value zero for all firms. Each firm has the same real internal rate of return, r, which in the absence of price changes is 25%. The quasi-rent stream expected for each machine is such that internal rate depreciation equals straight-line depreciation ($90.90 per year) and the book values of the machine at various ages equal its market values in the absence of price changes. Let the quasi-rents be collected at the end of each period.

The quasi-rent falling at the end of the first period, R_a, must be $999.90 (.25 × $3636.00 + $90.90) and that falling at the end of the second, R_b, must be $977.18 (.25 × $3545.10 + $90.90), etc. In the absence of any price changes the firm would report profits for the first two periods as follows:

	First Period	Second Period
Quasi-rent	$999.90	$977.18
Depreciation	90.90	90.90
Operating Profit	$909.00	$886.28

Let us assume now that the price level rises at the rate of 3% per year but that the prices and costs relating to the operations of this firm remain constant. The monetary figures given above should remain unchanged. The quasi-rent at the end of the first period represents its value in current (end-of-first-period) monetary units. Depreciation is stated on a current cost basis as before because the cost of the machine has not changed and the monetary values relating to its use are unchanged. In a perfect market then a firm could sell a year of machine services for $90.90 (in end-of-first-period monetary units), no more, no less. The firm's operating profit remains at $909.00.

There are, however, two changes of significance. First, the firm has incurred a real loss by holding the machine during each period while the price level rose. The real loss in the first period is 3% of $3636.00, or $109.08. In the second period the real loss is 3% of $3545.10 or $106.35. These losses are not attributable to operations but simply to holding assets while the monetary unit, our unit of measurement, deteriorated in value. Second, the figures for the first and second periods are no longer comparable because they are stated in monetary units of different dates. Each must be deflated or inflated as the case may be to monetary units of the same vintage whether that be be-ginning-of-first-period, end-of-first-period or end-of-second-period units.* The data appear below in present (today's) contemporary (to period reported) and beginning-of-first-period (base period) monetary units:[40]

| | First Period | | | Second Period | |
	Base Period	Contemporary	Present	Base Period	Contemporary (= Present)
Quasi-rent	$970.77	$999.90	$1029.90	$921.09	$977.18
Depreciation	88.25	90.90	93.63	85.68	90.90
Operating Profit	882.52	909.00	936.27	835.41	886.28
Real Loss	105.90	109.08	112.35	102.45	106.35
Net Gain	$776.62	$799.92	$823.92	$732.96	$779.93

The advocates of price level depreciation would ignore the real loss except to the extent that it is realized. This loss is actually realized only on the machine services used—in the first period, 3% of $90.90 or $2.73. This real loss, however, they proceed to include with depre-ciation, i.e., depreciation would be adjusted upward to $93.63 which would reduce contemporary operating profit to $906.27. As damaging,

* If we now stand at the end of the second period, there is ample reason to make the comparison in current monetary units. They are the ones with which we are now familiar.

however, is the fact that the depreciation figure of $93.63 would be unaffected by any change (should it occur) in machine prices and the current value of the services it renders. Yet for the $93.63 to represent the *current* value of services rendered the price of the *machine* should rise by just 3%. Given this fact $93.63 would represent *current* value regardless of the movement in the price level.

Jones has realized the importance of recognizing the full losses incurred when the price level rises faster than the individual prices that affect the firm.[41] His solution leads him, however, to classify these losses as a depreciation element. In contemporary prices his depreciation figures in the above example would be $199.98 in the first period and $197.25 in the second (in base period prices, $194.15 and $188.13 respectively). This interpretation leads him to conclude that "the rising price level and that alone has... greatly accelerated the true rate of depreciation."[42]

In a replacement context, however, this view would suggest that the rising price level has more than doubled the value of the services rendered by the machine in the first period. It would be more likely that the lower real profitability of this machine relative to alternative investments would *reduce* the demand for these services, lower the cost of the machine, and bring current cost depreciation charges (in contemporary dollars) below $90.90. As a tax matter the desirability of separating capital gains and losses from operating profit is evidenced by the differential treatment accorded the two types of gain in many countries.

We have assumed so far that internal rate depreciation and current cost depreciation are identical. This is not likely to be so. Identical machines may have different costs to different firms, may be used for different purposes and in a variety of ways; and firms may entertain different expectations about the quasi-rent pattern the machine will produce. When a difference arises between the two a choice must be made for policy purposes. We reiterate two reasons which dictate against internal rate depreciation.* First, the method assumes that the internal rate of return should be constant over the life of the asset. But this is a purely arbitrary assumption; there is no reason why such pattern should be expected to prevail generally. Second, internal rate depreciation is essentially a subjective matter because the internal rate itself depends upon the anticipated revenue stream. It is subject therefore to the many changes in opinion and judgment, logical and capri-

* See the discussion above, pp. 66–68.

cious, which initiate with the entrepreneur. Any policy must be based upon more objective grounds if the possibility of fraudulently perverting the policy is to be avoided.

c. *Subjective Depreciation.* The subjective value of an asset is affected when the price level and the expected revenues and costs change disproportionately. If the quasi-rent stream is unchanged but the price level rises, the same stream is discounted by a higher market rate of interest. Subjective value falls but the money rate of interest is just high enough to leave money income unchanged. As the quasi-rent is unaffected also, monetary depreciation is unchanged. The real values of income and depreciation are obviously lowered, however. Nevertheless, if machine cost is also constant, current cost depreciation will bear the same relationship to subjective value depreciation as it would in the absence of price level changes.

If the prices related to the expected quasi-rent stream rise over time at the rate, p', but the price level does not, the discounted value of each quasi-rent becomes

$$\frac{R_j (1 + p')^j}{(1 + i)^j} ,$$

instead of

$$\frac{R_j}{(1 + i)^j} ,$$

and subjective value rises. As the interest rate is unchanged income rises by interest on the increase in subjective value. But the first (and each subsequent) quasi-rent is higher also. Whether depreciation falls or rises given the rate of change (p') in expected input and output prices depends upon the entrepreneur's horizon and the pattern of expected inputs and outputs. The more distant the horizon and the smaller early quasi-rents with respect to later ones the more likely it is that income will rise by more than the rise in the first quasi-rent and that depreciation in that period will fall.

But the essential point for policy purposes remains the subjectivity of the approach. Because the values it involves can only be subjectively determined, a policy based upon the replacement of subjective value cannot be objectively applied. The volatility of the values, while of secondary importance, is another unfavorable factor. We conclude then that current cost depreciation which permits the replacement of the current (objective or market) value of expired asset services is the preferable basis for a depreciation policy designed to exempt the costs of replacement from taxation. It remains to be seen whether the admission of technological change will require any modification of this view.

C. CHANGES IN DEMAND AND TECHNOLOGY

We shall argue that changes in demand and technology are not important *theoretical* considerations in determining depreciation in replacement terms on machines already in stock. This statement should not be interpreted to mean that these changes have no effect on depreciation but rather that their impact can be incorporated into the preceding analysis without extensive modification. That such changes make the *practical* application of theoretical depreciation methods (notably current cost depreciation) more difficult goes undisputed. A consideration of changes in demand and technology should, then, serve two purposes: (1) to clarify and summarize the theoretical basis for current cost depreciation and (2) to acknowledge and identify some of the practical problems involved in its accurate application.

1. *Current Cost Depreciation Summarized*

Current cost depreciation is the culmination of four choices. First is the choice of objective values over subjective values. This is made on the grounds that objectivity is a paramount consideration in any policy matter. It implies a choice of societal values, imperfect as they may be, over individual values. There is also the fact that when depreciation charges are covered by current quasi-rents, the funds so designated are themselves objective and market-valued. The entrepreneur is immediately free to place a higher subjective value on them. We have seen also that under certain circumstances objective depreciation permits the maintenance of *both* objective and subjective values.

Second is the choice of current values over historic ones. The principal purpose of this choice is to place all values pertinent to the position and operation of the firm on a currently significant basis. This implies two things—that the significant values are current values and that these values are measured in current monetary units. Once current values are determined in current monetary units they can be restated in other monetary units (base period, perhaps) in order to facilitate the comparison of current values for different periods or points in time. It should be clear, however, that historic values adjusted for price level changes do *not* yield current values but only historic values stated in current monetary units.

Third is the decision to separate the value of expired services from changes in the value of services remaining in stock. Depreciation is usually reserved to denote the former; the latter represent capital gains and losses. The distinction serves to separate the *operating* activities of a firm from its *holding* activities. When depreciation, thus defined, is matched with the machine's quasi-rents, the returns attributable to the machine are related to the values of the services contributed by it. The difference represents the increase in the objective values of the firm that results from the firm's operation. If capital gains or losses on services remaining in stock are treated as a depreciation element, the resulting depreciation charge can no longer be construed as the value of *expired* services.

Fourth is the choice of a depreciation pattern to apply to current cost in determining the value of currently expired asset services. This problem is not peculiar to current cost depreciation but one point is worth reiterating. The pattern, in keeping with point one above, should represent objective or societal values not subjective or individual ones. This rules out the determination of a pattern that accords, for example, with internal rate depreciation unless this in turn happens to accord with relationships among market values.* The depreciation pattern must relate, of course, to the rate at which the individual firm uses machine services, but the value assigned to the amount used should be the market value.

2. *Reduced Profitability, Zero Obsolescence*

Changes in demand and technology affect the quasi-rents to be secured from operations involving machines already in stock at the time of the change.** An increase in demand will raise them; a decrease in demand will reduce them. Similarly, technological changes that are

---

* It is perhaps worthwhile here to add the suggestion that the market values related by the pattern should be vectoral values in the sense that they should be values *in* the flow of production, not the values these objects might have if sold on the market. Current cost in this sense relates to *purchase* cost not *opportunity* cost. A one-year old machine would be valued at its purchase cost (including transportation and installation) not at its value if sold. A difference between the two versions of value is largely attributable to market imperfections.

We abstract from this problem in the text because it is of secondary importance.[43]

** Changes that are anticipated will affect subjective values (and indirectly market values) even before the changes take place. But it is the fact of change, not whether it is expected or not, that concerns us here.

complementary, i.e., that reduce the cost of operating the machine in stock or reduce the price of products complementary to that produced by the machine, tend to increase quasi-rents; on the other hand, competitive changes in technology tend to reduce quasi-rents. It is largely the changes that are unfavorable to the stocked machine that concern us here.

A reduction in the size of the stocked machine's quasi-rents has the immediate effect of diminishing the profitability of the machine relative to other avenues of investment. We can distinguish three cases of importance:

(1) The reduction in profitability is *not intensive* in that it is not large enough to modify the planned use of the machine by any of the firms employing it. This results in *zero obsolescence*.

(2) The reduction in profitability is *not extensive* in that it applies only to one of the machine's multiple uses and the machine is employed in this use by but one of many firms that utilize the machine. The reduction is *intensive*, however, in that the machine will not be replaced in kind in the use affected. This results in *partial obsolescence*.

(3) The reduction in profitability is both *extensive* and *intensive*. This results in *total obsolescence*.

Reduced profitability which is nevertheless not serious enough to affect the employment of the machine will first reduce the subjective values related to the machine by the few firms who first anticipate the effect. As these subjective capital losses become more widespread there will be pressures exerted on the machine's market value. If the machine is already marketed at a competitive price, no alteration is likely to occur but if some excess profit exists in the industry manufacturing the machine and the firms buying it have some bargaining power, the market value is likely to be depressed and objective capital losses will appear.

Given uniform expectations concerning the new quasi-rents and machine costs, and assuming an infinite horizon for all entrepreneurs over which the new set of circumstances is seen to be stationary, subjective depreciation will equal current cost depreciation. If the machine's market values are unaffected, the impact of the reduced stream of quasi-rents will fall entirely on income, subjective or objective. If the machine's market value stabilizes at a lower figure, the impact will be divided between reduced depreciation and reduced income.

3. *Reduced Profitability; Partial Obsolescence*

A machine may become obsolescent in one use (1) because its supply price rises, (2) because the demand for the product so produced falls (and the reduced scale of operations can be more profitably carried on by other means) or disappears, and (3) a new machine is developed which is more profitable than the existing one in this use but not in others. But the occurrence of any of these events need not cause *immediate* abandonment of the machines in stock even though when they are in fact discontinued in use they will not be replaced in kind.[44] Therefore, the problem of determining depreciation on these machines during the lifetime remaining to them persists.

If this firm represents a small part of the total demand for the machine, the withdrawal of its demand will not affect materially the market price of the machine. The decline in subjective value within the firm will reduce subjective income and the reduced quasi-rents, when they are realized, will reduce objective income but current cost depreciation will be unaffected. The firm continues to use machine services whose market value is unchanged. The fact that the use to which they are put is uneconomic in the sense that the allocation of more machines (and the bundles of services they represent) to the same use would not represent an efficient use of resources is evidenced by the decline in income. Current cost depreciation again represents a meaningful view of replacement.

4. *Reduced Profitability, Total Obsolescence*

Total obsolescence of a multi-purpose machine is unlikely to occur because of shifts in demand; it would require a peculiar conjunction of events—the simultaneous and substantial reduction in the demands for all products produced with the aid of the machine. Total obsolescence is more likely to be the result of technological change, the development of a new machine that is competitive with the old one in *all* of its uses. Again, though physical replacement in kind is no longer anticipated as a result of the technological change, the machines already in stock may continue in service for a time and depreciation must be estimated on the machines for the periods included in their remaining lifetimes.

The existence of the superior machine does not affect the theoretical basis for current cost depreciation on the old one. The superior machine will tend to reduce (a) the quasi-rent stream associated with the old machine and (b) the objective value that can reasonably be assigned to it. Given these facts, the firms employing the machine suffer capital losses and current cost depreciation is reduced. In a replacement context, however, depreciation on the old machine should still be a measure of the value of the machine services the firm is actually using, not the value associated with some unutilized technique, namely, the superior machine.

But this value is no longer unambiguous. If the value assigned by society in the market place to machines of the old type falls below their minimum supply price, as total obsolescence implies, then the market for such machines, new, disappears—the factors of production amalgamated as a machine have a market value which is exceeded by the sum of the market values of the factors of production needed to produce the machine—reproduction cost exceeds market value. Which of these should serve, on a theoretical plane, as a basis for current cost depreciation? Clearly the value of the services the firm is using relates to the value of the factors of production cemented permanently as they are in the machine. That reproduction cost is completely hypothetical and irrelevant to the depreciation problem and to the values being consumed in production is evidenced by the fact that the machine has disappeared from the assembly line.

The clarification of this ambiguity on the theoretical level does not diminish at all the practical difficulties that total obsolescence creates for the estimation of current cost depreciation, but it is perhaps worth repeating that the effect of technological change on the computation of depreciation on existing machines is mainly a practical and not a theoretical matter.* Theoretical considerations indicate the *kind* of information necessary to compute depreciation on a current cost basis. Unfortunately technological changes may reduce the means available for estimating this data.

Markets for second-hand assets and their services are notoriously imperfect and often sporadic in their operation. When the machines being depreciated are being currently produced, we have a base price from which to estimate the values of their services. Technological change complicates the problem further when it leads to total obsolescence because this base price disappears. Other, often relatively arbitrary, methods of estimation must be resorted to such as reproduction cost, subjective value, appraisal, the values of competing machines, and price indexes for small groups of assets. A thorough discussion of these techniques cannot be attempted here. The essential point is that they

* The fact that changes in demand and technology which increase the profitability of the existing machine are seldom discussed in the literature on depreciation is itself prima facie evidence that the principal problem is not theoretical in nature.

are all estimates, not the values theoretically required. A few comments may be in order, however.

Reproduction cost is clearly too high as an estimate of the value of services currently utilized. Appraisals made by qualified people may serve the purpose by applying judgment to the results of the other methods but all too often one is led to believe that appraisers are estimating one or the other of the values which are themselves approximations. The value of the superior machine, appropriately adjusted, may yield a useful maximum figure. The ratio of the output of the old machine to the output of the new machine might be used to derive a value for the old machine from that of the new. But such a procedure abstracts from any shift in factor proportions occasioned by the employment of the new machine. Computing the value in such a way as to restore the profit rate that existed before the technological change implies the restoration of capital losses as well as the replacement of values currently utilized.[45] The use of specific index numbers is complicated by technological change because efforts to adjust for quality changes are not likely to be completely successful.[46]

One must grant the defects in these methods of estimation but if value replacement is conceded to be a useful concept for depreciation, it does not follow that current cost depreciation should be abandoned. The essential question becomes, Is there an alternative approach to depreciation which yields a closer approximation to value replacement than do the estimation methods discussed above? No definitive answer can be given but one can hazard the judgment that historic cost depreciation would be unlikely to yield a better approximation to current cost depreciation if only because it ignores *entirely* the events that have occurred since acquisition. Purchasing power depreciation is only historic cost depreciation adjusted for general, not specific, price changes. And the index numbers used in estimating purchasing power may be affected by quality change in much the same way as are index numbers for smaller groups of assets. It can also be said that a price index for a small group of assets is more likely to approximate changes in the price of an asset belonging to that group than is a price index for the universe of goods to which it belongs.

We conclude then that technological change and the obsolescence it creates do not affect the theoretical value of current cost depreciation as representing a meaningful concept of replacement. The additional market imperfections it introduces do, however, complicate the practical task of estimation. These difficulties should not be underestimated but on the other hand the errors involved should not be permitted to scuttle the whole approach. The replacement of the value of currently exhausted services remains an objective against which to measure the adequacy of depreciation charges in a replacement context.

III. CONCLUSION

We have explored in this study several concepts of replacement in terms of their economic significance and their relevance to the determination of depreciation charges under a variety of circumstances including stationary conditions, growth, price and price level movements, and changes in demand and technology. The study suggests that if depreciation is viewed as a measure of the funds necessary should the firm wish to replace exhausted service values, the concept of physical replacement, (maintaining a constant physical stock of machines) must be discarded and a concept based upon value, specifically current value, substituted for it. The significance of relating depreciation to the cost of physical replacement is seriously questioned.

It is also argued that if depreciation is to have relevance for anyone other than the individual entrepreneur, this current value must be an objective one. This conceptual choice does not preclude the possibility that objective and subjective depreciation estimates might be identical, however, and the circumstances conductive to such an identity are examined.

The impact of tax allowable depreciation techniques on total internally generated funds and thus on the after-tax profit rate is explored. The relationships developed are used to clarify the effects such depreciation techniques may have on the size, growth and composition of capital.

Finally the position is taken that capital gains and losses should be excluded from those changes in current value that are treated as depreciation because the one refers to the valuation of *forthcoming* services while the other relates to the value of *currently exhausted* services. This approach requires a knowledge of (1) current machine prices (to determine (a) the value of expired services and (b) the gain or loss on services remaining in the machine stock) and (2) changes in the price level (to determine real gains and losses and to compare the results of different periods). These two kinds of data are not substitutes, as some have suggested, but are instead complementary.

The view developed holds up well as a concept under the various dynamic conditions considered, but these conditions make its practical application more complex.

It is perhaps worth emphasizing that depreciation in this paper has been treated in terms of its adequacy as a measure of replacement. This has meant a preoccupation with matters of internal equity, with the appropriateness of the depreciation charge for the measurement of a firm's income from operations. Other considerations may over-shadow internal equity as a determinant of policy-oriented depreciation charges. The maintenance of full employment, the stabilization of prices, the stimulation of growth, the modification of investment patterns and the composition of output, and the comparable treatment of all economic sectors (considerations of external equity) are among those possible policy objectives which might be advanced by the mani-pulation of state-authorized depreciation charges. But depreciation charges are the obvious tool for promoting internal equity in the matter of replacement. It is not so clear that other tools, such as the mani-pulation of taxes, expenditures and monetary variables, cannot ac-complish the broader policy objectives more effectively than can depreciation charges. Certainly the burden of proof falls on those who would use depreciation policy to further these ends.

MATHEMATICAL APPENDIX[47]

The following variables are listed, generally, in order of appearance:

n = life of machine

t, time, can assume values between 0 and n.

t = n = present.

t = 0 = time at which oldest asset in present machine stock was acquired.

$g(t)$ = rate of new machine acquisitions at time t.

k = rate of growth of new acquisitions.

u = percentage of scrap value, S, to cost, C.

r = internal rate of return.

b = proportion of profit, rN, retained after taxes. $(1 - b)$ = tax rate.

c = proportion of after-tax profit retained in firm.

bcr = rate of retained profit.

p = rate of change in machine prices.

g = percentage of acquisition cost permitted as initial allowance.

The following definitional symbols are also employed:

A = current rate of new acquisitions; cost of current acquisitions.

G = number of machines in stock; valuation of machine stock if all machines were new.

$1 - z$ = average age of the machine stock.

N = book value of the machine stock.

D = depreciation.

R = cost of physical replacements, if made.

M = $D + uR$ = total machine funds = depreciation plus scrap value of retirements.

P = retained profit.

F = total internally generated funds.

X = reduction in reported profit.

Various subscripts are explained when first used.

A. GROWTH

1. *The Physical Stock of Machine Services*

Let $g(0) = 1$. Then $g(t) = e^{kt}$, and the current rate of acquisitions, A, is

$$(1) \qquad A = g(n) = e^{kn}.$$

The total number of machines in stock at present can be determined by integrating the expression for $g(t)$.

$$(2) \qquad G = \int_0^n g(t)\, dt = \frac{e^{kn} - 1}{k}.$$

As each machine in stock originally had a life of n years the maximum years of service life represented by the machine stock, if new, is

$$(3) \qquad n\, \frac{(e^{kn} - 1)}{k}.$$

A machine purchased at time t must have at time n, t years of service life remaining, and the total machine-years now remaining of any acquisition must be

$$(4) \qquad g(t)t = e^{kt}\, t.$$

The actual number of machine-years of use now remaining in the machine stock can be determined by integrating expression (4)

$$(5) \qquad \int_0^n g(t)t\, dt = \frac{e^{kn}\,(kn - 1) + 1}{k^2}.$$

The stable age distribution typical of a machine stock can be represented as the proportion, z, of the actual number of machine-years of service remaining in the machine stock to the machine-years that would be remaining if all machines in stock were new; i.e., expression (5) divided by expression (3), which simplifies to

(6)
$$z = 1 - \frac{1}{kn} + \frac{1}{e^{kn} - 1}.$$

2. *Straight-Line Depreciation*

When prices are constant and straight-line depreciation is used with a zero scrap value and dollar acquisitions at $t = 0$ are designated by 1, expression (1) represents dollar outlays at any moment and expression (2) represents the original cost of machines in stock at any moment. Because a machine purchased at t has by definition the fraction, t/n, of its value (and life) remaining the book value of the machine is given by

(7)
$$g(t) \frac{t}{n} = e^{kt} \frac{t}{n}.$$

The book value of the machine stock at the present is determined by integrating expression (7).

(8)
$$N_s = \int_0^n g(t) \frac{t}{n} \, dt = \frac{e^{kn}(kn - 1) + 1}{k^2 n}.$$

The ratio of book value to original cost is simply expression (8) divided by expression (2), which yields expression (6).

According to the straight-line technique, when scrap value is zero, the depreciation rate is $1/n$. Depreciation (zero scrap value), D_0, at the present is therefore $1/n$ times expression (2).

(9)
$$D_0 = \frac{e^{kn} - 1}{kn}.$$

As acquisitions at $t = 0$ were arbitrarily assigned a value of 1, the cost of running physical replacement, R, at $t = n$ is also 1. Therefore

(10)
$$\frac{D_0}{R} = \frac{e^{kn} - 1}{kn}.$$

The ratio of depreciation charges to the cost of new acquisitions is determined by dividing expression (9) by expression (1), which simplifies to

(11)
$$\frac{D_0}{A} = \frac{1 - e^{-kn}}{kn}.$$

More generally under the straight-line technique the ratio of total machine funds, M_s, to the cost of new acquisitions, A, is dependent also on the salvage percentage, u

(12) $$M_s = D_s + uR. \quad (R \text{ is set equal to } 1).$$

As depreciation is now taken on $(1 - u)\,G$.

(13) $$D_s = (1 - u)\,D_0 = (1 - u)\,\frac{e^{kn} - 1}{kn}, \text{ and}$$

(14) $$M_s = (1 - u)\,\frac{e^{kn} - 1}{kn} + u\,.$$

Dividing by $A = e^{kn}$ and simplifying yields

(15) $$\frac{M_s}{A} = (1 - u)\,\frac{(1 - e^{-kn})}{kn} + ue^{-kn}\,.$$

This in turn, simplifies to expression (11) when $u = 0$, and to R/A $(= e^{-kn})$ when $u = 1$, i.e., when there is no loss in machine value over its entire lifetime.

3. Diminishing Balance Depreciation

The true diminishing balance technique yields a depreciation rate, a, determined from the expression,

(16) $$e^{-an} = u.$$

Diminishing balance depreciation, D_d, is determined by applying this rate, a, to the net book value, N_d, of the stock of machines. Any acquisition, $g(t)$, has in the present, n, a value of $e^{kt}\,e^{-a\,(n-t)}$. The value of the total machine stock at present is the integral of this expression and diminishing balance depreciation is

(17) $$D_d = \frac{a\,(e^{kn} - e^{-an})}{a + k}\,.$$

Following a procedure similar to that used for straight-line depreciation and using e^{-an} for u reveals the amount of machine funds $(M_d = D_d + u)$ to be

(18) $$M_d = \frac{a\,e^{kn} - ke^{-an}}{a + k}\,.$$

The ratio of machine funds to the cost of new acquisitions is

$$(19) \qquad \frac{M_d}{A} = \frac{a + ke^{-n(a+k)}}{a + k}.$$

4. Initial Amortization Allowances

The granting of initial amortization allowances can now be introduced. The initial allowance permits the firm to deduct a part, q, of new acquisition cost, A, immediately. The initial allowance may be 1) an additional allowance above and beyond regular depreciation or (2) a substitute for that amount of depreciation. In the first case the new ratio, M_q/A, is

$$(20) \qquad \frac{M_q}{A} = \frac{M + gA}{A} = \frac{M}{A} + q,$$

where M/A represents the ratio for whatever depreciation method that is in fact used.

If the initial allowance displaces an equal amount of depreciation, it can be shown that the new ratio, M_q/A, is

$$(21) \qquad \frac{M_g}{A} = (1 - q)\frac{M}{A} + q = \frac{M}{A} + q\left(1 - \frac{M}{A}\right),$$

where M/A is the ratio that would obtain with the depreciation method used if it were applied without the initial allowance.

5. The Effect of Various Tax Allowable Techniques on After-Tax Profit Rate

The retained profit rate, bcr, can be related generally to various depreciation methods where total depreciation is limited to $(1 - u)\,A$ when it is assumed that the depreciation technique is consistent with a constant internal rate. Under any such system, retained profit, P, is

$$(22) \qquad P = bcr\,N.$$

Total internally generated funds, F, must equal

$$(23) \qquad F = bcr\,N + D + u = bcr\,N + M.$$

But when stable ratios have been attained all amounts are growing at the rate k. Therefore

$$(24) \qquad k = \frac{A - R}{G} = \frac{A - M}{N}$$

Expression (20) can be rewritten substituting

$$\frac{A - M}{k}$$

for N, and dividing by A.

(25) $$\frac{F}{A} = \frac{bcr}{k} + \left(1 - \frac{bcr}{k}\right)\frac{M}{A} = \frac{M}{A} + \frac{bcr}{k}\left(1 - \frac{M}{A}\right),$$

where M/A varies with the internally consistent depreciation technique that is appropriate for the type of machine utilized by the firm.

A firm operating machines which yield, with the internally consistent depreciation method, a ratio, M_1/A, may be permitted to use another amortization technique for tax purposes which yields a ratio, M_2/A. The effect this will have on the availability of internal funds to the firm depends on the firm's treatment of the tax saving. We can distinguish three cases but for all of them we can take as given the internally generated funds when only the internally consistent depreciation method is permitted.

(26) $$F = bcr\, N_1 + M_1.$$

Furthermore the tax saving, X, is in every case given by the tax rate, $(1 - b)$, applied to the reduction in reported profit, $(M_2 - M_1)$.

(27) $$X = (1 - b)(M_2 - M_1).$$

Case 1: The firm retains all tax savings, no more, no less. It follows immediately that the saving as a percentage of the cost of new acquisitions is

(28) $$\frac{\Delta F}{A} = \frac{X}{A} = (1 - b)\frac{(M_2 - M_1)}{A}.$$

From expression (24),

$$N_1 = \frac{A - M_1}{k}$$

It follows that

(29) $$\frac{\Delta F}{N_1} = \frac{X}{N_1} = \frac{k(1 - b)\dfrac{(M_2 - M_1)}{A}}{1 - \dfrac{M_1}{A}}.$$

Taking the partial derivative of expression (29) with respect to M_1/A yields

$$(30) \qquad \frac{\partial \left(\dfrac{\Delta F}{N_1} \right)}{\partial \left(\dfrac{M_1}{A} \right)} = \frac{k \, (1 - b) \left(\dfrac{M_2}{A} - 1 \right)}{\left(1 - \dfrac{M_1}{A} \right)^2} \, .$$

The derivative takes the sign of

$$\left[k \left(\frac{M_2}{A} - 1 \right) \right].$$

For growing firms, $k > 0$. If

$$\frac{M_2}{A} > 1 \, ,$$

the profit rate is raised more, the *higher* M_1/A; if

$$\frac{M_2}{A} < 1 \, ,$$

the profit rate is raised more, the *lower* M_1/A. For declining firms, however, for whom M_2/A must be greater than or equal to one, the profit rate must be either neutral with respect to M_1/A or declining as M_1/A increases. But for declining firms, a larger M_1/A means a less accelerated internally consistent depreciation technique. Declining firms, therefore, should favor more accelerated type machines unless a subsidy policy is strong enough, given the firm's rate of growth, to make

$$\frac{M_2}{A} > 1 \, .$$

Case 2: The firm shares the tax saving with owners. By definition the firm retains only

$$(31) \qquad \Delta F = cX = c(1 - b) \, (M_2 - M_1).$$

The saving accruing to the firm can readily be stated as a proportion of either A or N_1.

$$(32) \qquad \frac{\Delta F}{A} = \frac{cX}{A} = c \, (1 - b) \frac{(M_2 - M_1)}{A} \, .$$

$$(33) \qquad \frac{\Delta F}{N_1} = \frac{cX}{N_1} = \frac{ck(1-b)\left(\dfrac{M_2 - M_1}{A}\right)}{1 - \dfrac{M_1}{A}}.$$

Its derivative with respect to M_1/A has the same characteristics as expression (30).

Case 3: The firm bases its dividend policy on the new after-tax *reported* profit figure and distributes $(1-c)$ of that amount to owners. Before-tax reported profit is reduced by $b(M_2 - M_1)$. Therefore dividends are reduced by $(1-c)\,b\,(M_2 - M_1)$. The increase in funds available to the firm, F, is now composed of two elements, the tax saving and the dividend reduction.

$$(34) \qquad \Delta F = (1-b)(M_2 - M_1) + (1-c)\,b\,(M_2 - M_1)$$
$$= (1-bc)(M_2 - M_1).$$

As a proportion of A, this is

$$(35) \qquad \frac{\Delta F}{A} = (1 - bc)\frac{(M_2 - M_1)}{A}.$$

As a proportion of N_1, it is

$$(36) \qquad \frac{\Delta F}{N_1} = \frac{k(1 - bc)\left(\dfrac{M_2 - M_1}{A}\right)}{1 - \dfrac{M_1}{A}}.$$

Its derivative with respect to M_1/A has the same characteristics as expression (30).

B. Price Changes and Growth

Expenditures for machines may differ from one period to another not only because of real growth, k, but also because of the rate of change in machine prices, p. Let us assume that at $t = 0$ the price index stands at 1 and asset acquisitions are also 1; the present we denote as before by $t = n$.

The historic cost of any asset, $g(t)$, is now $e^{t(p+k)}$, and the historic cost of the present stock of machines, G^h, is by integration

$$(37) \qquad G^h = \frac{e^{n(p+k)} - 1}{p + k}.$$

The current cost of any acquisition, its cost if purchased new today, is $e^{t(p+k)} e^{p(n-t)} = e^{pn+kt}$, and the current cost of the existing stock of machines is

$$(38) \qquad G^c = e^{pn} \frac{(e^{kn} - 1)}{k} . \quad \text{(If } k = 0, G^c = ne^{pn}.)$$

1. Straight-Line Depreciation

Straight-line depreciation, zero salvage value, on the historic cost basis is

$$(39) \qquad D_s{}^h = \frac{e^{n(p+k)} - 1}{n(p+k)} .$$

On a current cost basis it is

$$(40) \qquad D_s{}^c = e^{pn} \left(\frac{e^{kn} - 1}{kn} \right) . \quad \text{(If } k = 0, D_s{}^c = e^{pn}.)$$

It follows that the appropriate price index for converting historic cost depreciation into current cost depreciation is

$$(41) \qquad \frac{D_s{}^c}{D_s{}^h} = \frac{(p+k)(e^{kn} - 1)}{k(e^{kn} - e^{-pn})} . \quad \left(\text{If } k = 0, \frac{D_s{}^c}{D_s{}^h} = \frac{pn}{1 - e^{-pn}} \right).$$

This is equal to one when $p = 0$ and greater than one when p is positive.

The depreciated historic cost of any asset is

$$\frac{t}{n} e^{t(p+k)} ,$$

and the depreciated historic cost of the present stock of machines is by integration

$$(42) \qquad N_s{}^h = \frac{e^{n(p+k)} (pn + kn - 1) + 1}{n(p+k)^2} .$$

The depreciated current cost of any asset is

$$\frac{t}{n} e^{pn+kt}$$

and the depreciated current cost of the stock is

$$(43) \qquad N_s{}^c = e^{pn} \left[\frac{e^{kn}(kn - 1) + 1}{k^2 n} \right] . \quad \left(\text{If } k = 0, N^{sc} = \frac{ne^{pn}}{2} \right).$$

2. Diminishing Balance Depreciation

Similar relationships for diminishing balance depreciation can also be derived. If prices are rising, the expected salvage value proportion is increased from u to ue^{pn}. Let this equal u' and let $e^{-a'n} = u'$, where $a' = a - p$. We can now proceed as in expression (16) through (19).

The depreciated historic cost of any acquisition is now $e^{t(k+p)}$ $e^{(p-a)(n-t)}$. Total machine funds on the historic cost basis, $M_d{}^h$, includes diminishing balance depreciation, which is $(a - b)$ times the integral of the expression for depreciated historic cost, and the salvage value of the retired machine, $e^{n(p-a)}$.

$$(44) \qquad M_d{}^h = (a - p)\frac{(e^{n(k+b)} - e^{n(p-a)})}{a + k} + e^{n(p-a)}$$

$$= \frac{(a - p)\ e^{n(k+a)} + k + p}{(a + k)\ e^{-n(p-a)}}.$$

Total machine funds on a current cost basis can be determined in a similar fashion. Any acquisition must now be valued at $e^{pn}\ e^{kt}\ e^{-a(n-t)}$. Integrating, multiplying by the current cost depreciation rate, a, and adding salvage value yields

$$(45) \qquad M_d{}^c = \frac{ae^{pn}\ (e^{kn} - e^{-an})}{a + k} + e^{n(p-a)} = \frac{ae^{n(k+a)} + k}{(a + k)\ e^{-n(p-a)}}.$$

The ratio of current cost diminishing balance depreciation to its historic cost counterpart is

$$(46) \qquad \frac{M_d{}^c}{M_d{}^h} = \frac{ae^{n(k+a)} + k}{(a - p)e^{n(k+a)} + k + p}.$$

These and related equations are summarized below for both the non-growth and growth situations:

3. *Some Relevant Expressions Summarized*

ZERO GROWTH EXPRESSIONS

	Base Period $(t = 0)$ Prices	Historic Cost Prices	Current $(t = n)$ Prices
G	n	$\dfrac{e^{pn} - 1}{p}$	ne^{pn}
$M_s = D_s$	1	$\dfrac{e^{pn} - 1}{pn}$	e^{pn}
N	$n/2$	$\dfrac{e^{pn}(pn - 1) + 1}{p^2 n}$	$\dfrac{ne^{pn}}{2}$
$\dfrac{M_s}{A} = \dfrac{M_s}{R}$	1	$\dfrac{1 - e^{-pn}}{pn}$	1

$$\frac{D_s{}^c}{D_s{}^h} = \frac{pn}{1 - e^{-pn}} \cdot \qquad \frac{M_d{}^c}{M_d{}^h} = \frac{a}{a - p(1 - e^{-an})} = \frac{a' + p}{a' + pe^{-n(p+a')}} \cdot$$

GROWTH EXPRESSIONS

(Real rate of growth $= k$)

(Nominal rate of growth $= k + p$)

	Base Period $(t = 0)$ Prices	Historic Cost Prices	Current $(t = n)$ Prices
G	$\dfrac{e^{kn} - 1}{k}$	$\dfrac{e^{n(p+k)} - 1}{p + k}$	$e^{pn}\dfrac{e^{kn} - 1}{k}$
$M_s = D_s$	$\dfrac{e^{kn} - 1}{kn}$	$\dfrac{e^{n(p+k)} - 1}{n(p + k)}$	$e^{pn}\dfrac{e^{kn} - 1}{kn}$
N	$\dfrac{e^{kn}(kn - 1) + 1}{k^2 n}$	$\dfrac{e^{n(p+k)}(pn + kn - 1) + 1}{n(p + k)^2}$	$e^{pn}\dfrac{e^{kn}(kn - 1) + 1}{k^2 n}$
$\dfrac{M_s}{A}$	$\dfrac{1 - e^{-kn}}{kn}$	$\dfrac{1 - e^{-n(p+k)}}{n(p + k)}$	$\dfrac{1 - e^{-kn}}{kn}$
$\dfrac{M_s}{R}$	$\dfrac{e^{kn} - 1}{kn}$	$\dfrac{e^{kn} - e^{-pn}}{n(p + k)}$	$\dfrac{e^{kn} - 1}{kn}$

$$\frac{D_s{}^c}{D_s{}^h} = \frac{(p + k)(e^{kn} - 1)}{k(e^{kn} - e^{-pn})} \cdot \qquad \frac{M_d{}^c}{M_d{}^h} = \frac{ae^{n(k+a)} + k}{(a - p)e^{n(k+a)} + k + p} \cdot$$

REFERENCES

1. Two streams can be identified in the literature. Among those who have stressed the income element are ERIK LINDAHL, *Studies in the Theory of Money and Capital* (London, 1939), esp. pp. 74–111; J. R. HICKS, *Value and Capital*, 2nd Edition, (London, 1946), esp. pp. 171–201; and F. A. HAYEK, *The Pure Theory of Capital* (Chicago, 1941). Those who have stressed the depreciation element are well represented by GABRIEL A. D. PREINREICH. One of his many articles is his "Annual Survey of Economic Theory: The Theory of Depreciation", *Econometrica* (July, 1938), pp. 219–241, hereafter called "Theory". An important contribution, which draws from both streams, is FRIEDRICH and VERA LUTZ, *The Theory of Investment of the Firm* (Princeton, 1951).

2. ROBERT EISNER, "Depreciation Allowances, Replacement Requirements and Growth", *American Economic Review* (December, 1952), pp. 820−831, and other articles; and EVSEY D. DOMAR, "Depreciation, Replacement and Growth", *Economic Journal* (March, 1953), pp. 1–32.

3. This term is borrowed from LUTZ, *op. cit.*, p. 102. The succeeding development of depreciation principles for such an enterprise draws heavily on this work and on various articles by G. A. D. PREINREICH (particularly his "The Economic Life of Industrial Equipment", *Econometrica* (January, 1940), pp. 12–44, hereafter called "Life").

4. Preinreich, "Life", *op. cit.*

5. *Loc. cit.*

6. See, for example, ERIK LINDAHL, *op. cit.*, pp. 74–111; Hicks, *op. cit.*, and his "Maintaining Capital Intact: A Further Suggestion", *Economica* (May, 1942), pp. 174–179; F. A. HAYEK, *op. cit.* and his "Maintaining Capital Intact: A Reply", *Economica* (August, 1941), pp. 276–280. The two articles are responses to A. C. PIGOU, "Maintaining Capital Intact", *Economica* (August, 1941), pp. 271–275, in which exception is taken to Hayek's presentation in *The Pure Theory of Capital*.

7. PREINREICH treats this approach as the central one ("Theory", *op. cit.*). More recently RALPH C. JONES has reiterated this view. See his *Effects of Price Level Changes on Business Income, Capital and Taxes*, (American Accounting Association, 1956) esp. pp. 111–113.

8. I have not located any references in which this situation is discussed. LUTZ (*op. cit.*, pp. 219–221) discusses the choice of depreciation method in terms of the necessity of choosing between the maintenance of subjective value or cost except where the two are identical. He (and others) is apparently unaware of the possibility of maintaining both when the objective depreciation charge itself has a higher subjective value.

9. PREINREICH has given emphasis to the arbitrary nature of the assumption. "No matter how far analysis and conjecture are carried, it is necessary to assume the form of the profit function either deliberately or by doing—perhaps unwittingly—something equivalent". ("Theory", *op. cit.*, p. 237).

   Both a constant income stream, the characteristic of subjective depreciation, and a constant internal rate of return are appealing concepts, but as we have shown the two are likely to be inconsistent with each other.

10. R. C. JONES, *op. cit.*, p. 112.

11. MYRON GORDON has drawn this distinction between the *base* and the *allocation technique* to be applied to it. See his "Depreciation Allowances, Replacement Requirements and Growth: A Comment", *American Economic Review*, v. 43 (Sept., 1953), p. 609.

12. Estimates of some important market value patterns can be found in GEORGE

TERBORGH, *Realistic Depreciation Policy* (Machinery and Allied Products Institute) 1954, pp. 39–47.

13. These factors have been discussed in more detail by F. and V. LUTZ, *op. cit.*, Chapter XII.

14. There is one exception which may be important in practice. Probability theory suggests that all of the machine in the stock will not have exactly the same life. Thus each machine in the stock will not be replaced at exactly the same time. This dispersion in asset lives will tend over time to even out the age distribution of the firm's machines. *See* G. A. D. PREINREICH, "Theory", *op. cit.*

15. It is similar to one appearing in F. and V. LUTZ, *op. cit.*, p. 148.

16. LUTZ, *op. cit.*, p. 150.

17. Some of the patterns of output growth that would warrant the steady reinvestment of depreciation charges during this interim period can be inferred from EDWARDS, "The Effect of Depreciation on the Output-Capital Coefficient of a Firm", *Economic Journal* (December, 1955), pp. 654–666.

18. Among the relevant materials dealing with depreciation and growth are E. D. DOMAR, "Depreciation, Replacement and Growth", *Economic Journal* (March, 1953), pp. 1–32; DOMAR, "The Case for Accelerated Depreciation", *Quarterly Journal of Economics* (November, 1953), pp. 493–519; ROBERT EISNER, "Accelerated Amortization, Growth, and Net Profits", *Quarterly Journal of Economics* (November, 1952), pp. 533–544; EISNER, "Depreciation Allowances, Replacement Requirements and Growth", *American Economic Review* (December, 1952), pp. 820–831. These authors seem to have overlooked an important earlier work in which some of their conclusions are anticipated, namely PREINREICH, "Theory", *op. cit.* In this work growth and changing replacement costs are both examined in terms of their effects on various book value, depreciation, and profit relationships. This is done for several different depreciation techniques.

19. This ratio for Manufacturing taken from *Statistics of Income* for 1953 (the year before accelerated depreciation was made generally permissible in the United States) was .56 which places it in the reasonable range indicated in Table 5. No special significance should be attached to the figure, however, because price changes and obsolescence factors are also involved.

20. See references in note 18.

21. It is perhaps ironic that EISNER chose to conclude an early and otherwise excellent article with the statement, "In this entire area (of depreciation-replacement relationships) economists must avoid explaining our developing world with models which ignore the phenomenon of growth". "Depreciation Allowances, Replacement Requirements and Growth", *op. cit.*, p. 831.

22. R. EISNER, "Depreciation Allowances, Replacement Requirements and Growth: A Rejoinder", *American Economic Review* (Sept., 1953), pp. 615–616. See also his "Depreciation Allowances and Replacements Restated", *The Controller* (May, 1954).

23. DOMAR, "Depreciation, Replacement and Growth", *op. cit.*, p. 5.

24. The role of scrap or salvage values is usually minimized and is often neglected. GEORGE TERBORGH in his *Dynamic Equipment Policy* (New York, 1949), suggests that it can often be ignored. Most authors of growth-replacement material have given it a small role, if any. Some empirical work on the size of salvage values would be helpful in evaluating the cost of assuming it to be zero.

25. Various efforts have been directed toward analyzing the effects of the actual amortization techniques permitted in England and the United States. DOMAR's article, "The Case for Accelerated Depreciation", *op. cit.*, treats the British system before the 1954–55 budget and U.S. systems before the 1954 change. Eisner's article, "Depreciation Allowances, Replacement Requirements and Growth", *op. cit.*, is based largely on pre-1954 U.S. experience. RICHARD GOODE, "Accelerated Depre-

ciation Allowances as a Stimulus to Investment", *Quarterly Journal of Economics*, (May, 1955), pp. 191–220 contains an analysis involving more recent British and United States techniques. The optimum amortization method for a firm in the United States is considered by RALPH C. JONES, *op. cit.*

26. DOMAR has argued ("The Case for Accelerated Depreciation", *op. cit.*, p. 508) that straight-line depreciation is internally consistent in the United States. EISNER, too, ("Accelerated Depreciation: Some Further Thoughts", *Quarterly Journal of Economics* (May, 1955), pp. 285–296) accepts the straight-line depreciation premise. On the other hand, some economists who have studied the characteristics of depreciable equipment carefully (TERBORGH, *Realistic Depreciation Policy, op. cit.*, for example; and JOEL DEAN, *Capital Budgeting* (New York, 1951); and many accountants (JONES, *op. cit.*, for example) suggest that a more typical pattern would require sharply accelerated charges. If the typical internally consistent pattern is more accelerated than the double rate declining balance method (a U.S. tax allowable technique), growth would still be penalized. The penalty would be less than with the straight-line technique but a larger rate of growth would nevertheless carry a larger penalty.

27. This proposition should not be confused with the second. A *positive* growth incentive exists if the allowable technique is accelerated relative to the internally consistent one; a *relative* incentive arises if the new allowable technique is more accelerated than the old one. This distinction is made by DWIGHT BROTHERS, "Public Policy Toward Tax Depreciation Allowances: A Study of Its Influence on Business Decisions and the Functioning of the Economy", unpublished doctoral dissertation, 1957, Princeton University.

28. EISNER has considered this problem more extensively in his "Accelerated Depreciation: Some Further Thoughts", *op. cit.*, pp. 285–296.

29. GEORGE TERBORGH, *Dynamic Equipment Policy*, pp. 189–194, presents evidence that pay out periods seldom exceed five years. B. S. KIERSTEAD has estimated effective entrepreneurial horizons at ten to twelve years. (*An Essay in the Theory of Profits and Income Distribution* (Oxford, 1953), p. 37).

30. DOMAR, "The Case for Accelerated Amortization", *op. cit.*, p. 508.

31. Among the more comprehensive earlier discussions are F. SCHMIDT, *Die Organische Tageswerbilanz* (Leipzig, 1929), and H. W. SWEENEY, *Stabilized Accounting* (New York, 1936).

32. EISNER is perhaps most clearly associated with this idea. See his "Depreciation Allowances and Replacements Restated", *The Controller* v. 22 (May, 1954), pp. 228, 248 and other works previously cited. MYRON J. GORDON has disputed Eisner's interpretation (*op. cit.*).

33. A table depicting critical rates of inflation given the rate of growth and asset life can be found in DOMAR, "Depreciation, Replacement and Growth", *op. cit.*, p. 11. The relationship between growth and inflation has also been explored by Eisner (see works previously cited).

34. R. C. JONES (*op. cit.*, pp. 107–110) uses such a concept implicitly when he discusses the effect of rising prices on depreciation. His approach is discussed more fully below.

35. E. CARY BROWN has argued the external equity considerations strongly in his *Effects of Taxation: Depreciation Adjustment for Price Changes* (Boston, 1952), pp. 76–78.

36. See for example, NILS VÄSTHAGEN, *De fria avaskrivningarna 1938–1951* (Lund, 1953), pp. 27–28, and E. O. EDWARDS, "Depreciation Policy Under Changing Price Levels", *Accounting Review* (April, 1954), esp. pp. 271–272. The most rigorous demonstration I have seen is WENDELL P. TRUMBULL, "Price-Level Depreciation and Replacement Cost", *Accounting Review* (January, 1958), pp. 26–34.

37. A recent exposition of this point of view can be found in Jones, *op. cit.*, Appendix A.

Another but briefer presentation is PERRY MASON, *Price-Level Changes and Financial Statements: Basic concepts and Methods* (American Accounting Association, 1956). See also TERBORGH, *Realistic Depreciation Policy*, Chapter 14.

38. WILLARD J. GRAHAM made this point in his "The Effect of Changing Price Levels on the Determination, Reporting and Interpretation of Income", *Accounting Review* (January, 1949). It has also been made in a study by the Taxation and Research Committee of the Association of Certified and Corporate Accountants, *Accounting for Inflation* (London, 1952). See also the forthcoming book by E. O. Edwards and P. W. Bell, *The Theory and Measurement of Business Income* (Berkeley, Calif., 1961).

39. TERBORGH, *op. cit.*, p. 117. The same approach is used by A. L. BELL, "Fixed Assets and Current Costs" *Accounting Review* (January, 1953), pp. 44–53, and G. H. WARNER, "Depreciation on a Current Basis", *Accounting Review* (October, 1954), pp. 628–633. A notable development of the view that the two adjustments are complementary can be found in J. E. KANE, "Structural Changes and General Changes in the Price Level in Relation to Financial Reporting", *Accounting Review* (October, 1951), pp. 496–502.

40. The classifications in the example appeared in the author's "Depreciation Policy Under Price Level Changes", *op. cit.* Examples and proposed accounting treatments for various combinations of price level and asset price movements are presented there.

41. JONES, *op. cit.*, pp. 107–110.

42. *Ibid.*, p. 108.

43. It is treated more thoroughly in a forthcoming book by EDWARDS and BELL, *op. cit.*

44. Precisely *when* such a machine should be abandoned does not concern us here. On this subject see, among others, GEORGE TERBORGH, *Dynamic Equipment Policy* JOEL DEAN, *Capital Budgeting*; and B. E. RIFAS, "Replacement Models", in *Introduction to Operations Research* (Churchman, Ackoff, and Arnoff, editors) (New York, 1956).

45. This appears to be HAYEK's view for anticipated obsolescence. See *The Pure Theory of Capital*, pp. 300–303. For unexpected obsolescence, however, he suggests the maintenance of income on the reduced capital value (pp. 307–308).

46. SIDNEY DAVIDSON has expressed considerable concern over the impact of technical change on the determination of current cost depreciation, "Depreciation and Profit Determination", *Accounting Review* (January, 1950), pp. 45–57.

47. The author wishes to acknowledge his indebtedness in constructing this appendix to the mathematical formulations that have preceded it. Particular note is due the following: GABRIEL A. D. PREINREICH, "Annual Survey of Economic Theory: The Theory of Depreciation", *Econometrica* (July, 1938), pp. 219–241; EVSEY DOMAR, "Depreciation, Replacement and Growth", *Economic Journal*, (March, 1953), esp. pp. 24–32; and JAMES TOBIN, "A Note ...", Appendix B in R. C. JONES, *Effects of Price Level Changes on Business Income, Capital, and Taxes* (American Accounting Association, 1956), pp. 182–184.

CHAPTER 3

DEPRECIATION PROBLEMS AND TAXATION*

DAVID WALKER

University College of East Africa, Uganda

I. INTRODUCTION

This chapter considers in a very broad and general way some problems that arise when taxes are levied at a fairly high rate on business profits. The particular problem with which we shall be mainly concerned is the treatment of capital expenditure as a cost of production for taxation purposes. We begin by considering the nature of capital expenditure and its role as a cost of production. In the second section we consider some of the problems that arise when an income tax is imposed on business profits and some of the ways in which the state can influence the level of investment expenditure through the income tax system. In these first two sections it will, for the most part, be assumed that we are dealing with an economy in which the general level of prices remains unchanged. In the third section this assumption is relaxed and some of the problems and difficulties that arise in connection with capital costs under an income tax system in a period of inflation are examined.

For the most part the problems under discussion will be fairly general in the sense that they occur in all countries and they will be considered as such. From time to time, however, reference will be made to the particular experiences and practices of various countries. Many of these references will be to the U.K. with whose tax structure and tax problems I am most familiar but reference to the tax systems of other countries will also be made. These various comments on particular countries and specific problems are mainly used as illustrative material, to give life and reality to the general proposition under discussion and are not meant in any way as a full treatment of the problem or event that is mentioned.

* This chapter was completed in June 1956 at a time when the writer was a lecturer in Economics in the University of Manchester, U.K.

II. CAPITAL EXPENDITURE AS A COST OF PRODUCTION

A. THE NATURE OF DEPRECIATION ALLOWANCES[1]

Profit or business income is the difference between the costs of producing a certain quantity of goods and the revenue produced by selling these goods. Costs of production may be divided into two main categories, capital expenditure and current expenditure. The distinction between these two types of spending is purely one of time and there is no sharp or fundamental distinction between them. In so far as the benefit accruing from a particular item of expenditure is exhausted during the accounting period in which the expenditure takes place it is revenue or current expenditure. In so far as the benefit is prolonged beyond the current accounting period it is capital or investment expenditure. If one takes as a single period a long succession of accounting periods it is obvious that capital and current expenditure merge together and become indistinguishable. The need for the distinction arises out of the necessity for computing figures of profit for relatively short periods of time, such as a year. When this has to be done account has to be taken of the fact that expenditure in a given time period—capital expenditure—is not entirely or even mainly a cost of producing goods in that period and that such expenditure has to be spread over a number of accounting periods if a misleading impression of business income is not to be given. And a misleading impression of the events of a given time period would be given if in computing the profits of a particular period the cost of an asset expected to yield services over many years was deducted from sales proceeds in the year of acquisition. The profits of that period would be underestimated and the profits of succeeding periods would be exaggerated.

The distinguishing feature of capital expenditure, therefore, is that it has to be spread over a number of accounting periods. Two main problems arise in doing this. The first is to decide the period over which the asset will be in use and providing services. The second is, given this life, to decide how to allocate or spread the cost of the asset over these various accounting periods.

The calculation of depreciation and obsolescence charges is the normal way in which capital expenditure is allocated to specific accounting periods. A firm when purchasing a capital asset makes an estimate of its useful economic life and then decides to allocate in some way the cost of the asset over this period. The annual allocations or instalments of cost are known as depreciation allowances or charges and are regarded and treated as part of the cost of production of the period to be set against sales proceeds before arriving at the profit of the period. If the actual life of the asset turns out to be less than the expected life the difference between the original cost of the asset and the sum of the annual depreciation charged to that time and any scrap value it may produce is treated as an offset to profits in the year when it is scrapped, and written off as an obsolescence charge. Over the life of the asset, then, its cost, minus any scrap value, is deducted from sales proceeds and reduces profits accordingly.

Broadly speaking no asset purchased by a business with the possible exceptions of freehold land and goodwill can retain its efficiency for ever and therefore have an infinitely long effective or economic life. If assets did have an infinite capacity for yielding services obviously the arguments that have been deployed above for justifying the allocation of their cost over a finite number of accounting periods would lose their force—but they have not.

Assets have a limited economic life for two main reasons. On the one hand they deteriorate through actual wear and tear in the process of production and indeed from the mere lapse of time; buildings for instance given a sufficiently long period of exposure will suffer seriously from the weather. The second group of reasons for a limited life is obsolescence; technological developments may occur which make the cost of operating a particular capital asset uneconomical, or there may be a shift in the demand for the product for the production of which the asset was purchased.

Traditionally the first set of reasons have been the ones used to justify systematic depreciation charges but it is becoming more and more obvious that in the modern scientific economy obsolescence in the broad sense is becoming a more important factor in determining the effective life of assets than wear and tear.

It has always been difficult to estimate at all exactly the economic life of an asset and, therefore, to decide the period over which it has to be depreciated. It is even more difficult at the present time in view of the importance of obsolescence relatively to wear and tear considerations. Nevertheless a decision has to be made and though this may mean, looking backwards, that too much or too little has been offset against profits in the early years of the asset's life, leading to too low or too high profits in the early period and correspondingly too high or too low profits in the later period, there is no doubt that these profit figures will give a fairer view of things than if either no account was

taken of capital costs or if the cost was written off in the year of acquisition or scrapping. Nevertheless it has always to be borne in mind
that estimates of expected economic life are only estimates and that
they will often be wrong and, thus, on this count alone annual depreciation charges may very often underestimate or overestimate the value
of the services yielded by an asset in a particular accounting period.

There are clearly an infinite number of ways in which the cost of
a capital asset can be spread over its expected life. Considerations of
administrative and accounting efficiency make it necessary, of course,
that for most assets a systematic and fairly simple method should be
used by most firms.

There are four methods of allocating the cost of an asset over its
expected life commonly used by business firms. Let us assume we are
dealing with an asset costing £100 and expected to last ten years.
The most simple way to allocate this cost is the so-called straight line
method in which the same amount is written off each year; in this case
one tenth of the asset's cost, £10, would be the annual depreciation
charge to be set off as an expense before arriving at profits. (We have
implicitly assumed no scrap value. If it had been expected that the
asset would be worth—as scrap—£10 at the end of ten years then £90
would have had to be written off over 10 years and the annual depreciation charge would then have been £9.) The second method is the
reducing balance method in which a certain percentage is computed
such that when it is applied to the written down value of the asset
produces scrap value at the end of ten years. As no reducing balance
rate can write off the cost of an asset completely there is a certain
flexibility here. A 25% rate would reduce the written down value to
6% of its cost at the end of ten years and a 20% rate to about 10% of
the original cost; the remaining unallocated costs would have to be
written off—less any scrap value—in the year of retirement.

The third method of cost allocation is known as the sum-of-digits
method. In this system the fraction of an asset's cost to be written off
each year is computed by first adding together the digits of the estimated life of the asset—in our case $1 + 2 + 3 + \ldots + 10 = 55$, and
then making the first year's depreciation charge ten fifty-fifths ($\frac{10}{55}$) of
the cost of the asset; the second year's depreciation charge nine fifty-
fifths ($\frac{9}{55}$) of the cost of the asset; the third year eight fifty-fifths ($\frac{8}{55}$)
of the cost of the asset, and so on—thus writing off the total cost of
the asset in the ten year period, as with the straight line method.

Fourthly we must consider the sinking fund method. In this system of cost allocation there is first computed the annual payment which if set aside each year and allowed to accumulate at compound interest would reach £100 at the end of the ten years. If we assume a 5% rate of interest this sum would be £7.95. The annual depreciation charge to be set off against sales proceeds using this method of cost allocation would be £7.95 *plus* the annual interest payments that are necessary on the growing capital sum in order to make £7.95 a year for ten years grow to £100. In the first year the charge would be £7.95; in the second

$$£7.95 + \frac{5}{100} \times £7.96 \text{ i.e. } £8.3 \text{ .}$$

In the third year it would be

$$£8.3 + \frac{5}{100} \times £8.3 \text{ .}$$

i.e. £8.8 and so on.

TABLE 1

DEPRECIATION CHARGES £100 ASSET, 10 YEAR LIFE

		Method							
Year	Straight line	Declining balance				Sum of digits		Sinking fund 5% rate of interest	
		25% Rate		20% Rate					
	Annual charge	Written down value	Annual charge	Written down value	Annual charge	Written down value	Annual charge	Written down value	Annual charge	Written down value
1	10	90	25.0	75.0	20.0	80.0	18.2	81.8	7.9	92.1
2	10	80	18.7	56.3	16.0	64.0	16.3	65.5	8.3	83.8
3	10	70	14.1	42.2	12.8	51.2	14.6	50.9	8.8	75.0
4	10	60	10.5	31.7	10.2	41.0	12.7	38.2	9.2	65.8
5	10	50	7.9	23.8	8.2	32.8	10.9	27.3	9.7	56.1
6	10	40	5.9	17.9	6.6	26.2	9.1	18.2	10.2	45.9
7	10	30	4.5	13.4	5.2	21.0	7.3	10.9	10.7	35.2
8	10	20	3.4	10.0	4.2	16.8	5.4	5.5	11.2	24.0
9	10	10	2.5	7.5	3.4	13.4	3.7	1.8	11.7	12.3
10	10	0	1.9	5.6*	2.7	10.7*	1.8	0	12.3	0

* If the asset was scrapped in this year and there was no scrap value these amounts — £5.6 and £10.7 — would have to be written off in year ten, making the total depreciation charges in this year £7.5 and £13.4.

In Table 1 there is computed the annual depreciation charge and each year's written down value of an asset costing £100 under each of these four main methods of apportioning capital expenditures. If one takes the straight line method, in which the annual charge is the same every year, as a standard, it is obvious that there is a marked difference between the Decreasing Balance and Sum-of-Digits method on the one hand and the Sinking Fund system on the other. Under the first two methods the annual depreciation charge begins much in excess of the straight line charge but fairly quickly falls till in year five it is below it and is still declining. On the other hand the annual depreciation charge under the Sinking Fund system begins below the straight line charge and does not exceed it till year six.

Argument as to which of these various methods is the best way of measuring annual capital costs of production given the expected economic life of assets has at times been strenuous. There is no complete or definite answer but a number of points can be made.

The main idea underlying the straight line basis—and it is a sound one—is the importance of time alone in limiting the services that an asset can yield; that many of the factors likely to limit the useful life of an asset are directly or indirectly related to its age. A second reason is its simplicity; it is a very easy system to operate. There are, however, two important objections to it. Firstly, if one expects sales proceeds and revenue or current expenses of production to remain more or less unchanged during each year of the asset's life then the rate of return on the capital employed measured by the written down value of the asset, will rise as the asset gets older which seems somewhat unreasonable. The position would of course, be worse under either of the declining charge systems but would, in part, be met by the Sinking Fund System. If however, one takes the view that revenue might be expected to decline or current costs of production to increase as the asset gets older, this would not be an objection against the straight line method and *a fortiori* the declining charge systems. The second objection to the straight line method is that it ignores the uncertainty surrounding the estimate of useful economic life. It is after all, an estimate and when an estimate ten years ahead is made what is really involved is that the Board of Directors think it highly unlikely that the asset will have to be scrapped earlier than after say, five or six years but will *probably* have to be scrapped after ten and certainly after thirteen or fourteen years. Given this attitude there is a lot to be said for the declining balance method for the writing off of a substantial part of an asset's cost in its early life is a way of taking into account the risks and uncertainties of the real economic world.

It is probably true to say that the method of depreciation should vary with the type of asset and industry. In an industry in which expected revenues, expected current costs of production and the economic life of the capital asset can be estimated with considerable certainty there is probably a lot to be said for the Sinking Fund method of allocating capital costs if revenues and current costs are expected to be more or less stable over the asset's life and the straight line method if revenues are expected to decline or current costs to increase by relatively small amounts. On the other hand if there is tremendous uncertainty or if the gap between current revenues and current costs is expected to increase very rapidly then one of the declining charge methods is desirable. As between these there is not much to choose. The Sum of Digits method has an advantage in that it writes off the whole cost of the asset over its estimated life but the percentage method is a more simple and straightforward one to operate from an administrative point of view.

We have suggested above that the purpose of depreciation charges is to allocate over a succession of accounting periods expenditure on capital assets. Just as expenditure on wages or on raw materials is a cost of production to be subtracted from sales proceeds before arriving at profit so too is the cost of machinery and buildings and patent rights; the only difference being that such expenditure results in the acquisition of assets which yield their services to a firm over a period of years. Capital consumption is an inescapable cost of production: no profit or income can result unless this cost has been allowed for. This view of the nature of depreciation allowances may be called the 'amortisation of cost' view or approach; the cost of capital assets and no more than the cost of assets have to be set off, over a period of years against sales proceeds as a cost of production. We have seen that it is not easy to estimate the effective economic life of assets and that there is room for a wide variety of methods as to how the cost should be allocated. Nevertheless the principle that depreciation allowances are an amortisation of cost, a spreading of cost over a fixed number of years, lies behind what has been said above.

Now this approach to the nature of depreciation allowances can be challenged from at least two sides. On the one hand it can be argued that the purpose of depreciation allowances is to reflect the fall in value of the capital asset during its effective life and, on the other hand, that the main purpose of depreciation allowances is to build up a fund sufficient to replace the asset when it wears out.

The first of these arguments is related to the common sense usage of the word 'depreciation'. It is quite common for an individual having just purchased a new car to say that it will depreciate by a substantial amount as soon as he has driven it a few miles. What is meant by such a statement is not that the car will have diminished in usefulness or in its capacity to yield services but that the *value* of the car in the sense of the price that its owner could get for it if he had to sell it in the secondhand market, would be much less than what he had paid for it. This way of looking at depreciation is to say that annual depreciation charges should represent the decline in value—in the sense of market value—that occurred during the year. This sort of reasoning can of course, be used to justify very heavy depreciation charges in the first year of ownership. Arguments can be deployed to suggest that this method of treating depreciation should be adopted by businesses. In particular, if one was wanting a snapshot picture of the value of a business at a given moment of time, this way of assessing aggregate accumulated depreciation might well be the best. There are however important arguments against it, even if we leave on one side as being relevant to the third section of this chapter the fact that in periods when the price of a particular asset is increasing no depreciation might be charged on an asset during a particular time period if this method of computing depreciation charges were used even though the usefulness of the asset had deteriorated. Moreover there is still the point that it is very difficult to know what the decline in the market value of an asset has been during the course of a year. For most capital assets there would be some considerable expense involved in calculating the depreciation charge at all exactly by this method; experts of various kinds would have to be called in to make valuations. And once the exercise is carried out on a rule of thumb basis there does not seem much difference in practice between this decline in market value method and the alternative 'amortisation of cost' arrangements as a means of spreading the cost of the asset over its effective economic life.

Another version of the decline in value approach, and one which is closely linked with some of the points we made in the previous section, is to look at the capital value of the asset not as a market phenomenon but as a reflection of the asset's expected income stream. If we look at depreciation in this way the annual depreciation charge becomes the decline in the asset's capital value during a given year, which in turn is the difference between the capital value of the asset's expected income stream at the start of one year and the start of the next. Table 2 illustrates the tremendous importance of the time distribution of the services yielded by the asset. An asset expected to last ten years

TABLE 2

DECLINE IN VALUE OF A CAPITAL ASSET EXPECTED TO LAST TEN YEARS AND TO YIELD
£ 1,000 OF INCOME ON THE ASSUMPTION OF A 5% DISCOUNT RATE

| | Constant income stream | | | Declining income stream | | |
Year	Expected income	Capital value of income stream at start of year	Decline in capital value during year	Expected income	Capital value of income stream at start of year	Decline in capital value during year
1	100	772.2	61.4	190	842.0	156.3
2	100	710.8	64.5	170	685.7	135.7
3	100	646.3	67.7	150	550.0	122.5
4	100	578.6	71.0	130	427.5	108.6
5	100	507.6	74.7	110	318.9	94.0
6	100	432.9	78.3	90	224.9	78.7
7	100	354.6	82.3	70	146.1	62.7
8	100	272.3	86.4	50	83.4	45.8
9	100	185.9	90.7	30	37.6	28.1
10	100	95.2	95.2	10	9.5	9.5

and expected to yield an income of £1,000 is considered. In the first instance it is assumed that the asset yields £100 in each year and in the second that the income is expected to fall from £190 in the first year by £20 each year to £10 in the final year. If we assume a given rate of discount it is possible to work out the capital value of the expected income stream at the beginning of each year. This is done in cols. (2) and (5) and the depreciation charge or annual decline in capital value is the difference between the value at the start of one year and the start of the next. This is worked out in cols. (3) and (6). What is interesting is the fact that with a constant income stream the depreciation charge increases year by year, whereas with a declining expected income the depreciation charge gets smaller as the asset gets older. It is obvious that the time pattern of the expected income due to a particular asset can have an important influence on the annual depreciation charge calculated in this manner.

The second alternative approach to depreciation charges is to regard them as a means of accumulating funds to replace the asset when its useful life is over. In discussing the effects of inflation in the third section of this chapter we shall have to examine in some detail the basis of this attitude towards depreciation. At this stage, however, I only want to indicate what the problem is about and in particular to try and show that the arguments between the supporters of the historical cost basis and the supporters of the replacement cost basis are arguments not so much about the nature of depreciation as an 'amortisation of cost' but about the nature of the cost that has to be amortised.

The problem is that in periods of rising prices the sum of depreciation charges computed in an orthodox accounting manner are not sufficient to pay for the replacement of an asset. If we are dealing with an asset which cost £100 ten years ago depreciation charges will only amount to £100 over the life of the asset. If prices have increased over the life of the asset the accumulated depreciation allowances will have to be augmented with other funds in order to replace the asset.

The recent Final Report of the British Royal Commission on the Taxation of Profits and Income[2] make the point that both the supporters of the 'amortisation of (historical) cost' principle as the basis for depreciation charges and the supporters of having depreciation charges linked to replacement cost recognised that it was necessary to write off as a cost of production expenditure on capital assets. Both schools of though were able to agree with the recommendation of the Institute of Chartered Accountants of England and Wales that "depreciation represents that part of the cost of a fixed asset to its owner which is not recoverable when the asset is finally put out of use by him. Provision against this loss of capital is an integral cost of conducting business during the effective commercial life of the asset and is not dependent upon the amount of profit earned."[3] The conflict arose over the interpretation of the phrase "that part of the cost of a fixed asset which is not recoverable when the asset is finally put out of use by him". As the Royal Commission put it: "There exist two theories each proceeding from a different conception of what is the cost of a fixed asset to its owner when that cost has to be taken as the basis of an annual provision for its amortisation. There is the basis of the cost of acquisition (minus scrap value) or there is the figure that would result from a current valuation of the asset (minus scrap value)."[4]

There is a real and important difference of opinion on this issue which we shall discuss later on.* Nevertheless—and this is the point that it is desired to emphasise at this stage—it is *agreed* that depreciation represents the 'amortisation of cost over the economic life of an asset'. The disagreement is whether cost means 'money cost' or 'real cost', whether allowances should or should not be made for changes in the value of money.

* See below, pp. 168–170.

B. Capital Costs and Investment Decisions

So far we have been looking backwards and on the assumption that a given capital asset has been purchased considering how its cost should be charged against sales proceeds as a cost of production so as to arrive at a 'fair' figure of profit during the years in which the asset is yielding services. It is now necessary to look forwards and discuss how expected capital costs affect investment decisions. We shall first of all discuss replacement or re-equipment investment decisions and then net investment decisions. The discussion at this stage will be at a fairly elementary level—more complicated considerations will be brought in later in the chapter.*

In considering whether or not to replace a particular asset the first thing to think about is, of course, future market or revenue prospects. Les us assume that an assessment has been made of expected demand or sales proceeds from a particular product and that this assessment is a favourable one. The next thing to do is to make estimates of the operating costs or current costs of production (including repair and maintenance expenditure) with the existing stock of capital and with the proposed new capital. The next stage is to lay down the rate at which the new proposed capital expenditure is to be depreciated and the minimum return to be expected on the capital.

The rate of depreciation is determined by the *expected* economic life of the plant. In highly speculative ventures this may be a very much shorter period than the physical life: a set of machines which might have a physical life of 20 years may only have an expected economic life of five years, and this has to be the depreciation period. The more risky the venture is and the greater the gap between physical and economic life, the higher is the depreciation rate. Similarly with the required expected returns on capital. The more risky the venture, the greater the possibility that the capital will be lost, the higher the minimum rate of return that will be necessary to induce an entrepreneur to invest.

In deciding whether or not to replace an existing plant due account has to be taken of the fact the old plant has already been paid for—that it may not have been completely written off in the books is of no consequence— while the installation of a new plant will involve the provision of fresh capital. This can be allowed for by excluding depreciation as an element in the cost of the old plant while including

* See below, pp. 161–168.

it when calculating the cost of the new process. The interest on the new capital has also to be taken into account as an operating cost in the new process.

Let us assume that the annual operating costs of the old plant is expected to be £200 per annum. Let us further assume that we are contemplating an investment (a replacement investment of course) of £100 in an asset expected to have an economic life of ten years. The operating cost of the new plant is estimated at £170 a year and as the depreciation charge would be £10 (assuming straight line depreciation), the total annual cost would be £180. In comparison with the old plant there is a saving of £20 per annum on an investment of £100 and therefore a gross return of 20%.

To indicate the importance of depreciation, let us now assume that due to risk and uncertainty it is decided that the expected economic life of the capital asset should be taken at 5 years. The annual depreciation charge now becomes £20 a year and the total annual costs of production with the new asset would be £190 a year yielding only 10% on the capital investment.

It is obvious that the calculation of depreciation charges is necessary before coming to a decision about whether a particular piece of equipment should be replaced. It is also interesting to note that, contrary to common opinion, it may be more difficult to establish the case for re-equipment in a highly progressive industry in which the whole plant may have to be written off in a short period of time and in which, therefore, the rate of depreciation is higher than in a more stable industry.

When considering additions to the stock of capital rather than replacements, similar comparisons have to be made. In this case, however, what has to be compared are the total costs of production—operating costs and depreciation—of the various alternative types of investment. For instance there may be two possible and reasonable ways of producing a given volume of output—one using more capital than the other and consequently less of the other factors of production. Let us assume that one method involves a capital expenditure of £200 and the other £400 and that in each case the expected economic life is 10 years; capital costs on a straight line basis are then £20 a year and £40 a year respectively. If we assume that operating costs are £170 a year in the first case and £140 in the second, thus making total costs £190 and £180, it is clear that the yield on the additional £200 of capital expenditure is only 5%; costs being reduced by £10 per annum for an additional capital outlay of £200. If we now assume that the assets have an expected economic life of five years and not ten, annual depreciation charges increase to £40 and £80 a year and total costs to £210 and £220 per annum and it is clear that the more capital using form of production is grossly uneconomic; the further £200 of capital resulting in an *increase* rather than a decrease in total costs of production.

Depreciation charges are an important cost of production and in considering the advantages and disadvantages of replacing a given piece of equipment or of installing a more or less capitalistic process it is clear that calculations of capital costs as well as of current costs of production are necessary if wise and economic decisions are to be taken.

III. TAXATION AND CAPITAL COSTS

A. GENERAL

We are concerned in this chapter with taxes on profits or business income. We have seen that income is the difference between sales proceeds and costs of production, capital and current, and that depreciation charges are the method by which capital expenditure is allocated to particular accounting periods. It follows that capital costs (depreciation charges) should be a cost for taxation purposes. If this is not the case then the tax would not be a tax on net income or profit but one on sales proceeds minus current costs of production. This would not be an *income* tax.

Obviously there are many possible degrees of grossness. On the one extreme is a tax levied on total sales proceeds or turnover—a sales or turnover tax—and on the other a true tax on net income which allows all costs of production as a deduction from sales proceeds. In between one could have a tax levied on value added or a tax on operating income (i.e. a tax on sales proceeds minus all expenses except interest payments) or finally as hinted at above a tax which allows all current expenditure as a deduction for income tax purposes but does not allow capital costs. Obviously an income tax should allow *all* costs of production as a fair deduction from gross revenue before arriving at the tax base.

Before we consider the treatment of capital costs we must first say something about the general question of costs of production under an income tax system.

In the absence of taxation there is no need for the State to interfere very much with the methods and conventions whereby business firms, relying no doubt on their professional advisers, draw up their accounts and determine what are profits and appropriations of profits and what are expenses or costs of production. If an individual who runs his own business treats as a cost of the business the wage of a man who acts as his butler, or the cost of the beer that he drinks, no one can really complain. Profits are lower and costs of production are higher than they would be under some other method of accounting but if the chap wants to present his accounts in this way it does not matter very much. It is true that when one man businesses become companies and there arises a divorce between management and ownership there is some need for the State to lay down certain broad rules of accounting procedure that should govern the accounts of such bodies so as to protect shareholders from exploitation and give them the opportunity of having some reasonable knowledge of the activities of the businesses that they own. Nevertheless, it is quite sensible for the State to lay down only very general rules and reasonable for it to take the view that broadly speaking shareholders are themselves responsible if they allow the Board of Directors of the companies that they own to deceive them.

Once however an income tax is introduced the whole position changes. If the tax is to be fair and equitable as between individual tax payers, the State has to produce a set of rules or laws which lay down what is and what is not a cost of production. And in the last resort the Courts will have to decide in particular cases whether a particular piece of expenditure is or is not a real cost of production. Rules or laws are absolutely necessary for the efficient working of an income tax system.

An important point which it is necessary to emphasise, is that the problem of what is and what is not a cost of production is the same with respect to current and capital costs. In principle there should be no difference. If a certain revenue expenditure is incurred in the course of carrying on the business and as a part of the business it is a cost of production and a proper deduction from sales proceeds for income tax purposes. Similarly if a certain capital asset was purchased in the course of carrying on the business and as a part of the business this expenditure should be a cost for income tax purposes. And conversely if a given expenditure of a revenue or a capital nature was not so incurred then it should not be regarded as a cost.

In this chapter it is not possible to go into detail as regards the specific rules that exist on this subject in any particular country but the following brief description of the U.K. system may be indicative of the form which the income tax law takes in the U.K. and other countries.

The remaining paragraphs of this section of the chapter relate to the British system of treating *current* costs of production. The way in which capital expenditure is treated in British tax law is somewhat complicated. In those parts of the 1952 Income Tax Act relating to what is and what is not income capital expenditure is *not* regarded as a cost of production; indeed capital expenditure in this part of the tax law is expressly disallowed. Then in a different part of the Act specific allowances for capital expenditure are mentioned. Neither in theory nor practice does the British income tax law recognise that capital expenditure is just as much a cost of production as current expenditure. Nevertheless a study of the British Law defining allowable *current* costs of production is useful as an example of what the Law should be for both current and capital costs.

In section 137 of the Income Tax Act 1952 there is set out a list of items, the deduction of which is not to be allowed as a cost of production for income tax purposes. The first item is the one that is relevant for the present purpose. It is expressed as follows: "any disbursements or expenses not being money wholly and exclusively laid out or expended for the purposes of the trade, profession or vocation". In this rather roundabout manner the Act lays down that all expenses are deductable which are made—wholly and exclusively—for the purposes of the business. Now it is obvious that in many cases it must be a matter of opinion whether a particular piece of spending falls within or without the rule in Section 137; the Courts have plenty of work to do. There are many cases on the subject and it would not be untrue to say that the effective law on the subject changes from time to time. A serious difficulty for example that has arisen in the U.K. over the question of the deduction of (current) expenses in recent years arises from a passage in the speech of Lord Davey in the case of Strong & Co., of Romsey Ltd., v Woodfield:—"It is not enough that the disbursement is made in the course of, or arises out of, or is connected with, the trade or is made out of the profits of the trade. It must be made for the purpose of earning the profits"[5]. In practice there is no doubt that the operation of this law has lead to some rather ridiculous results and both the Tucker Committee on the Taxation of Trading Profits and the Royal Commission have recommended to the

British Government that the Income Tax Act should be amended in such a manner as to make it quite clear that Lord Davey's dictum is no longer to have any compelling legal authority.[6]

So much for the general issue. A tax on profits by its very nature should permit a firm to deduct from its sales proceeds all the expenses that have been incurred in producing and selling the goods. The higher the tax rate the more important it is that this principle should operate. (It has also to be remembered that the higher the tax rate the more incentive a business man has to disguise consumption or personal expenditure as a cost of production.) It is appreciated that there will be border line cases in which perhaps only part of a particular piece of expenditure is for business purposes and the remainder is personal or consumption expenditure. In such cases some appropriate apportionment has to be made. It is also recognised that the dividing line between what is and what is not a cost of production may often be difficult to establish. Nevertheless the general principle is clear.

Given this general approach there are two main questions to consider. First the extent to which these principles are applied to capital costs in income tax systems and if they are not applied the arguments that are used to justify their exclusion. And second—and at a much more humdrum level—in those cases in which capital expenditures are deductible—the sort of rules which the taxation authorities lay down for dealing with these costs.

Income Tax Systems do not necessarily allow capital expenditure to be written off even when in their treatment of current expenditure they seem to recognise that an income tax is or should be a tax levied on the difference between sales proceeds and costs of production.

It was not till 1878—more than a generation after the introduction of the U.K. Income Tax in more or less its present form—that any relief for capital expenditure was given. Since that time there have been depreciation allowances for plant and machinery and since 1918 mills, factories and other similar premises which were regarded as especially susceptible to depreciation owing to vibration caused by plant and machinery have qualified for certain reliefs to compensate the owners for the exceptional wear and tear suffered by such assets. Nevertheless it is true to say that the present fairly comprehensive system of depreciation allowances in the U.K. dates only from the end of the second world war and—as we shall see—there are still some important forms of capital expenditure that cannot be written off for taxation purposes.

Legislation passed in 1944 and 1945 brought about an almost revolutionary change in the tax treatment of capital expenditures. This legislation followed an investigation by the Board of Internal Revenue (carried out at the request of the then Chancellor of the Exchequer, Sir Kingsley Wood) into the effects of business taxation generally and, in particular, into the treatment of capital expenditure for which no allowance was being made under the then existing income tax code. His successor, SIR JOHN ANDERSON (later LORD WAVERLEY) announced his conclusions after receiving the report of the Committee in his 1944 budget speech and the report formed the basis of the reforms of 1944 and 1945 which in essence have remained unchanged till the present time.

This legislation created six different types of depreciable asset; plant and machinery, industrial buildings, buildings and equipment used in scientific research, patent rights, agricultural buildings and works, mining assets; and it enabled capital expenditures on any of these assets to be written off by way of an annual depreciation charge as a cost for taxation purposes.[7] Expenditure on capital assets other than those listed above is not depreciable for tax purposes no matter how it may be treated in the accounts of the business.

It is clear that though the reforms of 1944–5 increased substantially the number of assets that can be written off for taxation purposes there are still some significant omissions. The most important of these are that the following types of capital expenditure are not depreciable for taxation purposes: (a) commercial buildings (i.e. shops and offices etc.) (b) lump sum payments for the use of an asset for a period of years, (c) expenditure on the adaptation of land such as tunnelling and levelling ground in connection with the construction of buildings, (d) expenditure by a mining concern for the purchase of a mineral area (even though annual royalty payments are deductible as a current cost), (e) the payment of a premium for a lease, and (f) expenditure on the acquisition of land and for the purchase of goodwill. The recent Report of the Royal Commission has recommended that the first four of these should become depreciable assets.[8] They would also like to permit premiums for leases to be depreciable but were unable to recommend this as they felt that if such premiums were deductible by the Leesee they should rank as taxable income of the lessor and they did not think it feasible for such payment to attract the full progressive rates of the personal income tax.[9]

It may seem odd that as accountants and economists have been agreed for so long that income is not true income unless provision has been made for the depreciation of wasting assets, that income tax was levied for so long—and is still so levied so far as concerns a number of assets—upon something which is not true income. Four important reasons seem to have been responsible.

The first one is an historical explanation. The British income tax developed in the days before sophisticated accounting techniques had been discovered and when it was introduced the rates of taxation were very low and no one was very much concerned with the effects of taxation and taxation definitions of income. In such a context it is possible to understand the non deductability of capital costs as with a cash-book system of accounting capital expenditure seems to represent a transfer of wealth from one form—say cash—into another—a machine —rather than a cost of production.

A second reason for disallowing capital costs was because of the fear of possible repercussions on the tax treatment of the income of persons. It was thought for a long time that if capital expenditure on physical assets was allowed as an expense for tax purposes similar allowances would have to be given for expenditure incurred in producing immaterial capital; such expenditure as that on education, professional training and books. As it was recognised to be extraordinarily difficult to allow this latter form of expenditure as a cost considerations of equity, that one taxpayer should be treated in the same way as another, made it necessary to resist claims for the grant of taxation depreciation allowances on material capital expenditure.

It is interesting to note that both these arguments received the support of the 1920 Royal Commission on the Income Tax. The Commission was able to state that: "For income tax purposes income is the surplus of receipts over the current expenditure necessary to earn those receipts regardless of any part of the receipts or surplus for the writing off or amortising the capital value of any assets that waste in the process of producing the income".[10]

A third reason is that it is not always clear (often much less clear than with a particular piece of current expenditure) whether an asset is or is not necessary to production therefore—by a big jump—there is the temptation to disallow all capital expenditure. There is some substance in this point however. It is difficult to know whether or not a new canteen, or a new sports pavilion, or a new block of offices is a necessary cost of production. Nevertheless it has to be admitted that these considerations do apply more or less equally to current as well as capital spending. When it is argued that high tax rates combined

with generous depreciation allowances—as in post-war Germany—
causes a lot of wasteful capital expenditure it is often forgotten that
high tax rates tend to encourage current expenditure as well. There
is perhaps one point of difference. In a society with no capital gains
tax or one which has only a low rate of tax on such gains, there may be
a considerable incentive to spend money rather extravagantly on
capital assets if such expenditure is allowed as a cost for income tax
purposes so as to be able in the future to obtain a substantial tax free
capital gain by selling the business. If such conduct became common
there might be a case—other things having to remain unchanged—for
not permitting certain capital expenditures to be depreciated for taxation purposes.

The final reason is a technical or administrative one. Expenditure
on the purchase or construction of commercial buildings and expenditure on the adaptation of land for instance, are likely to yield services
over many years. The rate of depreciation allowed would therefore
be very low and it is sometimes argued that the costs of working out
the right depreciation charge would not be worth the annual gain to
the taxpayer.

All the arguments that we have mentioned have had some effect in
limiting the availability and scope of depreciation allowances under
the British Income Tax. In recent years however, the tide of opinion
has been moving in the opposite direction. Inflation, very high tax
rates, the growing importance of the various accountancy bodies and
the recognition that investment may need encouraging have had the
effect of making the recent Royal Commission accept the general proposition: "that the income tax system should give relief in respect of
the wasting of all assets that are used up or consumed in the course of
carrying on a business." There is little doubt but that the government
will accept this principle and eventually put it into operation. The
battle in the U.K. at any rate seems to be won and it will not be long
before all capital assets can be amortised over their useful life. This to
the writer seems not only economically right and expedient but also
just.

In the U.S.A. it also took time for depreciation to be recognised
as a true cost of production. Once however it was so recognised all
capital expenditure on wasting assets (i.e. excluding capital expenditure
on freehold land and goodwill) soon became regarded as a true cost of
production. In the Civil War income tax legislation depreciation was
not even mentioned. In the first permanent Income Tax Act of 1894

it was expressly disallowed as a cost of production and it was not till 1909 that the Act of that year recognised that capital costs were a right and proper deduction from sales proceeds in arriving at taxable income and laid down that "a reasonable allowance for the depreciation of property" should be permitted. The present U.S.A. law states—and these words were first inserted in the 1918 Revenue Act—that "a reasonable allowance for the exhaustion, and wear and tear of property used in the trade or business including a reasonable allowance for obsolescence" should be permitted for tax purposes. The effect of the U.S.A. law has been very broadly that the cost of all wasting assets have been allowed as a deduction for tax purposes.

The normal method in which relief on capital expenditure is allowed for tax purposes is for the tax authorities to permit firms to write off their investment expenditure over a period of years agreed between the tax authorities and the industry concerned.

In the U.K. where the reducing balance method of depreciation is common for plant and machinery, the Board of Inland Revenue in conjunction with the representatives of the industries concerned determine the normal life of particular assets and this in turn produces the appropriate rate of depreciation to be applied to the written down value of the asset. [11] (Firms may if they wish depreciate in the straight line manner.) Over the life of the asset firms are permitted to write off the total cost but no more than the cost of the asset. To ensure this provision is made for an obsolescence allowance known as a balancing allowance to be allowed to the firm if, when the asset is scrapped or sold, the proceeds are less than the difference between the original cost of the asset and the written down value. If the proceeds are greater the excess is treated as taxable income, i.e. some of the depreciation charges already allowed are clawed back.

A similar procedure is followed in the U.S. The Bureau of Internal Revenue in conjunction with the industries concerned determine the normal life of assets which then produces an appropriate rate of depreciation.[12] Until very recently the straight line method was the normal one permitted by the U.S.A. tax authorities but now both the Sum of Digits approach and the Declining Balance method are permitted. Section 167 of the 1954 Internal Revenue Act provides for the use of the Straight Line method, Sum of Digits method and any other consistent method which will provide annual allowances such that deductions during the first two-thirds of the useful life of the asset do not exceed the allowance under depreciation computed according to the Declining Balance method. In former years, i.e. before the 1954 Internal Revenue Act the Declining Balance method of depreciation was a recognised one but it was limited in that the rate could not exceed 150% of the Straight Line rate. The new (1954) law permits a rate equal to 200% of the Straight Line method.

During the years before the changes in the law relating to depreciation which took place in the 1954 Internal Revenue Act, business men and economists in the U.S.A. had been much concerned with the fact that the tax authorities would only permit the equivalent of straight line depreciation over a period representing the full estimated useful life of the asset. This rather strict attitude towards depreciation charges dated from the middle of the 1930's. Before that date business men were allowed to depreciate their capital expenditure in any consistent manner. There is no evidence that business men misused their freedom which was taken away (by administrative action) in the 1930's to allocate their capital expenditure more or less as they pleased over varying accounting periods.

Most other countries have systems similar to that of the U.K. and U.S.A. An interesting exception was the well known Swedish system in operation from 1938–1951 in which firms were permitted to use whatever rate of depreciation they liked—even to the extent of writing off a machine's cost in a single year—subject, of course to the restraint that no more than the cost of the asset could be written off. As we shall see later in this chapter there are tremendous economic advantages in a scheme of this sort and it is interesting to ask why such systems are not more generally permitted. The objections to giving firms this freedom are largely budgetary given that it is not desired to hinder capital investment. The government would find it more difficult to estimate its revenue year by year, more detailed records of capital assets would have to be kept by taxpayers and tax collectors and expectations of tax changes might have substantial effects on the level of investment and that in a perverse direction, expected increases in taxation would tend to encourage the level of investment and expected decreases would tend to reductions. To the writer these do not seem to be important objections.

B. Taxation, Depreciation and Capital Spending

We have seen that Depreciation and Obsolescence allowances permit or should permit business enterprises to deduct over time capital expenditures as well as current expenditures from gross sales proceeds before arriving at taxable income. Obviously such taxation allowances must have a favourable effect upon the level of investment particularly in a period when tax rates are high.

The level of investment would be affected in two ways. On the one hand the desire to invest would be increased and on the other the ability to carry out a particular piece of spending (and the ability to borrow) would be improved. Let us assume that a business is contemplating installing a new machine costing £100 and is prepared to take the plunge only if it expects the asset to pay for itself in five years. Let us further assume that the expected life of the asset is five years and that the tax rate is 50%. It follows that in the absence of depreciation allowances the machine will have to increase the gross profits of the business by some £40 per annum if it is to be installed; equivalent to a gross return of some 40% per annum. If however the firm is permitted tax free depreciation allowances on the asset then it will only have to earn 20% gross to justify its installation. On the finance side the effect of receiving depreciation allowances on existing capital assets is to improve the firm's financial position thus making it easier for the firm to finance further investment both from its own resources and from the capital market.

It may also be argued that the picture we have presented in the previous section is a false one in that tax revenue is much reduced when depreciation allowances are permitted and that a fairer comparison would be between two situations in which the tax revenue is unchanged. In one there would be no depreciation charges (and relatively low tax rates) and in the other depreciation allowances and, therefore, relatively high effective tax rates. Even when this more rigorous comparison is made, the introduction of depreciation allowances is still favourable to investment for the burden of taxation is shifted from those firms employing a lot of capital to those firms employing a little and—in a dynamic sense—the burden is reduced upon those who invest and increased upon those who do not.

It follows from what has been said above that the government could fairly easily influence the level of investment by granting or withdrawing the right of depreciating capital assets for tax purposes, or indeed by altering the terms or conditions affecting the writing off of such spending.

It is obvious that not allowing the cost of a capital asset for tax purposes or allowing only part of the cost will have a depressing influence on the level of investment and similarly that allowing a firm

to write off *more* than the cost will have a favourable effect. It is also
fairly obvious that the higher the tax rate and the more important
depreciation costs are as a cost of production—the more help and the
more stimulating are taxation depreciation allowances.

What is not so obvious is the extent to which the timing of tax
depreciation allowances can affect investment decisions. We shall consider first of all a simple case and then proceed to look at more complicated situations.

An obvious instance when the speeding up of depreciation allowances
would stimulate investment is when the expected life of an asset as
laid down by the tax authorities is much longer than the number of
years over which the taxpayer *wants* to depreciate the asset. This sort
of discrepancy can easily arise. The tax authorities tend to think
in terms of physical life and 'normal' obsolescence and in terms
of 'averages'. If however the taxpayer is engaged in some very
risky undertaking one of the ways in which he makes allowance for
risk and uncertainty when contemplating investment decisions is to
say that the machine or asset will have to be depreciated in a short
period.

Let us suppose that a taxpayer is contemplating installing a machine
costing £100 and he is prepared to invest if (a) the machine pays for
itself in five years and (b) he makes 10% per annum profit on his £100
outlay. Now if there was no tax system in operation this investment
would be possible and worthwhile if the asset increased gross operating
profits (sales proceeds minus current costs of production) by £30 per
annum. £20 of this surplus would then be depreciation or capital costs
and the remaining £10 would be net profit giving the required 10%
return on capital outlay. Now let us suppose that an Income Tax is
imposed at a 50% rate but that the tax authorities permit the firm to
write off 20% of the cost each year i.e. allow a five year depreciation
period and straight line depreciation charges. In these circumstances
the asset would have to increase gross operating profits by £40 per
annum. Of this £20 would be capital costs and £20 gross profits which,
after the deduction of a 50% tax rate, would yield the required 10%
return on capital. If however the tax authorities would only permit
a 10% straight line depreciation rate (i.e. permit the firm to write the
asset off over a ten year life) the asset would only be purchased if it
was expected to increase gross operating profits by £50 per annum.
Of this £10 would be allowed tax free as a depreciation charge and
£40 would be taxed at the 50% rate leaving £20 which would provide

the additional £10 internal depreciation requirements and the 10% return on capital.

These simple and unsophisticated examples show the importance that taxation depreciation allowances and their timing can have on investment decisions.

We must now proceed to more complicated cases and consider the general reasons why Accelerated Depreciation is beneficial to investment. The term Accelerated Depreciation is used to cover all methods of deliberately speeding up the rate at which the original cost of assets (minus scrap value) may be deducted from gross profits for taxation purposes; it implies a concentration of depreciation allowances for tax purposes in the early years of an asset's life. In a later part of this section of the chapter we shall consider a number of alternative methods by which depreciation allowances can be accelerated; at this stage however—in order to get to grips with the underlying principles of the idea—it is proposed to consider the American method of allowing an asset to be amortised for tax purposes over a five year period even though the asset may have an effective life of say twenty years and an expected economic life of the same period.

Accelerated Depreciation of this type was introduced in the U.S. during the war for approved defence facilities and re-introduced during the Korean War and is still in existence. The term defence facilities has been interpreted quite widely; for instance the railways have qualified for the special depreciation allowance.

We have already seen that Accelerated Depreciation may offset the risk or uncertainty associated with a new piece of investment particularly when firms take this into account by shortening the time period over which they have to write off the cost of the asset. Accelerated Depreciation also makes the finance of new investment easier in that as compared with ordinary Depreciation Allowances it represents an interest free loan by the exchequer to the firm. For any single asset the loan has to be repaid but so long as a firm's investment outlays do not fall the loan does not have to be repaid. In these cases it represents a permanent tax reduction. But even an interest free loan is very useful! For with Accelerated Depreciation the firm receives the benefits of its tax free depreciation allowances earlier in time and money benefits at a near date are, of course, worth more than money benefits in the future.

Let us consider an asset costing £200 with a normal life of twenty years. With Straight Line depreciation allowances this means an annual depreciation allowance of £10 a year. This represents assuming a tax rate of 50%, a reduction in tax liability of £5 a year over 20 years as compared to a system in which there was no depreciation allowances. The present value of this benefit assuming a 5% rate of interest would be £62.3. If, however, the tax authorities permitted the firm to depreciate the asset over ten years, thus allowing annual depreciation charges of £20 a year and, therefore, reductions of tax liability of £10 a year for ten years the present value of this stream of benefits assuming a 5% discount rate, would be £77.2. By similar reasoning the present value of depreciation allowances spread over a five year period would be £86.5.

The higher the tax rate, the higher the interest rate and the more uncertain the business outlook the more likely it is that Accelerated Depreciation will help the level of investment. There is one important qualification however. The benefits of Accelerated Depreciation are only valuable to the taxpayer if they can be offset against income. If therefore high depreciation charges make total costs (from a taxation point of view) greater than total revenue the taxpayer will not benefit from the high permitted depreciation charges unless he is allowed to carry forward the loss against future income or carry it back against profits of previous time periods. In order for schemes of Accelerated Depreciation to have their full effect on the level of investment there is need for generous provision for carrying losses forwards and backwards. Nor must one forget that schemes of Accelerated Depreciation do not affect actual or expected revenues or sales proceeds. They remove deterrents to investment rather than provide new stimulants. It would therefore be wrong to expect schemes of Accelerated Depreciation to stimulate investment by any very great amount in a slump when entrepreneurs are very pessimistic about present and future demand conditions.

We have seen that with given tax rates Accelerated Depreciation has a stimulating effect on investment. An interesting way to indicate the importance of the benefit is to see what reduction in tax rates would have to take place with the normal depreciation period to make a particular investment proposition as attractive as a 50% tax rate combined with Accelerated Depreciation. The two tax systems are assumed to be the same if the discounted value of the tax concessions are identical. Assuming a £100 asset and a 5% discount rate, the discounted value of the tax concessions when an asset is depreciated over a five year depreciation period is £43.3. Let us assume the normal life of the asset to be ten years. The discounted value of £10 per year for ten years is £77.2. The benefits of the new rate of tax must have a present value of £43.3. Therefore the present value of the tax payments over a ten year period must be £33.9. This sum represents the present value of a tax rate of approximately 44% on a base of £10 a year. Accelerated Depreciation would of course tend to have a more important effect on the level of investment than such a general tax cut giving up the same revenue as it is a selective instrument; only the firms who invest benefit; whereas with a general tax reduction the relief would be spread thinly alike over investors, potential investors and non-investors.

There are a large number of ways in which taxation allowances for depreciation can be accelerated. In addition to the American method of permitting firms to depreciate assets in five years there are three other important methods that should be considered. First the Swedish method in which assets could be depreciated as rapidly as the taxpayer wished and we shall take the extreme case in which expenditure on capital assets is completely written off at the end of the assets first year of life. Second the British method of having initial and investment allowances and finally a straightforward doubling or trebling of ordinary depreciation rates.[13]

All except the British method are fairly obvious but initial and investment allowances need a little explanation. Let us assume a £100 asset with a ten year (normal) life and straight line depreciation. Then in the ordinary course £10 a year would be allowed as an expense for tax purposes. If now a 20% initial allowance is introduced the firm would be allowed to deduct in the first year an initial allowance of £20 plus the first annual allowance of £10—£30 in all—and then for the next seven years (year two to year eight inclusive) would be able to deduct £10 a year, thus completely amortising the asset. A ten year asset would be written off in eight years and—perhaps more important—30% of the cost would be written off in the first year and half of it during the first third of the asset's life. With a 40% initial allowance the asset would be written off in six years and no less than 50% in the first year of its operation. An initial allowance is a pure form of accelerated depreciation: it is a substitute at an early time period for annual allowances at a later time period. The cost and no more than the cost of an asset can be written off.

With an investment allowance it is different. If a 20% investment allowance is in operation a firm is permitted to write off £30 in the first year—£20 investment allowance and £10 the first year's annual allowance. At this stage then an investment allowance has the same effect as an initial allowance at the same rate. In contrast to the initial allowance however the investment allowance is granted in addition to and not as a substitute for the ordinary depreciation allowance; consequently in years two to ten inclusive £10 a year can be written off making a total tax free deduction from Sales proceeds of £120 for every £100 spent on capital assets qualifying for the allowance.

TABLE 3

THE PRESENT VALUE OF THE TAX REDUCTIONS BROUGHT ABOUT WITH VARIOUS FORMS OF DEPRECIATION ALLOWANCE

It is assumed (a) that the rate of tax is 50%, (b) that the rate of discount is 5% and (c) that we are discussing a capital asset costing £100.

Type of asset	Ordinary straight line depreciation	American 5 year straight line write off	Swedish one year write off	20% Initial allowance and straight line depreciation	40% Initial allowance and straight line depreciation	20% Investment allowance and straight line depreciation	Double straight line depreciation rates
10 Year life	38.6	43.3	47.6	41.9	44.4	48.1	43.3
20 Year life	31.1	43.3	47.6	36.6	41.2	40.6	38.6

Table 3 compares the present value of the different forms of accelerated depreciation for both a ten year asset and a twenty year asset. It is obvious that the American and Swedish methods are much more valuable than the British method for long lived assets. It is also interesting to note the rather small advantage that the investment allowance has over the initial allowance. Though on first examination an investment allowance would seem to be a much more powerful weapon for stimulating investment than an initial allowance because of the greater absolute reduction in tax liability the table brings out how slight is the difference when the distant benefits are discounted back to the present. Particularly if one is concerned with combating risk and uncertainty, or in providing finance to help investment at the time it is being carried out, there is much to be said for the methods which concentrate tax relief in the early years of an asset's life.

On the other hand the schemes which concentrate tax relief at the start of an asset's life have a number of disadvantages. The most important of these is that they tend to encourage investment in assets with a long life rather than in assets with a short life. In order to avoid such discrimination—if it is desired not to discriminate in this manner—a useful way of accelerating depreciation would be to increase all depreciation rates by a given proportion—50%, 100% or 200%, for example.

We have seen that Accelerated depreciation tends to encourage investment in a number of ways. It is equally true that slowing down the granting of depreciation allowances will—other things being equal —have a retarding effect on the level of investment. The Canadian government introduced a scheme of deferred depreciation in 1951 and the British government recognised the force of the argument by abolishing initial allowances in 1951 when they desired to reduce the level of investment and by abolishing investment allowances in 1956 for the same reason.

IV. CAPITAL COSTS, TAXATION AND INFLATION

A. THE PROBLEMS

We have argued that firms are or should be permitted to write off the cost of capital expenditure over the life of an asset and that the total tax free allowances granted to the owner of a depreciable asset should not in the normal way exceed its original cost. In a period of stable prices the sum of these tax free allowances will be sufficient to replace the asset at the end of its useful life. It follows that if over this period the whole of the net profit was ploughed back into the business these spendings would constitute additions to the capital stock. Similarly, if all net profit was given to the shareholders and spent on consumption goods the stock of capital of the firm under consideration would be maintained intact; it would have the same *real* capital at the end of the period as at the beginning.

In a period of rising prices however, the sum of the depreciation allowances cannot provide sufficient funds to replace the worn out assets. A machine which costs £100 some years ago may cost £200 to replace and since the sum of the tax free allowances can only add up to £100 the additional £100 which is required merely to maintain the company's real capital intact has to be found from taxed undistributed profits (equivalent on the assumption of a 50% tax rate to £200 of taxable profits) or from the capital market.

In considering the role of price changes, it is necessary to distinguish between changes in the price level of particular capital assets and changes in the general level of prices applicable to all capital assets. It would be impossible administratively and highly questionable in theory to attempt to relate Replacement Allowances or to calculate Revaluations with respect to price changes of particular assets. Impossible administratively as it is very rarely that a firm replaces a capital asset with an exactly similar piece of equipment. Indeed, often the old type of equipment is no longer available for sale and thus there would be no market price quotation for it. Dubious from a theoretical point of view for similar reasons, as the effect of technical development arising with the passage of time would have enabled a firm, in the absence of price changes, to obtain a new piece of equipment with the same amount of money which would make a greater contribution to total output than the old asset that is being replaced. Certainly, a discussion with respect to the change in the price level of particular assets, without there being a change in the general level of prices, would seem to fall outside the scope of this particular section of the chapter. Here we are concerned with problems arising from a change in the general level of prices with respect to capital assets purchased by firms, it being assumed either that the prices of particular assets do not diverge very much, or in the event of an attempt to meet the problem that a sufficient number of index numbers are calculated so as to ensure that rough justice is done.

In considering the effect of inflation on the real value of Depreciation Allowances, it is impossible to be completely accurate or completely just if we wish to be at all realistic. If we are considering possible taxation concessions or possible independent action by business men, the most that can be done is to approximate to the correct decision. There can only be a limited number of price index numbers used for revaluing Depreciation Allowances or the value of capital employed in a firm. If these index numbers are published by a government department, then, so long as there is a wide coverage and a sufficient number of them and the basis of them is clearly set out, no real hardship will be caused. Some companies will do rather well and some not so well, but, on balance, all will be rather better off than without a revaluation.

In the absence of taxation, there would be no real problem due to increases in the general level of prices. Prices and profits would rise together and though 'accountancy' depreciation allowances would be fixed in money terms profits would show a proportionately greater rise and firms should be no worse off. It is of course possible that a firm will base its prices on costing figures incorporating a depreciation charge based on the original cost of the asset. In this case of course its profits would not go up *pari passu* with the price level—but this would be the fault of the business man or his advisers not the result of government action or the play of economic forces.

The existence of heavy taxes on profits computed after allowance for historical cost depreciation complicates the whole matter and makes rising prices a much more serious phenomena for firms than it otherwise would be. The effects of the combination of rising prices and heavy tax rates have produced in the various countries that have suffered the phenomenon since the war demands from business men and economists that more generous depreciation allowances should be given for tax purposes, the underlying idea being that the system of depreciation allowances should be such as to have the same effect on the level of savings and investment and the firm generally in a period of stable or rising prices.

These arguments fall into two groups. On the one hand there are the essentially theoretical arguments; that as a matter of accounting or economic theory depreciation allowances in a period of inflation *should* be based upon the replacement cost of assets and that historical costs have no relevance to this computation. Individuals putting forward these arguments are often prepared to face the fact that the proceeds from the taxation of profits may have to be maintained and that given a change in the method of computing depreciation tax rates might have to be increased. What they are really pleading for is a re-allocation of the tax burden rather than a reduction in it. Firms with a lot of capital or with old capital would have their burden reduced at the expense of those with a small amount of fixed capital or with new capital. (This group may, however, believe even if they do not state it specifically that in a period of rapidly rising prices the increase in tax rates needed to maintain the revenue might be so great as to make it difficult from a political point of view for the rates to be increased fully to offset the new definition of taxable income. It follows that the revenue obtainable in a period of rising prices with an historical cost definition of income with little political disturbance might not be able to be raised in a period of stable prices.)

The second group of arguments are based on expediency considerations rather than theory; the claim being that the combination of rising prices and high taxes imposes such a burden on industry that the level of investment is much reduced and in the extreme case—the stock of capital is not maintained intact. It is also argued that firms make wrong decisions in periods of rising prices because they are mislead by the computations of profits based on the historical cost basis.

There are three possible ways of dealing with these problems. The first, and very difficult to introduce from a political point of view, is a substantial reduction in the rate of taxation levied on the profits of firms. This method of providing relief we will not consider. The second method is to allow firms to base their depreciation charges on the replacement cost rather than the historical cost of assets. The third method is to allow firms to write off their capital expenditure over a much shorter period than the estimated real economic life of the asset, i.e. Accelerated Depreciation.

B. REVALUATION

We shall consider, first of all, the two arguments noticed above for basing depreciation charges on the replacement cost of assets. Many witnesses appeared before the recent British Royal Commission on the Taxation of Income and Profits or submitted papers to it arguing along both these lines, and a useful way of considering the problems is to summarise very briefly the arguments that were deployed and the view the Commission took of them.

Perhaps the best argued theoretical case in favour of departing from the strict historical cost principle was developed in the memorandum submitted to the Royal Commission by the Association of British Chambers of Commerce.[14] Their argument may be summarised as follows. Taxpayers who carry on a business are taxed—unlike wage earners, salary earners or rentiers—on the difference between two totals sales proceeds and costs of production. An income and expenditure account has to be worked out before the taxable income of businesses can be determined. The two totals of income and expenditure for a given time period are expressed in pounds and it is most important that the unit of account should be the same for the two sides of the account; otherwise like will not be subtracted from like and a misleading (if not a nonsensical) result will emerge.

In a period of price stability this comparability between totals emerges if ordinary accounting conventions are followed. In a period of rising (or falling) prices, however, it does not for the depreciation charge on the cost or expenditure side of the account is in terms of prices of some time ago whereas all the other figures are in terms of contemporary prices, and pounds of current value. Costs are therefore underestimated and profits exaggerated. In order to get a true and proper picture of the events of a given time period the depreciation charges expressed in pounds of previous years have to be adjusted so as to make them comparable with the other figures in the income and expenditure account; in particular with the sales proceeds and current costs entries.

The British Chambers of Commerce suggested to the Royal Commission that the annual depreciation charge should be first calculated on the basis of traditional or historical cost principles and then written up in accordance with some index number of prices published by the government and that this written up figure should represent the allowable depreciation charge for taxation purposes, thus giving the same real treatment to taxpayers in periods of rising prices as they receive in periods of stable prices.

It was also argued that this form of (replacement) accounting for taxation purposes would approach much more closely than does the present (historical cost) form of taxation accounting to the economists' measure of income. Economists have, of course, many views as to the nature of income. A fairly generally recognised one, however, is that in any time period income is not true income unless the capital used to produce the flow of income is maintained intact. Professor Hicks has defined income in the following way. It is "the maximum amount which an individual can spend this week and still expect to be able to spend the same amount in real terms in future weeks".[15] It is obvious in this context that the capital costs of a given time period have to be measured in the prices ruling in the same time period.

It is, of course, an interesting question whether the economists' conception of income is the right one or even a useful one for taxation purposes. On the whole the Royal Commission did not think it was and this belief played some part—though not in my judgment a major part—in the process that eventually lead them to recommend no departure from traditional principles.

Two main considerations seem to have influenced their opinion on this point and were instrumental in producing their conservative conclusion on the theoretical issue.

First and I think most important, was the feeling that it would be wrong or unjust, to depart from a money base in favour of a real base in the one case of depreciation allowances and as it would be impracticable and perhaps even dangerous from an economic point of view to have general revaluations of money contracts, it would not be right to single out depreciation allowances for special and favourable treatment. This argument carried perhaps more weight than it deserved due to the fact that it was obvious that a revaluation of depreciation allowances would directly or indirectly benefit the owners of business assets—the ordinary shareholders—who tend to do rather well as compared to other income receivers in periods of inflation; and certainly better than other individuals who receive income from property. The Royal Commission quote with approval the recommendation of the Tucker Committee that "one objection common to all schemes (of replacement cost accounting) is that they involve giving preferential treatment to the owners of businesses as against other classes of taxpayer".[16] And this would be most marked if it is assumed that the revenue would have to be maintained, for the reduction in the tax payments of businesses would have to be offset by increased payments by other members of the community.

Though some witnesses, notably Professor F. W. Paish,[17] were prepared for certain money claims on businesses such as debenture interest to be revalued upwards in a period of rising prices no one was prepared to recommend or even to visualise the abolition of contracts in money terms, and yet from the Royal Commission's point of view it would be unfair to allow depreciation allowances to be written up unless this was done.

The Royal Commission were not prepared to recommend a reform that would make such a substantial change in the incidence of taxation. Some may think that they did not recognise sufficiently that inflation directly affects the tax burdens on business income and does not directly affect the tax burden on other types of income and that the introduction of replacement cost accounting far from conferring a privilege would only terminate an injustice. Points such as these emphasise it seems to me, the fact that the Royal Commission was not very interested in the theoretical arguments. If there had been clear evidence—and we shall see below that there was not—or indeed any evidence that the level of investment had been seriously affected by original cost depreciation or that firms had in their price policies or dividend policies been misled by computations of profit based on historical cost, the views of the Royal Commission on the theoretical arguments might have been different.

The second argument which the Royal Commission brought against the theoretical arguments of the replacement cost supporters was that such a system must be more complicated and administratively more difficult to operate than original cost depreciation. It quoted with approval the Chartered Accountants' view that "An important feature of the historical cost basis of preparing annual accounts is that it reduces to a minimum the extent to which the accounts can be affected by the personal opinion of those responsible for them" and comments later on that "in this respect always a matter of great concern in a tax code no method of revaluation has a similar efficacy".[18]

It is difficult to place much weight upon this last point in view of the fact that systems of revaluations have been operated in many European countries since the war and in view of the clear and detailed schemes for accounting and taxation reform presented to the British Royal Commission by—amongst other—such a body as the Association of British Chambers of Commerce.

The French taxation authorities have, for over twenty years, authorised the revaluation of fixed assets; the first scheme in which there have been a number of changes, notably in 1948, having been introduced early in the 1930's. The object of the scheme was to reduce the taxation burden brought about by the combination of historical cost taxation accounting, rising prices and the taxation of business profits. The method by which the relief is given is somewhat complicated but seems to work quite well. An index number is given to each year from 1914 representing the change in prices from that date. In computing and accounting for the annual depreciation charge the cost of the asset is multiplied by the index number appropriate to the date it was purchased. Thus in 1955 for example the cost of a building erected in 1944 will be multiplied by 194.4 this figure representing the (official) difference in the two price levels. This total will be the re-valued original cost. Then a re-valued written down value will be computed in a similar manner and finally a re-valued annual depreciation charge can be computed which is allowed for tax purposes; thus permitting the tax payer substantially greater tax free deductions than he would have had but for the revaluations.

In contrast to the French system, the Belgian government's revaluation of industrial buildings and plant which took place in 1947 was in intention at any rate, a once for all event. The broad principle adopted was that tax payers should be permitted to place a contemporary value on buildings and plant in use at the end of December 1945 and that depreciation charges for tax purposes would then be based on these values. In principle the value to be attributed to each asset was to be the true commercial value at that date. In practice however, this was impossible to operate; there were not enough trained valuers, so the government introduced a rule. No class of asset could be valued at more than two and a half times the value of the new asset before the war less depreciation based on the revalued cost. And prices had gone up by much more than two and a half times.

It is also interesting to note that the Belgian scheme was in principle confined to assets of a type which the government wished to favour though practical difficulties of line-drawing somewhat nullified the government's intention. It should also be noted that the tax payer when he came to replace his fixed assets would have to provide a part of the replacement cost out of taxed profits—as the scheme provided no tax free allowance to make good the inadequacy of depreciation charges before the revaluation.

The British Chambers of Commerce developed before the Royal Commission an index number scheme for putting depreciation charges on a replacement rather than on an historical cost basis. They proposed that the annual depreciation charge on the historical cost method should be first computed and that this sum should then be increased by a multiple representing the change in the price level since the asset was purchased, and that this new, revalued depreciation charge should be the effective one for tax purposes. At the end of the asset's life when balancing charges and allowances come to be computed they suggested that the computation should take place as follows. The historical cost of the asset should be written up to contemporary values by the appropriate index number: there should then be deducted the actual (revalued) depreciation charges that have been written off as a cost plus any scrap value. The difference between these two calculations would be the balancing allowance (if the revalued cost was greater than the amounts written off) or balancing charge (if the revalued costs were less than the amounts written off plus scrap value).

The Institute of Chartered Accountants put in a scheme for a Replacement Allowance. They wished depreciation charges to be computed in the ordinary way but when the time came for an asset to be replaced for the difference between the historical cost and the replacement cost to be allowed as an official deduction from sales proceeds.

There would seem to be good evidence to suggest that it is practicable to have a system of replacement cost depreciation and one feels that if the Royal Commission had found that British industry was being seriously affected by the rise in prices they would have found a way to provide relief for businesses—but they did not.

We have now to turn to the practical or expediency arguments that were put to the Royal Commission; that the combination of inflation and high tax rates have a bad effect on the level of investment. It is interesting to note straight away the Commissions conclusion with respect to the U.K.:—"Our final conclusion so far as the available evidence supported a conclusion was that we could not proceed on the basis that figures would establish the thesis that taxation is eroding the capital of productive enterprise by its method of calculating depreciation charges. We cannot support proposals for radical changes in the present system on any such ground".[19]

It is, of course, very difficult to establish by statistical or other reasoning whether or not investment in a country during a given period of time would or would not have been higher if a different depreciation policy had been followed. It is particularly difficult when, as in this instance important economic forces are operating in opposite directions. On the one hand inflation does tend to increase the effective burden of taxation as depreciation charges are undervalued in real terms. On the other hand however, rising prices are associated with good trade and business men's views of the future are very coloured by the present and on this count inflation has a favourable effect on investment.

It was not, therefore, surprising that the Royal Commission received a lot of conflicting and contradictory evidence on this aspect of their work. The Federation of British Industries put in some evidence based on the replies to questionnaires submitted by eighty member companies covering the period 1938–49.[20] This evidence purported to show that the post war level of taxation was having a serious effect on the level of company savings and investment. The Royal Commission also received evidence from the Trades Union Congress on this question and their evidence based on a random sample of firms taken from the accounts issued by Moody's Services Ltd., purported to demonstrate the opposite point of view.[21]

Not satisfied with these contradictory statements the Royal Commission asked the Board of Inland Revenue to carry out an investigation, the upshot of which was—as the Commission puts it —that "the

Board's survey did not show that anything that could be called an erosion of the capital of industry had taken place between 1938–1951. In particular the survey showed that the real value of plant and machinery had been maintained and some additions to it financed out of depreciation allowances (including initial allowances) themselves". The Royal Commission point out, however, that the real value of plant and machinery would not have been maintained intact out of tax free depreciation allowances if there had been no initial allowances.

There can be no doubt that these conclusions were extremely important in bringing about the rejection by the Royal Commission of the claims of business men and economists that the high effective burden of taxation on business brought about by the combination of high tax rates and inflation should be reduced.

TABLE 4

THE APPROPRIATION OF COMPANY INCOME IN THE U.K. 1938 AND 1955

	1938		1955	
	£ M	%	£ M	%
Dividends on Preference and Ordinary Shares	481	47	772	21
Other interest payments	160	15	442	12
U.K. Taxes on Income	95	9	884	24
Saving before providing for depreciation and stock appreciation	299	29	1596	43
	1035	100	3694	100

Source 1938 and 1948. National Income and Expenditure 1955 Table 29.
1955. Preliminary Estimates of National Income 1950–1955, p. 29.

It may seem surprising that the Royal Commission were able to reach the conclusion they did reach on this issue. Two important factors, however, have operated in the U.K. in the post war period so as to mitigate the bad economic effects of taxation and rising prices. The first of these has been the introduction of initial and investment allowances, the effect of which, in this context, will be discussed later in the chapter. At this stage all that need be said is that Accelerated Depreciation can alleviate pretty well completely the bad effects of rising prices. The second reason has been the tremendous fall in the post war period in the proportion of company income being distributed to shareholders. As can be seen in Table 4 though the burden of taxation has gone up dividends and interest payments have fallen so much that Gross Saving is a much higher proportion of company income than it was before the war. The reasons for this shift are many—high taxation, discriminatory taxation, requests by successive chancellors of the Exchequer for dividend restraint, inflation itself, in that dividends lag behind profits—but there can be no doubt that it has enabled companies to cope the more easily with the problem of inflation.

C. INFLATION AND ACCELERATED DEPRECIATION

The fiscal authorities of the U.K., U.S.A., and the British Dominions have been faced with the combination of rising prices and high tax rates and have not felt it necessary to go in for schemes of revaluation. There can be no doubt that the various forms of Accelerated Depreciation in operation in these countries have been an important factor preventing any bad economic effects. We can examine the assistance that Accelerated Depreciation can give in periods of inflation first in a very simple situation and then in a more sophisticated manner.

Let us consider the problem of replacing an asset which cost £100 ten years ago, the replacement cost of which is now £200. £100 will have been allowed as an expense for tax purposes against Sales proceeds. To replace the asset needs—in the absence of an Initial Allowance—some £100 from taxed profits. If however, there is an initial allowance of 40% in operation there will be no need for taxed profits to be called upon at all to maintain the firm's capital intact. The £200 of investment spending will yield an £80 initial allowance and a £20 annual allowance in year one which combined with the £100 permitted against the old asset is sufficient for the replacement. A 40% initial allowance takes care of the replacement problem of a ten year asset so long as the price level does no more than double over the period. It is obvious that there exists appropriate rates of initial allowance for assets of various lives and inflations of various magnitudes.

Let us now examine in a rather general manner the relationship between Depreciation Allowances and replacement requirements and for the moment let us assume conditions of price stability. Let us further assume that a company is in stationary equilibrium in that all its gross investment is for replacement purposes: that it has ten machines and that the age distribution of these machines is normal such that one machine is due for replacement, one is nine tenths depreciated and so on:* and that depreciation is carried out on the

---

* We have taken as an example a "mature" concern. The picture would be different for a new concern. If a business starts with a brand new factory composed of a large number of items of equipment all with varying lengths of life the management will

Straight Line basis. On these assumptions it is pretty obvious that the sum of the annual depreciation allowances is equal to replacement requirements for the firm as a whole. If the cost of each machine is £100 the sum of the straight line depreciation allowances on the nine old machines (£90) plus the first year's depreciation allowance on the new machine (£10) will be sufficient to finance the replacement of the tenth. The introduction of Accelerated Depreciation alters this equality and Table 5 shows the gap that arises between Depreciation Allowances and replacement requirements with five different varieties of Accelerated Depreciation and Table 6 shows in detail how the figures for one of these methods were produced. With the exception of investment allowances which lead to a permanent reduction in tax payments the other four examples (which are of pure accelerated depreciation) show that Accelerated Depreciation brings about a temporary (though substantial) gap between Depreciation Allowances and replacement requirements as compared to a state of affairs with ordinary depreciation.

We have assumed above that the price level is stable. If prices are rising this tax concession produced by Accelerated Depreciation provides some considerable assistance in overcoming the effects of the price change.

We must now complicate the matter a little by relaxing the assumption of an economy or firm in stationary equilibrium. Instead we shall consider a firm or economy in which the level of investment spending is growing at a constant percentage rate.[22]

Let us suppose first of all, that only ordinary Straight Line depreciation allowances are in operation. We have shown above that in static conditions annual depreciation allowances are equal to replacement requirements. It is pretty obvious that this equality will not hold if the business or economy is growing for, though what is required for replacement purposes is unaffected by growth, provision for depreciation will have grown as the capital stock has increased. Professor Domar has shown how the excess of depreciation over replacement depends on the rate of growth of investment spending and the length of the life of the asset. The greater the rate of growth and the longer the life of the asset the greater the excess of depreciation charges over what is required for replacement purposes.

normally find that for a period of years depreciation allowances (computed in the ordinary way) will exceed replacement requirements and that after this period they will be more or less in balance (assuming zero net investment). The excess depreciation allowances in the early life of the business are available for purpose other than replacing fixed assets.

TABLE 5

EXCESS OF DEPRECIATION ALLOWANCES OVER REPLACEMENT REQUIREMENTS

Ten ten year assets costing £ 100 each

Year	1 Year write off	5 Year write off	20% initial allowance	40% initial allowance	20% investment allowance
1	90	10	20	40	20
2	80	20	20	40	20
3	70	30	20	40	20
4	60	40	20	40	20
5	50	50	20	40	20
6	40	40	20	40	20
7	30	30	20	30	20
8	20	20	20	20	20
9	10	10	10	10	20
10	Nil	Nil	Nil	Nil	20
11	Nil	Nil	Nil	Nil	20
12	Nil	Nil	Nil	Nil	20
Total 1–12	450	250	170	300	240

TABLE 6

FIVE YEAR DEPRECIATION PERIOD (TEN YEAR LIFE) AND
REPLACEMENT REQUIREMENTS

Machines years	Depreciation allowances										Total depreciation allowances	Years replacement expenditure	Excess of depreciation over replacement
	1	2	3	4	5	6	7	8	9	10			
1	20	10	10	10	10	10	10	10	10	10	110	100	10
2	20	20	10	10	10	10	10	10	10	10	120	100	20
3	20	20	20	10	10	10	10	10	10	10	130	100	30
4	20	20	20	20	10	10	10	10	10	10	140	100	40
5	20	20	20	20	20	10	10	10	10	10	150	100	50
6	Nil	20	20	20	20	20	10	10	10	10	140	100	40
7	Nil	Nil	20	20	20	20	20	10	10	10	130	100	30
8	Nil	Nil	Nil	20	20	20	20	20	10	10	120	100	20
9	Nil	Nil	Nil	Nil	20	20	20	20	20	10	110	100	10
10	Nil	Nil	Nil	Nil	Nil	20	20	20	20	20	100	100	Nil
11	20	Nil	Nil	Nil	Nil	Nil	20	20	20	20	100	100	Nil
12	20	20	Nil	Nil	Nil	Nil	Nil	20	20	20	100	100	Nil

Table 7[23] shows the relationship between depreciation allowances and replacement requirements in a growing firm for ten year assets at different growth rates, on the assumption that depreciation is calcu-

TABLE 7

REPLACEMENT REQUIREMENTS AS A PERCENTAGE OF DEPRECIATION ALLOWANCES

	Rate of growth of investment spending		
	3%	*5%*	*10%*
Ten year life asset Ordinary straight line depreciation	86%	77%	58%

lated on a straight line basis. The gap between Depreciation and Replacement would, of course, be greater if one of the declining balance methods were used. We have assumed in these calculations that the price level is stable. If prices rise, however, it is obvious that up to some limiting rate of growth depreciation allowances will still exceed replacement needs. Broadly speaking it can be shown that so long as the rate of growth of *real* investment is greater than the rate of growth of prices replacement needs will be more than covered by Depreciation Allowances.

TABLE 8

ANNUAL RATE OF GROWTH OF PRICES WHICH MAKE DEPRECIATION ALLOWANCES (ORDINARY STRAIGHT LINE) EQUAL REPLACEMENT REQUIREMENTS

10 year asset

	Real rate of growth		
	1%	*3%*	*5%*
Rate of growth of prices needed to bring about equality	1.05	3.3	6.0
Rate of growth of money investment expenditures at which replacement will equal depreciation at above price growth rates	2.05	6.3	11.0

Table 8 illustrates this for a ten year asset and shows the rate of growth of prices needed to bring replacement needs into equality with depreciation allowances at various rates of growth of real investment expenditures. The important point to grasp is that if a firm is growing and if the price level is stable depreciation allowances exceed replacement needs and thus tax free funds are available for net investment purposes. In periods when the price level is rising these tax free resources are available to meet the added cost of replacement and as we have seen substantial increases in the price level can be offset by growth.

TABLE 9

REPLACEMENT REQUIREMENTS AS A PERCENTAGE OF DEPRECIATION ALLOWANCES

10 year asset

Depreciation method	Rate of growth of investment spending		
	3%	5%	10%
5 Year write off	79.6%	68.1%	46.4%
20% Initial allowance	83.5%	72.6%	51.8%
40% Initial allowance	78.9%	69.2%	47.2%
Ordinary straight line	(86%)	(77%)	(58%)

Accelerated Depreciation widens the gap between annual depreciation charges and replacement requirements and thus for a given group of assets and rate of growth a bigger increase in the price level can be absorbed with Accelerated Depreciation than with Ordinary Depreciation. In Table 9 the relationship between Replacement needs and depreciation allowances—when depreciation is accelerated (and, for purposes of comparison, ordinary straigt Line depreciation) is set out *after* the transitional benefits of accelerated depreciations have been allowed for, and it is obvious that Accelerated Depreciation can go a considerable way in helping firms to meet the problems of rising prices. There is no doubt that American and United Kingdom firms have benefited immensely from the various Accelerated Depreciation Schemes that have been in existence in these countries during and since the war and that Accelerated Depreciation has been an important factor in mitigating the potentially bad economic effects of the combination of high tax rates and rising prices.[24]

In this chapter we have argued that capital costs are just as much a cost of production as current costs and that depreciation charges which are the method by which capital costs are allocated to specific accounting periods should be recognised as a cost of production for Income Tax purposes and we noted some of the considerations that influence firms in their judgement of the particular method to adopt in writing off the cost of their capital equipment. We also considered the effects of capital costs and the allocation of capital expenditure to particular accounting periods on investment decisions and noticed the extent to which the various forms of Accelerated Depreciation could effect the level of investment spending. We then examined some of the problems that arise in a period of rising prices and some of the

possible remedies for the economic effects of historical cost depreciation accounting for income tax purposes; in particular we examined
the effects of growth and Accelerated Depreciation in helping firms to
meet these problems.

In conclusion the writer would like to make a suggestions which
though not explicitly developed in the chapter seems to him to be of
tremendous importance. It is considered that a most desirable reform
or change in Income Tax practice would be for firms to be allowed
more or less complete freedom as to the manner in which they depreciate their assets for taxation purposes. Not only would this ensure that
taxation would have a much less unfavourable effect on the level of
investment due to the various reasons noted above but it would also
substantially reduce the problems brought about by rising price levels
as firms could—if they wished—be able to write off assets very quickly
and thus get back the real value of their capital expenditures—as a
deduction from gross sales proceeds for income tax purposes—even
without introducing any special revaluation scheme. There seems very
much to be gained and little to be lost in giving firms a reasonably free
hand in choosing how they will allocate over time their spending on
capital assets for income tax purposes.

REFERENCES

1. For a good discussion of the whole question see GEORGE TERBORGH, *Realistic Depreciation Policy*, Machinery and Allied Products Institute, 1954.
2. The Royal Commission was appointed on January 2nd 1951 "to inquire into the present system of taxation of profits and income including its incidence and effects with particular reference to the taxation of business profits and the taxation of salaries and wages". Its First Report (Cmd. 8761) was published in February 1953, its Second Report (Cmd. 9105) in April 1954, and its Final Report (Cmd. 9474) in June 1955. The Royal Commission's comments on the taxation of business income are to be found in its Final Report. In their investigations into the problems of business taxation the Royal Commission had the advantages of having available to it the Report of the Committee on the Taxation of Trading Profits (Cmd. 8189, April 1951). This committee under the Chairmanship of Mr. (now Sir) Millard Tucker was appointed in June 1949, "to inquire into the methods of computing net trade profits for the purpose of charging them to income tax".
3. Institute of Chartered Accountants in England and Wales, *Recommendations on Accounting Principles*, IX, para. 90.
4. *Final Report* of the Royal Commission on the Taxation of Income and Profits, para. 344.
5. 1906, 5 T.C. 215, at p. 220.
6. *Final Report* of the Royal Commission, paras. 127–128. See also *Report* of the Tucker Committee, paras. 181–183.
7. The 1944 Finance Act introduced Depreciation Allowances for capital expenditure on scientific Research. The Income Tax Act 1945 brought into being in their

present guise depreciation allowances on the other forms of capital expenditure mentioned in the text.

8. *Final Report*, paras. 374–404.

9. See *Final Report*, paras. 850–871. See also *Report* of the Tucker Committee, paras. 214–228.

10. *Report* of the Royal Commission on the Income Tax, Cmd. 615, 1920, paras. 180–185.

11. In the U.K. the various depreciation rates for plant and machinery are set out in a Board of Inland Revenue publication, *Income Tax Wear and Tear Allowances for Machinery or Plant, List of Percentage Rates* (London, H.M.S.O. 1950). The actual procedure by which these rates are produced is rather complicated. The commissioners of Inland Revenue fix the life of the asset. Then there is calculated the rate of depreciation that will produce a written down value of 10 percent of the original cost by the time the asset is expected to be suitable only for scrap. The actual and operational rate of depreciation is then five-fourths of this calculated rate. The treatment of the other depreciable assets is somewhat different. Industrial Buildings, for example, are depreciated on a Straight Line basis and they are assumed to last fifty years. The cost basis is the original cost of the building and not as it is with plant and machinery the original cost to the buyer. Capital expenditure on scientific research may be depreciated over five years or in whatever *shorter* period of time the asset is expected to last. Capital expenditure on the acquisition of patent rights is depreciable on the Straight Line basis over a period of seventeen years or the life of the rights acquired, whichever is the shorter.

12. U.S. Bureau of Internal Revenue, Bulletin F, *Income Tax: Depreciation and Obsolescence, Estimated Useful Lives and Depreciation* (Washington Government Printing Office, 1952).

13. Initial allowances arose out of the inquiry into business taxation instituted by SIR KINGSLEY WOOD that we noted above (p.p. 156–178). They were given legal form in the Income Tax Act of 1945 and became effective as from April 1946. The 1946 rates of initial allowance were 20% for plant and machinery and 10% for industrial buildings and mining works. In the 1949 Finance Act the rate for plant and machinery was increased to 40%. The Finance Act of 1951 suspended initial allowances from April 1952 but they were restored a year later in the 1953 Finance Act at 20% for plant and machinery, 10% for industrial buildings and 40% for mining works. They were effectively superceded by the introduction of Investment Allowances in 1954 but on their abolition in February 1956 Initial Allowances were re-introduced. Investment Allowances were introduced at the following rates: 10 per cent for industrial and agricultural buildings and works; and 20 per cent for plant and machinery, mining works and scientific research assets.

14. *Minutes of Evidence* taken before the Royal Commission on the Taxation of Profits and Income, Sixteenth Day.

15. Hicks, J. R., *Value and Capital*, Oxford, p. 174.

16. *Report* of the Tucker Committee, para. 100. See also *Final Report* of the Royal Commission, paras. 255–356. For a full discussion of the issues involved see E. Cary Brown's volume, *Depreciation Adjustment for Price Changes* in the Harvard "Effects of Taxation" series, especially Chapter IV (Allowance of Replacement Cost Depreciation for Tax Purpose—Equity and Economic Effects).

17. Professor F. W. PAISH Minutes of Evidence, Day 9, p. 227, para. 16.

18. *Final Report*, para. 354.

19. *Final Report*, para. 343.

20. *The Effects of Inflation on Industrial Capital Resources*. A memorandum submitted to the Royal Commission by the Federation of British Industries.

21. *Supplementary Memorandum* submitted to the Royal Commission by the Trades Union Congress (Day 15).

22. There is a very substantial literature on these issues. The following are probably the most useful contributions and they contain most of the other references: E. D. DOMAR, "Depreciation, Replacement and Growth", *Economic Journal*, March 1953: E. D. DOMAR, "The Case for Accelerated Depreciation", *Quarterly Journal of Economics*, November 1953: R. GOODE, "Accelerated Depreciation Allowances as a Stimulus to Investment", *Quarterly Journal of Economics*, May 1955.

23. Calculated from the formula produced by Professor DOMAR in his Economic Journal article linking together Straight Line Depreciation Allowances and replacement requirement in a growing economy. Professor Domar shows that if R = annual replacement expenditures, D = annual depreciation charges, r = annual rate of growth of investment, m = life of assets, then

$$\frac{R}{D} = \frac{(1 + r)^m - 1}{Rm}.$$

24. In the U.K., for example, it has recently been shown that for most of the post war period total tax free depreciation allowances, i.e. the combined total of initial, investment and ordinary annual allowances, have exceeded the straight line depreciation charge on a replacement basis. The following table illustrates this:

	Company Depreciation £ M						
	1948	*1949*	*1950*	*1951*	*1952*	*1953*	*1954*
Depreciation (straight line) at replacement cost	280	300	330	390	450	480	510
Depreciation allowed for tax: annual allowance	207	220	241	253	273	313	363
Initial and investment allowance	95	184	232	236	109	97	142
Total allowed for taxation purposes	302	404	473	489	382	410	505

Estimates of Replacement Cost Depreciation are derived from an important paper by Mr. Philip Redfern of the Central Statistical Office, "Net Investment in Fixed Capital in the United Kingdom, 1938–1953" *Journal of the Royal Statistical Society* (Series A), Volume 118, Part 2, 1955.

CHAPTER 4

THE THEORY OF DEPRECIATION AND ENTREPRENEURIAL BEHAVIOUR

L. H. KLAASSEN, L. M. KOYCK

Netherlands Economic Institute, Rotterdam, The Netherlands

and

J. L. MEIJ, J. L. BOUMA

Institute of Industrial Economics, State University of Groningen, The Netherlands

I. INTRODUCTORY

It is usual in economic literature to distinguish between re-investment and net-investment, re-investment being treated as a separate phenomenon obeying to specific laws.*

The aim of this study is to gain somewhat more insight into the actual behaviour of the entrepreneur with regard to re-investments in order to make theory on this subject a bit more realistic. The results of the study have lead to some doubt with regard to the above made distinction and it is questioned whether this distinction can be maintained under all circumstances.

It very well might be, for example, that the producer is much more concerned with adapting his production-capacity to actual demand by means of retarding and accelerating scrapping than with determining the exact point of time on which replacement shall have to take place.

It will appear that a distinction has to be made between the enterpreneurial behaviour in a static or a continuously expanding economy on one side and that in a fluctuating economy on the other. In the first case one can speak of a real replacement decision viz. to scrap the old machine and to put a new one in its place. In a fluctuating economy however, the producer is concerned with scrapping old machines and buying new ones in order to keep his capacity in line with demand. In fact he then makes at least two separate decisions, one for scrapping and, not necessarily at the same moment of time, one for buying a new one.

In the first case the decision to scrap a machine is taken with the intention to replace it by a new one and in doing so, to maintain

---

* This distinction is important, of course, for profit determination: re-investment being an element of costs, whereas net-investments come from savings, either of the enterpreneur, or of others.

production-capacity. This is then replacement in the ordinary sense of the word, defined as the investment necessary to replace a machine put out of use, in order to maintain actual production-capacity. This is in opposition to net-investments, which are made in order to extend production-capacity.

From this definition it follows that the decisions to scrap an old machine and to replace it by a new one take place at the same or nearly the same moment. If not, one could not, following the definition speak of maintaining actual capacity.

In a fluctuating economy, however, the decision to scrap in a period of falling demand is often made in order to decrease production capacity whilst in periods of increasing demand this decision is postponed in order not to diminish capacity. The decision to buy a new machine on the contrary is made in periods of increasing demand.

In this respect the difference between a static or a monotonically expanding economy and a fluctuating one is therefore that in the first one only one replacement decision is made; in the second one two separate decisions, one to scrap and the other to buy a new machine, are combined in such a way that there is an optimal adaption of production-capacity to demand.

In connection with the foregoing, a theoretical analysis will first be given of the optimal behaviour with respect to re-investment in a continuously expanding economy (section II). These theoretical considerations will be compared with the actual behaviour of Dutch firms during the post-war period, which can be considered to fulfill the conditions of a continuously expanding economy (section III).

In section IV a theoretical analysis will be given of enterpreneurial behaviour in a fluctuating economy, followed by an empirical analysis of the scrapping of old ships and the building of new ones for the Dutch commercial marine in the interwar period (section V).

A summary of conclusions is given in section VI.

II. THEORETICAL CONSIDERATIONS ON REPLACEMENT IN A CONTINUOUSLY EXPANDING ECONOMY

A. THE PROBLEM OF REPLACEMENT IN ECONOMIC LITERATURE

Various theories have arisen during the last decades in regard to the problem of replacing durable capital goods and many practical views have been presented. We shall summarize the principle ideas of some selected theories, and at the same time add a few critical remarks.

In advance we state explicitly that a correct theory of replacement of durable capital goods should at the same time imply a solution of the problem of depreciation.

The amounts periodically written off for depreciation that are chargeable to the units of product in every period should reflect the degree to which the capital good contributes to the combination of productive means needed to obtain the desired products.

The sum total of the amounts written off during the whole lifetime of the machine must enable its replacement.

The different ways in which the problems of life-time and depreciation are dealt with are also decisive for the way in which the moment of replacement is determined. A rational determination of that moment can only be made by a comparison of the costs of continuing production with the old machine and that of production with a new one.*

Surveying the literature of the last decades, we find that there have been five different attempts to solve the replacement-problem.

First, one has started from a direct estimation of the life-time of the machine. In practice this results in choosing a depreciation period that has become usual in the branch. Though the formulae may be complicated in some cases they are no more than the application of rules of thumb, on which the determination of the amounts of depreciation is based. The moment at which the machine is put out of use is given by the estimated life-time.

Circumstances may have changed, however, so that the assumed life-time does no longer agree with the real one. In the case of a newly-developed machine, for instance, comparison of the cost of production with the old machine and that with the new one will determine the actual replacement. These costs of production are again based on an estimate of the remaining life-time of the old machine and an estimate of that of the new machine.

This method can be accepted in those cases in which the capital good is considered to be worn out as soon as it is no longer able to perform the services needed in the place where the machine is in operation. This may be caused by a quantitative as well as qualitative decrease of the products provided by the machine. It is said that the technical life-time has then expired. In some cases the estimation of this tech-

---

* How far margins of safety are to be taken into account in the various theories is a problem in itself. In its consequence it means that not every saving in costs, how ever small it may be, will be sufficient to cause actual replacement.

nical life-time can be estimated to a high degree of certainty.*

Second there is the attempt to determine the optimal life-time of the capital good as the period of use which involves the minimal average costs of production per unit of product obtained by means of that machine. This theory has been advocated by Taylor[1] and Hotelling[2].

If the price of the capital good is given and the course of the quantity of product and of the complementary costs over time is known as well as the interest of the capital invested and, eventually, the scrapping value, the costs of producing a unit of product only depend on the period during which the capital good remains in use, i.e. the life-time. It can, therefore, be asked at what life-time those costs will be a minimum. This life-time has been called by Taylor and Hotelling the economic life-time.

When the economic life-time has been determined in this way, the problem of depreciation must be considered as a problem of distributing the purchasing-price over the years of its life-time.

The problem of replacement has also been solved in this theory if all factors mentioned above have remained the same. Replacement should take place if the economic life-time as defined above has expired. The old capital good will be replaced at that moment by a new one of the same type. The assumption that all circumstances remain the same may be partly dropped as will be seen in the following.

When new and better types of capital goods enter into the market or if the circumstances under which production takes place change, the problem of replacement must be reviewed. In this case, replacement forms a special problem. The old apparatus will be kept in operation as long as its complementary costs (eventually augmented by the diminution of the scrap-value during the period of use) are less than the minimum-costs of the new machine.

Preinreich very properly observed in his article mentioned below that the problem is not quite as simple as this analysis would suggest. In the following pages we shall return to this remark when we shall try to offer a synthesis of this "minimal unit costs theory", and one of the other theories which is still to be treated. It will be shown that, while maintaining the principles of Taylor and Hotelling, many difficulties can be removed.

* It goes without saying that if in such a case the product of the apparatus remains quantitatively and qualitatively constant over the whole life-time, this does not imply any constancy of the depreciation. The course of the depreciation during the life-time will also depend on the behaviour of the complementary costs.

Further it has been argued that the optimal life-time can be determined by finding the period of use for which the goodwill is maximal. The goodwill of a capital good is the difference between the discounted value of the "quasi-rents" and the purchasing-price of the capital good. By "quasi-rents" or "net income" is meant the difference between the proceeds from the products* and the complementary costs.

Advocates of this theory are Preinreich[3], F. A. and Vera C. Lutz[4] and Schneider[5].

Elaborating Preinreich's theory, F. A. and Vera C. Lutz, as well as Schneider, deal with three cases of investment. First the single machine horizon, i.e. the entrepreneur confines himself to the life-time of a certain machine and renounces replacing it by a new one.

In this case the goodwill will have been maximized if the quasi-rent of the machine is equal to the interest on the salvage-value of the apparatus at the moment that putting out of use is considered**.

Secondly there is the case in which a finite and fixed number of replacements by identical machines will take place. As Schneider already observed, this is in practice an improbable case.***

In this second case the life-times of the several machines differ in the sense that the economic life-time of an earlier machine will be shorter than that of a later one because both the discounted value of the future quasi-rents decreases and interest on that value decreases as time passes, for the life-time of a machine is ended when the quasi-rents of the old machine becomes equal to the interest on its salvage value plus the interest on the goodwill of the finite series of future machines.

---

* Proceeds from sale of the products, or if the products are used in the same firm, the proceeds imputed.

** Eventually augmented by the interest on the depreciation of the salvage-value, if it is supposed, that this value decreases as the apparatus grows older.

Mathematical proofs of this and following statements are given by the authors mentioned.

These conclusions have been derived by the authors under the assumption that the rate of interest remains constant and that the quasi-rent of the capital good falls monotonically in time. For if the quasi-rent as a function of time does not fall monotonically—because for instance the demand curve of the product shifts in time to the left as well as to the right—the capital good may stay in active operation though its quasi-rent falls below the interest of the salvage-value c.q. below the interest of the salvage-value plus the interest of the future goodwill (as will be seen in the following two cases) because the quasi-rent may rise again above that level afterwards.

*** It seems much more realistic to assume that the process of production will be executed during a certain period of time in view of current and expiring concessions. The argument in this case will differ from that of a fixed number of replacements.

In the third case, there is an infinite series of replacements by identical machines. The economic life-time of the several machines is now always equally long irrespective of being earlier or later in the series. This life-time will end and a machine will be replaced as soon as the quasi-rent of the old machine becomes less than the interest on its salvage value plus the interest on the discounted value of the future good-wills of the infinite series of new machines. Because this series is infinite, that discounted value never decreases. So all machines in the series have the same economic life-time.[6]

Many objections can be raised against the goodwill theory. Hotelling rightly observed that the products of many durable capital goods are semi-consumable articles and, therefore, often used in the same firm. Therefore, no proceeds can be determined. More fundamental is the objection that the profit which arises from the whole combination of means of production is imputed exclusively to an individual capital good. As a result of this arbitrary imputation the capital good will stay in active operation until the profit has completely disappeared.

In the case of the single machine horizon (no replacement) this does not matter and is justified. The optimal duration of the production-process (i.e. for which the profit has been maximized) is calculated and, because no replacement will take place, the duration of the production-process is as long as the life-time of the capital good. Though the two concepts are different, in this case it is quite indifferent whether total profit is imputed to one means of production or to more. It will be clear that the case of the single machine horizon is not very realistic, but when it is realistic the conclusion is correct. This may happen when the total yield of the products is less than the total costs. Then replacement is not economically justified. The buying-price is, however, a sunk cost, so that the production will be continued until the complementary costs c.q. plus the interest on the scrapping value, are equal to the proceeds. The quasi-rents are then nil c.q. equal to the interest on the scrapping value. Only in this case can the yield have any influence on the optimal life-time of the machine.

In other cases, imputation of the total profit to the capital good only may have no effect if one supposes, as Schneider does, that the yield of the products is constant over time. But then the goodwill-theory amounts to a minimal costs theory of a form which differs from Taylor and Hotelling in the assumption that the quantity of products is constant over time. This assumption is not necessary and is a super-fluous restriction of the general validity of the theory.

It may be observed, however, that in considering the question of whether to replace an apparatus in use by a new one, a new difficulty arises in the goodwill method. For, one cannot state: if the discounted value of the net-yield of the new machine is higher than that of the old, replacement will be necessary. In this case one will have to examine at what life-time under present circumstances the remaining goodwill of the old machine will be maximal. Then for the same number of years the goodwill of the new machine will have to be determined. The replacement decision will be made by comparing these two results.

Finally, we believe that the advocates of the goodwill-theory offer no solution for the depreciation problem, for they do not consider the course of the services of the machine over time (i.e. the performances of the machine in the combination of means of production which results in the products). Their methods are, therefore, of little use for determining a rational system of "writing-off".

In the Dutch literature on industrial economics the life-time and the time of replacing capital goods have been determined by means of estimating the course of the value of the services during the life-time of the apparatus.

Such a theory has been inaugurated by Th. Limperg in his lectures at the Municipal University of Amsterdam and elaborated by J. L. Meij.[7] The argument presented by Meij can be summarized as follows*:

a. It is supposed that we know the course of the replacement value** of the total product of the machine (in combination with its complementary factors), at any moment of time, during the whole life-time. This means that we have a certain index indicating the proportion of the replacement value of the total product at any moment of time to the replacement value of the total product at another moment of time.

    The total product may vary in quantity and quality. If we can reduce differences in quality to differences in quantity the replace-

---

* We give the summary in a more or less mathematical form, in order to link it up to the next of our argument.

Originally Meij exposed his theory in a verbal way with graphical examples. From our mathematical presentation, it follows that there is no basis to the objection sometimes heard that arguing in this way is reasoning in a circle.

** As will be seen on p. 205 by the replacement value of the product we denote the minimal costs corresponding to the optimal method of production attainable for the firm in question.

ment value of the total product at any moment of time may be represented by

$$R_0 \cdot x(t) \tag{A}$$

in which R_0 is the replacement value of the unit of product which is to be determined. $x(t)$ is the quantity produced by the productive combination of the machine and its complementary factors at the moment of time t, differences in quality being reduced to differences in quantity.

We suppose that the machine has been bought at point of time $t = 0$.

b. The replacement value of the product at any moment of time is equal to the sum of the complementary costs $k(t)$ and the value of the nett-services of the durable capital good itself (indicated by $g(t)$) at the same moment.

Thus

$$R_0 \cdot x(t) = k(t) + g(t) . \tag{B}$$

c. The complementary costs function $k(t)$ is known. The price of the capital good C is given and constant:

$$\frac{dC}{dt} = 0 \qquad \text{,}$$

the lifetime of the machine is ended at $t = t_0$; t_0 is unknown and is to be determined.

d. The sum of the values of all the services during the whole life-time of the machine is equal to the price of the capital good. Thus:

$$\int_0^{t_0} g(t)dt = C \tag{C}$$

where t_0 indicates the moment of replacement which is to be determined.

e. The value of the nett-services of the capital good at the moment of replacement, t_0, is nil.

Thus:

$$g(t_0) = 0 . \tag{D}$$

From (B) it follows that:

$$\int_0^{t_0} R_0 \cdot x(t) \, dt = \int_0^{t_0} k(t)dt + \int_0^{t_0} g(t)dt . \tag{E}$$

From (C) and (E)

$$R_0 \cdot \int_0^{t_0} x(t) \, dt - \int_0^{t_0} (kt) \, dt = C . \tag{F}$$

From (B) and (D)

$$R_0 \cdot x(t_0) - k(t_0) = 0 . \tag{G}$$

The functions $x(t)$ and $k(t)$ are known, therefore from (F) and (G) the two unknowns R_0 and t_0 can be determined.

Further from (G):

$$R_0 = \frac{k(t_0)}{x(t_0)} \tag{H}$$

which implies that at the moment of replacement, t_0, the complementary costs per unit of product are equal to its replacement value.

For the sake of simplicity the price of the capital good has been taken constant and there has been renounced of any salvage value*. For the same reason the rate of interest is not taken into consideration. Its introduction would not make a fundamental change in the argument. All functions would be multiplied by $1/e^{it}$, the rate of interest being $100 \cdot i$ procent per year, compounded continuously. E.g. $R_0 \cdot x(t)$ would become $R_0 \cdot x(t) \cdot e^{-it}$; $k(t)$ would become $k(t) \cdot e^{-it}$. See p. 202 ff.

The argument given above holds especially for a capital good of the newest type. When an old capital good is considered, then we do not only know the *course of the replacement value* of the product, but also the *replacement value itself* if we know the quantity and quality of the product at every moment t. The product of the old machine cannot have a replacement value which is larger than that with production with the new apparatus, R_0, for the product can be replaced at that value, provided that the new type of machine can be used in the plant considered. If R_0 is known and we know the quantity of product $x(t)$ (where qualitative differences have been reduced to quantitative differences) then the foregoing argument will be slightly modified:

We know the replacement value of the total product of the old machine at any moment t, so: $R_0 \cdot x(t)$ is a *known* function.

---

* If the salvage value is taken into account then $C(t)$ can be taken as the difference between price and salvage value.

Again $$R_0 \cdot x(t) = k(t) + g(t) \qquad \text{(B')}$$

where $k(t)$ are the complementary costs incurred at a point of time t with production with the old machine and $g(t)$ the value of the performance of the capital good of the old type.

In this case also the value of the service of the old capital good is at the moment of replacement, t_0, nil. Thus:

$$g(t_0) = 0 \qquad \text{(D')}$$

From (B') and (D'):

$$R_0 \cdot x(t_0) = k(t_0) \therefore R_0 = \frac{k(t_0)}{x(t_0)} \qquad \text{(H')}$$

which implies that at the moment of replacement the complementary costs of the production with the old apparatus per unit of product are equal to the replacement value of the product as produced by the new machine. As $k(t)$ is known, from (H') t_0 can be determined.

Meij has stated explicitly that in his theory little account is taken of the influence of the actual replacement at a certain moment on all future replacements. We shall reconsider this point in our following arguments.

It is to be observed that this theory has essential significance for solving the depreciation-problem. If from (F) and (G) or from (H') R_0 and t_0 have been determined, the function $g(t)$ can be found. In a correct depreciation system during every short period of time, dt, an amount $g(t)$ should be chargeable to the products produced during that period dt, supposed that the course of the replacement value, and that of the complementary costs have been estimated correctly.

In our treatise of the next theory, the theory of Terborgh, more will be said about this estimate.

Terborgh[8] suggests a simple and easily applicable method for determining the moment of time at which a means of production should be replaced. The determination of the life-time and the solution of the depreciation-problem are moved to the background.

In Terborgh's line of thought the sacrifices connected with the use of a durable capital good are of two kinds.

In the first place the capital invested in the apparatus must be amortized in the period during which it is used. If the capital good has a direct salvage value, only the yearly decreases in that value need to be taken as sacrifices of the year concerned.

The second group of sacrifices consists of the increasing operating inferiority of the capital good in service, relative to the best apparatus that is available. This inferiority may manifest itself in the increase in complementary costs of production as well as in the decrease of the quantity and quality of the products.

The periodical increase in inferiority is determined by Terborgh as a certain amount per period, called the inferiority gradient. He supposes that the increase in inferiority is proportional with the time, so that the inferiority gradient is constant.

By quantifying the increase in inferiority as a sacrifice of production he can take it as one of the costs connected with the use of the apparatus considered. He then takes for any year the sum of the diminishing average capital costs—the interest and amortization of the capital invested divided over the number of service years—and the ever increasing inferiority—also calculated as a time-adjusted average over the same number of years. The time-adjusted average of the inferiority over the service life tends to increase as the life-time is extended, since the inferiority of a machine relative to its best current alternative tends to increase with age. On the other hand, the longer the period of service over which capital amortization is spread the lower is the average capital cost for the period. The lowest combination of time-adjusted average of capital costs and operating inferiority of the machine is called the "adverse minimum"[9].

In order to decide whether an old capital good (called the defender) should be replaced by a new one (called the challenger) the "adverse minimum" of defender and challenger must be determined. In calculating the "adverse minimum" of the defender only the capital costs of its salvage value at the moment of comparison are taken into account. The operating inferiority of the defender should be determined relative to its best current alternative. When the "adverse minimum" of the defender is lower than that of the challenger, replacement is not yet desirable; in the opposite case replacement is rational.

According to Terborgh, in general it holds that if an asset has become an appropriate object for a replacement analysis, its normal, or representative, operating inferiority will usually be rising faster than its capital costs (if any) are falling, giving a rising trend for the two combined. For this reason it could usually be assumed that the next-year total of these factors is the adverse minimum (this is the so-called "next-year analysis")[10].

Terborgh expressively points out that the application of the method indicated rests on two standard assumptions viz:

1. future challengers will have the same adverse minimum as the present one, and
2. the present challenger will accumulate operating inferiority at a constant rate over its service life[11].

It can be questioned whether these assumptions are realistic. The necessity to check the desirability of replacement every time a machine has been used during some period points to the contrary. If the first supposition were confirmed in practice such an examination would never be necessary. One would simply keep each capital good in service until its adverse minimum has been reached. At that moment it would be replaced by an identical new machine.

The period determined by the adverse minimum could be considered as the economic life-time on which the actual writing-off for depreciation of the machine and the actual amortization of the capital invested can be based.

In practice the replacement analysis for the asset in service will always serve as a check of the actual depreciation method and of the life-time on which that method has been based. This check becomes necessary if it can be assumed that the new machines do not have the same adverse minimum as that of the old apparatus we started from. Therefore we cannot accept Terborgh's assumption that a "next-year analysis" will be enough. It is contradictory to the consequences of his own theory. It is not at all certain that this check will not be necessary until the moment at which the operating inferiority will be rising faster than the capital costs are falling.

Since it is Terborgh's first objective to determine the moment of replacement he does not find an exact solution of the depreciation problem. The challenger requires an investment which is equal to its price, in the defender there cannot be invested more than its direct salvage value. The amortization of the capital invested (taking into account its interest) is divided equally over the service life. As the life-time is longer the yearly capital costs will accordingly be smaller.

Terborgh therefore does not consider the necessity of dividing the total capital cost in proportion to the yearly services of the machine. The distribution of the capital invested equally over the service life is therefore no depreciation method and is not intended to be such.

The weakest point of Terborgh's argument is in the concept of operating inferiority and the way in which this concept is used.

What does cause an apparatus to become inferior relative to the best available new one? If we suppose that the best available machine is of the same type as the old one, i.e. the new asset does not possess any improvements, while the value of the products and the value of the complementary costs have changed, then the following factors are relevant:

— rising of the complementary costs of production
— reduction of the quantity periodically produced
— diminishing of the quality of the units produced.

We usually call this "endogeneous factors of depreciation[12]", i.e. they are connected with the capital good in question.

As it is obvious from the supposition made a few lines ago there are also exogenous factors that make an asset inferior in service-capacity. These factors can be similarly summed up as follows:

— improvements of the quality of the products produced by the new capital good
— increasing of the quantity of product periodically obtained from it
— reduction of the complementary costs connected with production by means of the new capital good.

A comparison of the asset in use with the best available asset leads to the conclusion that the operating inferiority consists of three aspects: inferiority with regard to the complementary costs, to the quantity produced and to its quality.

Indeed these three can be quantified, but there is a great difference between the operating inferiority due to endogeneous factors, which appears by comparison of the service of the machine in use with that obtainable from an identical new machine (depreciation), and the operating inferiority that could appear by comparison of a new machine of the type in use with the best new machine currently available (obsolescence). About the course of this latter kind of inferiority through time nothing can be predicted with any certainty. On the contrary the course of the former (depreciation) can be predicted to a certain degree. It is, however, not very likely that the operating inferiority (depreciation and obsolescence) will accumulate linearly, since the maintenance- and repair costs will increase progressively with the growing age of the apparatus, and furthermore there is the chance of a decreasing of the quantity and quality of the product. In so far as the way in which operating inferiority develops is predictable, i.e. in so far it is due to endogeneous factors, we can compare the method of Terborgh with the theory of Meij, built on the statement of Limperg that the periodical depreciation should represent the value of the services of the capital good. For we can say that the operating inferi-

ority of an asset in use is duofold, viz: inferiority as to the complementary costs and inferiority as to the product.

These two categories of inferiority can be easily demonstrated by
means of the following graphical exposition of the determination of
the economic life-time after the theory of Meij.

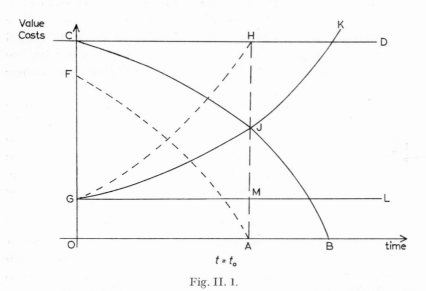

Fig. II. 1.

In the case represented by Fig. II.1 it is supposed that there is a
new capital good producing the same goods as can be made by the old
machine. The replacement value of a unit of product, assumed to be
known, is equal to the minimal costs of production with the new
machine.

The line CD represents the replacement value of the annual produce
of the best new machine currently available. OG are the complementary
costs of production with this best new apparatus, so GL is the complementary cost function for the new machine. The curve CB represents
the replacement value of the annual product of the old machine, while
the curve GK denotes the course of the complementary costs of production with this old asset. So CB is the graphical representation of
$R_0 \cdot x(t)$ and GK is the representation of $k(t)$. (See page 193).

We saw that at the moment of replacement the value of the service
of the old capital good should be nil. So:

$$R_0 \cdot x(t) = k(t).$$

This holds for the point of time $t = t_0$. The economic life-time in the theory of Meij is denoted by OA.

It is now clear that we can derive the inferiority, in the sense of Terborgh, from the distance between GK and GL and from the distance between CD and CB. The total inferiority at a certain moment is denoted by the sum of these two distances graphically represented by the curve GH. In Meij's theory at the moment on which the capital good should be replaced, the total inferiority HM has just become equal to the replacement value of the produce of the best new machine minus its complementary costs.

In Meij's line of thought too the moment of replacement can be determined by means of an estimation of the accumulation of the inferiority (for it amounts to estimating the course of the value of the services of the machine, the function $g(t)$ in the preceeding exposition of Meij's theory) represented in the graph by FA. (It should be observed that OG = FC). As can easily be seen the course of the value of the nett-services of the old machine is contrary to that of its inferiority accumulation *. Nevertheless Terborgh equally spreads the capital invested (augmented by a certain factor of interest) over the number of years of the service life and so arrives at a certain average per annum for each number of years. The accumulated amount of inferiority is treated in the same way. For he determines the total inferiority accumulated by the old machine compared to the best one available and divides the amount thus found (augmented by the same factor of interest) by the number of years of the service life the inferiority-accumulation refers to. Then he adds the two quantities—the time-averaged capital costs and the time-averaged inferiority— and observes at what number of years this sum is minimal. If the inferiority accumulation has been estimated correctly, Terborgh could determine an economic life-time

---

* Denote OC by $R_0 \cdot x(0) = \overline{R}$; $x(0)$ is the quantity produced at $t = 0$, and denote OG by $k(0) = \overline{K}$.

Then the total inferiority at a certain moment, $I(t)$, is equal to

$$I(t) = \{\overline{R} - R_0 \cdot x(t)\} + \{k(t) - \overline{K}\}$$
$$= \{\overline{R} - \overline{K}\} - \{R_0 \cdot x(t) - k(t)\}$$

$R_0 \cdot x(t) - k(t)$ is nothing else than the function $g(t)$ representing the course in time of the nett-services of the machine.

$$\text{So: } I(t) = \{\overline{R} - \overline{K}\} - g(t)$$
$$\text{or: } g(t) = \{\overline{R} - \overline{K}\} - I(t).$$

Therefore the course in time of the nett-services is inverse to that of the inferiority accumulation.

which agrees with that according to the theory of Meij, at least in the case of an old machine relative to a new type. He would proceed then virtually the same as Meij. Whereas Meij considers the inferiority differentially so to speak, Terborgh determines an average inferiority.

Terborgh does not estimate, however, the course of the inferiority over time but tries to deduct an inferiority gradient from the inferiority already accumulated by the equipment in use. It is clear that this method is not possible for equipment of a new type. It can therefore hardly be accepted when different types of apparatus are considered to replace assets already in use. For one would simply trace the influence of a factor working in the past for the new apparatus, which possibly is of quite a different quality and which will be used under different circumstances. The very fact that a replacement analysis appears to be necessary is a proof that the new apparatus is not quite identical to the old one or that the conditions under which it will be used in the future have changed. If it is supposed that nothing has been altered since the old machine was put into use, it would have served during the period in which the adverse minimum has been reached and then would be replaced by a new one with the same adverse minimum.

Meanwhile these difficulties only affect the way in which the inferiority gradient is deduced. The principle of Terborgh's method is not affected by this. There is, however, another objection against the manner in which Terborgh tackles the question of replacement, an objection more principal in character.

In order to determine the operating inferiority of some apparatus it is necessary to know the costs of production with the best machine currently available. This requires the knowledge of the adverse minimum of this new asset. This adverse minimum cannot be determined unless we know the operating inferiority of that new asset. Now we could find the complementary-costs-inferiority of the new apparatus relative to its initial state. The inferiority as to the quantity of product and its quality, however, cannot be quantified unless we know the costs of production with that best new machine itself. This requires knowledge of the service life of that machine, i.e. knowledge of the period of time in which its adverse minimum is reached. So we have got entangled in a vicious circle.

Terborgh has not detected this reasoning in a circle in his theory because he has not fully analysed the inferiority in its component parts. Since the concept of the operating inferiority is the core of his whole method, we cannot accept his theory as a right solution of the replacement problem, not to mention the way in which he distributes the capital costs over the service life and so leaves the depreciation problem unsolved too.

In the next part of our exposition we will try to synthesize the two above mentioned theories viz: the "minimal unit costs" theory of Taylor and Hotelling on one side and the theory of Meij on the other.

It will be shown that these two theories rest on the same principle only with this difference that Meij's version brings the depreciation problem to the forefront, while Taylor and Hotelling have focused their attention primarily on the moment of replacement.

B. A Synthesis

1. *Starting Point and Assumptions*

It is assumed that a firm is producing a certain well-defined product by means of one single machine in co-operation with complementary factors of production.

This product, which may be a consumable good, a semi-consumable article or a sort of service (using a certain department of a plant during a period of time), can be obtained through the method of production most appropriate to the firm, in a planned quantity, at minimal costs per unit of product, valued at replacement prices.

These costs* per unit of product depend on:

1. *the quantitative proportions* in which the various means of production are combined;
2. *the quantity of product which is to be produced at every moment of time,* depending on the situation on the market and the organizational and technological structure of the plant;
3. *the life-time of the machine,* that is the time during which it will stay in active operation;
4. *the replacement value of the machine and of the complementary factors of production;*
5. *the interest costs* as determined by the rate of interest and the production period.

About these five points we can make the following remarks:

We suppose that there is a fixed number of possible ways in which

---

* In this explanation we do not deal with the difference between costs of production, and losses caused by using less than normal capacity.

the production can take place. These possibilities depend among other things on the state of technology, which is taken as constant until further notice.

In order to find the optimal method of production, we have to form cost-functions for every possible method. For each of the cost-functions the optimum or minimum cost is to be determined with regard to the other variables.

By comparison of the several relative optima, the 'optimum optimorum' or the method of production best suited for the firm can be found and with it the actual cost-function. It is conceivable, that the entrepreneur is limited in his choice of the production method because of various historical, geographical or organizational reasons, e.g. the location, specialization on quality articles, the different types and qualities in which the means of production are to be obtained.

Exogeneous factors such as the situation in the labour-market might also play a role. Hence we shall assume that the optimal method of production is given.

The quantity of product that is to be produced at each moment of time (a small period dt), is given by $x(t)$. The function $x(t)$, representing the course of the quantity produced through time, is determined by the manager of the firm. One might imagine that the department concerned is an integral part of the organization of the entire plant.

x implies a quantity of product of a well-defined quality (differences in quality should be reduced to differences in quantity).

$x(t)$ may remain constant or vary monotonously in the course of time. For the definiteness of the results of the following theory it is not allowed that $x(t)$ fluctuates. It can be questioned, whether the firm can tolerate a decline of the quantity. This depends on fluctuations in the volume of sales or on the possibility of replacing the service of the machine and its complementary factors by another combination of the means of production.

The $x(t)$ required can, however, always be obtained by a combination of physical services of the machine and complementary factors. Decreasing the capacity of the machine does not necessarily mean a decrease of the quantity $x(t)$ produced by the complementary factors and the machine together.

In order to be able to apply the differential-calculus to the functions of t, we suppose that $x(t)$ is continuous.

The life-time of the machine is proportional with the course of time.

If we assume that the machine in question has been bought at a point of time $t = 0$, its age is denoted by t.

The replacement value of a means of production is taken as its value at the moment of *actual* replacement, assuming that there is perfect foresight. In determining the life-time of the machine no active role is attributed to the market-price of the product, it being supposed that the proceeds (market-value of the product) are higher than the replacement value of the product.

The influence of the rate of interest is not considered in our further explanation because introduction of this factor does not make a fundamental change in the argument, and its letting aside means a great simplification.

2. *The Optimal Life-time and Minimal Costs*

The type and quality of the durable capital good will be expressed in its replacement value C.

The type and quality of the machine is determined by the method of production (which we assumed being given) and the quantity which is to be produced with it at every moment of time. Once the machine is bought, its replacement value varies in time only as a price of this apparatus technically well-defined. This price variation of C in the course of time will be indicated by the function $C(t)$.

The durable capital good furnishes certain services. These services at any moment depend quantitatively and qualitatively on the life-time already gone by. The quantity and quality of these services will decrease in general in the course of time. In order to obtain $x(t)$ there must be incurred complementary costs in addition to the costs of the durable capital good.

The complementary costs k are, given the method of production, a function of the course of time (we assume that the complementary costs will rise over time), and the quantity $x(t)$ to be produced at each moment of time.

Thus:

$$k = k\{t,x(t)\},$$

henceforth indicated by $k(t)$.

Over the entire life-time, t, of the capital good the total quantity produced may be denoted as

$$\int_0^t x(t)\mathrm{d}t = X_{0,t}.$$

The total costs for this amount are equal to

$$\int_0^t k \{t,x(t)\} \, dt + C(t) = K_{0,t} + C(t).$$

We assume that the scrap value at the moment of disposing of the old machine is zero. If this scrap value is not zero, $C(t)$ is to be regarded as the difference between the replacement value and the scrap value.

If we indicate the costs per unit of product by R (replacement value of the product), then

$$R = \frac{K_{0,t} + C(t)}{X_{0,t}}. \tag{1}$$

By the replacement value of the product we denote the minimal costs R_0 corresponding to the optimal method of production. We have already supposed that this optimal method was given.

R_0 is attained if the equation

$$\frac{dR}{dt} = 0$$

is satisfied*, i.e. if:

$$\frac{X_{0,t} \cdot \{k(t) + \dfrac{dC}{dt}\} - x(t) \cdot \{K_{0,t} + C(t)\}}{(X_{0,t})^2} = 0. \tag{2}$$

The point of time determined by (2) we indicate as t_0. (2) can be written as:

$$\frac{k(t_0) + \dfrac{dC_0}{dt}}{x(t_0)} = \frac{K_{0,t_0} + C(t_0)}{X_{0,t_0}}. \tag{3}**$$

It follows that the costs per unit of product are minimal if the marginal costs per unit of product are equal to the average costs also per unit of product throughout the whole life-time of the machine. The point of time t_0, at which this requirement is fulfilled, indicates the moment at which the capital good should be replaced. We did not

---

* We do not take into consideration the sufficient condition for the minimum value and therefore the second order derivatives.

** $\dfrac{dC_0}{dt}$ is the value of $\dfrac{dC}{dt}$ at $t = t_0$.

take into account technical progress, so that the capital good is replaced by an identical one.

If the machine is not replaced at t_0 then the average costs per unit of product calculated over the whole life-time will exceed R_0. Given the objective already formulated, namely to produce x at minimal costs, the durable capital good will have to be replaced at t_0.

From (1) and (3) it follows that:

$$R_0 = \frac{K_{0,t_0} + C(t_0)}{X_{0,t_0}} = \frac{k(t_0) + \dfrac{dC_0}{dt}}{x(t_0)} . \tag{4}$$

If we assume that the replacement value* of the capital good is constant around the point of time t_0, which may be very realistic in practical calculations, so that

$$\frac{dC_0}{dt} = 0 ,$$

then it follows that

$$R_0 = \frac{k(t_0)}{x(t_0)} \tag{5}$$

which implies that at the moment of replacement, the complementary costs per unit of product are equal to its replacement value.

As we saw in equation (H) (p. 194), the same criterion for the determination of the economic life-time of a machine was used in the theory of Meij. (5) is identical to (H). It is observed that the supposition in Meij's theory that

$$\frac{dC}{dt} = 0$$

is not necessary, it is only necessary to suppose that

$$\frac{dC_0}{dt} = 0 .$$

Hence it is evident that Meij's starting point: "the value of the nett-service of the durable capital good is nil at the moment of replacement" agrees with the minimization of the costs per unit of product

$$(\text{given } \frac{dC_0}{dt} = 0) .$$

* c.q. the difference between replacement value and scrap value.

In the theory developed above the depreciation-problem has also been solved. For the value of the nett-service of the machine during a short period of time dt, (denoted by $g(t)$), contributed to the combination of the means of production for obtaining the quantity $x(t)$ is equal to*

$$g(t) = R_0 \cdot x(t) - k(t) .$$

When R_0 has been found, $g(t)$ can be determined. The products obtained during period dt should be charged with a writing off for depreciation equal to $g(t)$. Thus the value of the nett-services and depreciation are equal.

When we have determined from (4) the optimal life-time of the machine and the point of time of its replacement, can we say, if we actually replace it, that we take the economically right decision? That is not always certain. We must realize that our decisions have consequences for the future. For if we decide to buy a new machine, our decision exerts an influence on all subsequent replacements. If we still keep the old machine in active operation for some years, then all subsequent replacements will change not only as to points of time but also as to the kind and nature of the means of production.

Application of the equation (4) is therefore only justified if we suppose that the (minimal) costs of production with all subsequent replacing machines will be equal to the costs of production with the existing one.** In the next section we shall drop this supposition at least partly. We then assume that the costs of production with another means of production and by means of other technics can fall below that of production with the old machine. We shall, however, still suppose that these new (lower) costs will again remain constant for the future.

These assumptions are rather irrealistic but they are necessary to keep the theory lucide. By realizing these suppositions we know the restrictions of our theory.

In practice it will be necessary to check the correctness of the determined life-time and the depreciation connected with it, at every change in prices and every technical development.

It was tacitly assumed that the requirements as to the quality and the quantity of the product do not make replacement necessary at a

---

* See also the equation (B) on page 193.

** For if we should know that e.g. a machine will enter into the market next year, which will be able to work much more economically than the actual "challenger", one would have done better to postpone replacement though the cost of production with the actual challenger would justify replacement.

point of time earlier than $t = t_0$, i.e. that the technical life-time of the machine does not expire before $t = t_0$.

3. *The Influence of Technical Progress on the Moment of Replacement*

If some technical improvement takes place, the question arises whether the technical life-time of the capital good has expired. This may be the case if new products enter into the market, which are of a better quality and therefore cause the products of the older machine in question to become unsaleable. We suppose that such a phenomenon does not arise when asking what will be the influence of technical progress on the economic life-time.

We start from the foregoing equation (3) and we assume that the quantity produced in every period is constant, i.e.

$$X_{0,t_0} = t_0 \cdot x(t) \quad x(t) = \text{constant} . \tag{6}$$

From (6) and (3):

$$t_0 = \frac{K_{0,t_0} + C(t_0)}{k(t_0) + \dfrac{dC_0}{dt}} . \tag{7}$$

The influence of the technical progress on the moment of replacement depends on where the new invention has taken place. In the following we shall examine the different possibilities.

CASE I. Suppose a technical improvement takes place in the production of the type of the durable capital good, that is used by the firm in question. As a result the replacement value of the machine, $C(t)$ wil be diminished so that further on

$$\frac{dC}{dt} = 0 .$$

From (7) it is evident that this leads to a shortening of the economic life-time. If the replacement value falls gradually, i.e.

$$\frac{dC}{dt} < 0 ,$$

even an extension of the life-time may result in certain cases.

CASE II. Suppose now a new type machine is offered on the market. This new machine in co-operation with certain complementary factors can produce the same or a better *product* at a lower cost per unit. Assume further that this new machine can be used by the firm in question, then the *new—lower—replacement value of the product* will have to be taken as the starting point.

The out-of-date machine will not be replaced again by a machine of the same type. The replacement value of the old machine is therefore no longer actual; however, it has a scrap or salvage value.

The services of the machine during the rest of its life-time may have a value which is higher than the direct yield obtainable by selling or scrapping it.

There may be, for example, a profitable difference between the value of the products which can be produced during the rest of the life-time of the old machine on the one hand, and the complementary costs and the reduction of the scrap value on the other hand.

If R_n indicates the new-lower-replacement value of the product, t_x the point of time at which the invention takes place and $S(t)$ the variation of the salvage- or scrap value in time, we can state that there is an advantageous premium P equal to

$$R_n \cdot \int_{t_x}^{t} x(t)\mathrm{d}t - \int_{t_x}^{t} k(t)\mathrm{d}t - S(t) = P(t) . \tag{8}$$

This premium is maximal if

$$\frac{\mathrm{d}P}{\mathrm{d}t} = 0 ,$$

thus if

$$R_n \cdot x(t) = k(t) + \frac{\mathrm{d}S}{\mathrm{d}t} . \tag{9}$$

From (9) we can calculate the optimal point of time at which the machine can be replaced: t_n. If we put

$$\frac{\mathrm{d}S}{\mathrm{d}t} = 0$$

then it follows from (9)

$$R_n = \frac{k(t_n)}{x(t_n)} . \tag{10}$$

That amounts to saying that the old machine remains in the production process until its complementary costs per unit of product are equal to the new replacement value. In the normal case the machine was also kept in active operation until these two quantities became equal, (supposed $dC_0/dt = 0$) c.f. equation (5) *.

The complementary cost *function* belonging to the old machine in question has remained the same after the invention. The replacement value of the product to which it should be equal has, however, gone down. Since the complementary costs increase in the course of time, this equality (10) will be reached at an earlier point of time. This results in an advancement of the moment of replacement and a shortening of the economic life-time.

Supposing that $x(t)$ is constant over time we can illustrate this result with a graph (Fig. II. 2).

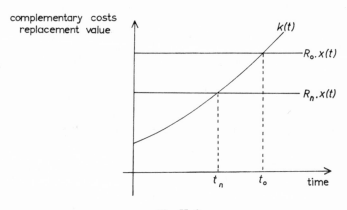

Fig. II.2

CASE III A. Suppose the technical improvement results in a fall in the *prices* of the *complementary factors*. Then in (7) K_{0,t_0} and also $k(t_0)$ at any moment t_0 will be smaller than would have been the case if the invention had not taken place. (It is tacitly assumed that the

---

* As to the solving of the depreciation-problem in this case, it can be observed that the value of the performance of the machine during the short period of time dt is equal to

$$g(t) = R_n \cdot x(t) - k(t) \ . \tag{I}$$

From (8):

$$R_n \cdot x(t) - k(t) - \frac{dS}{dt} = \frac{dP}{dt} \ . \tag{II}$$

If $\dfrac{dS}{dt} = 0$, from (I) and (II): $g(t) = \dfrac{dP}{dt} \ .$ (III)

So the periodical writing-off depreciation is equal to the marginal premium obtained during that period dt.

moment at which the invention is effective, indicated by t_x, precedes t_0 $(t_x < t_0)$.

If K_{0,t_0} falls relatively as much as $k (t_0)$* **, then on the righthand side of (7) (where $C(t)$ is constant and $dC/dt = 0$) the numerator will fall relatively less than the denominator, with the result that the quotient at any moment t_0 will be larger than was assumed before the invention (fall of prices). It follows definitively that t_0 will be larger. In this case the economic life-time will be extended.

CASE III B. Suppose that technical progress makes possible a change in the *method of production* with the "old" machine in question, resulting in a saving of complementary factors while the use of the durable capital good is unchanged.

If for the rest of the life-time the proportion

$$\frac{\int_{t_x}^{t_0} k(t)dt}{k(t_0)}$$

remains constant, i.e. when the reduction of costs is proportional for any moment following t_x the economic life-time will be extended.

This follows from (7) where $C(t)$ is constant and

$$\frac{dC}{dt} = 0 .$$

For any moment t following t_x the quotient on the righthand side of the equation (7) will be larger than was assumed before the invention took p'ace, because the numerator (in which there are constant factors) falls relatively less than the denominator. So t_0 will become larger and the economic life-time extended.

In the cases I and II we noticed a shortening of the life-time and in the cases III a and III b a lengthening.

---

* All complementary factors used before the point of time t_x will be valued at the lower prices (replacement value). These lower replacement values of the factors of production determine the new replacement value of the product, for if the durable capital good would be replaced, some or all cost functions combined with it, when expressed in monetary value, would run at a lower level, though physically they remain the same. These new cost functions exert an influence on the life-time of the capital good which has not changed in type. It is not plausible that an identical durable capital good would have a different life-time, because it has worked up in the beginning of its life-time complementary factors only at different prices whereas it has been physically used in the same way.

** The actual proportion depends on the quantitative proportion in the course of time of the various components that constitute together the complementary factors and the relative changes in price of the various factors.

When the cases I and III occur together, this results in a shortening of the life-time if the replacement value of the durable capital good falls relatively more than that of the complementary factors. As wages form a substantial part of the complementary costs and large labour savings with a given machine cannot be expected, technical progress as a whole will very likely tend to shorten the economic life-time. This conclusion especially holds good, because case II will be the most general in a period of technical progress.

4. *The Influence of the Expansion of the Economy on the Moment of Replacement*

As the starting point of our explanation we take equation (3)

$$\frac{k(t_0) + \dfrac{dC_0}{dt}}{x(t_0)} = \frac{K_{0,t_0} + C(t_0)}{X_{0,t_0}} . \tag{11}$$

The moment of time t_0 determined by this equation denotes as we have seen the moment at which the capital good should be replaced.

We assume that the quantity of product to be produced during any short period of time reflects the possibilities of sale in the market.

Therefore $x(t)$ will increase in an expanding economy.

We have already assumed, that the complementary costs at any moment depend on the course of time and on the quantity produced at that moment.

$$k = k\{t, x(t)\} . \tag{12}$$

The function k increases with the course of time. The degree of this increase over time will depend on the total quantity of the product which has been already produced since the machine was put in active operation.

Hence we suppose that dk/dt will be larger according as $X_{0,t}$ will be larger*.

$X_{0,t}$ will be larger according as $x(t)$ will be larger. Hence we suppose that dk/dt will increase as $x(t)$ will increase.

The expansion of production will not have an influence on the replacement value of the capital good already in use. Considerations as to the quantity to produce played a role in the past when the machine was bought. So $C(t)$ will not change ceteris paribus with changing $x(t)$.

* $X_{0,t} = \int_0^t x(t)dt.$

It is plausible that the complementary costs at any given moment of time will increase proportionately with the increase of production at the same moment, as long as the capacity of the machine is used less than in a certain degree*. Let us call this critical point the point of full capacity.

Beyond the point of using full capacity, the complementary costs as a function of the quantity produced at the same moment will increase progressively.

Therefore in our analysis we shall distinguish between

A. the phase of the expansion of the economy (the increasing demand for the product of the firm) until the moment at which capacity is in full operation.

B. the phase in the expansion beyond this point.

ad A. We suppose that prices will remain constant, hence

$$\frac{dC_0}{dt} = 0.$$

An increase of $x(t)$ at a certain moment indicated by $t = T$ will cause a proportional rise of the complementary costs at the same moment

$$\frac{dk}{dx} = \text{constant} .$$

In this phase the extension of production will have no influence on the technical life-time of the capital good.

From (11),

$$\frac{dC_0}{dt} = 0$$

(constant prices), it follows:

$$\frac{k(t_0)}{x(t_0)} = \frac{K_{0,T} + K_{T,t_0} + C(t_0)}{X_{0,t_0}} ** \tag{13}$$

T is the point at which the extension of demand takes place; following T $x(t)$ goes on rising or remains constant on the higher level. If $x(t)$ increases from $t = T$, the function $k(t)$ runs steeper beyond this

---

* This proportionality means that dk/dx is constant.

** $K_{0,T} = \int_0^T k \{t, x(t)\} \, dt$ and $K_{T,t_0} = \int_T^{t_0} k \{t, x(t)\} \, dt$.

point because dk/dt increases. Hence the lefthand side of (13) will increase at any moment beyond $t = T$.*

Of the righthand side of (13) the terms $K_{0,T}$ and $C(t)$ are constant, i.e.

$$\frac{K_{0,T} + C(t)}{X_{0,t}}$$

will fall more rapidly according as $x(t)$ increases after T. The other term of the righthand side of (13)

$$\frac{K_{T,t}}{X_{0,t}}$$

will rise less than

$$\frac{k(t)}{x(t)} \quad ** .$$

On balance the quotient on the righthand side will, compared with the starting situation, fall or at any rate rise less than the quotient of the lefthand side of (13).

The final result depends to a high degree on the length of the period $0 - T$ during which the machine has been in active operation before the change in demand occurs.

Hence the lefthand side of (13) will rise with rising t, the righthand side will fall in value or at any rate will rise less than the lefthand side. Therefore these two functions will satisfy the equation (13) at an earlier point of time.

Graphically we can illustrate this result in Fig. II. 3. In an expanding economy with constant prices the economic life-time of the durable capital goods tends to shorten as a result of the increase of production. It is supposed that the complementary costs rise proportionately with the quantity at any moment. If the rise in complementary costs is less than proportional, no definite result can be obtained.

---

* The rise in $k(t)$ will not be weighed out by falling marginal costs per unit resulting from increasing production.

** $\qquad \dfrac{K_{T,t}}{X_{0,t}} = \dfrac{K_{T,t}}{X_{0,T} + X_{T,t}} \qquad$ The relation between $\dfrac{K_{T,t}}{X_{T,t}}$ and $\dfrac{k(t)}{x(t)}$

is one of average costs to marginal costs. If these functions rise the average costs function will rise less than the marginal costs function. In this case $K_{T,t}$ not only is divided by $X_{T,t}$ but by the larger factor $X_{0,t}$. Hence the rise is still more slowed down.

ad B. In this phase, in which the capacity of the machine is fully in operation, we should ask, in the first place, if the technical life-time of the capital good has now expired. This can happen if the machine can no longer perform its task quantitatively or qualitatively. If this is not the case we must examine the influence on the economic life-time.

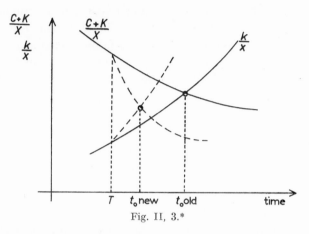

Fig. II, 3.*

Again we take as a starting point equation (11) and suppose that the prices will remain constant.

The progression on the lefthand side of the equation will be strengthened because an increase in production $x(t)$ will therefore result in a more than proportionate rise of the complementary costs. So dk/dx increases with increasing $x(t)$. The righthand side will rise relatively less because of the same considerations as given in note ** on page 213.

Hence the conclusions of the preceding analysis are all the more valid.

The value of such an argument, however, becomes doubtful for a continuously expanding economy, for the entrepreneur is able to avoid such an increase of costs by enlarging his firm with one or more similar machines. It is plausible that this will be his optimal conduct.

So we drop the assumption of a single machine but still restrict ourselves to the expanding economy in which replacement in the ordinary sense of the word still takes place. We suppose that an increase of production will be made possible by extending the capacity in the

* The solid curves relate to the course of the costs as it would have been if the increase of production had not taken place. The dotted lines indicate the actual course as a consequence of the expansion.

sense of buying new machines (with complementary factors of production).

In this case the results obtained remain formally the same, for as before, the problem is treated similarly for each machine separately.

The difference between this situation and that of the business-cycle is that in an expanding economy the producer has some definite ideas about the future. He is supposed to know that the production-increase is not a temporary one and will react accordingly. During the business-cycle he reckons with the possibility of a falling demand in the near future and this will influence his replacement behaviour materially.

Concluding this section we can state that our results will hold for a regularly expanding economy but that the problem has to be treated separately for a fluctuating economy.

In the next section actual enterpreneurial behaviour during the postwar expansion period in The Netherlands will be analysed.

III. ACTUAL ENTREPRENEURIAL REPLACEMENT BEHAVIOUR

A. INTRODUCTION

As a check on the conclusions reached in the foregoing section and in general to get more information about the actual behaviour of the entrepreneurs with regard to reinvestments we set up an inquiry concerning the replacement investments in 50 Dutch enterprises.

The enterprises involved belong to the industrial sector (the electro-technical industry, chemical industry, food-stuff industry, textile industry, engineering industry and the printing industry), the transportation sector and agriculture. The enterprises investigated were in general of a relatively large size.

For guiding the inquiry a questionnaire was used which in the first place collected information about the organisational aspects of replacement investments as compared with net-investments, in the second place about the factors influencing the replacement decisions, in the third place about the calculating aspects of reinvestments and finally about the scrapping of the replaced capital goods, in particular the degradation of equipment in the own enterprise and the second-hand market for disposed equipment.

In the following we will present the most important results of the inquiry. We notice that the information received refers to the post-war period, which, as Figure III. 1 shows, can be regarded as a period of steady expansion.

B. Terminology, Problems of Classification

From the first part of this study it clearly appeared already, that the distinction between replacement and expansion investments,

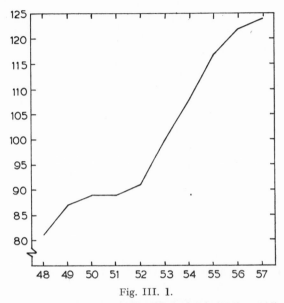

Fig. III. 1.

Real national income in The Netherlands (1953 = 100)
Source: The Netherlands Central Bureau of Statistics

although commonly used in theory, cannot be maintained strictly in practice.

As a consequence of technical progress machines having better performance and efficiency are produced. Replacement of a machine by an exactly similar type (the so-called technical replacement) does not frequently occur. Mostly the new equipment will not be identical with the old (economic replacement). When the new machine has a larger size and/or higher speed and therefore a greater capacity than the old one, we have to do with a mixed investment (replacement and expansion investment). In practice this is called a replacement investment, even when it serves to achieve the normal growth of the plant.

On the other hand, some concepts which are in practice not always considered as reinvestments, correspond to our definition. We here refer to the replacement not of the entire capital good, but of one or more parts of it. If such a part is replaced by an identical one, we speak of a revision; when it is replaced by an improved one, we shall speak of rebuilding. So revision can always be considered as a replacement investment. If rebuilding enlarges the capacity of the machine it constitutes a mixed investment.

It is clear that both revision and rebuilding prolong the technical life-time of the machine as a whole. Rebuilding will extend the economic life-time of a machine as well; revision only in as far as technical development permits.

As long as expansion and technical development in the industry considered continue revision will not occur frequently, especially not in the larger enterprises. In general only machines not being largely affected by obsolescence will be revised and as a matter of fact even then only when revision is cheaper than total replacement of the machine.

Rebuilding is of more importance. The necessity for it arises for large installations which are engaged permanently, so that the possibility of complete replacement seldom exists. Rebuilding will also be preferred to complete replacement, when the technical development is concentrated on certain vital parts of the installation. In both cases rebuilding will be cheaper than complete replacement.

C. Factors which Influence the Replacement Decision

In dealing with investment plans the industry makes no organisational difference whatsoever between economic replacement and net-investment. The investment plans are generally made at the highest level of management. Only the planning of the so-called technical replacement is sometimes left to the judgement of the lower staff.

As to the objects of reinvestment, the priority schedules set by the top management are not fixed but variable. The priority of certain investments will be strongly dependent upon the circumstances of the enterprise at a certain moment and on her purposes at that moment. The plans are mostly made for one year. In several cases, however, changes are made in the plans during their execution.

The post-war period is characterized by a strong expansion of industry combined with an accelerated technical development. New techniques, which sometimes mean a revolutionary development as well as the introduction of many new or improved articles, characterize this period.

Although of course, the foregoing does not hold to the same extent for all industries and all enterprises, one may say that the rapid technical development in this period increased the importance of economic obsolescence as a reason for reinvestment. In correspondence with the theoretical observations in the foregoing section, replacement of machines in this period often took place, long before the technical wastage made it necessary.

Moreover it appeared that acceleration of replacement by one enterprise induced the other enterprises of the same branch of industry to an accelerated replacement too. This "imitation" is not always based on pure economic motives. Considerations of prestige also play an important role.

The necessary means for the accelerated replacement were sufficiently available in this period of expansion which in general was characterized by large profits and therefore a good liquidity position.

It appeared that in addition to the technical progress in the particular sphere of the enterprise and its liquidity position at a given moment, the rate of replacement investments of an enterprise is positively influenced by its sales expectations*.

Needless to say that not only the sales-expectations but also the actual sales have a positive influence on the rate of reinvestment, because the latter determine the intensity of use of the equipment and consequently its economic as well as its technical life-time.

The influence of the fiscal climate on the volume of replacement investments must not be overestimated. The tax-facilities, granted in the Netherlands in the period considered, were not of such proportions, that they could influence to a large extent the replacement decisions. For the small private enterprises which are subject to a strongly progressive income-tax the fiscal climate is of more importance.

It is evident that for industries where the technical progress is more gradual the economic obsolescence of the equipment is of less importance. Here replacement mostly will not take place before the technical wastage of the equipment makes this necessary.

The same applies to the replacement of machinery which fulfills a less important role in the production and in general is not much influenced by the technical development.

Finally the technical development causes the production units to

* Though the postwar situation can be considered as one of steady expansion without fluctuations of any importance, there might have been some uncertainty about the future development of sales for the *individual* enterprise. Therefore in this period the expectations with regard to future sales are also important in determining the moment at which replacement takes place. The regularly expanding economy can be seen as a limiting case of a dynamic economy (see following section).

become bigger and more expensive. Therefore there will always be some smaller enterprises, which because of their limited production volume or lack of means cannot immediately introduce the technical developments. These enterprises too will often replace on the basis of technical wastage of their equipment.

Summing up, one may say that the rate of replacement of the equipment and therefore the volume of the reinvestments in a certain period for an enterprise are determined by:

1. the extent of technical progress in the particular sphere of the enterprise;
2. the sales and the sales expectations of the firm;
3. the liquidity position of the enterprise which is mainly determined by its profits and to a considerably less extent by the fiscal climate.

In the enumeration given here one might miss some factors which could be expected to influence the replacement decision too. It appeared however that in practice, in the enterprises investigated, these factors are not considered important in this connection. Some of these factors may be:

1. the rate of interest and the situation on the capital market;
2. the accessibility to the capital market for the enterprise;
3. the expectations about supply and prices of capital goods;
4. the rest-value of the machinery used by the enterprise in question and the facilities of its old equipment.

Concerning (1) and (2) it may be remarked that interest charges only form a small part of total expenditures for replacement investment. As for the situation on the capital market, we observed that in this period the greater part of the reinvestments has been auto-financed.

For this reason the situation on the capital market as well as the accessibility to the capital market of the individual enterprise in this period had no significant influence on the replacement decisions.

As regards (3) the enterprise is, generally speaking, hardly able to adapt the rate of replacement to the price-fluctuations of the capital goods. This is caused for instance by the time needed for the realisation of the replacement (among others the length of delivery time).

In so far as (4) concerns, in industry exchange-facilities for old equipment in general are not customary. The rest-value of equipment is mostly of such a small magnitude that it does not influence the replacement decision.

D. CALCULATING ASPECTS

As suggested in the foregoing section some comparison between the costs of production with the old and the new equipment will in general be made. The form in which these calculations take place differs highly. No general rule could be detected. Only in the rare cases that replacement takes place at the end of the technical life-time of the machine such a calculation is practically meaningless. In this case namely the enterprise is obliged to replace. In the case that new techniques improve the quality of a product, a sharp calculation turned out to be impossible because a factor like the probable loss of sales resulting from production with the old machine can hardly be calculated a priori.

Only in few cases with regard to this problem we found the prevalence of rigid ideas (such as the famous short pay-off rule) which Terborgh[13] describes as "industrial folklore".

The book-value of a machine proved to be of no importance for the replacement decision. The depreciation-policy may however influence the liquidity position and through this may influence the replacement decision.

E. THE DESTINATION OF REPLACED EQUIPMENT

The replacement decision implies two elements, namely the purchase of a new capital good resp. a part of it and the abolition of the old one.

In principle the abolition of a machine can take place in 3 forms:
  1. degradation (in the same enterprise)
  2. sale;
  3. scrap.

Ad 1. Degradation in the same enterprise takes place when the machine is used in another function where the requirements are less precise than in the former function. The possibility of such a degradation in own enterprise however greatly depends on the structure of production in the firm. This possibility will often be present when the enterprise produces products in different qualities (for example, printed matter). An other form of degradation within the firm can be found in case the machine is to be used as reserve-equipment.

Ad 2. In this case the machine will have a degraded function in another enterprise. The machine will be sold on the second hand market. This especially will be possible when the machinery has a more or less universal character, for example cars, lathes, presses, looms. The abolition of more specialised machines—so far as abolition occurs —must be affected by private sale.

The buyers on this second hand market may be enterprises whose production requires lesser qualities of the machines than the production of the selling enterprise. A second category might be enterprises of smaller size, which are unable to keep up with technical developments.

It is clear that these enterprises may belong to the same industry as the selling enterprise as well as to any other.

Ad 3. When down-grading or sale of a machine is impossible the machine will be destroyed by the enterprise or sold for scrapping. The sale of an installation is often undesirable. Several motives can be important here: competition (the desire to keep own production methods secret) the aim to lessen overcapacity in the industry, the fear of bringing the industry into discredit by using old machinery. For the last case we refer to the organised destruction of obsolete machines in the Dutch printing industry.

IV. SOME THEORETICAL CONSIDERATIONS CONCERNING INVESTMENT AND DESINVESTMENT IN A FLUCTUATING ECONOMY

We shall now turn to a somewhat more dynamic interpretation of the theory of reinvestment. As said in the introduction it cannot be considered unlikely that a producer maintains a production unit even if its economic life-time calculated in the conservative way of section II has expired.

He will try to adapt his capacity in an optimal way and it very well might be that in the long run his costs are not minimised by acting according to the theory mentioned in section II B.

To illustrate our argument we shall once again adapt the notation of section II, and consider a firm, having several similar machine-units producing a certain good. One of the machines at point of time t_0 has reached its optimal life-time in the traditional sense of the word and, under "normal" conditions should be replaced. At this point of time however, the demand for the product increases and an additional machine is needed. The producer now can follow two policies. The first is buying two new machines and scrapping the old one. The second is buying one new machine and producing as well with the old one. We shall denote these two policies by Policy I and Policy II.

Let us assume further that the enterpreneur from different sources has formed some idea about the production increase for the period $t - T$. More specifically he makes (right or wrong) the assumption that the probability that the increase will be of a permanent character is α and therefore will be temporary with a probability $1-\alpha$. For the sake of simplicity we assume that there is no doubt about length of the period $t-T$ if the increase of production is temporary.

The producer now has to choose one of the policies mentioned, and it is reasonable to assume that he will prefer the policy which, given his probability-estimate, will give him the smallest additional costs.

He will therefore first calculate these additional costs for all alternative possibilities with regard to the period $t-T$.

Situation 1. The producer chooses Policy I and the production increase is permanent.

Denoting by Δx the additional quantity to be produced during the period $t-T$ the additional costs of production during this period (with the new machine) will be equal to

$$\bar{K} \cdot \Delta x \tag{4.1}$$

when we denote by $\bar{K}$ the (minimum) average costs with which a machine in the firm "normally" is producing.

Situation 2. The producer chooses Policy I and the production increase is temporary. In this case a part of the total costs of the new machine together with the complementary costs of the additional production have to be considered as the costs of production of this additional quantity. We do not take total costs of the machine because sooner or later, in the course of time, one of the other machine-units will have to be replaced, and this can be done by the additional, relatively new, machine. The costs of maintaining the machine until that time together with interest on the capital invested have to be considered then as an element of the additional costs. We put these costs proportional to C and denote them by λC.

Total additional costs in this situation are therefore equal to

$$\bar{K} \Delta x + \lambda C \tag{4.2}$$

in which $\bar{K}$ again stand for minimum average costs of producing a quantity Δx.

Since λ and C are positive, (4.2) exceeds (4.1) in value.

Situation 3. The producer chooses Policy II and the production increase is permanent. This situation means that the enterpreneur produces against average costs above the minimum value $\bar{K}$. We assume this costs to be $\bar{K}'\Delta x > \bar{K} \Delta x$.

Situation 4. This situation is equivalent to situation 3 because it gives rise to the same additional costs $K'\varDelta x$.

Summarizing our results we find the following four possibilities with regard to the additional costs.

Policy \ Production increase	Permanent	Temporary
I (replacement)	$\overline{K}\,\varDelta x$	$\overline{K}\varDelta x + \lambda C$
II (no replacement)	$\overline{K}'\varDelta x$	$\overline{K}'\varDelta x$

Now, as stated before, α equals the probability that the producer assumes the production-increase to be permanent.

The mathematical expectation of additional costs in choosing Policy I then will be

$$E\mathrm{I}\,(K) = \alpha\overline{K}\varDelta x + (1 - \alpha)\,\{\overline{K}\varDelta x + \lambda C\} =$$
$$= \overline{K}\varDelta x + (1 - \alpha)\,\lambda C . \qquad (4.3)$$

The mathematical expectation of additional costs in choosing Policy II are obviously equal to $\overline{K}'\varDelta x$

$$E\mathrm{II}\,(\overline{K}) = \overline{K}'\varDelta x . \qquad (4.4)$$

Denoting by D the difference in costs-expectation between Policy I and Policy II we find

$$D = (1 - \alpha)\,\lambda C - (\overline{K}' - \overline{K})\,\varDelta x \qquad (4.5)$$

$\overline{K}' > \overline{K}$

If $D < 0$ he will choose Policy I and for $D > 0$, Policy II will be chosen.

It appears that the sign of D depends on the size of α. If α is near to unity, which means that the producer is practically sure that the production increase will be permanent, he will choose Policy I and buy the new machine. If on the other hand, α is near to zero, D tends to be positive, especially when C is large compared with the difference in complementary costs.

Now α, during the business-cycle cannot be treated as a constant. In the beginning of the boom the producer will be very careful not to overestimate the importance of an increase in demand and as a result will give a low value to α. Scrapping will fall. As production rises further the α will rise and he will gradually buy more new production units. At the same time the rate of fall in scrapping will decrease. At the top of the boom some time-lag in the actual buying of new machines is probable with regard to delivery-periods. Then he will decrease his capacity by increased scrapping and decrease investment in new machinery.

Summarizing we find that during the boom scrapping is likely to fall and new investments are likely to increase. During the depression the reverse is to be expected, new investment may show a time-lag with regard to the level of production.

V. A CASE-STUDY. THE DUTCH MERCHANT MARINE

It will now be our task to test the foregoing theory in a practical example. It will be clear that in principle every branch of industry, in which a sufficiently great number of interchangeable units of capital goods with a relatively long life-time in comparison with the phase of the business-cycle is used, could be taken. Examples are e.g. spindels in spinning industry, railway-carriages in a railway-corporation, elec-tro-motors in several branches, etc.

It is a pity that during the pre-war period the registration of durable production goods took place only incidentally or in scattered places and therefore it is very difficult, if not impossible to collect the neces-sary data.

The only time-series that seemed appropriate were those of ship-building and ship-scrapping. The lifetime of ships can be considered to be sufficiently long for our purposes, and for the Dutch commercial marine the necessary data are available for the interwar-period.

The data are to be found in Statistical and Econometric Studies of The Netherlands Central Bureau of Statistics[14]. From this source the figures have been taken for the period from 1923 until 1938.

The data are given in the following table. In this table the following is meant by:
1. New ships: the tonnages of ships newly built for the Dutch merchant marine and the ships bought in foreign countries as a percentage of available tonnage at the beginning of the year.
2. Scrap: the tonnage scrapped or sold to foreign countries, also as a percentage of available tonnage on the 1st of January.

TABLE 1

Some Data about the Dutch Merchant Marine from 1923 to 1938

Year	New tonnage added*	2-years moving average	Tonnage scrapped*	2-years moving average
1923	5,7		5,2	
		5,0		4,8
1924	4,2		4,3	
		3,4		3,5
1925	2,6		2,6	
		3,7		2,9
1926	4,7		3,1	
		5,6		4,1
1927	6,5		5,1	
		6,8		3,9
1928	7,0		2,6	
		6,8		2,2
1929	6,6		1,8	
		7,8		2,5
1930	8,9		3,1	
		6,9		4,4
1931	4,8		5,7	
		3,2		6,6
1932	1,6		7,4	
		1,0		7,4
1933	0,3		7,3	
		1,1		6,2
1934	1,9		5,1	
		2,7		5,8
1935	3,4		6,4	
		3,5		4,9
1936	3,6		3,3	
		4,5		2,0
1937	5,4		0,7	
		7,7		1,2
1938	10,0		1,7	

* In % of the total tonnage at the beginning of each year.

To get insight into the fluctuations of these percentages during a business-cycle they have been compared with the movement in the Private Gross National Product of the U.S. in billions of 1953 dollars [15], the data of which are given in Table 2.

All data relate to the interwar period, because the postwar period has to be considered as an example of a monotonically expanding economy.

In accordance with the conclusions reached in the foregoing section,

TABLE 2

GROSS NATIONAL PRODUCT U.S.

(constant dollars)

Year	Private gross national product (billions of 1953 dollars)	2-years moving average	Year	Private gross national product (billions of 1953 dollars)	2-years moving average
					146,3
1923	137,9		1931	141,1	
		137,3			129,9
1924	136,7		1932	118,6	
		143,5			115,9
1925	150,3		1933	113,1	
		154,0			118,0
1926	157,7		1934	122,8	
		158,0			131,0
1927	158,2		1935	139,1	
		159,2			146,6
1928	160,1		1936	154,0	
		164,4			161,2
1929	168,8		1937	168,3	
		160,2			163,1
1930	151,5		1938	157,9	

Note: private gross national product is total gross national product less compensation of general government employees.

it is evident from the Figs. V.1, V.2 and V.3 that the additions of vessels are highly correlated in a positive sense and the withdrawals in a negative sense with fluctuations in the G.N.P.

From these Figures it appears further that the percentage of tonnage added has fluctuated from about 1% in the lower turning point to about 8% in the upper turning point. The fluctuations of the percentage of tonnage withdrawn range from 1% in the upper turning point to 8% in the lower turning point. So it is evident that the greater part of the additions of new and the withdraws of old vessels move independently of each other. Therefore we can say that in a fluctuating economy the traditional concept of replacement with regard to vessels is relatively unimportant. This is in accordance with the explanation given in the foregoing section.

VI. SUMMARY OF CONCLUSIONS

What we stated above indicated that with regard to replacements a distinction ought to be made between the behaviour of the producer

Tonnage of vessels
added (●) resp. removed (×)

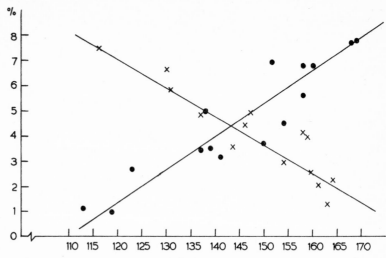

Private gross national product U.S. (billions of 1953 dollars)

Fig. V.1.

The relation between the tonnage aded (●) respectively removed (×) (in per cent of the total tonnage at the beginning of each year) and the Private Gross National Product U.S. (billions of 1953 dollars) for the period 1923–1938. Both the percentage of vessels added and vessels removed are expressed for each year as a two-year moving average, the first with a time lag of six months. In the second relation the Private Gross National Product is taken as a two-year moving average.

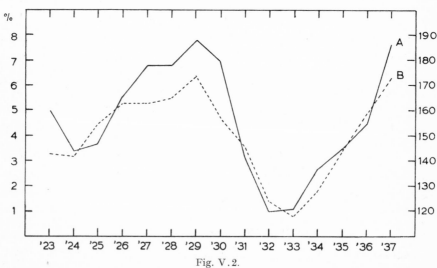

Fig. V.2.

A = Tonnage of vessels added (in % of total tonnage at the beginning of each year), two-year moving average;

B = Private Gross National product U.S. (billions of 1953 dollars), six month earlier.

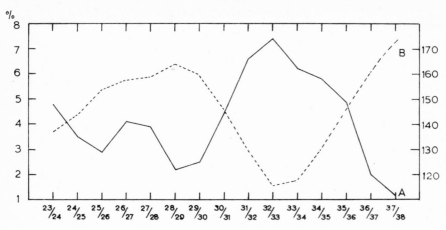

Fig. V.3.

A = Tonnage of vessels scrapped (in % of total tonnage at the beginning of each year);
B = Private Gross National Product U.S. (billions of 1953 dollars);
    Both curves represent two-year moving averages.

in a static or continuously expanding economy and the behaviour in
a fluctuating economy.

In the first case one can generally speak of a real replacement
investment in the ordinary sense of the word, defined in the literature
as the investment necessary to replace a capital good put out of use,
in order to maintain actual production capacity. From this definition
it follows that the decision to scrap an old machine and to replace it
by a new one must take place at the same or almost the same time.

From our theoretical analysis of the replacement behaviour in a
regularly expanding economy, we may deduce—under the given
assumption—at what moment the producer will replace a machine by
a new one. This is the moment when the average costs are minimal.
At this point the optimal economic lifetime of the machine is reached.

The introduction of technical progress into the theoretical analysis
will in general tend to shorten the economic life-time of a machine.
Especially in periods in which many new inventions take place this
will be actually the case.

We observed from our inquiry that the postwar period is characterized by a strong expansion of the industry combined with an accelerated
technical progress. In this period new techniques have developed and
new or improved articles have been introduced. So in this period
replacements become often necessary, long before the machines are
technically worn out.

It appeared further that besides the technical progress in the period concerned, future expectations with regard to sale and liquidity position of an enterprise are important in determining the moment of replacement.

The distinction between replacement and expansion investments causes difficulties in practice with regard to an exact measuring of the volume of replacements. This is because replacement of a machine by a like-for-like type (technical replacement) does not occur frequently. Often the new machine has a larger size and higher speed and therefore a greater capacity (mixed investment).

The introduction of the businesscycle in our theory has important consequences for the traditional replacement conception. The reason is that by purchasing a new and by disposing of an old machine in a dynamic economy the attention of the producer is directed in the first instance to an optimal adjustment of his own production capacity to his sales fluctuations.

In this situation withdrawal and purchase of a capital good do not necessarily take place at the same point of time.

The adjustment of the actual production capacity to the sales fluctuations takes place through
a. holding in use of the old equipment in the expanding economy;
b. accelerated scrapping of the old equipment in the contracting economy.

This means that during the upward economy scrapping is likely to fall and new equipment is likely to increase.

During the depression the reverse is to be expected.

In order to test the above theory we analysed the variations of the additions and withdrawals of vessels in the business cycle during the interwar period. In accordance with the given theoretical analysis it appears that the additions of vessels were highly positively and the withdrawals strongly negatively correlated with the business cycle. Our conclusion is that in a fluctuating economy the traditional replacement conception is quantitatively unimportant and that in the replacement decision one then has to distinguish between the scrapping decision and the decision to buy a new unit. They can be separated by a shorter or longer period of time. It is clear, however, that this conclusion only holds good in a situation where a more or less large group of durable goods of different ages exists.

The effect of the policy just described is that a certain degree of elasticity in the totality of durable means of production can be reached that enables the enterprise to adapt itself more or less to economic fluctuations.

REFERENCES

1. J. S. Taylor: A Statistical Theory of Depreciation, *Journal of the American Statistical Association* (Dec., 1923).
2. H. Hotelling: A General Mathematical Theory of Depreciation, *Journal of the American Statistical Association* (Sept., 1925).
3. G. A. D. Preinreich: The Economic Life of Industrial Equipment, *Econometrica* (Jan., 1940).
4. F. A. and Vera C. Lutz: *The Theory of Investment of the Firm* (Princeton, 1951).
5. E. Schneider: *Wirtschaftlichkeitsrechnung* (Bern/Tübingen, 1951). Schneider does not use the term "goodwill". By him the same concept is called "Kapitalwert". For a good summary of many theories see also: H. von Briel: *Die Ermittlung der wirtschaftlichen Nützungsdauer von Anlagegütern*, Zurich 1955.
6. The authors Luts finally deal with the case that the entrepreneur must take a decision to replace his old machine by a new apparatus *now* available or to postpone replacement until a new type of capital good will become available at some more or less distant point of time in future. In this way obsolescence of the present types is taken into account. In some cases it may be rational not to take a new machine of the present type but to wait until the new type enters into the market. When this will be true is indicated by the authors *op. cit.*, p. 110.
7. J. L. Meij: *Leerboek der Bedrijfshuishoudkunde* I (Principles of Industrial Economics), (The Hague, 1954); *Het vervangingswaardeprobleem bij duurzame productiemiddelen* (The Problem as to Replacing Durable Capital Goods), (The Hague, 1956).
8. George Terborgh: *Dynamic Equipment Policy* (New York, 1949), *MAPI Replacement Manual* (New York, 1950) and *Realistic Depreciation Policy* (1954).
9. Terborgh, *Dynamic Equipment Policy*, pp. 63–64.
10. Terborgh, *op. cit.*, p. 85.
11. Terborgh, *op. cit.*, p. 64–65.
12. Terborgh uses the term "deterioration" rather than depreciation. Deterioration is reflected in the decline, or retrogression, of its operating performance as compared with the performance that would be obtainable from an identical new machine. Obsolescence appears in the growing operating inferiority of such a replica of the existing unit in comparison with the best new machine currently available. Terborgh, *op. cit.*, p. 61.
13. George Terborgh: *Dynamic Equipment Policy* (New York, 1949), p. 187.
14. *4th Quarter 1955;* Volume 10, nr. 4, p. 153.
15. Figures taken from *"Potential Economic Growth of the United States During the Next Decade"*, Joint Committee on the Economic Report (Washington, 1954).

SUBJECT INDEX

NAME INDEX